Instructor's Man

to accompany

Purchasing and Supply Management

Twelfth Edition

Michiel R. Leenders
University of Western Ontario

Harold E. Fearon
Center of Advanced Purchasing Studies

Anna Flynn

Fraser Johnson
University of Western Ontario

Prepared by
Michiel R. Leenders
University of Western Ontario

Elaine Carson
University of Western Ontario

Boston   Burr Ridge, IL   Dubuque, IA   Madison, WI   New York   San Francisco   St. Louis
Bangkok   Bogotá   Caracas   Kuala Lumpur   Lisbon   London   Madrid   Mexico City
Milan   Montreal   New Delhi   Santiago   Seoul   Singapore   Sydney   Taipei   Toronto

McGraw-Hill Higher Education

A Division of The McGraw-Hill Companies

Instructor's Manual to accompany
PURCHASING AND SUPPLY MANAGEMENT
Michiel R. Leenders, Harold E. Fearon, Anna Flynn and Fraser Johnson

Published by McGraw-Hill/Irwin, an imprint of the McGraw-Hill Companies, Inc., 1221 Avenue of the Americas, New York, NY 10020.
Copyright © 2002, 1997, 1993, 1989, 1985, 1980, 1975, 1970, 1962, 1957, 1952, 1948
by the McGraw-Hill Companies, Inc. All rights reserved.
The contents, or parts thereof, may be reproduced in print form solely for classroom use with
PURCHASING AND SUPPLY MANAGEMENT
provided such reproductions bear copyright notice, but may not be reproduced in any other form or for any other purpose without the prior written consent of The McGraw-Hill Companies, Inc., including, but not limited to, in any network or other electronic storage or transmission, or broadcast for distance learning.

2 3 4 5 6 7 8 9 0 HAM/HAM 0 9 8 7 6 5 4 3 2

ISBN 0-07-237061-0

www.mhhe.com

TABLE OF CONTENTS

Introduction	ix
The Case Context	x
PowerPoint Presentations, Transparency Masters And Electronic Quiz Access	xii
The Review and Discussion Questions	xii
The Use of Reports	xii
Exhibit 1	xiii
Exhibit II	xiv
Exhibit III	xvi
Course Design Options	xvii
Special Interest Groups	xix
Examinations	xix
The Use of Audio-Visual Support and the Internet	xx
The Use of Visitors to Class	xxi
Quizzes and Commentaries	xxi
Chapter 1 — The Challenge of Purchasing and Supply Management	**1**
Quiz	2
Case 1-1 Commercial Laundry Products	6
Case 1-2 Custom Equipment (A)	10
Case 1-3 The Purchasing of Co-Op	16
Chapter 2 — Objectives and Organization for Effective Purchasing and Supply Management	**21**
Quiz	22
Case 2-1 Goodlife Club	27
Case 2-2 Duchess University	30
Chapter 3 — Procedures and Information Flows	**35**
Quiz	36
Case 3-1 Mike Wesley	40
Case 3-2 UIL Inc.	44
Case 3-3 Artsell Inc.	48

iv   **Table of Contents**

Chapter 4 — Technology and E-Commerce   51

    Quiz   52
    Case 4-1   Somers Office Products Inc.   56
    Case 4-2   Cable and Wireless plc   61
    Case 4-3   Establishing e-Business Standards at Deere & Company   69

Chapter 5 — Quality Specification and Inspection   73

    Quiz   74
    Case 5-1   St. Ann's Hospital   78
    Case 5-2   Dorman Printing Inc.   81

Chapter 6 — Quantity and Delivery   85

    Quiz   86
    Case 6-1   Roger Gray   90
    Case 6-2   Connecticut Circuit Manufacturers   94
    Case 6-3   Abbey Paquette   99
    Case 6-4   Corn Silk   104

Chapter 7 — Supplier Selection   109

    Quiz   110
    Case 7-1   Lancaster Life Insurance Co.   114
    Case 7-2   Quotech Inc.   118
    Case 7-3   Bid Evaluation and Custom Equipment (B)   121
    Case 7-4   Industrial Products Corporation (IPC)   133

Chapter 8 — Outsourcing, Supplier Relations, and Supply-Chain Management   137

    Quiz   138
    Case 8-1   Saucy Foods Limited   142
    Case 8-2   Paron Metal Fabricating Inc.   147
    Case 8-3   Super Stamps and Products Inc.   151

Chapter 9 — Price Determination — 155

Quiz — 156
Case 9-1 Global Heat Exchangers Inc. — 160
Case 9-2 MasTech Inc. — 163
Case 9-3 Chevron Corporation: The PC Selection Team — 168
Case 9-4 Price Forecasting Exercise — 180
Case 9-5 Commodity Purchasing Game — 186

Chapter 10 — Purchasing Logistics Services — 199

Quiz — 200
Case 10-1 Great Western Bank — 204
Case 10-2 Geo Products — 206
Case 10-3 Specialty Brewers — 210

Chapter 11 — Investment Recovery — 215

Quiz — 216
Case 11-1 Nova Stamping Company — 220
Case 11-2 Ornex — 223

Chapter 12 — Legal Aspects of Purchasing — 227

Quiz — 228
Case 12-1 Brassco — 232

Chapter 13 — Research and Measurement — 235

Quiz — 236
Case 13-1 Red Sea Corporation — 241
Case 13-2 Chemical Treatment Company (CTC) Ltd. — 246

Chapter 14 — Global Supply Management — 251

Quiz — 252
Case 14-1 Global Pharmaceuticals Ltd. — 256
Case 14-2 Marathon Oil Company International — 260

Chapter 15 — Public Purchasing — 265

    Quiz — 266
    Case 15-1   City of Roxborough — 270
    Case 15-2   Don Willit Associates — 273
    Case 15-3   TriCity — 277

Chapter 16 — Capital Goods Acquisition — 281

    Quiz — 282
    Case 16-1   Mark Appleton — 286
    Case 16-2   Casson Construction — 289

Chapter 17 — Services Purchasing — 293

    Quiz — 294
    Case 17-1   Erica Carson — 298
    Case 17-2   Talbot County School Board — 301
    Case 17-3   Scope Repairs — 305

Chapter 18 — Strategy in Purchasing and Supply Management — 313

    Quiz — 314
    Case 18-1   Saint Mary's Health Center — 318
    Case 18-2   Heat Transfer Systems Inc. — 323
    Case 18-3   Custom Windows Inc. — 328

Appendix — 335
    PowerPoint Presentation

CASE COMMENTARIES IN ALPHABETICAL ORDER

	Chapter	Page
Abbey Paquette	6	99
Artsell Inc.	3	48
Bid Evaluation and Custom Equipment (B)	7	121
Brassco	12	232
Cable & Wireless PLC (A)	4	61
Casson Construction	16	289
Chemical Treatment Company (CTC) Ltd.	13	246
Chevron Corporation: The PC Selection Team	9	168
City of Roxborough	15	270
Commercial Laundry Products	1	6
Commodity Purchasing Game	9	186
Connecticut Circuit Manufacturers	6	94
Corn Silk	6	104
Custom Equipment (A)	1	10
Custom Windows Inc.	18	328
Don Willit Associates	15	273
Dorman Printing	5	81
Duchess University	2	30
Erica Carson	17	298
Establishing e-Business Standards at Deere & Company	4	69
Geo Products	10	206
Global Heat Exchangers Inc.	9	160
Global Pharmaceuticals Ltd.	14	256
Goodlife Club	2	27
Great Western Bank	10	204
Heat Transfer Systems Inc.	18	323
Industrial Products Corporation (IPC)	7	133

	Chapter	Page
Lancaster Life Insurance Co.	7	114
Marathon Oil Company International	14	260
Mark Appleton	16	286
MasTech Inc.	9	163
Mike Wesley	3	40
Nova Stamping Company	11	220
Ornex	11	223
Paron Metal Fabricating	8	147
Price Forecasting Exercise	9	180
Quotech	7	118
Red Sea Corporation	13	241
Roger Gray	6	90
Saint Mary's Health Center	18	318
Saucy Foods Limited	8	142
Scope Repairs	17	305
Somers Office Products Inc.	4	56
Specialty Brewers	10	210
St. Ann's Hospital	5	78
Super Stamps and Products Inc. (B)	8	151
Talbot County School Board	17	301
The Purchasing Co-op (R)	1	16
TriCity	15	277
UIL Inc.	3	44

INTRODUCTION

These notes are designed to assist instructors using the text: *Purchasing and Supply Management*. The intention is to help the instructor have an effective and enjoyable experience while the class participants are likewise engaged in a stimulating learning environment. A participative way of learning and teaching is recommended on the philosophy that learning by doing is more effective than learning by listening.

The purpose in preparing this Instructor's Manual is to provide suggestions which may be helpful to instructors who are using *Purchasing and Supply Management* in regularly organized classes in undergraduate or graduate schools, colleges, industrial firms, service organizations, institutions, or trade associations. The manual should not be made available to students. The suggestions are based on the experiences of teaching the cases and exercises in our classes at The University of Western Ontario, Arizona State University, and in executive development programs for managers and practitioners.

This text reflects the major changes taking place across the world in management philosophy. Total customer satisfaction, e-procurement, total quality management, total cost of ownership, outsourcing, continuous improvement, time compression, world class competition, supply chain management, focus on value added activities, environmental concerns, benchmarking, partnering with suppliers and strategic alliances, supplier rationalization and strategic long term procurement or supply management have all been incorporated into the text and cases in this edition.

Also, for the reader's ease, the outline of each chapter and key questions facing practitioners introduce each new major topic area addressed and margin notes provided further guidance.

The central theme of this text deals with supply efficiency **and** effectiveness.

Effectiveness is concerned about the fit between purchasing objectives and strategies and organizational objectives and strategies.

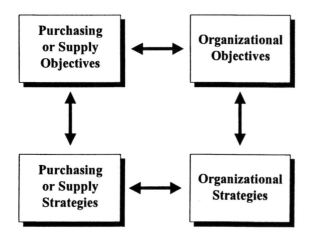

It is the double arrows relationship that truly reflects supply effectiveness. In other words, it is not only how can supply ensure that organizational objectives and strategies are appropriately enforced by the supply function and supplier, but **also** how should organizational objectives and strategies be changed to reflect opportunities and challenges on the supply side?

This is the essential focus of this text, now in its eighth decade, to ensure the continuing advancement of purchasing and supply management. The cases have been selected to identify the full range of ways in which this may be accomplished.

THE CASE CONTEXT

All of the cases were obtained from real organizations and companies and are based on actual experiences. There is seldom just one answer, or just one way of thinking about a business problem. Consequently, there generally is no one "right" answer for the problems presented in the cases. It is important that the student make a decision and that such a decision be based on a definition of the issue or problem, and on a careful and thorough analysis of the pertinent facts and a consideration of the alternative courses of action which may be available.

A few small cases have been included at the beginning of each chapter's case section. These can be used for in-class reading and immediate discussion, if desired. They also provide a gradation of relatively easy at the start to more difficult cases at the end of each chapter. What makes the case material of particular interest, even to instructors who may not wish to discuss them formally in class, is the opportunity for students to learn a tremendous amount about current materials problems and practices by just reading them. Samples of organization charts, forms, reports, contracts, and correspondence are included in cases where relevant. Thus, the cases and their contents offer a unique opportunity for reinforcement of chapter readings.

All cases have been written with the concept of an underlying corporate or organizational mission and strategy. In this context the relevant question for all case material becomes:

> "How can the supply function be managed to contribute effectively to organizational objectives and strategies?"

Although the corporate strategy and mission may not be explicitly stated in every case, reasonable assumptions may be made using the industry and other case information as a guide. For example, a company supplying electrical power to industrial and domestic users is in a totally different position from a chemical firm, a hospital, or an electronic corporation. The ratio of dollars spent in the purchasing and materials area to the corporation's sales (or total budget), the absolute dollar value, and the opportunities for improvement and their impact on the organization's financial outlook are simple preliminary guides to determine strategic potential.

Instant availability and the impact of quality have become matters of increasing concern in the past few years. Similarly, price control over vital items has presented a new dimension of strategic worries. It is the adoption of a forward look with concern for the future rather than the efficient filling of current requisitions that is sought in this text. Moreover, we see a major distinction between efficiency and effectiveness.

Almost all of the case material at the end of each chapter has been reported in such a fashion that the initial cases are brief, relatively easy, and dealing with fundamental issues. The later cases in each chapter become progressively more difficult. Thus, it is possible to use this text for both introductory and more advanced courses. It should be possible with more advanced groups to assign several of the small cases simultaneously.

For those anxious to use the case material extensively, the following comments and reference materials may be of particular interest.

Teaching by the case method is a challenging experience which requires a thorough knowledge of the case to be taught and a carefully thought-out program to achieve the teaching objectives. It is recommended that those who wish to explore the many variations possible in teaching by the case method and developing a case course read the text: *Teaching with Cases* by J.A. Erskine, L.A. Mauffette-Leenders and M.R. Leenders, published by the University of Western Ontario, Richard Ivey School of Business.

The brand new text *Learning with Cases* by the same three authors is a small book for use by students to explain the effective use of cases. It is also available from the same source.

The third case method book from the same authors: *Writing Cases* explains how cases are written and may be particularly useful for those who wish to understand the origin of cases.

Anyone wishing to order these texts or a case from an earlier edition of *Purchasing and Materials Management* not included in this edition can do so from Ivey Publishing, Ivey Management Services, c/o Richard Ivey School of Business, The University of Western Ontario, London, Ontario, Canada N6A 3K7. Telephone: (519) 661-3208. Fax: (519) 661-3882. E-mail: cases@ivey.uwo.ca. Website: http://www.ivey.uwo.ca/cases.

POWERPOINT PRESENTATIONS, TRANSPARENCY MASTERS AND ELECTRONIC QUIZ ACCESS

Instructors wishing to use PowerPoint presentations, transparencies of text diagrams or the chapter quizzes can access the McGraw-Hill website The transparency master at the start of each new chapter, can be used in previous classes to signal the next subjects to be raised, or during chapter introduction or discussion, or even later in review.

A useful tool for lectures, a PowerPoint presentation to accompany the text will be available on the website (http://www.mhhe.com/leenders12e). The slides will include tables and graphs from the text. This presentation material is shown six to a page in the Appendix of this Instructor's Manual.

THE REVIEW AND DISCUSSION QUESTIONS

The review and discussion questions at the end of each chapter are directly geared to the chapter readings and the answers will be found on the appropriate pages in each chapter. Their order has been scrambled, so that students will not simply start at the beginning of the chapter and go forward. The questions have been carefully selected to highlight the most important sections of each chapter and form an excellent base for review.

THE USE OF REPORTS

The writing of reports, if directed properly, can be a useful learning experience in studying procurement. One type of report which has been used successfully as an assignment for a term paper is a Product Buying Report. This report can be used to have students do field research with a specific company to obtain the information needed. Presented below in Exhibit I is a suggested form for assigning the report.

Exhibit I[1]

PRODUCT BUYING REPORT

In the assigned report, you are expected to present the information a buyer should have in order to purchase a specific product intelligently. This report should not be solely a factual presentation of commodity data but should reflect your concept of the function of a buyer. Therefore, in selecting and presenting the facts in your report, you should indicate--where it is not apparent--what use a buyer might make of these facts. The inclusion of extraneous and useless data will detract from the effectiveness and grade of your report.

There is, of course, no formula or check list which can be followed in determining the information which a buyer needs for sound purchasing. While the decision as to the data to be covered is, therefore, a matter for individual decision, the following topics are suggested for your consideration:

1. The intended use of the product and the requirements to be met by the item purchased.
2. The available products which might meet these requirements and their characteristics. (In discussing the characteristics of these products, the grades, classifications, and properties which distinguish one product from another should be defined.) From the available products, one may be selected for detailed investigation.
3. The technical data required in specifying and inspecting the selected product.
4. The materials and/or parts entering into the selected product and some analysis of their sources and availability.
5. Methods of manufacture, provided that they are significant in selecting suppliers or in appraising quality.
6. Sources from which the product can be obtained.
7. Factors affecting the supply, demand, price, and inventory of the selected product. An analysis of general business conditions is not intended.
8. Detailed sources of information on the selected product.

Your report should indicate by footnotes or otherwise the **specific** source of all data presented. Joint reports will not be accepted unless specifically approved by the instructor in advance.

The buying of commodities is of major importance to many companies, and consequently the student of procurement should know as much as possible about how to acquire the essential information and recognize the influences which affect the determination of the price of any commodity. Assigned readings will provide information on the operation of commodity exchanges, the factors affecting

---

[1] The assignment for a Product Buying Report was distributed to the students on the first day of class; the report was due just before the end of the term (approximately three months later). It was assigned in addition to the price forecast.

demand and supply of a commodity, and the technical or commercial grading standards used. One way of stimulating a student's interest in what happens to a specific commodity in the marketplace is to assign the Exercise in Price Forecasting. Another variation of assigning an exercise in price forecasting is shown in Exhibit II.

There are a variety of ways of handling the commodity forecast included in the chapter. Included here are some further details and some different options as to how to proceed. Basic differences between them lie with the number of people that are part of the commodity forecasting group, and the amount of explanation necessary to justify the forecast. Also, the price forecast and commodity commitment included in Exhibit III includes personal presentations in class.

Exhibit II

Each member of the class will be expected on or before _____, _____, to select one commodity traded on a regular exchange, signing his or her name after this selection. Not more than two persons may select one commodity. Any member of the class who has not indicated his or her choice on or before _____, _____, will be assigned a commodity.

On _____, _____, each person will be expected to hand in a statement containing the following data:

1. Name of commodity selected.
2. Grade of commodity on which price is quoted.
3. Price of commodity as of _____, _____
   (Where the quotation applies only to a particular city, that point should be named; thus, No. 2 hard, winter wheat at Chicago.)
4. Specific source of this quotation.
   (Give the name of the publication, data, and page. Sources are to be confined wholly to published information; no interviews will be permitted.)
5. **Anticipated price** (on comparable basis with that used in paragraph 3 above) as of _____, _____.

An analysis of the reasons for anticipating the price as forecasted will be accepted but is **not required**. Joint reports will not be accepted. Each forecast must be the individual's own forecast. **The final grade given on this assignment will be based entirely on the accuracy of the forecast.**

COMMODITY FORECAST

Fill in and return by _____p.m., _____, _____.

Name of Commodity_____

    Grade_____

Price on _____, _____ _____
(If quotation is applicable to a given market only, give name of city.)

Source (Give publication name, date, and page.) _____

_____

Forecasted price as of _____, _____ _____

Student's name _____

Another version of the commodity report, using larger groups and class presentations, is shown in the text in Chapter 8.

Another type of report which directs attention to commodity price movements and their effect on the finances of a company is shown in Exhibit III. The student is expected under certain assumptions to recommend an inventory policy for the ensuing three months and the ensuing nine months.

Exhibit III[2]

INVENTORY POLICY REPORT

Assume the following conditions:

1. The commodity which you have been assigned is a product of such importance to your company that continued operation is impossible without working amounts of the item.
2. There is now on hand a thirty-day stock of the item and outstanding orders for the immediate delivery of an additional thirty-day stock.
3. The company has adequate financial resources to pursue any inventory policy that seems wise.
4. The company has accepted orders from customers which will tax its manufacturing capacity for the next two months.
5. The company need not be an actual company, but it should be placed within a specific industry which complies with the conditions under paragraphs 1 and 2. For example, if your commodity were carbon black, you should assume that your company is either a rubber manufacturer, an ink manufacturer, or a paint manufacturer.
6. If any of the above assumptions are not realistic for your commodity, explain why, and make more realistic ones.

Problem

What inventory policy would you recommend (a) from June 1, _____, to September 1, _____, (b) from September 1, _____, to March 10, _____?

Note

- The recommendations should be an expression of the writer's own reasoned judgement, not merely a composite of what others may have said or written.
- The report is not to exceed 1,500 words.
- The **specific** source of all data on which your conclusions are based should be indicated.

A third type of commodity report is concerned with the procurement channels through which an assigned commodity moves from the producer to the end buyer. this report requires the names of the major producers; the channels through which the commodity moves (or may move) to reach the user; a rough estimate of the percentage of the total of the assigned commodity moving through each channel; and the names of potential sources from which , in a specific geographic area, a supply could be secured.

---

[2] This report was distributed to the students one month before its due date. It was assigned in addition to the Price Forecast.

COURSE DESIGN OPTIONS

This text lends itself for use in a variety of courses such as 40-session courses, a 25-session course, a 15-session course, as well as shorter seminars for specific groups, topics, or industries. For example, in 25 sessions of 1 ½ hour classes in a graduate course the following outline is used:

Sessions	Cases and Exercises	Chapter Readings
1	Assign Commodity Price Forecast and Discuss Commercial Laundry Products in class, after reading in class	
2	Custom Equipment (A)	1, 2
3	Duchess University	2
4	Artsell Inc.	3
5	Establishing e-Business Standards at Deere & Company	4
6	Dorman Printing	5
7	Corn Silk	6
8	Quotech	7
9	Bid Evaluation	6, 7
10	Paron Metal Fabricating	8
11	Saucy Foods Limited	8
12	Commodity Purchasing Game	9
13	Chevron Corporation: The PC Selection Team	9
14	Specialty Brewers	10
15	Ornex	11
16	Brassco	12
17	Red Sea Corporation	13
18	Marathon Oil Company International	14
19	TriCity	15
20	Casson Construction	16
21	Scope Repairs	17
22	Heat Transfer Systems Inc.	18
23	Custom Windows Inc.	18
24	Commodity Forecasts	9
25	Course Review	

For a 15-session introductory course at the college or undergraduate level, a different selection of materials is advised. It is also advised that certain sections of the chapters not be assigned, since they can be seen as more advanced. A suggested possible outline for such a course might be:

Sessions	Cases and Exercises	Chapters
1	The Purchasing Co-op (R)	1
2	Goodlife Club	2
3	Mike Wesley	3
4	Somers Office Products Inc.	4
5	St. Ann's Hospital	5
6	Roger Gray	6
7	Lancaster Life Insurance Co.	7
8	A review and midterm examination session	
9	MasTech Inc.	9
10	Great Western Bank	10
11	City of Roxborough	15
12	Erica Carson	17
13	A Visitor to Answer Questions on Any Aspect	
14	A Review Session	
15	An Exam	

SPECIAL INTEREST GROUPS

Special interest groups can easily be accommodated with the case materials. For example, the public institutions include:

Duchess University, City of Roxborough, Don Willit Associates, Tri City, Scope Repairs and Talbot County School Board

Nonmanufacturing or service organizations include:

The Purchasing Co-Op, Goodlife Club, Great Western Bank, Lancaster Life Insurance, Don Willit Associates, St. Ann's Hospital and Saint Mary's Health Center.

Similar listings can be extracted for small businesses, manufacturing organizations, or topic areas as has already been done in the chapters. The nature of cases is such that the same case could be used in different places, depending on the instructor's preference. For example, Talbot County School Board is a public organization, but has been included in another chapter. Almost all of the cases in Chapter 6 and many of the others have price implications and could conceivably be used in connection with Chapter 7. An instructor not satisfied with the case selection available for any one chapter might inspect some of the other chapters for the possibility of substitution.

EXAMINATIONS

Included in every chapter in the text are questions for review and discussion. All, or any of these would make good examination questions. Even if these were used only for five to fifteen minutes, they are quite appropriate.

In this instructor's manual are included multiple choice and true or false questions for every chapter. These may be reproduced and used for examinations for those instructors wishing to do so. No permission is required from the publisher for this purpose.

For those wishing to use cases for examination purposes, the following comments may be helpful. It is possible to use a case as a three or four hour final exam in this course. Under those circumstances students are welcome to bring their own books and notes into the exam room. One is the Harvard Business School Case Services, Harvard Graduate School of Business Administration, Soldier's Field, Boston, MA 02163. Website: http://www.hbsp.harvard.edu. Another is Richard Ivey School of Business, University of Western Ontario, London, Ontario, Canada N6A 3K7. Website: www.ivey.uwo.ca/cases. The European Case Clearing House website (ECCH) is: http://www.ecch.cranfield.uk.ac. These clearing houses are an excellent continuing source of new case material, which may be ordered from their bibliographies. Clearly, the material in this book can also be used for examination purposes and the following options might be seriously considered for longer examinations of the three to four hour type.

Saint Mary's Health Center, Heat Transfer Systems, Custom Windows, Scope Repairs, Super Stamps, Saucy Foods, Commercial Laundry Products, IPC, Specialty Brewers, Custom Windows, Chevron and Global Heat Exchangers, Corn Silk, Cable and Wireless PLC, Global Pharmaceuticals..

For short 1 - 2 hour examinations the following cases in the book are excellent:

Goodlife Club, Quotech, Brassco, and City of Roxborough.

THE USE OF AUDIO-VISUAL SUPPORT AND THE INTERNET

Well-selected videos and slides can be used to stimulate interest and add to the learning process. No video should ever be used unless it has been previewed by the instructor and he or she is convinced that the video will fill a teaching objective which he or she has in mind.

Many of the major producers of raw materials have produced videos which do excellent jobs of showing how the materials are produced, and in some instances the channels through which the materials move to market.

The National Association of Purchasing Management, Inc., 2055 East Centennial Circle, P.O. Box 22160, Tempe, AZ 85285-2160 has developed a substantial number of video and slide presentations. There is a reasonable rental charge for most of the programs. NAPM will provide a current list of what is available upon request to the Tempe, Arizona office.

The new one hour video by Mike Leenders about Purchasing Management and Reverse Marketing is available in three languages (English, French, and Dutch) from Video Management in Brussels. It is an excellent reinforcer of the key messages in this text. It can be ordered from: Video Management, Rue du Marais 33, 1000 Brussels, Belgium, telephone: 32 2 219 94 97 or International Tele-Firm Enterprises, 47 Densley Avenue, Toronto, Ontario M6M 5A8, telephone (416) 241-4483 or 243-2958, fax (416) 243-3287.

The Internet is a wonderful source of a large variety of information and its usefulness continues to expand.

Websites can be used to provide company and industry information, commodity exchange data and coverage of interesting topic areas. The Report on Business and the NAPM Purchasing Managers Indexes on Manufacturing and Non Manufacturing as well as the Ivey Purchasing Managers Index in Canada provide useful monthly updates on national business activity.

Students can access supplier catalogs, price components, compare offerings and develop a buying plan just using web data.

Copies of key diagrams have also been reproduced in transparency form to facilitate classroom reinforcement.

In these instructor's notes we have also included multiple choice and true and false questions for each chapter. The correct answer for each question is shown in the margin. The instructor should take care when reproducing these questions to keep the answers off.

THE USE OF VISITORS TO CLASS

Our experience shows that inviting visitors to classes, for almost any level of course, can be an interesting way to provide a change of pace and to add reality to the class readings and materials. Such people may have special expertise, for example, in commodities, public procurement, transportation, value analysis, or in certain commodities. There may also be people with a substantial amount of generalized experience which can be used near the end of the course to discuss almost any aspects of the supply function.

Sometimes, field trips to purchasing offices in the area can also be arranged.

QUIZZES AND COMMENTARIES

The remainder of this manual contains the transparencies and quizzes for each chapter and the instructor's notes for all the cases and exercises. They have been arranged in the same order as they appear in the text.

CHAPTER 1

The Challenge of Purchasing and Supply Management

Topics Covered

From Purchasing to Supply Management
    Purchasing and Logistics
Significance in Material Dollars
Decision Making in the Purchasing/Supply Management Context
The Differences between Commercial and Consumer Acquisition
Contribution of the Purchasing/Supply Management Function
    A Dual Supply Perspective
    The Direct and Indirect Contribution of Supply
Professionalism in Purchasing
Challenges Facing Purchasing and Supply Management over the Next Decade

Business-to-Business E-Commerce
Supply-Chain Management
Measurement
Purchase of Nontraditional Goods and Services
Contributions to Corporate Strategy
Recognition by Senior Management
Questions for Review and Discussion
References
Cases
    Commercial Laundry Products
    Custom Equipment
    The Purchasing of Co-Op

QUIZ RESPONSES

E   1. Purchasing has the potential to contribute to which of the following organizational objectives:

       a. profit.
       b. return on assets.
       c. competitive position.
       d. corporate social policy.
       e. all of the above.

C   2. In the typical United States manufacturing firm, purchases of materials (including capital equipment) account for what percentage of the sales dollar?

       a. 30 to 39.
       b. 40 to 49.
       c. 50 to 59.
       d. 60 to 69.
       e. 70 to 79.

A   3. The profit-leverage effect of purchasing means that:

       a. a dollar saved in purchasing has an effect on profits that is substantially greater than an extra dollar of sales.
       b. a good buyer can exert a good deal of leverage on a supplier.
       c. combining purchases gives "clout" or leverage to the buyer.
       d. good purchasing should be able to reduce prices paid by at least 10 percent.
       e. none of the above.

D	4.	Supply chain management refers to:

a. managing the sourcing process, obtaining materials, and maintaining relationships with key suppliers as directed by internal users.
b. managing the acquisition of supplies needed by governmental, usually military, entities.
c. managing supplies for maintenance, repairs, and operations (MRO) in the manufacturing sector only.
d. managing the flow of materials, services, and information from key suppliers, their suppliers, and their suppliers' suppliers to the end customer.
e. managing and monitoring the status of raw materials as a current asset all the way through to finished goods inventory. |
| C. | 5. | Purchasing in the early 21st century is characterized by:

a. reactive strategies and adversarial relationships.
b. short-term thinking and emphasis on price.
c. integration with the total business process.
d. tactical, transaction-based orientation.
e. competitive bidding and awards based on lowest price. |
| D | 6. | To contribute to organizational strategy, the purchasing department should:

a. buy from local suppliers.
b. double the return on assets (ROA).
c. buy from minority suppliers.
d. keep management informed of opportunities.
e. buy only from one supplier. |
| E | 7. | Purchasing is a potential source of information about:

a. current and potential customers.
b. acquisition candidates.
c. new marketing techniques.
d. distribution systems of suppliers.
e. all of the above. |

D | 8. One of the most basic, fundamental questions in supply management is:

   a. should we have a single source of supply for a specific purchase or multiple sources?
   b. should we order small quantities to avoid inventory charges or large quantities to get volume discounts?
   c. should we drop an existing supplier because of a slight price discount from a potential supplier?
   d. should we make or buy the needed good or service?
   e. should we make a long- or short-term agreement with a supplier?

B | 9. The return on assets effect (ROA):

   a. is an example of an indirect contribution of supply management.
   b. measures the impact of a purchase price reduction on the inventory asset base and the firm's performance.
   c. is caused by increasing sales at a greater rate than the cost of materials is increasing.
   d. is the result of reductions in the carrying cost of inventory.
   e. means that a dollar saved in purchasing has an effect on return that is substantially greater than an extra dollar of sales.

B | 10. Performance of the supply management function can be viewed in two contexts:

   a. trouble avoidance and opportunistic.
   b. trouble causing and reactive.
   c. quality oriented and value-driven.
   d. price sensitive and hard-nosed negotiating.
   e. none of the above.

True and False

F   1. The total purchase sales ratio (the percentage of sales dollars paid out to suppliers) varies little from industry to industry.

T   2. Purchasing can do much to influence management strategy and social policy to help develop local businesses, assist minority-owned businesses, and protect the environment.

T   3. Among the most significant challenges facing supply managers are applying business-to-business e-commerce tools to supply, problems with measuring results, gaining recognition of top management, and lack of involvement in buying nontraditional goods and services.

T   4. The North American Industry Classification System (NAICS) replaces the Standard Industry Code (SIC) as a means of categorizes industries.

F   5. Since outlays for purchased materials are greatly exceeded by labor and other costs in most manufacturing companies, purchasing cannot contribute much to permanent cost control.

F   6. The single most important step in achieving the potential of the purchasing function in a company is changing the name of the function from purchasing to supply management.

T   7. Purchasing and supply management has evolved from a transaction-based, tactical function to a process-oriented, strategic one.

F   8. Business-to-business e-commerce tools have little applicability to the purchasing process.

T   9. One of the best recognized barometers of business activity is the NAPM Report on Business which normally appears on the second business day of each month.

F   10. The Center for Advanced Purchasing Studies is the research arm of the International Federation of Purchasing and Materials Management (IFPMM).

Commercial Laundry Products (COLP)

Teaching Note

IMMEDIATE ISSUE

Are there potential savings by consolidating all of the boxes into one supplier order?

BASIC ISSUES

1. The advantages of consolidation.
2. The interaction between order quantities and prices.
3. The use of economic order quantities.
4. Understanding supplier costs.

SUGGESTED STUDENT ASSIGNMENT

1. Are materials savings possible with consolidation?
2. What is the implied set-up cost in the quotes provided?
3. Given this set-up cost, what would be the economic order quantity if we assume a carrying cost of 2% per month for this material?
4. What does your answer to question 3 imply?
5. What other considerations might enter into the order quantity calculation?
6. What would be your decision if the supplier offered to provide boxes on a daily delivery basis, provided you agreed to award a total annual contract for 10 million boxes at $250,000?

POSSIBLE DISCUSSION QUESTIONS

1. What are the advantages of consolidation?
2. What are the disadvantages of consolidation?
3. Why might COLP want to discontinue the use of co-packagers?
4. What else needs to be discussed with the printer?
5. Are there other alternatives that could be considered?

DISCUSSION

This is an interesting situation with an opportunity for lots of calculations. Moreover, the calculations provide some surprising answers! Let's take each of the questions one by one.

1. Are material savings possible with consolidation?

Under the current system COLP is paying $49.00 per 1000 for 1 million boxes for a total of $49,000 and $30.00 per 1000 for 9 million boxes for a total of $270,000 for a total cost of boxes of $319,000. This is the purchase price paid only and no information is given on current order quantities. Therefore, it is not possible to include any carrying charges for any of this packaging material. **(in-house cost)**

When we compare the $319,000 to the new prices quoted we find that in order quantities of 500,000 the annual cost would come to $295,000; annual order quantities of 750,000 would go down to $268,700; 1,500,000 would be $247,710; and at 2,000,000 per order it would drop to $239,930. None of these figures contain any carrying costs either. They tend to suggest, however, that some significant material savings may still be possible by consolidation. Moreover, the order quantity has a major impact on the actual savings achieved.

2. What is the implied set-up cost in the quotes provided?

We can use the supplier's quote to calculate an implied set-up cost. For example, if we used the order quantities of 500,000 and 750,000 we can come to the following conclusion:

at 500,000 order quantity the cost is $X + 500 \times (Y) = 29.5 \times 500 = 14,750$
at 750,000 order quantity the cost is $X + 750 \times (Y) = \$20,152.50$
∴ $250 Y = 5,402.50$ and $Y = \$21.61$ per 1000

$X = \$3,845$

Therefore, the set-up cost implied by these two quotes is $3,845.00 and the cost per 1000 is $21.61

When we do similar calculations for 1.5 million and 2 million order quantities, we find that at 2 million $X + 2000 Y$ is $47,860; $X + 1500$ is $37,155. Therefore, $500 Y = \$10,715$ and $Y = \$21.43$, and $X + 2000 Y$ is $47,860 from which $2000 Y$ is $= \$42,860$ and X is $5,000. Therefore, at the higher volumes the set-up cost is $5000 and the variable cost is $21.43 per 1000.

This is a rather surprising finding. There are several possibilities for this. One is that the supplier is not quoting consistently. Another is that two different processes may actually be used to produce these boxes and that at the higher quantities a different type of equipment might be used. It is also possible that the supplier may be able to get some quantity discount on the materials and be able to quote a slightly lower material cost at the higher quantities.

3. Given this set-up cost what would be the EOQ if we assume the carrying cost of 2% for this material?

If we use the $3,845 set-up cost the EOQ = $\sqrt{2 \times 10,000,000 \times 3,845 \div .24 \times \$21.61} = 3.85$ million. If we use the $5,000 set-up cost and the $21.43 per 1000 variable cost the EOQ = $\sqrt{2 \times 10,000,000 \times \$5,000 \div .24 \times \$21.43 \text{ per } 1000} = 4.41$ million.

4. What does your answer to question 3 imply?

The answer to question 3 implies that Joan Walters did not ask for quotes in higher order quantities and that she should check these out with the supplier. She is asking for quantities in much too low a range at the moment. Total cost calculations at different order quantities show an interesting pattern as follows:

Order Quantity	Purchase Price	Order Cost	Total Cost
4 million	$226,800	$10,286	$237,086
2 million	$239,930	$ 5,143	$245,073
1,500,000	$247,710	$ 3,857	$251,567
750,000	$268,700	$ 1,945	$270,645
500,000	$295,000	$ 1,297	$296,297

5. What other considerations might enter into the order quantity calculation?

Clearly, the ability to forecast specific product requirements is a crucial factor in any of these calculations. Also, the obsolescence of the package design is a further issue. If Joan orders a certain configuration of boxes and the demand runs higher for one type than another, will she get stuck with a large inventory of extra boxes? She achieves purchasing savings by printing multiple boxes on an individual sheet but may incur obsolescence and other costs as a result. She should ask the supplier to give her options on the mix of boxes that she can enter onto any sheet of 20 boxes.

No information is given about available space to store the boxes. It is, at the moment, assumed that in the 24% carrying charge, all appropriate costs have been included. This may not be the case. A higher carrying cost would reduce the economic order quantity. We are also assuming here that sufficient capital is available to tie it up in inventory should this be required.

6. What would be your decision if the supplier offered to provide boxes on a daily delivery basis, provided you agreed to award the total annual contract for 10 million boxes at $250,000?

The lowest total cost possible by taking full ownership of the boxes and storing an average of 2 million boxes at a time with a 4 million boxes order quantity was $237,000. It sure sounds as if it would be worth it to have the supplier do all the storing plus run the risk of varying product demand. It had better be understood that such flexibility is required before any contract is signed along these lines. The supplier has the advantage that it can store the boxes at it's own manufacturing costs rather than it's selling price. If COLP could order boxes on a daily basis and have immediate delivery without any hassles, this would certainly be worth at least $13,000 to them. Even at $250,000 there is a total saving of at least $69,000 compared to the current option of what is paid for the material with co-packagers under the current mode.

It is very important to do the appropriate calculations in this case and to recognize that different students may end up with some slightly varying answers on these questions. It is obvious that the supplier is not consistent in his price quoting and that Joan should have asked for even larger quantities than she did. Obviously, there are many other considerations that go into the decision to quit using co-packagers beyond just a simple question as to how much is paid for the boxes themselves.

Custom Equipment (A)

Teaching Note

This case is part of a series case, with the case Bid Evaluation as the immediate follow-on in chapter 7. Custom Equipment (B) is in the teaching notes for the Bid Evaluation case and can be handed out in class during the Bid Evaluation discussion. Custom Equipment (B) presents a different option (an in-house vendor store) not previously considered.

IMMEDIATE ISSUES

1. How to reduce the number of wire and cable suppliers within a specific time frame?
2. How to improve the total cost of ownership of wire and cable requirements?

BASIC ISSUES

1. Supplier selection and criteria for selection.
2. Supply base reduction.
3. Inventory management.
4. Total cost of ownership.
5. The role of a new employee in purchasing.
6. Single sourcing.

SUGGESTED STUDENT ASSIGNMENT

If you were in the position of Matt Roberts, what would be the best way to proceed with the Wire Management Program given the available resources?

POSSIBLE DISCUSSION QUESTIONS

1. What are the most important factors to consider when deciding on a supplier?
2. If the company goal is to reduce costs, is the WMP an appropriate method to accomplish this objective? Should Matt try to suggest a better method for reducing purchasing costs?
3. Why is it important to take time when selecting a supplier?
4. What considerations are most important to CE in supplier selection?
5. Why not have more than one supplier?
6. Is any additional information required for Matt to make his selection?

7. How can Matt find out more information about the suppliers in a short period of time? What are his internal or external resources that he should consider?

ANALYSIS

Matt is new to CE and he wants to show he is capable of completing any assignment he is given. He doesn't know anyone in CE very well and is unfamiliar with CE's current suppliers and their capabilities.

To reduce the vendor base, the supplier's fit with CE's current needs must be taken into consideration. Although cost savings are important, reducing the time to market is also important, especially for CE's customers. Therefore, Matt should be leaning toward whichever supplier is most responsive to CE's 'rush' requirements, and can also offer competitive pricing. The supplier must be large enough to stock almost anything required, or have access to it in a short time, due to the possibility of specified products. It also must have the agility of a small supplier. Ideally, the vendor should consider CE's business to be important enough to be well-serviced.

Matt should arrange to visit each of the potential suppliers in person, especially since they are local. A personal visit will allow him to observe the supplier's facility, warehouse, and get an impression of the supplier's motivation to supply CE. The financial viability and future goals of the organization should also be considered when assessing if a fit exists.

Having a single-source of supply would allow CE to take advantage of quantity pricing. CE and the chosen supplier may also be able to improve processes together, leading to a reduction in administrative expenses. As a purchasing agent, Matt will be able to focus his time on other procurement issues. However, with only one vendor, continuity of supply cannot be ensured. Therefore, the idea of having two suppliers, or at least a back-up supplier, must be considered. Two or three suppliers are still a reduction in the supplier base.

Two suppliers may be used in various ways. One could supply certain products, while the second provides others. Alternatively, one could supply regular items, and the second could supply rush/specialty products. There are numerous ways to arrange what each supplies. The benefit is that CE has a smaller chance of being without the products it requires. The suppliers may also be more conscious of pricing, especially due to product overlap. There is a possibility of collusion, but with commodity products, CE could always gauge the market periodically. The major downside is that both suppliers may not provide as good pricing as they would being the only source.

Matt is receiving some informal evaluation from various employees at CE, but he cannot justify the validity of their statements. He is also unfamiliar with potential personal connections that the employees have with the suppliers. The comments of the receiving manager, who kept some records on supplier performance, could be a valuable source of objective information.

Alternatives

1. **Gather more information / do not make selection**

    a. Use time to collect information through supplier visits.
    b. Contact the suppliers' current comparable customers to get their opinions on the suppliers' performance.
    c. Matt, as a new employee, wants to prove his abilities as a good decision maker, but needs to collect more data before making a decision. He also wants to please his manager, who originated the WMP.

    Gathering more information and establishing personal contact with the potential suppliers will give Matt the opportunity to assess which are capable of fulfilling all of CE's requirements. He wants to do his best with the WMP, and should know more about the electric suppliers. It will allow him to understand which suppliers are most capable of fulfilling all needs and he will get a qualitative feel for who is the most-likely candidate prior to receiving the bids. This alternative may be used as a first step, but will not satisfy the WMP objective.

    The records kept by the receiving manager regarding supplier performance need to be analyzed carefully. Matt should sit down with him, since not everything will be included in the written records.

2. **Choose one best candidate**

    a. Select the most capable supplier and ask if they would like to supply all CE's wire and cable requirements.
    b. This would save a lot of time, and Matt could justify his selection with the receiving manager's records.
    c. More time could be given to negotiating with a preferred supplier, rather than analyzing numerous bids.

    This might be a good option if Matt had a few years experience dealing with the suppliers. Matt may not be the best candidate to assess a supplier's capability without having first-hand experience. Negotiating an improved total contract may be more advantageous than a bidding process. However, suppliers tend to make their best effort when they know there is competition and there is a possibility of losing business. Past performance records are a good, but not perfect indication of a supplier's future performance. Finally, since Matt is relatively new, his negotiating skills may require honing, and he may not fully understand all details required for effective negotiation. This alternative would not be the best choice in this circumstance.

3. **Choose two best candidates (or even three)**

   a. Similar to option Alternative #2.
   b. By selecting two suppliers from the initial base, Matt has the opportunity to observe the suppliers handle various requests.
   c. Given that reducing the 'time to market' is very important to CE's customers, it would be beneficial to have a second supplier to further guarantee availability.

   Although it should not be difficult to choose the best two suppliers from the group, many of the reasons for not choosing Alternative #2 are applicable here.

   CE may not achieve its best potential cost reduction goal if there are still two or more suppliers. Using two suppliers, Matt may be able to select the best candidate for wire and also the best for cable. Alternatively, he could choose the supplier who had the best prices for both products, and also keep the second best supplier. In time, he could negotiate with the one that excelled in performance; thereby going from 6 suppliers down to 2 (or 3), and even down to a single source. This alternative is possible only if his manager approves having more than one supplier, otherwise it cannot be chosen.

4. **Use a bidding process**

   a. Send out a request for suppliers to quote all of CE's annual wire and cable requirements.
   b. A bid submission can be an excellent method for assessing a supplier's capability. Information is gathered and analyzed to make a more informed decision.
   c. This was mentioned in the case as the process CE's customers use to choose a supplier for a project. Therefore, it is quite acceptable within the automotive industry.
   d. Only ask the most qualified suppliers to submit bids → Must consider supplier's actual ability to supply before asking to quote. This can be achieved by initially implementing Alternative #1.

   There is quite a lot of information that can be gathered about suppliers, especially if the bid requests specific information. Some of the most creative ideas can be proposed simply by asking the bidding supplier to explain why they would make the best fit with our organization. When the suppliers realize what is required of them, they may arrive at the conclusion that servicing the organization may be more than they anticipated. In other words, it is an opportunity for the supplier to opt-out of the selection process.

   Bid preparation can take a few days and cost the supplier a considerable amount of money. It's not fair to ask a large number of suppliers to prepare quotes, only to select the most obvious and favored choice from the beginning.

Suppliers that are aware of their competition will usually have a "very sharp pencil" when quoting, especially if the business is desired. Therefore, this process can be more effective than negotiation in many cases, which saves a lot of time on both sides.

A negative aspect of bidding is misinterpretation by the buyer regarding certain aspects of the quote. A supplier may be quickly excluded from the process if this occurs. To avoid this occurrence, companies occasionally allow a post-bid meeting to discuss the proposal in detail. This meeting is sometimes beneficial in creating improved proposals. Again however, meetings take time and cost money.

5. **Use a bidding process and then negotiate final agreement**

   a. Similar to Alternative #4, but with the added ability to negotiate aspects of the proposals. The bid analysis allows narrowing of the potential suppliers.
   b. This alternative is attractive especially if there are aspects of the most attractive bid(s) that could be improved upon.

The bidding process is effective in choosing one best candidate, but there may be aspects of that supplier's proposal that can be improved upon. Terms, certain product prices, or delivery may not be as favorable as that found in other proposals, which creates the possibility of negotiation and discussion. Similar to other alternatives, the negotiation process takes time and therefore increases costs. Yet, if potential benefits of post-bid negotiation are possible, it is worth the effort. This alternative is possible, especially since Matt will possess a greater understanding of the suppliers' abilities after the bids are returned to him, and because there is less time pressure to make a selection. Employ this Alternative if discrepancies exist in the chosen bid proposal.

Recommendation

As Matt, I would initially implement Alternative #1 to gather more information about the potential suppliers. It would be possible to meet and visit all suppliers in less than one week, considering they are all local. Information gathering would allow Matt to get to know suppliers and enable him to determine the most capable suppliers.

Then I would implement Alternative #4 by sending out a request to bid to the best-qualified suppliers asking suppliers to quote the total package. The bid request would include CE's current annual and forecasted requirements for all wire and cable.

Suppliers would be encouraged to include innovative ideas to handle CE's requirements. If prices are relatively even, an interesting plan detailing how the supplier could better service CE may set the supplier apart from the group.

Their reasons for making this recommendation include: fairness, objectivity, the desire to meet managerial expectations, and the potential for achieving a greater total cost reduction.

Key Points

1. Purchaser should not make such an important decision with incomplete information.
2. Employees' opinions and advice are helpful but can be biased. Everyone has his favorite, but it may not necessarily be in the best interest of the organization as a whole.
3. The assignment of the WMP may be a test to see how the new purchasing agent reacts, a way to meet others and familiarize himself with the suppliers, a method of understanding important factors to purchasing within Custom Equipment. It's also a way to assess Matt's analytical and interpersonal skills.
4. A good method for finding out about a supplier's performance is to contact another organization currently using them. Ask them to comment on various positive and negative attributes of the supplier.
5. Visiting a supplier, if possible, will allow the buyer to assess many aspects, including size, stock available, number of personnel, systems and processes in place, and general culture of the organization. A catalogue may be available to see exactly which products are stocked.
6. Single sourcing may lead to a closer relationship and the opportunity for further cost savings. Therefore, reduction is costs may not be limited to this particular situation. New ideas and methods can be developed.

The Purchasing Co-op (R)

Teaching Note

IMMEDIATE ISSUE

Determine how best to promote the growth of the purchasing co-op.

BASIC ISSUES

1. Consortia purchasing.
2. Supplies management.
3. Source selection.
4. Small business/entrepreneurship.

SUGGESTED STUDENT ASSIGNMENT

1. As Margaret Warren, what would you do to promote the growth of the purchasing co-op?
2. How would your action plan change if the purchasing co-op involved organizations with combined purchases in the million dollar range?

SUGGESTED DISCUSSION QUESTIONS

1. What are the advantages and disadvantages of a purchasing corsortium?
2. Is the idea of rotating purchasing responsibilities among consortium members a good idea?
3. Should Margaret charge for her purchasing experrtise?
4. Does this consortium have a long-term future?
5. What are the challenges of buying for a small business?
6. How large could this consortium grow?
7. What members make best candidates for consortium buying?

DISCUSSION

1. As Margaret Warren, what would you do to promote the growth of the purchasing co-op?

Answering this question requires the student to recognize that "the tasks of arranging purchases, understanding purchasing terminology, and finding and reaching suppliers, while necessary, and normally considered non-value added activities for small business types." For many of these small business owners, the production aspect of the business is what they do best. Additionally, students need to realize the informal arrangement and management of the purchasing co-op described in the case. When deciding on how to promote the growth of the purchasing co-op, the student should:

(a) Articulate the benefits Margaret anticipated in the formation of the purchasing co-op (i.e., more purchasing and price clout). The case makes it clear that there are purchasing cost savings of about 20 per cent, but if any of the other businesses are like Margaret's, then these savings are not necessarily noteworthy (the 20 per cent figure is an approximation as not all the co-op members employ accurate accounting software). Shipping lead times averaged two to three days and shipping costs on a purchase of $200 equalled $10, further demonstrating that price and cost reductions (one of the main drivers to form such co-operatives) was, in hindsight, not that big of an attraction for members. As the co-op grows, however, price and cost reductions may become increasingly important.

(b) Articulate the unintended benefits achieved in the formation of the purchasing co-op (i.e., better customer service from vendors, better understanding of running a small business through shared experiences and practices among co-op members);

(c) Recognize the importance of the Local Business Women's Association in identifying other businesses (not necessarily competitors) who produce products or have business needs similar to Margaret's'; and

(d) Recognize that "growth" refers to both the size of the co-op group (e.g., at what size would some of the administrative duties become burdensome as all the co-op management tasks related to the order are done by a single individual in turn; however, a larger co-op group may allow for subgroups of co-op members to purchase "with clout") and the direction of the co-op group's purchases (e.g., the group experimented first with essential oils and then included labels, wrapping, etc. Photocopying and printing services were now being considered — based on other small businesses students may relate to, are there other business material needs that Margaret's co-op group should consider? This may facilitate a discussion of what some of these common business needs of small businesses are).

The price and cost reductions will become more important as Margaret's sales of Utopia Soap products increase. The student can estimate some of Margaret's present and potential material needs that she would purchase through the co-op. For example, the case notes that each bar of soap costs $1. Based on Exhibit 1, 30 cents of that relates to essential oils. Given that the price of a 467 millilitre bottle of essential oil costs $100, that means that 330 bars of soap can be produced from each 467 millilitre bottle assuming no waste. Margaret's 1999 sales are $10,000 (the case states that a small percentage of sales are made directly by Margaret, so assume 95 per cent sales from retailers and wholesalers, five per cent sales sold direct, indicating 3,300 soap bars sold), meaning that she needed 10 bottles of essential oils (assuming that there are no differences in essential oil prices). With a 25 per cent growth in sales over the coming year (or 4,125 soap bars), that translates to a need for 13 bottles of essential oils. To attain the three-year goal of $100,000 in annual sales (assume increase due to sales to retailers and wholesalers, or 33,300 soap bars), Margaret will need to purchase 100 bottles of essential oils. Undoubtedly, she will have to increase her batch size as her volume grows. Related to this growth may be an expansion of the soap product line, resulting in more varied materials needs and more complex production requirements. This analysis focused only on essential oils, but the key issue is that even for such a small-scaled operation indicate that this handmade soap operation is not Margaret's core business, but one of several; what might the businesses of the other five co-op members resemble?), there are benefits in forming such an informal purchasing arrangement.

2. **How would your action plan change if the purchasing co-op involved organizations with combined purchases in the million-dollar range?**

Johnson identifies the following nine reasons for purchasing collaboratively:

- Price and cost reductions due to increased volume
- Staff reductions
- Product and service standardization
- Improved supplier management capabilities
- Specialization of staff
- Customer service
- Higher profile through a purchasing collaboration
- Expanded role of purchasing
- Transition of products through ABC categories

Such collaborations could take the form of informal groups meeting regularly to discuss purchase issues to the creation of formal, centralized consortia whose objective is to manage the members' supply activities. Purchasing co-ops are quite common in the public sector (e.g., health-care co-ops and public agency co-ops), where competition amongst co-op members is not an issue.

Johnson also identifies areas of difficulties associated with implementing such purchasing collaborations:

- Co-ordination costs
- Uncertainty
- Standardization of practices and compliance
- Governance
- Free riding
- Declining effect of cost savings

The purchasing co-op Margaret arranged, due to its scale, has largely avoided some of these pitfalls. It has made a positive impact — so far — in terms of improved customer service and supplier management. However, as it grows, it seems logical that price and cost reduction will become a more important driver for purchasing co-op success. Related to this growth would be the greater need for a more formal co-op arrangement to reduce some of the difficulties Johnson mentioned. One interesting question worth discussing is whether Margaret, given her purchasing background, should begin to charge the other co-op members for "managing" the co-op and applying her professional expertise herself instead of passing the supply task around.

CHAPTER 2

Objectives and Organization for Effective Purchasing and Supply Management

Topics Covered

Objectives of Purchasing/Supply Management
Purchasing's Prime Decision Authority
Organizational Structures
Organization for Purchasing and Supply Management
    The Chief Purchasing Officer (CPO)
    Purchasing Reporting Relationships
    Supply Relationships with Other Areas of the Firm
    Specialization within the Purchasing/Supply Function
Purchasing Activities and Responsibilities
    Purchasing Activities
    The Influence of Industry Sector on Purchasing Activities
Supply Organizational Structures for Single Business Unit Firms
Supply Organizational Structures for Multi Business Unit Firms
    Hybrid Purchasing Organizational Structures

Managing Organizational Change in Purchasing
Teams and Teaming
    Cross Functional Teams
    Managing Cross-Functional Teams
    Teams with Supplier Participation
    Teams with Customer Participation
    Co-Location of Purchaser with Internal Customers
    Supplier Councils
    Purchasing Councils
    Consortiums
Conclusion
Questions for Review and Discussion
References
Cases
    Goodlife Club
    Duchess University

QUIZ RESPONSES

B | 1. In many process industry firms such as oil and gas, chemicals, glass and steel:

a. purchasing departments play a key role in each step in the materials cycle, from product design to production.
b. there are likely two supply organizations, a specialized group that handles raw materials, and one that acquires materials, supplies and services that support the operation of facilities.
c. most purchases are for resale.
d. purchases may represent a small percentage of total expenditures.
e. non-production purchasing is outsourced and expertise in production purchasing is developed inhouse.

D | 2. In an organization that does not use cross-functional sourcing teams, which of the following should not be within purchasing's decision authority?

a. select the supplier.
b. use whichever pricing method is appropriate.
c. monitor contacts with potential suppliers.
d. determine the specifications.
e. determine the price and terms of the agreement.

D | 3. Which factors have a major influence on purchasing's level in the organization:

I. the ratio of purchased material and outside services costs compared to either total costs or total income.
II. the credentials of the existing purchasing personnel.
III. the nature of the products or services acquired.
IV. the size of the supply base.
V. the extent to which supply and suppliers can provide competitive advantage.

a. I
b. I and II.
c. III and IV.
d. I, III, and V.
e. I, II, III, and IV.

C	4.	Firms commit resources to cross-functional team development to:

a. promote diversity in the workplace.
b. give purchasing ownership of tasks and problems.
c. achieve time-reduction targets.
d. give internal user ownership of tasks and problems.
e. cross-train employees in case of downsizing. |
| E | 5. | In a recent survey of purchasers and design engineers about their relationship and roles in the design stage:

a. there was a high level of congruence in most responses.
b. there was no congruence in any of the responses.
c. more than 90 percent of purchasers reported that they initiated the contact with engineers.
d. more than 90 percent of the engineers reported that they initiated the contact with purchasing.
e. both purchasers and engineers reported that purchasing handles price negotiation. |
| A | 6. | A purchasing consortium:

a. consists of two or more independent organizations that combine their requirements for materials, services and capital goods to gain better pricing, service and technology from suppliers.
b. speeds up the purchasing process, but does not usually result in price concessions from suppliers.
c. results in price concessions from suppliers, but usually does not speed up the purchasing process.
d. consists of two or more divisions of the same organization that combine their requirements for materials, services and capital goods to gain better pricing, service and technology from suppliers.
e. is a form of collaborative purchasing used only by the public sector to deliver a wider range of services at a lower total cost. |

A | 7. Which of the following should not be an objective of purchasing?

    a. customize, where possible, the items bought.
    b. minimize inventory.
    c. achieve harmonious working relationships with other functional areas in the organization.
    d. maintain and improve quality.
    e. improve the organization's competitive position.

E | 8. The primary factor which has led firms to adopt centralized-decentralized purchasing, in which the purchasing function is centralized on a division or plant basis, but decentralized on a corporate basis, is the:

    a. possibility of obtaining discounts.
    b. concept of completed staff work.
    c. principle of integrated functionalism.
    d. threat of antitrust action.
    e. profit-center concept.

D | 9. The organizational structure (centralized, decentralized, or hybrid) of the supply function:

    a. has little influence on how purchasing executes its responsibilities, how it works with other areas of the firm, or the skills and capabilities needed by the supply personnel.
    b. influences how purchasing executes its responsibilities, but not how it works with other areas of the firm, or the skills and capabilities needed by the supply personnel.
    c. influences how purchasing works with other areas of the firm, and the skills and capabilities needed by the supply personnel, but not how it executes its responsibilities
    d. influences how purchasing executes its responsibilities, how it works with other areas of the firm, and the skills and capabilities needed by the supply personnel.
    e. influences the skills and capabilities needed by supply personnel, but not how it executes its responsibilities, or how it works with other areas of the firm.

A   10.   The 1995 CAPS study on roles and responsibilities found that purchasing had a:

   a. moderate involvement in outsourcing and an expectation of increased involvement.
   b. high involvement in information systems, financial, and technology planning.
   c. high involvement in corporate strategic planning and risk management.
   d. slight involvement in new-product development
   e. moderate involvement in governmental relations, countertrade, marketing planning, and corporate mergers and alliances.

True and False

T	1.	The materials management group manages the contract after it is signed, directs the flow of materials and services from the supplier, and keeps track of the supplier's delivery and quality commitments.
F	2.	Some of the advantages of a centralized purchasing structure are speed of response, effective use of local sources, and undivided authority and responsibility.
F	3.	For large firms, collaborative purchasing might be viewed as anti-competitive by the U.S. Department of Justice and there are generally no safeguards that can be put in place to address such regulatory issues.
T	4.	Sources of supply talent and information technology are two issues that were identified by a recent CAPS study on implementing structural changes to move toward centralization.
F	5.	In a hybrid purchasing structure, those tasks which are more effectively handled on a business unit basis include establishing policies, procedures, controls, and systems.
F	6.	The activities performed by those in supply management organizations differ greatly depending on the size of the company.
F	7.	Some of the disadvantages of decentralization are narrow specialization and job boredom, lack of job flexibility, and a tendency to minimize legitimate differences in requirements.
T	8.	The executive to whom the CPO reports gives a good indication of the status of purchasing and the degree to which it is emphasized within the organization.
T	9.	Purchasing councils are generally comprised of senior purchasing staff from the company and are established to facilitate coordination among the business units, divisions or plants.
T	10.	Industry sector influences purchasing's responsibilities.

Goodlife Club

Teaching Note

IMMEDIATE ISSUE

How to get cooperation from the Dallas center managers in the new centralized purchasing system.

BASIC ISSUES

1. Centralization vs. decentralization of purchases.
2. Implementation of a new purchasing system.
3. The value added or the rationale for purchasing expertise in an organization.

SUGGESTED STUDENT ASSIGNMENT

1. If you were Sally Newton what would be your analysis of the purchasing situation at Goodlife?
2. What problems are you facing now?
3. What alternatives might you consider and why?
4. What action would you take and why?

POSSIBLE DISCUSSION QUESTIONS

1. How would you characterize purchasing at Goodlife before Sally arrived?
2. Was her idea to centralize a good one?
3. What would be the advantage and disadvantages of the new system for a center manager? For Goodlife and its owner?
4. Would you have proceeded the same way as Sally?
5. What might you do now?
6. As a Dallas center manager what arguments would you advance for not cooperating?
7. How could Sally deal with these arguments?
8. Are you surprised at what happened?

ANALYSIS

This is an interesting case which can be used to explore the basic tenets of the need for a purchasing profession. What can purchasing contribute to organizational objectives and strategies and how should this be accomplished?

In this context, it is evident that Sally represents a case of the blind leading the blind. She can claim no professional expertise, she is still very young and inexperienced and is likely to lack significant credibility. Her appointment to this task shows management's perspective on the function. Nevertheless, she may well be right — that centralization might be advantageous to Goodlife. The first common sense evidence comes from the area of price paid.

Sally is certainly proceeding at a great pace. Hired in January, she has within a few weeks a centralization plan approved and is busy implementing it in February. She may be too fast.

A tour of each of the centers to discuss needs, problems, and opportunities, resulting in a better understanding of the nature of requirements, where the dollars are spent and where the strategy requirements lie and what their future needs might be would have been a logical starting point. This should have been followed by some careful market research to get a feel for the available suppliers and their ability to meet Goodlife's future requirements. A subsequent matching of needs with market opportunities could then reveal the best way to deal with the process of acquisition for Goodlife.

For example, does standardization of shampoos, body lotions, forms, towels, etc. make sense for Goodlife or not? If so, should we have a contract of one year or longer with single preferred sources, or deal through distributors who can handle a range of requirements? Should center managers arrange directly with suppliers to release against the common contract or should releases be only handled by Sally? Should suppliers ship directly to each center and with what frequency?

Should purchasing be involved in the acquisition of telephone services, office systems, the rental or purchase of real estate, power, insurance, equipment, advertising, etc.?

To Sally's credit — she is trying to hustle and a common sense approach is probably the only way she can start. But it denies the existence of a legitimate body of knowledge and expertise in the field. Moreover, she will quickly get caught in the trap of filling requisition after requisition and get caught up in all of the detail of the function, including chasing late deliveries, without a clear vision as to where her greatest contribution can come from. For her own education she should quickly enroll in a good quality "introduction to purchasing" course locally. She should join the local NAPM group and make contact with some special mentors.

She should also sit back and work out exactly what she is trying to accomplish and why that is good for each center manager and Goodlife — in the short and long run.

For example, the Dallas resistance is normal, but potentially dangerous. A Dallas center manager could easily argue: 1) I know more about this business than Sally does. 2) I have more purchasing expertise than she does. 3) I know exactly what I want and can get it faster than she can. 4) I can get better laid down prices in Dallas than she can. 5) By working together in Dallas we cut our workload and have a good thing going. 6) Don't fix what ain't broke.

And the Dallas center manager who argues this way may well be right on all counts.

The first and primary reason for the existence of a purchasing function in an organization is that the organization is better off with it than without it. Standard arguments are given in the text — but include better value in the short and long term, freeing up time for other functional people to concentrate on their core functions, improve cash management and control, get suppliers who can assist the organization to satisfy its customers better, etc. Notice that all of these arguments are based on the assumption that specialized expertise is required to achieve maximum benefits.

It would be extremely surprising if a survey of center heads did not reveal a great commonality of requirements in both products and services. Without an overview of the total funds spent with suppliers and the time taken to perform procurement tasks currently, it is difficult to determine whether Goodlife is big enough to justify a fully experienced person in the purchasing area.

As is typical in many small businesses, the owner manager may well reserve the major dollar expenditures for him/herself, leaving the paperwork and the small stuff for a clerical assistant. This may be true for Jim Stewart, Goodlife's owner/manager.

Sally should proceed carefully from where she is. Aside from improving her personal qualifications in the materials management area, she should make sure that she does a good job for the center managers who are willing to use her services. She should also be willing to modify her routine to fit specific center needs. Given the large geographical area of Texas, the option for local purchases of perishable, high transport cost items, or emergency requirements needs to be established. She has to put a high emphasis on responsiveness and be very careful not to promise things she cannot provide — like one week delivery.

She should visit the three Dallas managers and find out from them why they are not cooperating. Perhaps she will find that she can use some of their suppliers to serve all 19 locations. Perhaps their system is superior to hers.

The advantages of combining volume to achieve clout may be lower prices or higher quality or greater supplier responsiveness. Opting out by individual center managers destroys supplier confidence in purchasing's ability to deliver the volume forecasted. Thus, the whole tenet of Sally's centralization scheme is thrown into doubt by the action of the Dallas managers.

One interesting side aspect may well be that these managers are paying more attention to purchasing issues than before, resulting in net benefits to them and Goodlife. The threat of centralization may achieve some of the same benefits as actual centralization.

It is interesting to see the class reaction, initially highly supportive of Sally, switch to greater concern for the center manager and the ultimate customer of Goodlife. If total customer satisfaction is the driving force for this business — the question becomes — How can Goodlife's future suppliers help ensure Goodlife's future success in satisfying its customers? What Sally has to do is find out the best way to help in achieving this. And her challenge is shared by every purchasing professional in the world.

Duchess University

Teaching Note

IMMEDIATE ISSUES

1. How to structure the purchasing department?
2. How to staff the current vacancies?

BASIC ISSUES

1. Purchasing organization structure.
2. Staffing levels and headcount.
3. Purchasing efficiency and effectiveness.
4. Purchasing in a service organization.
5. Criteria for performance measurement.
6. Staff motivation
7. Supply in a budget tightening environment.

SUGGESTED STUDENT ASSIGNMENT

If you were in the position of Jim Haywood:
1. What would be your assessment of the current organization structure of the purchasing department?
2. How would you fill the two remaining vacant positions?
3. What changes would you make and why?

POSSIBLE DISCUSSION QUESTIONS

1. What is an appropriate headcount?
2. How do you motivate purchasing employees to work efficiently and effectively?
3. Are there advantages to the current structure? Disadvantages?
4. Do the current vacancies represent a problem or an opportunity?
5. Why would the University appoint someone without any supply background director of purchasing?

ANALYSIS

This is much more than an organizational structure case. Although there are many facts missing from the case (the age and experience of each purchasing department employee are simple examples), the case is useful to raise a host of issues. The organizational structure question needs to be resolved in an environmental context that is certainly not a friendly one for purchasing. Clearly, the department ranks low on the university totem pole in terms of reporting line, budget priority, and headcount pressures. The appointment of a relatively low ranked finance department employee without any supply background to the position of director of purchasing six years ago is symptomatic of the university administration's respect for the purchasing function. In the past six years headcount reduction (particularly in senior purchasing positions) and budget cuts seem to have been favored over supply efficiency and effectiveness. And there is no indication that in the years ahead this internal perspective will change. This is a tough environment in which to fashion a well functioning supply group.

The Current Organization Structure

The current organization structure with four tiers for 14 people in total just does not make any sense in today's philosophy of flat organization structures. It is clearly a way for Jim to avoid having to get involved in the details of acquisition, given his lack of supply background. It also allows for internal opportunity for promotion from junior buyer to senior buyer to purchasing manager to director of purchases. The current structure separates physical plant from the rest of the campus requirements. Such a separation is one of the popular options available, whereby the purchasing group focuses on different major end user groups.

What is surprising is that both Jim (with only 3 direct reports) and Theo (with 5 direct reports) feel they spend too much time supervising.

The unexpected loss of three employees represents both a challenge and an opportunity to rethink not only the department's structure but also its mission.

Purchasing Effectiveness

Exhibit 2 in the case represents an admirable wish list, which shows Jim's employees have lots of ideas as to how the current purchasing group can still improve. The key questions are: who is going to do these and what is going to be dropped to free up time?

Moreover, purchasing effectiveness requires a highly skilled and highly motivated group of purchasing professionals. Questions like headcount, job rotation, training, opportunity for advancement and recognition and adequate pay are central to achieving high purchasing performance. Unfortunately, Jim himself seems to have more of a cost cutting and headcount mentality than worrying about purchasing's effective contribution to university effectiveness. Like many financial people he values what is easily counted rather than what is important. That he has been willing to live with a four-tier structure for six years is indicative that rocking the boat is not his favorite pastime.

If he is not willing or able to come up with proposals that justify a certain headcount, pay and expertise level to pursue major supply opportunities (you have to invest money if you want a return), then he will have to continue managing within an ever tightening noose on the department's budget.

Vacancy Options

The simplest vacancy option is to hire people for the vacant positions without changing any job descriptions. This will in all likelihood meet the university expectations.

A different approach is to ask, "How many people and of what kind do we need to pursue the initiatives mentioned in Exhibit 2?" If the total exceeds 14, then a proposal for additional hires needs to be prepared. If the total is within 14, then what additional skills have to be brought in?

For example, a purchase analyst position might be particularly useful to support almost all of the items listed in Exhibit 2. It might be possible to create one or more systems contracts for all heating, plumbing and electrical supplies or even to create an in-house vendor store if total volume warrants it. This might do away with the need for the junior buyer position in physical plant. Similarly, the same possibility might exist for scientific and lab supplies and office supplies. No information is available on the staffing in physical plant and other stores on campus, but their outsourcing might be a possibility.

Given that purchasing's contribution should be both operational and strategic and that almost all of this department's focus has been on the operational side, significant strategic opportunities still exist.

Aside from the list in Exhibit 2, insourcing and outsourcing, alliances with other educational or public institutions, e-commerce and improved internal and external relations could be added. That represents an ambitious program of improving purchasing's effectiveness and moving it to a strategic mode. Such a direction might argue for splitting the organization into operational and strategic sides, appropriately staffed with the necessary skills.

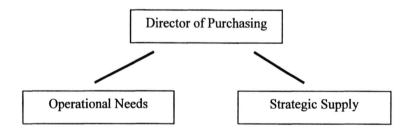

The Organization Structure Revisited

On the assumption that Jim Haywood will not voluntarily resign his post, a key decision he must make is how flat he intends to make his structure. He currently has four tiers with one job, Elvira Castor's with a dual reporting line. Maintaining this structure is one option, as discussed earlier. Going to three tiers would be possible if Jim took on the general campus reports as well as the two senior buyers in Physical Plant and Theo Vaslow, giving him ten direct reports. A two-tier structure would have Jim with 13 reports. After six years in the job Jim should have picked up enough experience in supply to flatten the organization by at least one tier. Whether he is ready to move the whole supply organization into a more strategic mode is up to him.

Chapter 3

Procedures and Information Flows

Topics Covered

Objectives of Purchasing/Supply Management

Purchasing's Prime Decision Authority
Organizational Structures
Organization for Purchasing and Supply Management
    The Chief Purchasing Officer (CPO)
    Purchasing Reporting Relationships
    Supply Relationships with Other Areas of the Firm
    Specialization within the Purchasing/Supply Function
Purchasing Activities and Responsibilities
    Purchasing Activities
    The Influence of Industry Sector on Purchasing Activities
Supply Organizational Structures for Single Business Unit Firms
Supply Organizational Structures for Multi Business Unit Firms

Hybrid Purchasing Organizational Structures
Managing Organizational Change in Purchasing
Teams and Teaming
    Cross Functional Teams
    Managing Cross-Functional Teams
    Teams with Supplier Participation
    Teams with Customer Participation
    Co-Location of Purchaser with Internal Customers
    Supplier Councils
    Purchasing Councils
    Consortiums
Conclusion
Questions for Review and Discussion
References
Cases
    Goodlife Club
    Duchess University

QUIZ RESPONSES

C   1.   The greatest opportunity to affect value in the purchasing process is in:

         a. the supplier selection decision.
         b. the determination of price and terms.
         c. need recognition and description.
         d. analysis of potential suppliers.
         e. follow-up and expediting.

B   2.   If the buyer wants to give potential suppliers the chance to recommend alternative solutions and make the offers subject to negotiation, he or she will typically issue a:

         a. request for quotation (RFQ).
         b. request for proposal (RFP).
         c. request for information (RFI).
         d. request for bid (RFB).
         e. request for suggestions (RFS).

E   3.   An example(s) of the type of information that purchasing and supply provides to others in the organization is(are):

         a. source, product, and price information.
         b. economic conditions.
         c. competitive conditions.
         d. a and c.
         e. a, b, and c.

E   4.   Small dollar value purchase orders might realistically be dealt with by:

         I. increasing the number of standardized items.
         II. putting purchases on blanket orders.
         III. entering into a stockless buying contract.
         IV. giving users a corporate purchasing card.
         V. implementing EDI or an e-procurement application.

    a. I and II.
    b. III and IV.
    c. I, II and IV.
    d. II, IV, and V.
    e. I, II, III, IV and V.

A 5. Corporate purchasing cards are issued to:

    a. internal customers who select suppliers from a preferred supplier list to purchase certain preapproved goods and services.
    b. purchasing department personnel to speed up the acquisition of rush orders and small value orders.
    c. internal customers who may then evaluate suppliers, and select the supplier the cardholder prefers.
    d. internal customers to purchase high-dollar, production materials of a highly technical nature.
    e. purchasing department personnel to eliminate purchase orders and individual invoices.

D 6. One type of information coming into purchasing and supply from external (outside the buyer's company) sources is:

    a. sales forecasts.
    b. economic order quantities.
    c. cost studies from make or buy decisions.
    d. general market conditions.
    e. long-term future requirements of the buyer's organization.

C 7. The bill of material (BOM) includes:

    a. the total quantity of materials/parts needed to meet annual production projections.
    b. the total quantity of material/parts to meet next month's production projections.
    c. the total quantity of material/parts needed to make one end unit.
    d. a list of potential suppliers for each item needed to make one end unit.
    e. none of the above.

A | 8. Pareto's Law:

a. is also known as ABC analysis.
b. states that purchasing can impact an organization's return on assets.
c. states that purchasing can impact the organization's profitability.
d. defines the point at which a legally binding contract is in effect.
e. is also known as the economic order quantity.

B | 9. In stockless buying or systems contracting:

a. the main application is for major raw materials (the "A" category of purchased items).
b. generally, the inventory of all items covered by a contract is stored by the supplier.
c. there typically is a lengthening of supplier lead times.
d. the price is determined at the time of shipment.
e. all of the above.

D | 10. The document which provides general guidelines as to how problems are to be handled by the purchasing department is known as:

a. standard operating procedure.
b. data form.
c. training manual.
d. policy manual.
e. data processing manual.

True and False

T	1.	A bill of material (B/M) is used primarily by firms which make a standard item over a relatively long period of time.
F	2.	There are no good reasons why the buying organization should pay an invoice before the goods have been received, inspected, and accepted.
F	3.	Rush orders, which cost more to handle, can never be justified in a well-run purchasing operation.
F	4.	A purchase order must include quality control methods, a cancellation clause, and an arbitration clause.
F	5.	Contracts with third party MRO suppliers are designed to provide the buying organization with all or most of its MRO requirements as quickly and easily as possible even if prices are higher and service levels are lower than was provided in-house.
T	6.	The purchasing department should be involved in writing specifications, or at a minimum, have the right to question specifications.
T	7.	Follow-up is the routine tracking of an order to assure that the supplier will be able to meet delivery promises.
T	8.	The basic purchase records which should be maintained are a purchase order (PO) log, a PO file, a commodity file, and a supplier history file.
T	9.	A blank check purchase order includes a signed, blank check along with the purchase order so that the supplier can enter in the amount due and deposit the payment.
F	10.	Early purchasing involvement refers to the practice of buying requirements in advance of actual need to ensure supply availability.

Mike Wesley

Teaching Note

IMMEDIATE ISSUE

How to avoid future production problems and cost overruns.

BASIC ISSUES

1. Role of supply in production planning.
2. Procedures and information flow.
3. Quality management.
4. Production scheduling.
5. Process analysis
6. Project management.
7. Inter-company coordination and organization structures.
8. Outsourcing.
9. ISO 9000.

SUGGESTED STUDENT ASSIGNMENT

As Mike Wesley, what is your assessment of the problems associated with the Fine Foods print job? What action would you recommend and why?

POSSIBLE DISCUSSION QUESTIONS

1. Do you think anyone is to blame for the problems with this job? If so, who?
2. How much authority do you think Mike has to change things?
3. Should these problems have been caught? Do you think this just is bad luck?
4. Diagram the production process at Wesley. How is this job unique?
5. What do you think of the supplier's response?
6. How does Wesley schedule it jobs? How do you think they should be scheduled?
7. Does Wesley have the proper organization structure for the type of business that it is in?
8. What changes would you make? Who has to be involved in making these changes?

DISCUSSION

A good place to start is to understand the nature of Wesley's business. First, Wesley competes on quality, dependability, and flexibility. Quality here is defined as complex jobs, requiring special operations and high tolerances. Dependability refers to on-time delivery and when required, rush delivery. Flexibility is defined as an ability to produce non-standard jobs. The case infers that Wesley does not compete for high volume, generic jobs, where supply decisions are based largely on price. Clearly the company must be able to handle jobs effectively and efficiently like the one for Fine Foods.

Second, Wesley processes its jobs in batches. Exhibit TN1 outlines the process flow for the Fine Food job. Although this job progressed through each of the six departments at Wesley (art, camera, plate, press, bindery, and shipping), the activities within each department may change from job-to-job. For example, part of the Fine Foods job was outsourced to a bindery department. The non-standard nature of this process makes it more difficult to detect and correct quality problems at the source.

There are two factors that influence the ability of Wesley's management to oversee its production operations. The first is systems control, including quality systems and operations procedures. Some students will recognize the opportunity for Wesley to use project management concepts in their operations. Because of the unique nature of most of Wesley's production, project management techniques could be used to plan, control and re-plan "special" jobs, especially those requiring outside resources. For example, the critical path method can be used to estimate delivery dates, and make adjustments to meet customer targets. PERT diagrams can be used to understand the sequencing of tasks.

Although Wesley is ISO certified, one should question how well the company follows its procedures. A systems review is evidentially required. The company should do this anyway as part of the ISO review process.

Presumably the production manager uses some kind of system to schedule, plan and control projects after the business is awarded. A review of his system is also required.

SOME POSSIBLE SOLUTIONS

There are some simple things that Mike could suggest that would greatly improve the existing system. An obvious suggestion would be to implement a work order system which describes exactly what work has to be done and where. Systems and controls at Wesley are far too informal. Forcing everyone to sign-off at their phase in the manufacturing process is one simple way of formalizing this system. Students may offer other suggestions, which will have to be evaluated on the basis of their reasonableness for the situation.

The second factor is organization structure. From a general standpoint, one has to question the traditional functional nature of an organization that is being asked to oversee individual projects. As work moves between departments and among functions, the different groups don't seem to know the specifics of the projects, each interpreting events and information from their unique perspective. Communication and coordination are problems here.

It is interesting to note the role of the sales representative in this company. The sales representative is responsible for "sheparding" the estimate and quotation through the system, then he hands it over to the production manager and waits at the shipping dock for the finished product. An opportunity exists to integrate sales and operations by getting the sales representative more involved in project planning and control activities. Wesley should get more value from its sales representatives than simply acting as order-takers. They can be valuable in coordinating activities with outside sources and negotiating delivery requirements with customers.

Timing of an implementation plan is less of an issue here than in most cases. Unlike many of the cases that the students have seen, there is not a deadline that has been imposed. The motivation is strong, however, to get something done soon. Mike not only needs to prevent a reoccurrence of the of the problem, but also respond to Fine Foods.

Another issue is the responsibility and authority of Mike Wesley. It is safe to assume that Mike is a descendant of the founder, and may own part of the company as a result. Clearly he has a substantial interest in improving company operations. However, like many other small family businesses, decision-making is most likely decentralized. The "old" way of doing business may be just fine as far as the other, more senior, members of the family are concerned.

The question may be less what has to be done, as opposed to how to change a business that has been around for almost 100 years. Implementing even the smallest of changes in such an environment can be a challenge. This is further complicated by the fact that Wesley has a unionized workforce. Any proposed changes in work rules will have to be negotiated with the union. Watch for sweeping, general recommendations by students that fail to take the environment at Wesley into account.

Procedures and Information Flows   43

TN1

PROCESS FLOW: FINE FOODS JOB

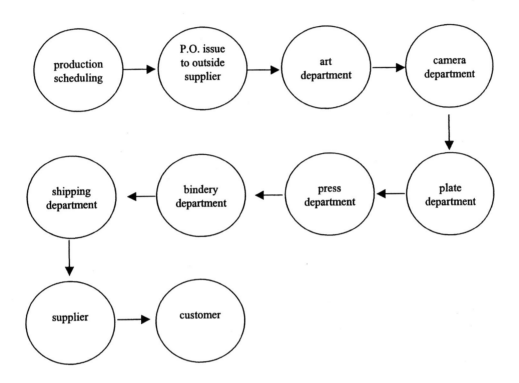

UIL, Inc.

Teaching Note

IMMEDIATE ISSUE

How to eliminate or significantly reduce rush orders.

BASIC ISSUES

1. Procedures and information flows.
2. Fixed order quantity models.
3. Fixed period models.
4. Vendor managed inventories.
5. Acquisition of indirect materials and supplies.
6. ABC analysis.
7. Systems contracts.

SUGGESTED STUDENT ASSIGNMENT

1. As Jim Sinclair, what is your analysis of the situation regarding the rush orders?
2. Which approach would you prefer, inventory holding cage or outsourcing?
3. What action would you take and why?

POSSIBLE DISCUSSION QUESTIONS

1. Which system is appropriate for acquisition of C items, a minimum – maximum system or a time-based system?
2. How much money do you think Jim might save if he adopted a blanket purchase order system?
3. Which option is more effective, inventory cages or blanket POs? Can you think of any other ways that Jim might approach this problem?
4. What issues might Jim's boss be concerned with? What questions might he ask Jim?
5. What is the cost of a stock-out?
6. What do you estimate the costs are for processing rush orders? How does this relate to the cost of the purchased item?

ANALYSIS

A common problem faced by many purchasing professionals is how to minimize acquisition costs and resources associated with C items in order to focus efforts on the acquisition of A items. However, failure to assure availability for low cost, low value items can cause as much problems for supply managers as issues related to supply problems for the most expensive production materials.

Jim Sinclair is using a minimum-maximum system to control inventory of welding, hardware and MRO supplies. These items are trivial in terms of cost – often costing less than a dollar each. However, the current system requires the user to record transactions in order to track inventory levels. When the inventories hit the reorder point, an order is placed with the supplier to replenish the stock. Students should be asked to describe and evaluate the current system (sometimes called a reorder point system or a fixed quantity model). They can be asked when such a system should be used and whether the system makes sense in the situation described in the case.

The minimum – maximum system used by UIL is more appropriate for A items, where there are advantages to controlling inventory levels and managing trade-offs between order costs and holding costs. The minimum – maximum system has the advantage of lower average inventories compared to fixed period systems, but a major disadvantage is the higher administrative costs. (Chapter 6 provides good coverage inventory systems.) Minimum – maximum systems require accurate information, and it appears that UIL employees see little value in recording transactions associated with low cost items.

Jim Sinclair would be better off using a fixed time period system for welding, hardware and MRO supplies. While such a system would require holding additional inventory, it has the advantage of reducing transaction costs significantly. Using the breakdown provided in the case, students can evaluate the number of POs issued based on the spend, using the 3,454 POs issued in the eight month period:

Percentage of Total Spend	Percentage of Total POs Issued	Number of POs Issued
Less than 1%	25%	864
Less than 4%	60%	2,072
Less than 8%	73%	2,521
Less than 30%	94%	3,247

Furthermore, the case also indicates that Jim expects to eliminate 637 transactions, or 18 percent of POs, if the outsourcing alternative is chosen.

Students can be asked to estimate the transaction costs associated with processing a PO. The case does not provide any hard data, but the students should be able to create a list of activities, such as issuing the PO, filing, expediting, matching invoices with POs, paying the invoice, etc. Most estimates will likely range from $30 to $75. Using a cost of $50, and assuming that Jim could eventually eliminate 2,000 invoices, the cost savings opportunity is $100,000. However, the flaw with this approach is that not all of the $50 cost is variable. The real savings is the opportunity cost of re-deploying staff, such as Jim Sinclair, to more productive activities. For example, if Jim Sinclair could dedicate more time working with key suppliers, UIL engineers or sales representatives, he could identify opportunities to reduce costs and enhance revenues. Consequently, the real issue relates to the "value of time".

Evaluation of Alternatives

The case describes two alternatives – outsourcing materials management to suppliers or re-establishing inventory cages. Inventory cages are overkill for inexpensive C items. As described above, adopting a period-based system is more attractive.

The outsourcing arrangement proposes that the suppliers would control the inventory and replenish based on a fix review period. While the general approach (e.g., fix period review) seems appropriate, there remain concerns regarding inventory control and product costs.

With respect to cost, items representing 8 percent of the total spend accounted for 73 percent of the total number of POs. If a systems contract is restricted to these items, a 12 percent price increase for all items only represents a 1 percent increase in total cost (e.g., increase from 8 percent of costs to 9 percent of costs). However, eliminating more than 2,000 POs would likely free up staff time and provide opportunities for cost reductions in other areas by attacking the remaining 92 percent of the spend. This seems like a good trade-off.

Other Options

Jim Sinclair might want to explore other options before finalizing his decision. First, he may want to explore a similar outsourcing arrangement, but ask the suppliers to provide the material on-site on consignment. This has the advantage of making the suppliers responsible for the inventory carrying costs, and since Marin charges UIL for capital, this option would be attractive to UIL management as a means of reducing invested capital. This approach also addresses Jim's concern regarding responsibility for obsolete stock.

Another option that Jim may consider is adopting purchasing cards. This strategy may take some time to implement and would be best suited for items that are not immediately required for operations. However, p-cards have the advantage of flexibility for the user while providing opportunities for providing spending controls.

What Should Jim Sinclair Do?

It would appear that the outsourcing arrangement will only affect 18 percent of the total invoices and Jim Sinclair may have to look at several iterations. Re-evaluating the inventory systems and developing a range of supply arrangements based on systems contracts should help alleviate the problem and reduce the number of POs significantly. Some purchasing professionals tend to focus too much on the acquisition price. However, Jim needs to consider the value to the organization and take into consideration total cost factors, such as transaction costs, expediting costs and costs of a stock-out. Jim will likely need to combine his approach of systems contracts and period-based review systems with a p-card system.

Artsell Inc.

Teaching Note

IMMEDIATE ISSUE

Decide what recommendations to make at the team meeting regarding integration of the Pur Pay accounting system and the Maximo purchasing system.

BASIC ISSUES

1. Procedures and information flows.
2. Information systems and ERP systems.
3. Procurement cards.
4. The procurement accounting interface.

ASSIGNMENT QUESTIONS

1. What is your evaluation of the three alternatives Tom Pepper identified? What are the advantages and disadvantages of each?
2. What recommendations would you make at the team meeting at noon and why? What information would you collect in preparation for the meeting?

POSSIBLE DISCUSSION QUESTIONS

1. If the decision was going to be made strictly on the basis of cost, which of the three options looks the best?
2. What criteria other than cost do you want to use to evaluate the alternatives?
3. Can we realistically expect the PeopleSoft system to be implemented on schedule? How would your recommendations change if you knew the People Soft system would be delayed by a year?
4. How well has the IT department managed this project?
5. Would you be prepared to scrap the Maximo system and go back to the old system?

ANALYSIS

This is a classic example of poor system integration and the headaches that such problems cause. The context is important in the case and the students should take into account the timing pressures. First, Tom Pepper only has two hours before the team meeting. Any information collection and analysis has to be done in a hurry. Second, the case does not say who will be at the meeting, but there will likely be representatives from purchasing (maybe Carrie Denton), accounting and IT. Any recommendations will have to address the concerns of the stakeholders. Third, the roll-out date for the Maximo system was January 1, which only leaves nine days. However, after taking Christmas and New Year's holidays into account, Tom might only have two or three working days. Finally, this project has been on going for approximately a year. Canceling it now or making a significant change to its direction will reflect poorly on Tom Pepper.

Discussion of Alternatives

There is some financial information that should be incorporated into the analysis. It appears that Artsell has $80,000 - $100,000 invested in the system. This estimate is based on the $30,000 - $50,000 cost and assumes that the cost for two full time staff for six months was $50,000. From the perspective of Tom Pepper, deciding not to go ahead with the system could raise questions concerning his judgment.

The case also provides some rough cost estimates regarding the three options identified. Manually matching the invoices will cost $30,000 per person. However, the case does not indicate how many people would be needed. Tom should get this information before the meeting. Based on 200 invoices/day, accounting would need to process 25 invoices/hour. This will likely require 1 –2 people, and represents a cost of $30,000 - $60,000/year.

This option has several potential problems. First, delays of PeopleSoft implementation could extend the period when extra staff would be required. Second, manually processing invoices could create quality control problems. For example a 1 percent error rate would represent approximately 500 invoice processing errors per year (assuming 200 invoices for 250 days) and a 5 percent error rate would result in approximately 2,500 invoice processing errors per year. Artsell will incur additional costs as a result of dealing with such problems.

The second option was hiring a programmer for six months to create the interface between the Pur Pay and Maximo systems. Such a person is would likely be expensive and might cost $30,000 - $40,000 for the six month period. Tom should get a cost estimate from the IT department prior to the meeting at noon.

This alternative also has the problem of a six-month lead time. Consequently, Tom will need to make arrangements to manually process invoices during this period, at a cost of $15,000 - $30,000 for staff, not including costs caused by processing errors. In addition, Tom will need to locate, interview and hire the programmer, which might take a few weeks. Furthermore, he expects that the programmer should be able to complete the job in "at least" six months. It might very well take much longer, adding additional costs.

The third option is to scrap the Maximo system and adopt a p-card. The case suggests that existing staff could handle the administrative activities and the bank would handle all design aspects for the cards, but suppliers would need to invest $250 - $500 for software and installation. It is not clear from the case whether the software was for Artsell only, or could be used for other p-card users. Tom should clarify the capabilities of the software before the meeting. However, assuming that the software had applications for all p-card users, many suppliers may already have the necessary capabilities. Before going ahead with this alternative, Tom should get an estimate regarding the availability of suppliers with p-card software. Such information would not likely be easily available for the meeting, but the bank might be able to provide a rough estimate.

Adopting a p-card system would also take several months. Tom would likely want to ask for proposals from two or three more p-card suppliers and once a system was selected, staff would need to be trained. Tom is likely looking at several months before the system could be set-up and functional. Even then some staff may be reluctant to use the cards and the adoption rate will likely never hit 100 percent, resulting in additional manual processing of invoices.

Deciding on a Course of Action

The analysis suggests that there are not any short-term fixes for the problem and he will likely need to make arrangements for manually processing the invoices starting in January, regardless of the course of action selected. In preparing for the meeting, Tom needs to spend the next couple of hours getting some information ready:

1. How many people will be needed to manually process the invoices?
2. How much will it cost to hire a programmer and how long will it take to hire a competent individual?
3. How many of our suppliers are p-card enabled and how long will it take to train staff and implement a new p-card system?

Tom should also talk to his counterpart at the Pennsylvania plant regarding the interface between their systems to see how they handled this problem.

Finally, another option is to do nothing. If Artsell is facing additional costs of more than $100,000, in a worst-case scenario, the plant manager may decide that the benefit is not worth the added costs.

CHAPTER 4

Technology and E-Commerce

Topics Covered

Glossary of Terms
Computer Use in Purchasing and Supply Management
    Software
    Application Service Providers (ASP)
    Hypertext Markup Language (HTML) versus Extensible Markup Language (XML)
Efficiency Improvements through Technology
    Effectiveness Improvements
    Bar Coding and EDI
    XML versus EDI
    Intranets and Extranets
e-Procurement Applications
    Implementation Challenges
    Role of Purchasing in e-Procurement
    Electronic or Online Supplier Catalogs
    Industrywide Informational Databases
Auctions and Reverse Auctions
e-Marketplaces
Implications for Purchasing
Conclusion
Questions for Review and Discussion
References
Cases
    Somers Office Products Inc.
    Cable and Wireless PLC
    Establishing e-Business Standards at Deere & Company

QUIZ RESPONSES

E   1.   Computerized purchasing systems:

       a. improve operating efficiency, but often negatively impact buyer-supplier relationships.
       b. assists the buyer with daily transactions, but do little to aid long-term decision-making.
       c. decrease processing time, but increase the chances for error.
       d. provide more accurate information quickly, but hinder integration with other functional areas.
       e. free buyers from repetitive tasks to focus on more value-adding activities like building supplier relationships.

A   2.   Bar coding systems are useful in purchasing in:

       a. receiving inbound materials and order generation.
       b. incoming inspection and quality control.
       c. obtaining price quotes.
       d. determining the availability of items from suppliers.
       e. transmitting purchase orders.

D   3.   The successful implementation of an EDI system will result in:

       a. an increase in total costs of doing business.
       b. disruptions in just-in-time systems.
       c. slower worldwide communications.
       d. increased integration of supply and manufacturing processes.
       e. Increased need for personnel in purchasing.

C 4. Computerizing the purchasing process will result in:

   a. an increase in clerical effort because of the need for more data entry than in a manual system.
   b. a negative impact on buyer-supplier relationships because of the impersonal nature of electronic communications.
   c. an ability to reduce the total cost of doing business by enabling just-in-time systems, bar-coding applications, integrated manufacturing, and electronic funds transfers.
   d. poorer negotiation planning and preparation because of the time spent accessing and analyzing data.
   e. a decline in operating performance because of the volume of information to be analyzed and considered before making a decision.

B 5. E-procurement applications are:

   a. closed systems that require a Value-Added Network (VAN) to enable a buyer and seller to transmit data electronically.
   b. web-based tools used to improve the efficiency and effectiveness of purchasing.
   c. systems that process data to assist purchasers in selecting from among alternatives.
   d. systems that use a series of parallel rectangular bars and spaces in a predetermined pattern to encode letters, numbers, and characters.
   e. Systems that provide decision making assistance via an interactive question-and-answer session with a human.

A 6. An eMarketplace:

   a. is a web site on which member companies buy and sell their goods and services.
   b. is a web site on which
   c. is an electronic forum in which buyers can post requests for information (RFI).
   d. is an electronic arena for open auctions.
   e. is for companies in the same industry only.

| E | 7. | When assessing e-commerce service providers, the following issue(s) should be considered:

a. scalability or the ability of the software to grow with the buyer's needs.
b. compatibility with, or ease of migration from, existing software.
c. the supplier's technical reputation and experience with supply chain software.
d. long-term viability of the service provider.
e. All of the above.

| C | 8. | Online auctions have been most effective when:

a. the good or service is unique or highly customized.
b. the organization owns the technology to run the auction.
c. the good or service has the characteristics of a commodity.
d. there are a limited number of suppliers available.
e. the market conditions favor sellers.

| A | 9. | Online supplier catalogs typically contain two types of information:

a. product specification data and transaction data.
b. product specification data and photographs.
c. transaction data and shipping information.
d. prices and shipping information.
e. product descriptions and product photographs.

| E | 10. | The main benefit(s) of e-procurement is(are):

a. it reduces the purchases made outside of existing contracts.
b. cycle time is reduced on the purchase of indirect items.
c. communications are faster and less-paper-intensive.
d. b and c.
e. a, b and c.

True and False

F	1.	Early in the 21st century, the most widely adopted use of the Internet in procurement was to purchase direct materials.
T	2.	Electronic Data Interchange (EDI) allows direct hookup with a supplier to obtain price quotes, determine availability, transmit a PO, and obtain service information.
T	3.	The fax machine and the computer are the two most important technological tools in everyday purchasing operations.
F	4.	Expert systems, computer programs that mimic problem-solving behavior of human experts, already exist are widely used by supply managers.
T	5.	Digital signatures ensure the authenticity of the sender by use of a pair of keys (one public and one private) that can only encrypt and decrypt each other.
T	6.	An extranet is an organization's web site that provides limited accessibility to person's outside the organization and often is used to link buyers with actual and potential suppliers.
T	7.	An online reverse auction is when a buyer, wishing to purchase certain items, invites specific suppliers to bid against one another using the Internet as the auction arena.
F	8.	ERP software systems are programs that manipulate data for a specific purpose, such as processing a purchase order, but do not interface with software for other functions or processes.
T	9.	An online catalog is a digitized version of a supplier's catalog that may be customized to include the specific items, prices, and other terms and conditions negotiated by the buyer and seller.
F	10.	Digital signatures are not legally binding in the United States.

Somers Office Products

Teaching Note

IMMEDIATE ISSUE

How should George Bellows respond to the acquisition of its supplier by a competitor?

BASIC ISSUES

1. Supply chain management.
2. Supplier development.
3. e-Commerce.
4. Supplier alliances.
5. Merchandising.

SUGGESTED STUDENT ASSIGNMENT

As George Bellows, what is your analysis of the situation at Somers? What action would you take and why?

POSSIBLE DISCUSSION QUESTIONS

1. How has e-commerce changed the office supplies business and how well is Somers positioned to compete? What is Somers' competitive advantage?
2. Is there any need to take immediate action? How much time does George have?
3. Should Somers get out of the office supplies business altogether?
4. Would you be concerned about relying on one supplier from computer supplies in this situation? Why or why not?
5. What do its customers want from Somers and how can its suppliers help provide this service?
6. What would you say to Wahby? What would you say to Fairmont Canada? What would you say to Wayne Fitzsimmons?

ANALYSIS

The Marketplace and Competitive Environment

Somers is a retailer and reseller of office and computer supplies, office furniture and office design services. It is the office supplies segment of its business that is the focus of the case.

First, let's look at the situation from the perspective of Somers' customers. Office supplies are viewed as low dollar value purchases, with high transaction costs relative to total value. However, companies have viewed this as a ripe area for easy cost reductions. As a consequence, many firms have adopted business processes to lower transaction costs, such as p-cards and electronic catalogues and requisition systems. It has also been commonplace to use single sourcing, also in an effort to reduce transaction costs, but also to negotiate supplier price reductions and to institute better controls and reporting. Consequently, Somers' customers would not carry a large inventory; would expect convenient, low cost fulfillment processes; and would expect same- or next-day service.

Many purchasers have some experience in this area and can talk extensively regarding the procurement issues. It is necessary, however, to translate this analysis into implications for Somers, and ultimately its supply requirements. Therefore, it would be useful to create a list of key success factors:

- Low cost customer order processes.
- Low prices/costs.
- Speed of delivery.
- Wide selection of products.
- High order fulfillment rate.
- Reliable deliveries.
- High order accuracy rate.

Implications for Supply

The ultimate success of Somers is dependent on its ability to use its supply base to develop these capabilities. Given its relatively small size, the company must be particularly effective at using its supply base to compete with its much larger competitors. For example, Somers needs suppliers that provide:

- A large selection in order to help its high order fulfillment rates.
- Same day and next day service to provide speed of service and keep its costs down by limiting the need for excessive inventories.
- On time delivery and order tracking capability to help its delivery performance.

- Competitive pricing.
- High quality to avoid customer complaints and returns.

In the office supplies segment, purchase costs might represent 70-80 percent of the sales price, so supply plays a critical role in the company's profitability and performance in the eyes of its customers.

Fairmont Situation

Fairmont Inc., Fairmont Canada's parent company, has begun to dabble in the resale end of the supply chain, competing against its traditional customers. Fairmont was following the trend set by Dell Computer that operated extensively through direct sales and avoided both resellers and retailers. It would be worthwhile spending time in class to explore the influence in e-commerce applications on the supply chain and the implications for Somers. It would appear that Fairmont decided to use its e-commerce capabilities to eliminate a link in the supply chain, moving downstream into the commercial segment. Meantime, Somers is still dependent on less efficient catalogues and paper-based order systems.

It appears that Fairmont is being sold and split-up into its two business segments: the U.S. distribution business is going to Roancroft, and MSC, a Somers competitor, is picking up Fairmont Canada, perhaps with an eye to expanding its Canadian market share.

It appears that Somers has two problems. The first is what to do about Fairmont. The second problem relates to whether similar changes are going to follow and how the company should be positioning itself in the supply chain.

Fairmont Canada Decision

There are a number of questions that George Bellows should ask before making a decision concerning Fairmont Canada:

- *How much time does he have?* At this point the deal has been announced, but no one, including Wayne Fitzsimmons, has given George a specific deadline to take action. It would appear that he has some time to ask some questions and collect information before making a decision. Given the importance of its supply relationships, George does not want to rush into a situation. One of the interesting aspects of the supply relationship between Somers and its office and computer supplies wholesalers is that the switching costs are high as the result of integration of systems and product offerings.
- *What information should be collected?* Since George has some time, the key point is what information does he need and where can he get it? An obvious place to start is with Fairmont Canada. However, at this point, they might not have any information themselves, since the acquisition has just been announced. However, given a few days or maybe a week or two, senior

management at Fairmont Canada will have a "party line" concerning its future direction. It seems reasonable for George to request a meeting with appropriate senior members of Fairmont management as quickly as they can provide him with such information.
- In the meantime George should start to collect information regarding alternate supply arrangements. It appears that he has been using Fairmont Canada as his primary source while using Wahby occasionally, likely as a back-up source. It also appears that Wahby does not have a strong Canadian presence, but George should start the process of identifying what their interest might be in expanding their relationship with Somers and their capabilities in this regard. It would be useful to look at a minimum of two other potential suppliers as well.
- At this point George is collecting information and preparing a back-up plan. He does not have to change suppliers.
- *What should be done with Wahby?* The easy answer to this question is nothing, at least right now. In all likelihood, Wahby, and other potential vendors wanting to take advantage of this situation, might approach George. However, he should wait until it becomes evident that a change is required.
- *What should George say to Wayne Fitzsimmons?* George will need to explain his strategy to Wayne in order to reassure him that appropriate steps are being taken to protect the company's interest. In a worst case scenario, Fairmont Canada might cut-off relationship with Somers, and Wayne will want to know how quickly George could react to such a situation. Wayne's biggest concern will be that George is on top of the situation.

A Long-Term Perspective

Senior management at Somers can perhaps be criticized for not reacting faster to the threat of information technology applications to the supply chain. It might be that the company cannot afford the necessary investments in this area. If so, it might have to retrench into the office furniture and office design services segments. However, automating fulfillment processes through Internet and Intranet applications is becoming a competitive necessity as end users look for opportunities to reduce transaction costs and improve service.

Presently Somers is dependent on catalogs, which can be costly to reproduce, update and distribute. Moving to web based systems can help the company keep its product offering current, update prices regularly and reduce printing and administrative costs.

TEACHING STRATEGY

Class can start with a size-up of the industry and the changes that are occurring as a result of e-commerce applications. Relying on student experiences ordering office supplies can be useful. This can then be followed by a discussion of the contributions that supply can make at Somers.

Finally, discussion can move to the Fairmont Canada situation. Start with the timing and sense of urgency. Some students might want to take immediate action and clearly this should be discussed.

Eventually discussion should move towards assessing what information needs to be collected and how George Bellows should respond to Wayne Fitzsimmons.

You can save time at the end of the class to discuss the general business issues of e-commerce implications for the supply chain. Appreciate, however, that control of such matters is beyond the scope of George Bellows' influence.

Cable and Wireless plc (A)

Teaching Note

IMMEDIATE ISSUE

Evaluate archival storage services and marketing papers as candidates for the e-Auction pilot project.

Decide on criteria for evaluating potential on-line bid service providers.

BASIC ISSUES

1. e-Purchasing and e-Commerce.
2. Internet and technology in supply.
3. Supplier relations.
4. Competitive bidding.
5. Price determination.
6. Cost savings projects.
7. Project management.

SUGGESTED STUDENT ASSIGNMENT

1. What is your assessment of archival storage services and marketing papers as candidates for the e-Auction pilot? Would you be in favor of using either of these commodities? If not, what other commodities might you consider and why?
2. What service arrangement would you want from your on-line bid service provider?
3. As Ninian Wilson, how would you proceed? Be prepared to share your plan with the class.

POSSIBLE DISCUSSION QUESTIONS

1. List other commodities that might be candidates for e-Auctions. Do any of these make better sense for the pilot?
2. What would you say to Clauws Records Services, who is expecting to receive the three-year contract based on the RFQ?
3. What are the advantages and disadvantages of conducting an e-Auction for C&W? How about the suppliers?

4. What parameters would you set for the on-line service provider? How much would you be willing to pay for this service? Would you expect the suppliers to also pay a fee for participating?
5. Ideally, how many suppliers would you want to participate in the e-Auction? What is the minimum and maximum number you would want?
6. What is the difference between an e-Auction and a RFQ?

ANALYSIS

C&W e-Procurement Initiative

The e-procurement initiative is but one aspect of the e-Business initiative at C&W. C&W has embarked on an ambitious corporate-wide e-procurement initiative, led by members of senior management. The company appears to be evaluating opportunities to introduce e-commerce, in part to reduce overall costs. And although not specifically indicated in the case, this initiative was also driven by a need to gain credibility in the marketplace – implementing e-Business programs would be an important factor supporting the use of C&W's services. Class discussion can delve into why senior management might support such an initiative and the anticipated benefits.

The e-Procurement Pilot

Class discussion should include an evaluation of the pilot project and its potential objectives. Students should be asked to describe the benefits of the pilot and list the deliverables that such a project could provide. In other words, why bother with a pilot project and what new information should it provide?

The actual objectives of the pilot phase of the project, as defined by the company, were:

- Conclude and recommend the appropriate solution/tool required to support the three main e-procurement concepts: e-Transacting, e-Sourcing and e-Intelligence.
- Identify and recommend the appropriate levels of integration both between the various components of the solution and with other internal and external systems and exchanges.
- Define the necessary organizational and process changes. Outlining the management information and audit capabilities recommended for user, manager, finance and purchasing needs.
- Reconfirm the overall business case.
- Gain approval for the full rollout, including the priority sites, categories and integration steps.
- Demonstrate the capability in a live environment
- Investigate the revenue opportunities presented by e-procurement.

e-Auctions

A student should be asked to describe the reverse auction process and explain how the e-Auction would work. Essentially, the reverse auction process described in the case would involve a dynamic pricing arrangement, where suppliers and buyer are connected via a secure Internet link and special software, all provided by the on-line bid service provider. The auction is designed to run over a specific period, while most have rules about extending the bid time provided new bids are being submitted. Eventually the suppliers bid-down the price until the bid ends. Suppliers submit their bids anonymously, typically from their office, in real time or "live". Only the buyer knows the identities of the bidders, while the bidders receive feedback concerning the current lowest offered price. In most reverse auctions, the price drops substantially during the final minutes.

If time permits, time can be spent to discuss the different types of auctions. For example, 1) seller controlled rising price auctions (traditional auctions likely most familiar to students); 2) seller controlled declining price auctions (e.g., Dutch flower auctions); 3) buyer controlled declining price auctions (e.g., reverse auctions).

Completing a reverse auction requires a substantial amount of work on the part of the buyer. Students should be asked to consider what preparatory steps should be included in the e-Auction process. A possible sequence is:

- Introduction to on-line bidding
- Category/commodity analysis
- Supplier analysis
- Auction parameter definition
- Prepare offering description
- Supplier training
- Configure auction
- Conduct auction
- Post-auction analysis
- Supplier selection

Conducting an e-Auction obviously requires a substantial amount of time, effort, resources and costs. Note also that much of the work can be described at "good purchasing practice" and the actual e-Auction process itself may provide limited benefits. The real value added could be provided from analyzing suppliers and commodity requirements, and then structuring competitive bids.

Advantages and Disadvantages

There are a number of reasons why firms might consider using e-Auctions:
- Opportunities for significant cost reduction through real time supplier competition
- Increased efficiency and speed of RFQ and bid process

- Access to new market and supplier information, such as supplier costs and bidding processes
- A method to consolidating supply

e-Auctions also have a number of potential benefits for suppliers:
- Introduction of new business opportunities
- Fair and open competition in the bidding process
- Increased market knowledge
- Ease of quoting

There are also a number of potential disadvantages of e-Auctions for the buying company:
- Costs and resources of preparing for the auction
- Costs and fees for the on-line service provider
- Prices may not decline – potential increase in costs
- Information sharing with suppliers
- Disrupting long-term supply relationships

From the suppliers' perspective, there are also a number of potential disadvantages:
- Low margins/costs
- Commoditization of products
- Cost of learning new technology and preparing for auction
- Disclosure
- Fairness – Who are the other parties and do they have special information?

Commodity Analysis

A key issue raised in the case is when should firms use reverse auctions? The questions that Ninian Wilson faced were: Is either archival services or marketing paper appropriate for a reverse auction? Furthermore, what other commodities might be considered candidates for future reverse auctions? An interesting aspect of this case is that for the two commodities under consideration, one was a service and the other was a product.

There are a number of different approaches that might be used to help flush out the appropriateness of reverse auctions. A simple approach would be an illustration through the use of a 2 × 2 matrix:

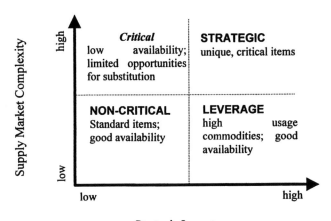

This matrix can be used as a basis for class discussion regarding commodity characteristics and the suitability for reverse auctions. Reverse auctions are best suited for non-critical and leverage items. These categories are characterized by good availability and opportunities to make supply decisions on the basis of price. Commodities in the strategic quadrant are suited for alliances and partnerships, meanwhile proposals and negotiations can be used for commodities in the critical quadrant.

Archival Services

Archival services can be described as a non-critical item for C&W. Indications are that after Wendy Ellis consolidated requirements under a three year bid, the price actually increased from £399,000 (three years at £133,000) to £423,000. Only about £3,000 of this increase could be attributed to fireproof storage.

When Wendy Ellis asked for quotes she did not anticipate conducting a reverse auction. Consequently, Clauws Records Services might be frustrated with Ninian's proposal to conduct an e-Auction and could suggest that it should be awarded the contract. However, Ninian claims that the potential benefit is 20 to 30 percent, suggesting potential savings of £85,000 to £125,000. Of course, costs of conducting the auction would still have to be taken into account, such as fees from the on-line bid service provider.

Whether or not to use archival services under these circumstances can be leveraged as a point of debate in class. The key issues are the suitability of archival services and how to convince the existing suppliers to participate. A reasonable is that Wendy Ellis pre-qualified each of the six vendors as part of the original RFQ process. Furthermore, the RFQ price from Clauws provides a good benchmark for the trial. However, the students must also consider the implications of the e-Auction on supplier relations. Specifically, how will the suppliers react and what can be done to encourage their participation?

Marketing Paper

The situation with marketing paper is much different from archival services. The spend is substantially higher, which would suggest higher risk and greater potential reward. Ninian appears to be considering conducting an e-Auction for C&W's corporate requirements, which would be much more complex, compared to the archival service alternative. However, the existence of a contract for C&W's U.K. requirements suggests that basis for comparison of the pre and post auction costs.

One interesting contrast to archival services is the commodity nature of paper products. Understanding the current market conditions might be useful information before making a final decision.

On-Line Bid Service Provider

A major consideration for Ninian Wilson was the selection of an on-line bid service provider. This part of the class discussion should focus on the supplier selection criteria, which might include:

- software capabilities
- reporting features: graphs, real time reporting
- implementation lead time
- integration with current C&W systems
- cost
- training and support
- experience

C&W needs a stand-alone solution for this auction, not an open bid on an Internet exchange or portal. Furthermore, Ninian Wilson will have to decide how to evaluate proposals from suppliers. For example, if the suppliers are not deemed to be equally capable, then the bids can be adjusted accordingly.

Finally, how much should Ninian be prepared to pay for the service? His options include a flat rate, a percentage of the contract or savings, and even have the bidders kick in. Table TN 1 provides a comparison of the reverse auction fee structures, based on certain estimates of contract costs and savings. This analysis underscores the wide variations of approaches taken by e-Auction service providers. An interesting point of debate in class can center on the logic and suitability of these pricing models.

Table TN 1

REVERSE AUCTION FEE COMPARISON

Commodity	IA-TECH (flat fee)	e-Procure (percent of contract)	e-Procure (shared savings)
Archival Services	£12,000	£12,000 (based on contract of £400,000)	£12,000 (based on savings of £80,000)
U.K. Marketing Papers	£25,000	£27,000 (based on contact of £1.2 mm)	£36,000 (based on savings of £240,000)
Marketing Papers	£50,000	£42,500 (based on contact of £1.2 mm)	£150,00 (based on savings of £1 mm)

TEACHING STRATEGY

This case can be used as a platform to explore opportunities and challenges associated with new technology-based procurement tools. Class discussion can follow the analysis provided in this teaching note, beginning with an exploration of the general concept of e-Auctions, using C&W as one example of company starting into a comprehensive e-commerce strategy. At some point during the discussion the instructor might want to provide a short lecture on e-procurement issues and reverse auction applications.

The class discussion can then focus on the issues facing Ninian Wilson. Specifically, which product makes sense for the pilot, archival services or marketing paper? Furthermore, what other commodities might be candidates? Finally, how can Ninian get cooperation from suppliers, how should he evaluate on-line bid service providers and how much should he pay for the service.

WHAT HAPPENED

C&W decided to start with archival services. The six original vendors were invited to submit bids for a three year contract and four agreed to participate, including the lowest bidder from the original RFQ. The auction lasted approximately 70 minutes, the initial 30 minute period plus 40 minutes of extended time (bid rules stipulated that the auction would run for five minutes past any new bids to overcome situations where bidders would submit bids at the last second of the auction). The final submission indicated a saving in excess of 26% over the currently agreed rates – a saving in excess of £100,000. The chart below plots bid progress during the e-Auction.

C&W contracted with IA-TECH, and paid a flat fee of £12,000.

On the heels of this success, Ninian Wilson was planning to conduct an e-Auction for C&W marketing papers requirement. Additional categories for e-Auction were being evaluated and proposed as part of the "Project Y€$" e-Procurement program.

While C&W did not believe that savings of the magnitude achieved in the archiving auction are guaranteed every time, it was considered to be an extremely valuable tool. In addition to the 'bottom line' benefits, advantages in the form of operational efficiencies such as speed to tender and response, automation/standardization of the Request for quotation (RFQ) process and market place awareness can be realized.

The chart plots bid progress during the course of the e-Auction. The e-Auction ran for an initial 30 minutes with 40 minutes of extended time. The lowest bid received bettered the RFQ costs by 26%.

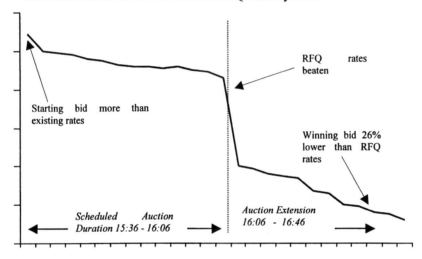

15:36 15:45 15:53 15:55 15:58 15:59 16:00 16:06 16:13 16:18 16:25 16:30 16:40 16:46

Approximately two weeks later C&W decided to conduct an e-Auction for its corporate requirements for marketing paper. The biding structure was set-up so suppliers could bid on its regional requirements for U.K., European, U.S. or Asian requirements. The results were much less impressive. Only three suppliers participated in the e-Auction, after five had committed to participating. Only one bid was placed for the European contract and no bids were placed for the U.S. or Asian contracts. The final bid for the U.K. contract was 4% below the existing contract, representing an annual saving of £48,000.

Establishing E-Business Standards at Deere and Company

Teaching Note

IMMEDIATE ISSUE

Develop a preliminary plan for Deere's e-business supply chain technology standards.

BASIC ISSUES

1. e-Business
2. Technology standardization and implementation.
3. Decentralized organizational structures.
4. Using technology to reduce costs and inventories.
5. Supply chain integration.
6. Systems and process management.

STUDENT ASSIGNMENT QUESTIONS

1. How can Deere's supply management group use e-business to improve its competitive position?
2. What specific problems might Paul Morrisey face in establishing technology standards for e-business transactions?
3. As Paul Morrisey, what recommendations would you make to your boss in two weeks and why?

POSSIBLE DISCUSSION QUESTIONS

1. Where would you start? How would you spend the two weeks?
2. What information do you think your boss wants? How will you get it for him?
3. Do you think Deere should use a consultant to develop its e-business strategy?
4. What does Deere's supply chain look like? What opportunities does Deere's size and dominance provide?
5. What problems and resistance can you expect from the business units? How would you suggest Paul Morrisey deal with these issues?
6. Do you think Deere should join a B2B exchange? Which one and why?
7. Do you think that Deere should start a new B2B exchange? What other companies would you suggest be asked to join?
8. What technology platform options does Deere have for its standard? What criteria would you use to evaluate the different technologies and suppliers?

DISCUSSION

Deere is about to launch an e-business initiative and Paul Morrisey has the daunting task of developing a preliminary plan for the supply management organization. The context of the case is important. First, Paul has two weeks before his plan and recommendations are due to his boss. This gives him time to collect information and do some research. It is appropriate to ask the students how they might use the two weeks. For example, should they talk to technology systems providers, benchmark other large companies, interview suppliers, collect articles and other research information, etc?

Second, the approach taken by Deere is worth commenting. Many large companies would hire consultants and spend millions on a study. Deere has evidently decided to use internal staff for the project, as far was we know. Furthermore, Paul does not appear to be a technology expert, and has a background in operations, marketing and supply.

Third, this assignment appears to be an initial pass, and is not a presentation for the Board of Directors, for example. This situation likely provides Paul with some flexibility in terms of presenting options as opposed to a "final solution". His boss may want to know his various options and costs before passing it up the line to the senior ranks.

THE DEERE SUPPLY CHAIN

Deere is a large company with a dominant position in the supply chain. This position should allow Deere to exert pressure on many of its suppliers. However, Deere also deals with other large companies, such as commodities for electronics, tires, third party logistics providers and engines. Coercing these companies to adopt a new technology standard will be more difficult and costly compared to Deere's smaller suppliers that heavily rely on the company for business. Therefore, it seems unlikely that Deere will be able to force a solution on its supply chain and Paul needs to consider which solutions provide the best fit with the diverse needs of its supply base.

One place for Paul to start is to understand what steps other companies in the industry have taken. For example, is there technology platform that has been adopted by other players in the industry? It would be useful if he could even narrow the options down to two or three prominent technology systems providers.

Paul should also investigate existing B2B industry portals related to Deere. The option exists to follow the lead of other sectors, such as chemicals, automotive and the airline industry, and create a dominant industry portal as part of a strategy of standardization.

The Deere Supply Management Organization

Deere has a very decentralized organization structure and getting the business units to agree on a common standard will be a difficult. Furthermore, there are likely significant differences between the business units with respect to suppliers and business processes. Consequently, Paul should evaluate how and where such differences exist and assess the implications for his project.

One approach to achieving organizational buy-in for the new standard would be to involve the business units through participation on an e-business technology council or taskforce. This group could be part of the existing Deere Electronic Commerce Council. The creation of such a body will permit business unit input and provide assurances that their concerns are aired and taken into consideration where possible. Furthermore, visibility of such a group helps promote a sense of openness in the decision-making process.

It seems unlikely that the business units have done any work in the area of e-business technology development yet, but Paul should check.

Issues for Paul Morrisey

There are a number of areas that Paul should investigate in preparation for his meeting in two weeks. First, recommending an e-business technology standard implies selection of a technology solutions supplier. However, this is an industry where the future is uncertain – new players are constantly entering with new products and services, existing players are merging and some are going broke. There are hundreds of possible solutions providers and attempting to predict the future and understand which companies will remain in the market with the best products and services will be tricky. Paul must make a careful assessment of potential suppliers and avoid, if possible, a situation where the supplier goes out of business or the supplier exits to the market or merges with another company and stops supporting our technology platform.

Second, as described above, Paul should also spend time conducting a preliminary analysis of the current situation regarding:

1. e-Business technology
2. e-Business initiatives in the heavy equipment industry

Paul should be able to describe the background in which his recommendations are being presented.

It seems unlikely that Paul will be able to develop a final solution in two weeks. He would be better off to educate his boss on the current environment and focus on the process that the company should follow to implement an e-business technology standard. Ultimately, visible top management support will be required to make the initiative a success.

CHAPTER 5

Quality Specification and Inspection

Topics Covered

Determination of Need
    Early Supply and Supplier Involvement
Methods of Description
    Description by Brand
    "Or Equal"
    Description by Specification
    Miscellaneous Methods of Description
    Combination of Descriptive Methods
    Sources of Specification Data
Standardization and Simplification
Quality, Suitability, and Best Buy
    Quality
    Suitability
    "Best Buy"
    Service and "Best Buy"
    Determining the "Best Buy"
Total Quality Management (TQM)
Quality
    Quality Dimensions
    Reliability
    The Cost Of Quality
    Continuous Improvement

The Malcolm Baldrige National Quality
Award and ISO 9000
    ISO 9000 Quality Standards
Quality Function Deployment (QFD)
Inspection and Testing
    Testing and Samples
    Inspection
    Quality Assurance and Quality Control
Process Control
Supplier Certification
    Adjustments and Returns
Questions for Review and Discussion
References
Cases
    St. Ann's Hospital
    Dorman Printing Inc.

QUIZ RESPONSES

D | 1. An advantage of buying by brand or equal is that:

    a. it provides evidence that thought and careful study have been given to the need and the ways in which it may be satisfied.
    b. it establishes a standard for measuring and checking materials as supplied.
    c. it provides an opportunity to purchase identical requirements from a number of different sources of supply.
    d. it shifts the responsibility for establishing equality or superiority to the bidder.
    e. it provides the potential for equitable competition by ensuring that the suppliers are quoting for exactly the same material or service.

B | 2. The purpose of identifying the function of an item to be required is:

    a. to provide the mathematics for a suitable inspection program.
    b. to assist in the determination of what represents acceptable value.
    c. to avoid having to purchase a branded item.
    d. to avoid substitution.
    e. to avoid engineering-purchasing arguments.

B | 3. Quality Function Deployment (QFD) is a method for:

    a. determining the match between a commercially available material, good or service and the intended functional use.
    b. developing new products in less time and at less cost.
    c. determining the mathematical probability that a product will function for a stipulated period of time.
    d. determining the ability of the organization to make the "best buy".
    e. improving purchasing/supply and engineering relations to increase efficiency and effectiveness.

C | 4. The best type of inspection to use is:

   a. 100 percent inspection.
   b. carried out by a commercial testing laboratory.
   c. dependent on the nature of the purchase.
   d. continuous sampling.
   e. sequential sampling.

D | 5. A buyer may be compelled to purchase by specification when:

   a. a high degree of supplier expertise or skill is required and difficult to define exactly.
   b. the internal user's preferences are impossible to overcome.
   c. a supplier holds a needed patent.
   d. an opportunity exists to purchase identical requirements from a number of different sources of supply.
   e. he or she wishes to leave it up to the supplier to decide how to make the most suitable product.

E | 6 Early supply involvement may be achieved by:

   a. staffing the supply area with engineers.
   b. co-locating purchasing people in the engineering or design areas.
   c. using cross-functional teams on new product development
   d. b and c
   e. a, b, and c

A | 7. JIT and MRP:

   a. both require high quality product to be delivered on time.
   b. both require sequential sampling.
   c. have substantially different quality requirements.
   d. require the presence of the purchaser's Q.C. staff on the supplier's premises.
   e. both require daily submission of OC curves from the supplier to the purchaser.

C | 8. Description by brand:

   a. may be a preference of an internal user, but it is never a necessity.
   b. is the least risky and lowest cost approach to attaining "best value."
   c. may be a necessity because the manufacturing process is secret
   d. should always be discouraged by the buyer.
   e. is usually an indication that a supplier has unduly influenced someone in the buyer's organization.

E | 9. ISO 9000 quality standards:

   a. try to provide common quality standards across the United States.
   b. measure customer satisfaction and continuing improvement.
   c. were established by the International Supply Organization.
   d. were first issued in the U.S. and later adopted worldwide.
   e. require an on-site audit by an accredited third party.

C | 10. Supplier certification programs:

   a. ensure that all suppliers in an industry produce goods of comparable quality.
   b. were originally instituted in the automotive industry because of the large number of purchased parts.
   c. seek to ensure that certified suppliers are capable of meeting specifications and quality standards.
   d. are gradually being abandoned because the goal of zero defects is unrealistic and costly.
   e. are difficult to implement because the mathematics of statistical quality control are not very well established.

True and False

F   1. The Malcolm Baldrige National Quality Award was created by the Internal Standards Organization to recognize companies that excel in quality achievement.

F   2. Total quality management (TQM) is a philosophy and system focused on applying product quality concepts to the behavior of top management.

T   3. Suitability refers to the match between a commercially available material, good or service and the intended function.

F   4. The real costs of quality are frequently overstated in an organization.

F   5. "Best buy" refers to the successful matching of the most suitable technical features to the best available supplier.

T   6. Standardization and simplification must be balanced against suitability and uniqueness to lower costs, improve quality, and offer consumers the appearance of extensive options.

T   7. The allocation between buyer and seller of the costs incurred when materials are rejected is affected by the kind of material rejected, trade customs, the buyer's cost accounting procedures, and the positions of strength of each organization.

F   8. Process capability refers to the ability of the process to meet production goals consistently.

T   9. Statistical process control (SPC) is a technique for testing a random sample of output from a process in order to detect if nonrandom changes in the process are occurring.

F   10. The original version of ISO 9000 checked for actual customer satisfaction, and registration guaranteed a quality product or service.

T   11. Disposal considerations may affect the specifications of an item to be acquired.

St. Ann's Hospital

Teaching Note

IMMEDIATE ISSUE

What should be done about the disposable surgical drapes contract?

BASIC ISSUES

1. What is the balance between clinical preference and cost? How much is clinical preference worth?
2. Is clinical preference the same as quality?
3. What are the ethical implications of considering the change in Alpha's rebate terms?

TEACHING OBJECTIVES

1. To demonstrate a problem in supplier relations.
2. To discuss what quality means in a hospital.
3. To show how purchasing decisions are made in a hospital setting.
4. To discuss an ethical issue in the contract bidding process.

SUGGESTED STUDENT ASSIGNMENT

1. As Hal Watkins, Director of Purchasing, what decision would you make, and why?
2. How would you explain your decision to Alpha and Tyler?

POSSIBLE DISCUSSION QUESTIONS

1. What are the alternatives available to Hal?
2. How would Alpha and Tyler likely react to each of those actions identified above?
3. How important is clinical preference in a hospital? How much are you willing to pay for clinical preference?
4. Is there anything wrong with what Alpha Products did in changing their rebate terms to improve their standing in terms of the surgical drapes contract?
5. How might this situation be different if it was set in a private sector firm?

ANALYSIS

Hal can either choose to buy from Alpha or Tyler.

Both suppliers will be upset by this, since the drapes contract represents a significant increase in business for both of them: the contract is worth $400,000; Alpha's current business with the hospital is $500,000 and Tyler's is $800,000. Both suppliers, because of the course of events also feel that they deserve the contract.

The Prime Vendor Agreements are a significant benefit to St. Ann's, and Hal does not want to jeopardize them: purchases under the agreements are $1.3 million; rebates are 1.5% - 2. In addition to the financial benefits the closer relations with Alpha and Tyler make it easier to manage supplies.

Technically, Hal should not consider the new rebate terms from Alpha in making his decision. The decision should really be made on the basis of the bids made last year and Tyler should get the contract. However, with the pressure from the nursing staff to choose Alpha, and the now, inconsequential price difference, he is in an awkward position.

One key fact so far ignored in the analysis is the frequency of discards on the Tyler product. It only takes a 5% occurrence rate for the two prices to become equivalent. Hal might do well to talk to the nurses and find out how often it happens that a drape does have to be discarded because it slipped on to the floor or for some other reason and to find out what delays and other problems drape replacement causes.

The case has a number of interesting issues attached to it. Under a prime vendor agreement does a vendor have different rights from a standard vendor? For example, can the vendor expect additional business on products not initially covered under the prime agreement? If the vendor gets a product tested and it is successful can the vendor automatically expect the business? Obviously, in the hospital situation we see that the hospital purchasing staff wants to maintain the advantage of competitiveness, while also trying to obtain the benefits from prime vendor agreements. How purchasing can maintain price competitiveness under prime vendor agreements is a key issue.

That both vendors are interested in this business is clear, just because of the volume alone. It is rather strange that so much time has passed since the original quotes. It is not really fair to allow one side to requote and the other one to maintain its price from a year earlier. The simplest action at this point is to allow both vendors to come in with one final quote and to handicap the price of Tyler's product by the rate of discards. For example, if the Tyler has a 2% discard rate, its total price should be increased by 2% to allow for this.

Hal has to be careful that his dealings with both vendors are such that he does not endanger the prime vendor agreements already in place. One good question is how Alpha can lower its price by an extra $80,000 over a one-year time. Does this mean that this is a high profit or high margin item or that the original price agreements made with these vendors have allowed for lots of latitude?

Is it not possible for Hal to check with other hospitals using the same products to see what kind of prices they are being charged? It really seems as if he is depending on the competitive process to do a lot of the work for him. Is it possible that, if he had not asked for a test of the Tyler product, he might have ended up paying substantially more for these drapes?

This is a fascinating case and should generate lots of discussion.

It is useful to end up on an ethics note. It is not fair to allow one side to requote and not the other at the same time under these circumstances. Given that a retest of the other product was ordered and too much time has passed, the original quotes really can no longer be considered as valid.

Dorman Printing Inc.

Teaching Note

IMMEDIATE ISSUE

What action to take concerning a new supplier, Mareden Ltd.

BASIC ISSUES

1. Quality.
2. Specification.
3. Supplier selection.
4. Total cost of ownership.
5. Supplier relations.
6. Supplier partnerships.
7. Commodity management.

SUGGESTED STUDENT ASSIGNMENT

As Alex Szabo, what is your analysis of the situation at Dorman Printing? What action would you take regarding Mareden and why?

POSSIBLE QUESTIONS FOR DISCUSSION IN CLASS

1. Why did problems occur in the print shop when Alex had already tested a sample of the ink?
2. How much longer do you think Dorman's suppliers will put up with Alex's antics?
3. What kind of commitments do you want from John Field?
4. Is this even a problem that Alex should be concerned with?
5. What do you want to do about the new equipment?

ANALYSIS

The Quality Issue

Despite Alex's belief that he has a strong group of supportive suppliers, he appears to be constantly prepared to try someone new. As we see here though, if things don't work out Alex has to leverage his goodwill and get his old, reliable suppliers to cover for him. One has to wonder how many times he can get away with such antics.

At first appearance, this seems to be a pretty basic problem and it would be easy to dismiss Mareden as a potential supplier. However, there are some interesting twists here. First, should Alex even be spending his time on this issue? Based on an annual expenditure of $800,000 and a 5 percent cost savings, Alex could save $40,000 per year. Not bad for a small company, but it ignores the bigger picture. However, as demonstrated in the case, such savings can be easily lost through costs of poor quality. The opportunity cost at Dorman of downtime on their presses is likely in the $200 per hour range, assuming a three-year payback on a $1.5 million new press ($1.5 million at 4,000 hours/year is $125 and does not include variable costs such as labor). Consequently, the $40,000 in savings would be eliminated with just 200 hours of downtime. It appears that the costs of switching can be high.

Second, the case indicated that Alex had taken some samples from the trade show and that initial tests proved favorable. This raises a question concerning the quality of the sample compared to the quality of the ink used in the production run. It also might indicate a poor test on the part of Dorman. Either, way Alex needs to get to the bottom of this issue.

Third, it appears that raw material can influence production processes and that specifying material characteristics at the machine design stage should be standard practice. This raises two important questions for Alex -- can the ink from Mareden run in other equipment at Dorman and what will he do about the new piece of equipment? It might very well be possible that the Mareden ink could run on other equipment in the press shop. John Field indicated that he could get technical support, who might be able to assist in making this determination. As well, a significant concern for Alex should be establishing and qualifying a reliable ink supplier for the new equipment.

Supplier Relations

Ink and paper represent the two important inputs into Dorman's production process. (Other important costs include labor, capital and energy.) However, at least for ink, Alex appears to take a short-term approach to supplier selection. This might not be wise if the ink supplier is critical for proper operation of the printing machine and quality of the final product. For example, changing ink suppliers might be difficult and costly in terms of poor quality, lost production and customer satisfaction. The implication is that selection of ink suppliers has important long-term implications for Dorman. It appears that Alex might want to consider another approach.

Ideally, Alex needs identify one or two good ink suppliers. He needs support in terms of product consistency and long-term pricing. For example, what happens if a supplier decides to stop production of a line that Dorman requires for one of its new printing machine? Alternatively, what new product advances are being made that might reduce costs or improve quality? Alex should understand supplier product management plans and track innovation opportunities. Price negotiation is only a portion of his commodity management responsibilities.

It would appear that Alex might have a bigger problem here than he had counted on. Despite his long tenure in the industry, he does not appear to be aware of the need to take a strategic approach to selecting suppliers to help the company compete successfully in an industry where quality and cost are critical determinants of success. This is a good application for buyer-supplier partnering.

CONCLUSIONS

This is an interesting situation. The problem with Mareden, however, is only the tip of the iceberg. The real issue in this case is recognizing the proper approach needed to select and develop suppliers for important commodities. Alex needs to clarify his current supply needs and take steps to identify appropriate suppliers. Working with these vendors should be his priority.

It certainly appears that Mareden can offer some potential savings, but it remains to be seen whether its products can be used at Dorman. Its machines might not be designed to use Mareden ink and the $40,000 in savings would be a mirage -- quality costs would more than off-set these savings.

A good place to start for Alex would be to make an internal assessment of his ink supply needs and match this with the vendor base, including a plan for the new equipment Consolidating with a few vendors makes sense here to gain some clout and credibility. In the long-term, this might represent the best opportunity for reductions in total costs.

TEACHING SUGGESTIONS

You can start the class by asking the students what they want to do about the situation with Mareden and what action they would take. Their initial comments will likely focus on the short-term tactical issues related to the problems with the recent printing job. Many of the students will want to dump Mareden and revert back to the previous supply relationship and consider the problem solved. However, the students should be pushed to consider the issues of relationships with existing suppliers, total cost of ownership and finally the implications of the new equipment. Press the students to assess how supply decisions affect the performance of the company and evaluate what Alex Szabo should be doing to help Dorman compete successfully on price and quality.

Once the students recognize the magnitude of the problem here for Alex, discussion can move towards the information that Alex needs and how he can collect it. He should look internally at the equipment requirements, and externally at the supplier base and develop a commodity strategy.

CHAPTER 6

Quantity and Delivery

Topics Covered

Time-Based Strategies and Quantity Decisions
Classification of Purchases
    ABC Classification
Forecasting
    Forecasting Techniques
Inventories
    Inventory Costs
    The Functions of Inventory
    The Forms of Inventory
    Inventory Function and Form Framework
    Controlling Inventory through Process Management
    Managing Supply-Chain Inventories
Stockless Purchasing Systems
Determining Order Quantities and Inventory Levels
Managing Independent Demand--Economic Order Quantity Models for Cycle Inventories
    Fixed Quantity Models
    Fixed Period Models
    Probabilistic Models and Service Coverage

Managing Dependent Demand--Material Requirements Planning (MRP)
    Structural Trees
    The MRP Plan
    MRP Inputs
    MRP Lot Sizing
    Modern MRP Systems and Capacity Requirements Planning (CRP)
Distribution Requirements Planning (DRP)
Purchasing Implications of MRP
Enterprise Resource Planning (ERP) Systems
Just-in-Time (JIT)
    Deliberate Inventory Level Reduction
    JIT Implications for Supply Management
    Implementing Lean Supply
Questions for Review and Discussion
References
Cases
    Roger Gray
    Connecticut Circuit Manufacturers
    Abbey Paquette
    Corn Silk

QUIZ RESPONSES

B   1.   "A" items in ABC analysis are:

        a. reviewed infrequently.
        b. particularly critical in financial terms.
        c. normally carried in large quantities.
        d. ordered infrequently.
        e. commonly managed by carrying inventory.

D   2.   In Kanban systems:

        a. large raw material inventories are necessary.
        b. great product variety is usually preferable.
        c. the Kanbans are discarded daily.
        d. the typical inventory level is counted in minutes and hours.
        e. large buffer inventories are usually carried.

A   3.   When a carpet manufacturer predicts carpet sales by using building permits issued, mortgage rates, apartment vacancy rates, and so on, this is an example of:

        a. a causal model.
        b. a deterministic model.
        c. a qualitative forecasting technique.
        d. a time series forecasting technique.
        e. a repetitive pattern modeling tool.

C   4.   On an annual requirement of 100 items spread evenly throughout the year, any purchaser has an opportunity of buying all 100 units at a price of $100 each, or buying 10 units at a time at a price of $120. If the inventory carrying cost is 25 percent per year and assuming no ordering costs:

        a. buying 100 at a time will save the company $1100 per year.
        b. buying 100 at a time will save the company $2,000 per year.
        c. buying 100 at a time will save the company $750 per year.
        d. buying 100 at a time will save the company $2500 a year.
        e. buying 100 at a time will save the company $3000 a year.

A | 5. | Closed-loop MRP:

a. requires a check between shop floor control and capacity and the master production schedule.
b. is a system which closes the loop between the supplier and the purchaser.
c. is an MRP system in which all invoices are checked by accountants.
d. requires a check between the master production schedule and the inventory on hand.
e. allows the departmental unit manager freedom on the sequence of jobs to be done in that department.

E | 6. | A buffer inventory is:

a. a stock accumulated for a well-defined future need.
b. an inventory to cut down the noise between two departments.
c. an inventory which is expected in the future.
d. an inventory carried to buffer the impact of a significant price increase.
e. an inventory to protect against uncertainties in supply and demand.

A | 7. | Service coverage:

a. is the portion of user requests served by the buffer stock.
b. is the ability of purchasing to meet the demands/needs of its internal customers.
c. is the accuracy of the EOQ model in a given time period.
d. remains constant over time for a given organization.
e. targets are easily set.

D | 8. | Stockout costs:

a. are easy to assess in most organizations.
b. are generally about equal to or less than the cost of carrying additional inventory.
c. do not include present and future lost contribution on lost sales and customer goodwill because these are difficult to quantify.
d. can vary depending on whether it is a seller's or a buyer's market.
e. are higher when it is a seller's market.

Chapter 6

D 9. JIT requires:

a. monthly deliveries.
b. receiving docks open 24 hours a day.
c. large cycle inventories.
d. frequent deliveries of relatively small quantities.
e. a superior MRP system.

C 10. When a carrying cost of inventory is expressed as a percentage:

a. the lower it is, the lower the economic order quantity.
b. it usually exceeds 57.5 percent per year.
c. it needs to be multiplied by the laid down cost of the item to calculate a dollar carrying cost per unit in the typical EOQ formula.
d. it must exclude the insurance cost of inventory.
e. it is usually the same as the borrowing cost of the organization.

B 11. Capacity requirements planning (CRP):

a. ignores the human resources required, but provides information on needed machine resources.
b. performs a similar function for manufacturing resources that MRP performs for materials.
c. is essential to minimize in-house inventories.
d. uses ABC analysis as an integral part of the process.
e. calculates the service level by dividing the average inventory carried by annual sales.

True and False

F	1.	ABC analysis categorizes purchases or inventory into different groups, normally based on number of items and supply market risk.
T	2.	For the supply management function, time-based strategies that impact competitive advantage relate to cycle time reductions and greater coordination of materials and information flows.
T	3.	The primary objective of EOQ models for cycle inventories is to balance the costs of carrying extra inventory against the costs of purchasing or making more frequently.
F	4.	Uncertainty regarding lead times in MRP can normally be handled by centralized shop floor control.
T	5.	A concerted set-up cost and time reduction program generally impacts cycle inventories.
F	6.	In MRO inventory management, scheduled maintenance requirements can be seen as independent demand requirements.
F	7.	One disadvantage of the Kanban system is that there is a need for elaborate computer support.
F	8.	In fixed period inventory models, orders are placed when the reorder point is reached.
F	9.	Since all types of inventory perform a decoupling function, there is no unique category of inventory called decoupling inventory.
T	10.	DRP refers to the application the time phasing logic of MRP to the distribution function.

Roger Gray

Teaching Note

IMMEDIATE ISSUE

Address the plant materials management problems, characterized by stockouts and high inventory levels

BASIC ISSUES

1. Systems and controls.
2. Management information systems.
3. JIT.
4. Total supply chain costs.
5. Planning and forecasting.
6. ABC analysis.
7. Logistics and transportation.

SUGGESTED STUDENT ASSIGNMENT

1. As Roger Gray, what is your analysis of the situation at Anderson Plastics? What alternatives do you have to address the materials management problems at the plant?
2. What action would you take and why?

POSSIBLE DISCUSSION QUESTIONS

1. What steps should Roger Gray take before he makes a decision?
2. Should Roger write his own software program? What do you think will be the reaction of head office?
3. Do you think Roger Gray's situation is common or uncommon? Why?
4. As Roger Gray, what further information would you like to have?
5. What alternatives might you consider here?
6. How would you rate Anderson's JIT practices?

ANALYSIS

Size-up

This is a very familiar problem to many purchasers and plant materials managers: incorrect and late information leading to poor supply performance. A common response is to blame the information system, and ask the IT group to fix it our design a new one. Others prefer to point to inaccurate records because those who use the system fail to record their transactions properly. Successful organizations find ways of dealing with these problems, as must Roger Gray.

The problems experienced by Roger Gray are typical of MRP- and MRPII-type systems. These systems provide the benefits of planning what to order and produce and when, which helps to keep costs down by minimizing inventories and avoiding unnecessary set-ups. The difficulty is that they require accurate data. Using data that is not accurate or is outdated leads to bad decisions.

The case also suggests that factors other than the materials management system were contributing to the problems. However, focusing on IT issues alone will not adequately address the problems.

An important factor here is the high cost of a stockout. Failure to meet delivery requirements would result in customer downtime, which carries tremendous costs, particularly for Anderson's automotive customers. Automotive OEMs charge their suppliers $300,000 to $400,000 per hour of downtime. Consequently, control over inventories is essential. Perhaps the fact that delivery reliability is important is one reason why Roger does not get criticized for carrying too much inventory.

Finally, Anderson supposedly is operating in a JIT environment. It would appear, however, that the plant has failed to adopt JIT practices, while its customers (and likely its competitors) have. This problem is demonstrated by unreliable deliveries from suppliers, poor control of inventories and poor planning and coordination of production. Class time can be dedicated to how well Anderson is doing with respect to JIT and what steps might be taken to improve their performance in this area. It would appear that they have a long way to go.

Possible Alternatives

Before making any decisions, Roger Gray may consider any of the following:

- Asking around other plants to see how they handle their materials management system problems. Chances are they, too, are experiencing similar difficulties and may already have developed a solution which Roger Gray could use.
- Get some help or advice from a qualified programmer either inside or outside the organization to determine the best system design and time to completion.
- Call head office to see if they have any interim solutions available.

In addition, before proceeding, Roger Gray should talk the problem over with his boss and make sure that doing anything on his own isn't contravening company policy.

Assessment of Two Alternatives

The two most obvious options to students are creating a new software program and/or carrying more inventory. These are evaluated below.

Option	Pros	Cons
Carry more inventory	- quick solution - never criticized by superiors	- poor inventory management practice - doesn't help to keep track of products and suppliers - constrained by available space - short-term solution only
Build new system	- shows initiative to management - will cut down work in long-term	- will take time (too much time and how long?) - not compatible with corporate systems - potentially won't work - only useful to Gray, not others ion company - may not solve problems

This analysis demonstrates that neither of these options are likely to be satisfactory and other alternatives need to be explored.

Other Alternatives

There seems to be an element of risk involved with writing this software with little corresponding reward. A more logical solution is to make adjustments to the current system which can be accomplished easily, while spending time trying to get to the root of the materials management system problems, such as varied production runs (perhaps due to a break down of communication between line management and purchasing) and the poor transportation system (switch carriers, or move from rail to truck). There are a number of related issues, which if addressed properly, could help improve the performance of the materials management systems.

A good place to start might be to look procedures for plant scheduling and control. For example, aggregate planning, master production scheduling and short-term scheduling procedures. Using basic planning and scheduling systems will help address problems early.

It certainly appears that Roger should re-assess transportation activities. Either the mode or vendors, or both, must be changed. Production problems because of transportation delays should not be tolerated – too many other options exist.

Training, communicating and following up with employees can address poor record keeping. Data reliability will improve once they understand the importance of such reports.

Using ABC analysis to control inventories might be a helpful approach here until the new system is installed. For example, Roger might want to hold high levels of C and B items and review their inventory levels only periodically, while paying closer attention to the A items. If he is responsible for 550 items and assuming total plant sales of $30 million and purchases of $20 million, this might suggest a breakdown of:

	# Products	% Products	% Total Value	$ Value
A items:	55	10%	70%	$14 million
B items	165	30%	20%	$ 4 million
C items	330	60%	10%	$ 2 million

FINAL CONSIDERATIONS

An easy, but completely unacceptable solution is to simply suggest that Roger should hire a programmer for a few days to fix the problems with the current system. Students that advocate such a course of action fail to take into consideration the complexities of the problems here. Implementing a properly functioning materials management system will take a great deal of work and be expensive. Furthermore, the fundamental problems of scheduling, planning and vendor selection must also be addressed if the performance of the materials management group is to improve. Using an ABC inventory system, coupled with proper materials planning and control, is Roger's best option.

Connecticut Circuit Manufacturers

Teaching Note

IMMEDIATE ISSUE

Develop appropriate recommendations, for presentation at the general management meeting the following day that will address the problem of late deliveries to customers.

BASIC ISSUES

1. Inventory management
2. Strategic supply
3. Customer service
4. Customer focus
5. Organization of the purchasing group
6. Changing product mix and the impact on purchasing
7. Commodity management

SUGGESTED STUDENT ASSIGNMENT

As Jack Veber, what is your analysis of the situation at Connecticut Circuit Manufacturers? What recommendations would you make at the general management meeting regarding the customer delivery problems and why?

POSSIBLE DISCUSSION QUESTIONS

1. What is more important here, customer focus or commodity focus?
2. What are the main differences between customers in the Contract Products and Design Products segments? What are the implications for purchasing?
3. How receptive do you think Al Cooper will be to your recommendations? How do you want to handle this matter with him?
4. Do you think you have enough information for the meeting tomorrow? What other information might be useful.
5. How can purchasing help CCM achieve its growth targets?

ANALYSIS

This case deals with the issue of customer focus and the implications for inventory control and the purchasing group. Although company sales are not provided in the case, based on the financial information in the exhibits, CCM appears to be a small or medium size company that is owned and operated by a group of entrepreneurs. The company also appears to be competing successfully in what can be described as a competitive industry.

CCM has a relatively small customer base, with only five customers. Students should recognize that under current circumstances, CCM cannot afford to lose a customer, especially as a result of controllable factors such as delivery performance. The growth potential in the Design Product customer group makes protecting these customers even more critical.

The case identifies CCM's customers as either Contract Product customers or Design Product customers. The characteristics of each group differs substantially:

	Design Product	**Custom Products**
Nature of Relationship	one-time, custom orders	ongoing orders
Customer Priorities	quality, delivery, service	quality, delivery, price
Growth Potential	40% per year	10% per year
Current Sales	500 - 1,000 units	4,000 - 5,000 units

This analysis demonstrates the differing needs and characteristics of CCM's customers. The exhibits provide additional information with respect to CCM's customer base and purchases. Exhibit TN1 combines data from Exhibits 1 and 2 in the case to establish and average cost per component. Exhibit TN2 uses the data from Exhibit 2 to identify the average cost per item for each customer.

This analysis indicates several relevant issues:

1. Although Design Products amount to only 10 to 20 percent of unit production (i.e. 500 -1,000 units out of a possible 4,500 - 6,000) the total value of purchases for these circuit boards is 70 percent of the total (i.e. total material value for Customer A and Customer E). This would indicate that Design Products represent a substantial amount in terms of sales in terms of dollar value.
2. As indicated in Exhibit TN2, the average cost per item is substantially higher for Design Product customers (Customers A and E) compared to Contract Product customers (Customers B, C and D)
3. Integrated circuits and printed circuit boards represent approximately 74% of total purchases.

The implication is that management has created a new customer segment, Design Products, which should be managed differently from its traditional customer base, Contract Products. This has implications for company inventory systems and the structure of the purchasing group.

The purchasing group at CCM plays an important role in the production control function of the company. Orders appear to be released to vendors based on confirmed orders. These orders appear to be placed by the buying group, not released by the production department based on blanket P.O.s. This maybe due to the unique nature of the products, price fluctuations between orders, or both. Either way, purchasing appears to work closely with production.

A POSSIBLE SOLUTION

The problem facing CCM is how to control inventory and material costs while still meeting the needs of its customers. In order to address these issues, CCM may want to segment its inventory policies based on customers and commodities.

First, the company may want to consider focusing inventory control activities on the high value items: integrated circuits and printed circuit boards. This could be accomplished by keeping minimum qualities of the high volume, low value items on-hand. It may also be advisable to explore opportunities to standardize low cost items between customers where possible. Admittedly this will be difficult with the Contract Product customers, but is definitely worth exploring.

Second, CCM should consider switching from the current commodity buying structure to organizing the purchasing group based on customers. For example, Veber may handle Custom Design purchases and Cooper could be responsible for Contract Product purchases. This move would allow the buyers to gain specific knowledge with respect to products for their customer base. The analysis in Exhibit TN2 seems to indicate that the value and perhaps the complexity of purchased items differs between Contract Products and Design Products. Consequently, there may be greater benefits in understanding the similarities of purchased components based on customers rather than by commodity segment.

Students should be sensitive to the position of Jack Veber. He has only been with the company for two months. Al Cooper has been with the company for over fifteen years. Although management may be eager to listen to new suggestions and insights, Veber should approach this situation with caution regarding his relationship with Cooper. The recommendation to re-structure the buying group based on customer focus is consistent with Veber's background, according to the information in the case. Veber should not be seen as simply attempting to change the system at CCM based on his previous management background. One approach to over-come this problem would be to discuss this matter with Cooper prior to the general management meeting in order to get him on-side.

TEACHING SUGGESTIONS

Asking students for their alternatives and action plans early would be a useful teaching approach to this case. You might have to push the students to get the financial analysis out, but it is important to have someone present the data in Exhibits TN1 and TN2 at some point early in the analysis. A practical way of accomplishing this task to make transparencies of both exhibits beforehand and simply get someone to present their analysis as part of the discussion related to action plans and alternatives. Putting the exhibits up as overheads, and asking how the data can be used, should trigger an appropriate response from one of the students. This analysis should create debate in class related to commodity versus customer focus, which can be supplemented with analysis related to the differences between the two customer segments. A key question to be raised is, what is more important customer or commodity differences?

A key point in the case is the role of the supply function and how its focus and orientation can affect customer service performance. Students should be made to appreciate that differences related to customer segmentation can be important to supply, as can be differences related to commodities. It is a careful balancing act, and maybe one reason whey companies continually tinker with their organization structures.

Exhibit TN1

ANNUAL COMPONENT PURCHASES

Item Name	# Types of Item	Annual Orders (parts)	Buyer	Total Annual Purchases	Average Cost
Integrated Circuits	73	50,000	Cooper	$250,000	$5.00
Resistors	95	500,000	Veber	$50,000	$0.10
Printed Circuit Boards	20	7,000	LeBlanc	$105,000	$15.00
Connectors	15	14,000	Cooper	$35,000	$2.50
Cables	10	8,000	Veber	$24,000	$3.00
Screws, Nuts, Washers	50	448,000	LeBlanc	$15,680	$0.04
Total	263	1,027,000		$479,680	$0.47

Exhibit TN2

ANNUAL COMPONENT PURCHASES

ITEM NAME	CUSTOMERS					
	A*	B	C	D	E*	Total
Integrated Circuits	15	10	20	3	25	73
Resistors	15	40	18	12	10	95
Printed Circuit Boards	4	3	5	1	7	20
Connectors	2	4	3	1	5	15
Cables	2	2	2	0	4	10
Screws, Nuts, Washers	8	12	10	10	10	50
Total # Items	46	71	58	27	61	263
Total Material Value	$135,000	$50,000	$80,000	$14,680	$200,000	$479,680
Average material value/item	$2,935	$704	$1,379	$544	$3,279	$1,824

* Design Product Customers

Abbey Paquette

Teaching Note

IMMEDIATE ISSUE

How to address the president's demand to radically reduce inventory carrying costs.

BASIC ISSUES

1. Inventory management.
2. Economic order quantity (EOQ) model.
3. Vendor managed inventories.
4. JIT.
5. Inventory control systems.
6. Cycle counting.
7. ABC analysis.
8. Total cost of ownership.

TEACHING OBJECTIVES

The objective of this case is to provide material for the discussion of the benefits of good supply chain management practices by providing an example of an organization challenged to reduce its inventory costs. Class discussion can include trade-offs of holding inventory, JIT delivery systems and approaches to inventory control.

SUGGESTED STUDENT ASSIGNMENT

As Abbey Paquette what recommendations would you make? How would you implement the changes that you have suggested? Support your recommendations with suitable analysis.

Optional question:

What is the economic order quantity for the BD-517? What action does this suggest you should take?

POSSIBLE DISCUSSION QUESTIONS

1. What is the course of action you plan to present to Chisholm on Monday?

2. How long will your plan take? Where do you want to start and why?
3. What improvements should be made to the present management systems?
4. What additional information do you need and where do you plan to get it?
5. What do you plan to say to your suppliers? What might they want from you in return?
6. What support do you need from manufacturing operations, finance/accounting, and marketing?
7. How much money can we save on the BD-517 by moving to weekly deliveries?
8. Is it realistic to get inventory holding costs down to zero? What might be a more realistic number?
9. What is included in inventory carrying costs? Why?

ANALYSIS

Size-up

It looks like Isaac Chisholm has been brought in to shake things up at PII. If their inventory management systems are any reflection of how the rest of the company is run, he should be able to find plenty of areas for improvement.

Let's start with some case facts. Chisholm indicated in his e-mail that PII has $2.5 million in annual inventory carrying costs and David Ellis claims that PII uses a 20 percent rate to calculate inventory holding costs. This would suggest that inventory levels are approximately $12.5 million. Assuming materials represent 50 percent of sales, total purchased components are approximately $25 million per year. Therefore, inventory turns are only two times per year – not very good.

Inventory Carrying Costs

An important issue here is how PII measures its inventory holding costs. As indicated by David Ellis, the company is using a rate of 20 percent, which is high if you assume that cost of capital might only be 8 – 10 percent. What might make-up the additional 10 – 12 percent?

There are several costs of holding inventory in addition to financing costs. Examples include insurance, damage, pilferage, warehousing, inplant movement, record keeping and inventory audits. It is worthwhile spending time in class discussing the actual costs of holding inventory.

BD-517

The BD-517 can be used as an example of the effects of declining inventory levels. Currently, the BD-517 is ordered in batches of 2,000, which represented four weeks of stock. This relationship is represented graphically in Figure TN1 below. Note that this analysis does not include consideration of safety stock.

Assuming constant usage, the average inventory is 1000 pieces, with an annual cost of $5,350 (1,000 pieces × 20% × $26.75). Many students will argue for batch sizes of 500 pieces, which represents one week of stock. At this batch size the average inventory level drops to 250 pieces, as shown in Figure TN2. The annual holding costs under this scenerio are $1,337.50 (250 pieces × 20% × $26.75).

EOQ Application

The case suggests that the variable costs of placing an order are $50. Using the EOQ formula to determine the optimum order quantity, the following solution is provided:

$$EOQ = \sqrt{\frac{2DS}{iC}} = \sqrt{\frac{2(25,000)50}{.20(26.75)}} = 684$$

The analysis suggests that a batch size of closer to 680 pieces provides an optimal balance between ordering and holding costs. This represents an annual holding (and ordering) cost of $1,830.

From Chisholm indicates that he would like to see the inventory holding costs "reduced to zero by year-end". This is not a realistic objective. Every system has inventory, even if it is only one piece. Secondly, inventory can serve useful purposes such as protecting against uncertainty and decoupling operations. The real question for PII is what reasonable objective should be established and what should be done to achieve it? With $12.5 million in inventories, clearly opportunities exist, but the ultimate target must be reasonable and the approach well thought-out.

An interesting aspect of this case is the atmosphere at PII. It appears that Chisholm has the entire organization on edge. The email to Abbey Paquette resulted in her dedicating a week of analysis to the inventory issue. Assuming of course that Chisholm is reasonable, what he might want is a substantial reduction in inventory carrying costs. Abbey's focus should be on developing a plan that addresses areas of opportunity, not necessarily ridding the company of every piece of inventory.

Alternatives and Action Plan

There are a number of steps that Abbey could recommend to Chisholm in the meeting:

- Order quantities should be reviewed, and opportunities to reduce them should be explored. The EOQ formula could provide good benchmarks in terms of ideal order quantities. However, changing these will involve negotiations with suppliers. The supplier of the BD-517 may indicate that its batch sizes are limited to increments of 500 pieces, forcing a decision between lot sizes of 500 and 1,000 pieces. Ultimately, PII could examine opportunities to lower its ordering costs, perhaps through information technology applications, which would allow it to further reduce order lot sizes.

- Use ABC principles. Abbey should start with the A items as part of her review process. The B and C items, characterized by lower volumes and/or costs, offer less opportunities to reduce inventory holding costs.
- Institute cycle counting. Verifying inventories will help avoid stock-outs and ordering material that is already in stock.
- Assign responsibility for inventory records. It appears that with the loss of the inventory clerk, responsibility for inventory records has not been assigned. Controls and procedures must be installed to address this weakness in the system. Training may be required for the fork lift operators.
- Some of the inventory may be safety stock, used to protect against uncertainty in demand. Abbey could involve sales/marketing and operations to examine methods of communicating and forecasting demand. Such information can be used to make decisions concerning safety stock, potentially reducing current levels.

Some students might suggest that PII should move to a JIT system and push inventory onto the suppliers. Athough JIT does have some applications at PII, implementation is a very involved process, and would represent a fundamentally different approach to business. Many students underestimate the challenges of installing a JIT system. The above comments suggest that basic inventory management principles can be used at PII to reduce their costs.

TEACHING SUGGESTIONS

Class can start by reviewing the opportunities at PII. Get an understanding of how much inventory PII carries and discuss what a reasonable objective might be in terms of reducing inventory carrying costs. For example, if inventory turns are only two times per year, then what is a reasonable goal? Can Chisholm's objective of zero inventory carrying costs be achieved? Discussion can include what costs are included in the 20 percent holding costs, and the trade-offs associated with reducing inventory levels.

Discussion can then concentrate on Abbey's investigation. What did she learn? How can this information be used? What do the students think of the process that she followed?

Save time for a discussion of the recommendations and action plan. Role playing can be used here, simulating a conversation between Chisholm and Paquette. Push the students hard to lay out what they want to do and how they plan to accomplish it. Make sure they are specific with their recommendations.

Quantity and Delivery 103

Figure TN1

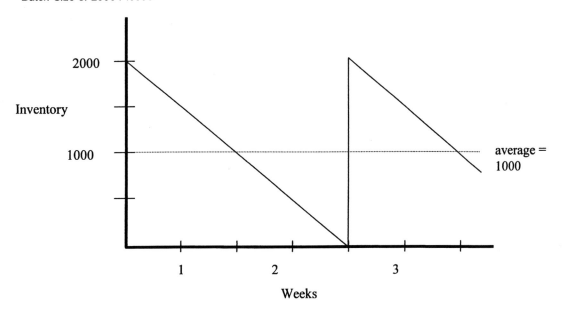

Batch Size of 2000 Pieces

Figure TN2

BATCH SIZE OF 500 PIECES

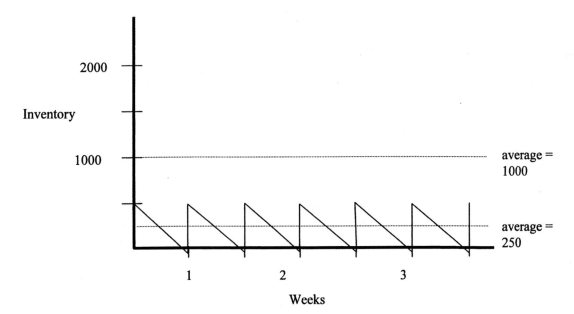

Corn Silk

Teaching Note

IMMEDIATE ISSUE

What should be done about supply commitments in reaction to a significant reduction in production?

BASIC ISSUES

1. Role of supply in production planning
2. Supplier management
3. Forecasting
4. Production scheduling
5. Commodity purchasing
6. Commodity trading
7. Inter-company coordination
8. ABC analysis

SUGGESTED STUDENT ASSIGNMENT

As Kim Hutton, what is your assessment of the corn supply problem at Corn Silk Inc. and what action would you recommend and why? Support your recommendations with suitable analysis.

QUESTIONS FOR DISCUSSION

1. How bad is the situation? How much extra inventory are you forecasting for January? For February? For March? When do you expect the storage bins to reach capacity?
2. What are the costs of holding extra inventory?
3. Why did Kim have to find-out about the production cut-back by overhearing a conversation in the office?
4. Which suppliers should we contact? Why?
5. Do you think Kim should just "wash the contract"? What are the risks if she does that?
6. What do you think the reaction of the suppliers will be if you ask them to delay shipments? Will you be able to reach them or will they be on vacation?
7. What long-term action is required here? What would you suggest to the general manager?
8. Who is at fault for Kim not knowing about the reduction in production? The purchasing, operations or sales departments?

DISCUSSION

This case requires the students to perform some calculations to grasp the issues and to develop a reasonable set of alternatives.

A good place to start is to assess the production operations in Iowa and Minnesota. From the data provided in the case, the following analysis can be performed:

	Iowa	Minnesota
Average annual corn purchases	$40 mil.	$27 mil.
Cost per bushel	$2.50	$2.50
Annual volume (bushels)	16 mil.	10.8 mil.
Capacity (bushels/day)	50,000	30,000
# days at capacity	320	360

Although the case does not come out and say it, this looks like a 7-day per week continuous operation when at capacity. Most likely the plant shuts-down for major holidays, such as Christmas, New Years Day, etc., plus an annual holiday period for two to three weeks. Understanding this allows the following calculations:

Analysis of Monthly Requirements 7-Day Operation (in bushels)

	Jan.	Feb.	March	Total
Number available days (see Exhibit)	25	28	35	88
Capacity (@80,000 bushels/day)	2.000 mil.	2.24 mil.	2.800 mil.	7.040 mil.
Production at 70% capacity	1.400 mil.	1.568 mil.	1.960 mil.	4.928 mil.
Supply (bushels; see Exhibit)	1.899 mil.	1.522 mil.	2.528 mil.	5.949 mil.
Supply - production differential	.499 mil.	(.046) mil.	.568 mil.	1.021 mil.
Number days over supply	6.2 days	(0.6) days	7.1 days	12.8 days
Excess storage needed (bushels)	.179 mil.	.133 mil.	.701 mil.	
Storage cost (@ $0.03/bushel)	$5,370	$3,990	$21,030	$30,390

This analysis indicates that although there is a problem, it does appear to be manageable, and things are a little better than they might have been. Students that assume a five-day per week operation will have a much different analysis of the situation. For example:

Analysis of Monthly Requirements 5-Day Operation (in bushels)

	Jan.	Feb.	March	Total
Number available days	22	20	23	65
Capacity (@80,000 bushels/day)	1.76 mil.	1.6 mil.	1.84 mil.	5.2 mil.
Production at 70% capacity	1.232 mil.	1.12 mil.	1.288 mil.	3.64 mil.
Supply (bushels; from Exhibit)	1.899 mil.	1.522 mil.	2.528 mil.	5.949 mil.
Supply - production differential	.667 mil.	.402 mil.	1.24 mil.	2.309 mil.
Number days over supply	8.34 days	5.3 days	15.5 days	28.86 days
Excess storage needed (bushels)	.347 mil.	.749 mil.	1.989 mil.	
Storage cost (@ $0.03/bushel)	$10,410	$22,470	$59,670	$92,550

Clearly the course of action will be dictated by how the students evaluate the magnitude of the problem. However, it does appear that the seven-day operation scenario is the more reasonable of the two.

Assuming a 7-day operation, Kim has a problem starting in January, which grows in March. With approximately a 6-day oversupply in January the storage bins should be able to handle all but two days of the excess. In March she will have to accept 568,000 bushels of corn in excess of production requirements. At $0.03 per month storage costs, assuming the storage bins can handle 4 days of inventory, CSI will have to store 701,000 bushels. This represents a total cost of $30,390 and $21,030 per month thereafter.

Note that these costs are only a portion of the expenses CSI will incur. Students should recognize that focusing on available storage space only, ignores the more important issue that CSI will have over $2.6 million in excess inventory (1.021 bushels at $2.50 each). Other costs that should be considered include interest changes, costs for double handling, and spoilage, not to mention the working capital that is tied-up. Consequently, if CSI is holding $1.021 million in excess inventory, the extra holding costs could represent about 2 percent per month (24 percent per annum) or $52,000 in addition to the $30,390 incurred by the end of March. Clearly something must be done about this problem.

Exhibit 1 in the case provides a list of suppliers and their delivery commitments. A reasonable way to approach this is to perform an ABC analysis in order to determine where high-volume purchases are concentrated. An ABC analysis is provided below. Note that students may make breaks in different areas, but the general message of the analysis should be the same: approximately a quarter of the suppliers represent 70 percent of Kim's purchases.

Focusing on the seven or so high volume suppliers makes the most sense for Kim. It does not make sense to target the low-volume suppliers to address the January and March over supply. It is reasonable to expect that the nature of the relationship between CSI and its largest suppliers is such that they will be able to accommodate Kim's request for a delay of some shipments. This assumes that Kim will be able to reach the suppliers. We need to make-up nine days, assuming we are prepared to use the storage bins to capacity.

The case indicates that some suppliers are not available during this period. However, it is safe to assume she would be able to reach some of the "magnificent seven".

ABC Analysis

	Supplier	3-Month Volume
A Items:		
	F	25157.16
	D	18917.65
	E	17761.37
	N	11899.68
	B	11726.27
	A	10574.59
	S	10446.83
Total A Items		106483.55 (n = 7; 27%)
B Items:	J	7703.97
	I	5148.57
	T	5015.82
	P	4693.04
	C	4040.59
	G	3753.62
Total B Items:		30355.61 (n = 6; 23%)
C Items:	O	2590.88
	U	2509.42
	V	2495.76
	R	1365.62
	K	1243.03
	W	767.08
	H	756.78
	X	746.94
	Q	695.53
	L	493.87
	M	477.42
	Y	81.31
	Z	49.02
Total C Items:		14272.66 (n = 13; 50%)

Other Considerations

A reasonable question to ask here is: Why is the situation not worse? If Kim had obviously not placed orders to meet planned production. There are two possible reasons. First, maybe she suspected that production in the first quarter would be cut. She may have heard other conversations suggesting cut-backs. Second, this may not be the first time that she has been burned. She could, therefore, regularly plan to make purchases on the open market, such as the Chicago Board of Trade.

Students may view the alternative of "washing" the contracts as a simple way out of the problem. However, they need to consider the costs of such a move. There will certainly be administrative costs, but there may also be costs associated with double-handling the corn, extra transportation costs, etc. There are not guarantees that the spot price will be the same, so CSI may take a loss. As a percentage of the total value of the product, storage for a few months is pretty low.

What is going to happen in April? If Kim is going to push-back deliveries, what happens if CSI decides to extend the drop in production for another month, or even a full three months again?

An issue that most students will pick-up on is inter-departmental communication and the role of purchasing in forecasting. Given the nature of single product dependence and the high value of corn purchases, purchasing should be involved in production planning at CSI. Failure to involve purchasing could be very costly. Obviously this is an issue that should be addressed with the general manager. Even a 2% savings in material costs (i.e. holding, spoilage, etc.) as a result of better planning would save the company $1.34 million each year!

Another important issue addressed in this case is the role of purchasing in commodity trading and speculation. Kim's role is to make short-term purchase arrangements to support operations. Her job is not to speculate on the price of corn. Commodity trading is a risky business, best left to professionals. Some students may suggest that Kim should simply sell the corn and take a profit or loss. Getting in the habit of doing this is dangerous. The safest plan here is to manage the inventories and supply arrangements. In the long-term, Kim should resolve the communication problems, and avoid situations that suggest market speculation. However, those students that want to advocate selling the corn on the open market should be able to provide some criteria regarding an appropriate price. For example, what is the break-even point at which the company is indifferent between holding the corn or selling it on the open market? If they are going to recommend selling, they should be able to say at what price. This calculation is dependent on what the students feel the holding cost is. An appropriate estimate should incorporate a value significantly higher than the $.03 storage costs.

CHAPTER 7

Supplier Selection

Topics Covered

Sourcing and Supplier Section
The Supplier Selection Decision
    Risk Assessment and Risk Management
    Decision Trees
    Sources of Information about Suppliers
    Ethical Dealings between Sales
    Representatives and Purchasers
    The Internet
    Narrowing the List
Supplier Evaluation
    Existing and Potential Sources
    Informal and Formal Evaluation of
    Current Suppliers
    Other Evaluation Criteria
The Evaluation of Potential Sources
    Technical, Engineering, and
    Manufacturing Strengths
    Management and Financial Evaluation
Additional Source Selection Considerations
    Single versus Multiple Sourcing
    Manufacturer or Distributor?

Geographical Location of Sources
Supplier Size
Joint Purchasing with Supplier
Purchasing for Company Personnel
Social, Political, and Environmental
    Concerns
Ethics
    Gifts and Gratuities
    Trade Relations
Overall Supplier Selection Considerations
Questions for Review and Discussion
References
Cases
    Lancaster Life Insurance Co.
    Quotech Inc.
    Bid Evaluation
    Industrial Products Corporation (IPC)

QUIZ RESPONSES

B 1. In the portfolio matrix, characteristics of goods and services in the leverage quadrant are:

   a. substitution is difficult, switching suppliers is difficult, and few available suppliers can meet the technical or capacity needs.
   b. substitution is possible, switching suppliers is possible, and several sources of supply are available.
   c. substitution is difficult, switching suppliers is difficult and few suppliers are available because of a unique specification.
   d. substitution is possible, switching suppliers is difficult, and many suppliers are available.
   e. Substitution is possible, switching suppliers is possible, and few suppliers have the technical expertise.

D 2. The supplier selection decision:

   a. can be seen as a decision making process undertaken in an environment of certainty.
   b. is based on a uniform set of weighted criteria that can be applied to every purchase.
   c. should always be preceded by a formal supplier evaluation and rating.
   d. can be depicted by a decision tree identifying options, evaluation criteria, and probabilities of success and failure.
   e. should be based on quantifiable factors such as price and delivery, and ignore social and political issues.

A 3. Action(s) that a buyer can take to avoid, mitigate, transfer, limit, or insure against risk is(are):

   a. hedging in a commodities market.
   b. requiring bid or performance bonds.
   c. not doing business in certain countries.
   d. a and b.
   e. a, b, and c.

B | 4. Gifts and gratuities:

   a. no matter how small, cannot be justified in a well-run purchasing organization, and should never be accepted.
   b. given to buyers by suppliers may lead to the perception of bias or subjectivity in the purchasing process.
   c. can be accepted as long as the buyer's supervisor is informed of the action.
   d. are acceptable if the buyer receives them from an international supplier rather than a domestic one.
   e. of even a nominal nature inevitably lead to commercial bribery.

E | 5. Small suppliers:

   a. are most suited for large dollar "A" requirements.
   b. usually represent very low risk to the purchaser.
   c. tend to have a strong financial base.
   d. should not be considered for longer term contracts.
   e. may provide an attractive local supply alternative for B and C requirements when responsiveness and flexibility are important.

D | 6. Which of the following statements supports relying upon a single supplier for a purchase:

   a. no ongoing long-term contract exists with a preferred supplier.
   b. supply assurance is increased by having one supplier totally reliant on the order.
   c. there are no patents, trademarks, or copyrights involved.
   d. the order is small.
   e. concerns exist about supplier capacity for future volume.

E | 7. The extent and depth of the analysis of potential suppliers is dependent on:

   a. the number of available suppliers.
   b. the expertise of the purchaser.
   c. the cost and importance of the item.
   d. the lead time available.
   e. all of the above.

C | 8. Supply base rationalization:

a. is an explanation why a particular supplier has been chosen for a particular requirement.
b. is an excuse by a supplier for poor delivery.
c. is an attempt to reduce the total number of suppliers to an organization.
d. is most appropriate when on-time delivery is the key issue.
e. is a master scheme of categorizing suppliers by dollar volume supplied and geographical location.

C | 9. In many organizations, standards of conduct for purchasing personnel:

a. distinguish between the treatment of customers, employees and suppliers.
b. instruct buyers to see suppliers only when the buyer's position is stronger.
c. stress the need to avoid all obligations to sellers except strict business obligations.
d. none of the above.
e. a, b, and c.

B | 10. Supply management's role in environmental considerations:

a. is limited because environmental issues have little impact on the phases of the acquisition cycle.
b. is expanding because the goal of zero environmental impact affects every phase in the acquisition cycle.
c. is expanding because purchasing has primary responsibility for specification writing.
d. is limited by the product design developed by design engineers.
e. is limited to precisely following government laws and regulations concerning hazardous materials.

True and False

F   1. Site visits to suppliers are of little use to supply managers because of their subjective nature.

T   2. Multiple sourcing is normally defended on the basis of supply security.

T   3. There is considerable debate over whether the Internet will help or hurt small businesses.

F   4. An executive roundtable discussion between top managers from the buying and selling organizations is an example of a formal supplier evaluation.

T   5. Weighted point evaluation systems rate suppliers by assigning weights and points to each factor in the analysis to derive an overall score.

F   6. Compliance with domestic content rules can lead to price discounts on goods.

T   7. To use supplier's references effectively, the buyer should ask for a reference of similar size and objectives, talk to people with firsthand knowledge of the relationship, and ask open-ended questions.

T   8. Reciprocity is the practice of demanding that suppliers purchase a set amount of goods and services from the buying firm.

F   9. Buyers should always expect to receive samples free of charge from suppliers.

T   10. The buyer's assessment of the risk associated with a supplier is influenced by whether it is a non-critical, leverage, bottleneck, or strategic purchase.

Lancaster Life Insurance Co.

Teaching Note

IMMEDIATE ISSUE

How to reply to an angry sales representative trying to use trade relations.

BASIC ISSUES

1. Reciprocity.
2. Sales-purchasing relations.
3. The development of purchasing policies.

SUGGESTED STUDENT ASSIGNMENT

If you were Glenn Williamson what would be your analysis of this situation and how would you reply to the sales representative and why?

POSSIBLE DISCUSSION QUESTIONS

1. Should customers receive preferred purchasing treatment? Why or why not?
2. If this were a manufacturing company instead of an insurance company, would this change the situation?
3. If this were a public organization and the "customer" a major tax payer, would it be handled differently?
4. How does the history between these two companies affect the situation?
5. Who else at Lancaster might be interested in this situation?
6. Does the size of the insurance account make a difference?
7. Why do sales representatives like reciprocity?

ANALYSIS

Obviously, Lancaster is a large company, with a wide range of insurance lines. It is successful in terms of earnings and must have at least several million customers at an average of $700 premium per customer. Employee benefits account for just over 20% of total premium income and less than 20% of earnings. Group insurance as a commodity product appears to be largely sold on price.

With purchases of supplies of $20 million per year and premium income of $1.5 billion, supplies purchases account for only 1.5% of total premium income.

It is interesting to note that in the past decade a serious attempt has been undertaken to centralize purchases and to ensure good value for money spent.

In an insurance company like this one, marketing, underwriting and pricing and claims would be major departments and purchasing would be seen as a minor administrative group.

MASTER PRINTER INC.

Master Printer appears to be a supplier which had difficulty making the switch to the modern reality of competition. Previously it supplied high quality printing and good service at very high prices without competition. Direct contact with marketing allowed Master Printer to charge sufficiently high prices to cover what may well have been exuberant costs. Their significant deterioration and sale to a new owner might be clues that they should no longer be considered a prime supplier.

Obviously, last spring Master Printer was not awarded a $22,000 printing order which they quoted at least $6,000 high on. It is not clear from the case that they have bid on and received or missed additional orders since that time.

RECIPROCAL BUYING

It is not difficult, especially with the insurance business to see the problems with reciprocity. If supplies run about 1.5% of total premium income and other purchases another 5 or 6%, it is very difficult to offer any kind of an equivalent volume of business to potential insurance customers. Even if only group customers at 20% of premium income put on pressure for reciprocity, the very best Lancaster could do is buy 1/3 of total premiums earned from any one customer. And that assumes that reciprocity is deemed acceptable.

The problem with reciprocity always has been and still is the dependence on factors other than value to make servicing decisions. In this particular instance the supplier happens to be high priced. In other instances it could be late delivery, unacceptable quality or questionable service.

Sales representatives, especially if they are commission agents, will try every trick in the book to secure or keep business. Trade relations, the euphemism developed for reciprocity, are clearly an angle no aggressive sales representative will miss if other options are not working.

Actually, trade relations arguments may make a sales staff lazy and, in the long term, ineffective. Lancaster cannot survive as an insurance company if its offerings, prices and services are not competitive. It cannot secure enough premium income if purchases have to drive the sales potential.

To be congruent with its own value approach to its insurance customers, it is appropriate for Lancaster to insist that its suppliers, be they also customers or not, must provide competitive value.

As a complete aside, it is interesting to note that what by law is forbidden to private companies actually flourishes in the public procurement field. Countries can and do insist on domestic content or offsets and states, provinces and cities have local preference rules.

The idea that a good customer should receive some recognition "all other things being equal" is accepted in the policy manual of many organizations. Many commentators bemoan the difficulties associated with the looseness of that wording. That judgement is called for is not a bad thing in itself. Obviously, a purchaser with a multi-million dollar customer who bids $100 higher than another non-customer supplier on a $100,000 contract may not face any great dilemma in this decision, even without customer or sales pressure, "all other things being equal."

The difficulties always occur at the margin. How much of a higher price, lower quality, worse delivery or service can still be tolerated before the sourcing decision will change?

In this case a $6,000 premium on a $22,000 printing contract hardly qualifies a $100,000 group premium per year on which the company is likely to earn about $3,000 at best.

Clearly, Lancaster sales representatives should not be encouraged to pressure suppliers to buy insurance. As a matter of fact, it would be bad practice to send a list of suppliers to the marketing group to encourage their staff to go after them.

THE SALES REPRESENTATIVE

Glenn Williamson has to tell the sales representative on the phone that Lancaster purchases cannot be used to secure sales contracts. If a company like Master Printer will only place its group insurance with actual customers for its printing, there is nothing Lancaster can do about that practice. But it is up to Lancaster to provide insurance that is competitive in the market place. It is understandable that the sales representative, facing a $3,000 commission drop is not particularly interested in the finer nuances of trade relations. Glenn should not discourage the sales representative from talking to his supervisor. Sales supervisors and managers should be well aware that Lancaster cannot offer to buy from its insurance customers without assuring superior value.

Glenn, as an old hand in this business, has to gauge whether this is just one of those isolated incidents that come up once in awhile, or whether this is a good time to approach the sales and marketing group to clarify the corporate stance on reciprocity. In any case, it probably is worth one or two calls to supervisors or managers in group insurance to let them know about the call from the sales rep and Glenn's response.

THE MATTER OF POLICY

In a company as large as Lancaster there has to be a reasonable statement of policy on trade relations. It has to be agreed to by the sales and marketing groups and must be understood by purchasing and sales personnel. If the current policy falls short or if it is incomplete, spending some time improving it and discussing it may well be worth while.

For the few really "tough-nut" cases that crop up each year, Glenn might well ask for the assistance of appropriate sales and underwriting managers to review these on an ad-hoc basis. Unilateral purchasing action without consultation may create resentment and prevent opportunities to discuss the purchasing perspective with other members of the management team.

Quotech Inc.

Teaching Note

IMMEDIATE ISSUE

Which supplier should Emily Trent source tubing requirements from?

BASIC ISSUES

1. Supplier selection.
2. Price vs. service.
3. New vs. existing suppliers.
4. Consolidated purchasing.
5. Total cost of ownership.
6. Multi purchase sites and multi supplier sites.

SUGGESTED STUDENT ASSIGNMENT

If you were in the position of Ms. Emily Trent, which supplier would you choose? Why?

POSSIBLE DISCUSSION QUESTIONS

1. What factors should be considered in making this supplier selection decision?
2. How is this purchasing decision influenced by other firms in the Loading Docks Division?
3. Is it necessary to "console" the firm losing the order?
4. What role should past performance play in supplier selection?
5. What should be the total role of a "lead" buyer?

ANALYSIS

1. In essence, Emily's decision boils down to weighing the relative costs/benefits of sustaining a long term relationship versus keeping sourcing options open. While the marginal monetary cost savings may well prompt the student to consider this decision a "no-brainer" in favor of Marmon Keystone, especially if this supplier's warehousing services are considered, there are two major constraining factors: First, there is an acknowledged need among purchasing firms to "have one foot in the market" as a credible threat to suppliers, should they begin to get complacent. Dual sourcing is a strategic way of keeping suppliers honest, as Emily mentioned. Second, hands are

tied by the consolidated purchase decisions that the three companies comprising the Division make. This brings up an additional issue worth discussion. To what extent does consolidated buying benefit <u>and</u> hurt the firm? This is discussed at length in the next answer.

2. One of the major, and most sought after, benefits of consolidated purchasing is the buying power that accumulates as a result of the pooled volume of the purchasers. The success of consolidated purchasing, however, rests on two very necessary factors. First, there should be continuous and close coordination among the pooling purchasers, so that product specifications and quality expectations may be worked out effectively. Furthermore, the pooling purchasers must recognize and plan for the very real possibility that sourcing decisions that may be the most appropriate for the group may not be so for every member of the purchasing group. Preferred individual supplier relationships may be damaged, and local imperatives pushed aside, as large-scale decisions are made. This does not suggest that consolidated purchasing should not occur. Rather, students must be made aware of the need to balance the consolidated purchasing decision carefully, so as to take advantage of the cost savings, even while minimizing dysfunctional supplier relationship outcomes.

   Emily's decision is also impacted considerably by the corporate wide cost reduction initiative, demonstrating how company-wide objectives matter to individual decision makers.

3. Some students may wonder why it is necessary to "console" the supplier losing the business for tubing. After all, it is a bona fide business decision to source, and personal feelings shouldn't enter. The answer to this question is two-fold. It should first be pointed out that business relationships are not just cut-and-dried, and price-based. Rather, as business relationships progress and mature, they are characterized by considerable and growing levels of flexibility and understanding on the part of both parties. We see evidence of this in the case. Second, even if feelings of camaraderie may not be present, it makes sound business sense, nevertheless, to nurture supplier relationships. In modern purchasing, the reduced inventory levels and zero-tolerance manufacturing systems make vendor-supplier relationships very important. Incorrect or hostile conduct with a supplier at one point in time could come back to haunt the vendor in future sourcing situations. As such, the "consolation order" could play a vital role in assuaging any supplier alienation.

4. Given that the Canadian company purchased $300,000 from Marmon Keystone last year, they were a major purchaser for this supplier. It might behoove Emily to discuss Marmon Keystone's performance on this business with the Canadian purchasing manager. John Stevenson's willingness to switch to Castle may be an indication that Marmon Keystone's Canadian operation did not perform as well as its Cleveland counterpart. It would also make sense for Emily to put a Total Cost of Ownership hat on to establish the real worth of Marmon Keystone services to her. Are they worth more than $18,000?

   Another alternative is to let the Canadian and Virginia units buy from Castle and for Emily to stay with Marmon Keystone. Although the notion of pooling purchase requirements assumes that clout will result in better value, this may not always be the case.

Many purchasers might give Marmon Keystone another chance to lower its prices. This will depend on the company's bid policy. If Quotech and MHD and HH want to establish a "one quote and it had better be your best one" policy and presence in the marketplace, such a requoting option would not be wise.

It is interesting that the cost of switching suppliers is often assumed to be zero in North America. It reduces the complexity of purchasing decision making, but is also likely to result in a fair number of foolish decisions.

Bid Evaluation

Teaching Note

This case is a follow-on case to Custom Equipment (A) in chapter 1 and can be used in combination or separately.

IMMEDIATE ISSUE

How to evaluate supplier bids and the criteria for selection.

BASIC ISSUES

1. Supplier selection.
2. Single sourcing.
3. Bid analysis.
4. Use of a post-bid meeting.
5. Standardization, qualification and substitution.
6. Non-response of suppliers to request for bid.
7. Dealing with a new supplier.
8. Supplier selection.
9. Criteria development.

SUGGESTED STUDENT ASSIGNMENT

If you were in the position of Matt Roberts:
1. What would be your analysis of the criteria and weights of the evaluation, and the scores assigned to each supplier?
2. Any further observations?

POSSIBLE DISCUSSION QUESTIONS

1. Do you agree with the criteria chosen for evaluating the suppliers' bids?
2. Do you agree with the assigned weightings? If not, what are more appropriate weights? For example, should the pricing criteria be increase to 40 percent or greater?
3. Is a post-bid meeting a good idea? How about a pre-bid meeting?
4. Were you surprised at the bids?
5. Why would some suppliers decline to bid?

ANALYSIS

An initial concern is the fact that only 40 percent of the suppliers submitted completed bids to CE. However, four bidders still make for a fair and objective bidding process. Matt should not be overly concerned.

Bannister is currently offering the best price for wire, and PCC has the most favorable cable prices. The difference in price between Bannister and State is about $59,000, which is quite significant. Bannister has no performance record at CE, although they service large and well-known companies. Unfortunately for Bannister, Matt was not able to give them any score for past performance (20 percent of the bidding company's total score) or delivery (15 percent of total score) since they haven't done any recent business with CE. However, when one considers their favorable pricing and terms, perhaps less weight should have been assigned to performance and delivery. It is possible that these should not have been included in Matt's evaluation, since it is not a fair comparison of companies. However, both of these criteria are significant to CE's operations.

Bannister would have placed first if past performance and delivery criteria were removed. Perhaps it would also be prudent for Matt to call one of Bannister's current customers, such as Alcatel, and speak with them regarding performance issues. He would then be able to assign them a score for these two criteria, rather than leaving them blank. Bannister has excellent product availability and potential for electronic data transfer and funds payment due to its size and systems.

Since CE already purchases its Newflex cable from PCC and they had the second-best total pricing, Matt may want to consider going with PCC as the sole supplier. PCC has a great past performance record and its salesman is quite capable. However, looking at other aspects of the vendor analysis, it has manual systems and its management team is not as strong as its competitors. It has less favorable payment terms of Net 15 days, which are similar to many smaller firms, and it will not be able to provide EDI in the near future. These vendor aspects are important, but not critical to CE's operations.

State's inability to supply Newflex could be seen as a reason to quickly dismiss them, since Kelvin cable has never been fully tested on a CE job. Changing to a more expensive cable would also be going against Matt's initial assignment of reducing the total cost of wire and cable. State's reputation, serviceability, and delivery will have to pull it a long way to make up for the almost $60,000 difference in total package price compared with Bannister.

One aspect keeping State in the running is that CE could potentially save $8,000-12,000 by testing the Kelvin cable free of charge on a project. That savings will go directly to CE's bottom line increasing the profitability of that job. In the big picture State has been awarded the most points on Matt's 'Bid Comparison' (Table 1), however with such a significant difference in price, compared with the other bidders, one begins to wonder if Matt has assigned sufficient weight to the pricing criterion.

Eastern seems to be a generally good supplier all-around. Its pricing is average; it has the best terms, and a good future outlook. If CE wants to go with a larger company versus more of a custom shop, Eastern may be the best choice. It has the size, the stock, and fast delivery, but it may not be as quick to respond to urgent product requests. CE's requirement for rush items may be 'lost in the shuffle', according to the reputation of its inside sales representative. If chosen as the WMP supplier, Matt may wish to stipulate that CE's account be handled with increased priority.

Based on CE's current $800,000 expenditure on wire and cable, a comparison between payment terms for Eastern and PCC, using a 10 percent rate of return, means that an extension of 30 days in payment would save CE an extra $550/month ($800,000/12*.10/12). Comparing Eastern's 45-day payment terms with those of State Electric (Net 30 days), Eastern's terms still save CE $275/month. Cash availability is good for any business.

Two companies, State and Eastern, made high dollar bids for CE's obsolete stock. Whether or not they actually care about re-selling the products, they have probably made a successful impression upon Matt's manager. These figures were subtracted from the total wire and cable cost in Matt's 'Bid Comparison' (Table 1).

Alternatives

1. **Do nothing**

    Don't make a final decision until the post-bid meetings have been conducted, to see if anything new and interesting is revealed. Matt has carefully analyzed the quotes and does not believe there are any misunderstandings.

    Although he has determined that the most promising quote relative to CE's requirements is that of State Electric, he should not make a decision yet. He can begin to create some questions to ask of all the suppliers at each respective meeting. Any discrepancies or misunderstanding can be resolved at that time.

2. **Choose State, since it performed the best in Matt's evaluation**

    The savings of $8,000-12,000 that would result from trying the Kelvin cable on a job is significant. However, the difference of $59,000 between the Bannister quote is also significant. Although price is important, there are many components that constitute an outstanding supplier. CE has developed a very good relationship with its sales representative. Also, State has its own trucks, which may allow for tighter control over the delivery schedule.

    All aspects of State's bid were clear, and Matt should feel confident in his decision. State's overall score was the best, which should lead Matt to select them as the supplier for the WMP at this time.

3. Adjust the weight assigned the pricing criterion upward, in order to reflect the intended purpose of the WMP

Currently, the pricing criterion accounts for 35 percent. Since achieving a lower total cost of CE purchases is a key goal for the WMP, the weight assigned to pricing should be increased past 40 percent. If this were done, Eastern would achieve the highest total score. As more weight is placed on pricing and taken away from other criteria, Eastern's total score would remain the highest, until eventually the best overall score would be that of Bannister.

Matt could adjust the weight of the pricing criterion to 50 percent and select Eastern as CE's wire and cable supplier. They are currently only a single point behind State, but their pricing is significantly better. There is also a good possibility that Matt could convince Eastern to provide CE with a different inside sales representative.

Going into the post-bid meeting, there would have to be some significant changes for Matt to not choose Eastern.

4. Remove the delivery and past performance criteria to enable equal evaluation of suppliers

As it stands now, Bannister has virtually no chance. To even the field, Matt should perhaps remove the past performance and delivery criteria from the comparison. However, in the big picture, those aspects are important to CE's operation.

5. Gather more information

It may be possible to get more information about the suppliers by calling some of their current customers, such as Alcatel for Bannister. Having a score for past performance and delivery would give Bannister a more fair chance in the bid comparison.

A problem with this alternative might be that the suppliers deal with their respective customers differently, particularly depending on the account's overall importance. At any rate, an interview with another customer of each supplier will give Matt a better understanding of each vendor's strengths and weaknesses.

6. Adjust a combination of criteria and weights

Altering the criteria and their associated weights can easily allow Matt to sway his decision whatever way desired. However, these decisions were made objectively, prior to receiving the bids. They were approved by Matt's manager and should not be tampered with or adjusted at this time.

7. **Choose the best-priced supplier for wire AND the best-priced supplier for cable → have two suppliers**

Combining the best-priced supplier for wire (Bannister) with that for cable (PCC) would create a total price of $804,000. This figure allows CE to save an additional $20,000 from the original lowest bid price submitted by any vendor. However, both companies scored below State and Eastern in Matt's overall Bid Comparison.

Matt should speak with the representatives from each company to assess the feasibility of this 'splitting' proposal. It is unlikely that the suppliers' respective prices will remain as they appear currently, however, a $5,000-$ 10,000 additional savings is significant. It is possible that both companies leveraged their respective strengths to arrive at a lower total combined price. Therefore, they would not be able to offer such attractive pricing individually.

Another advantage of having two suppliers is that one backs-up the other. Even if one of the suppliers was having problems, CE could source the product from its other supplier.

It would be useful to get more information regarding the suppliers, if possible. Matt could speak with, or even interview current similar-sized customers from each supplier. However, the suppliers would probably recommend speaking with their favorite, largest, or most loyal customers, which may not give an accurate reflection.

Performing some analysis with the current information available would be useful, but wait until after the post-bid meeting to make a final selection.

Pricing is important, but Matt realizes that other aspects, including vendor performance, must also be considered. Selecting purely on the basis of lowest total price would negate all of Matt's prior analysis.

Key Points

1. Price issues → Price is important, especially here when dealing with commodity products. The importance of pricing is increased when there is little product differentiation and similar product availability
2. Past performance is just that, a measure of the past. Although many believe it to be a good indicator for future performance, there are many factors that influence performance. Unless there are significant changes in processes or management, however, performance is likely to remain consistent.
3. The size of the vendor isn't necessarily a benefit → Although larger suppliers typically stock more items, the scale of their operations could actually impede the order fulfillment process. A larger company, even a more established business, may not be able to meet the needs of its customers as successfully as its smaller, niche competitors.

4. Serviceability → Businesses specializing in custom orders usually have frequent 'rush' requirements. The better a supplier's ability to modify its current processes, the easier it will be able to handle its customers' requirements.
5. Relationship → The more in-tune with its clients' requirements, the better able the vendor will be to serve them. Suppliers today must be willing to learn about the customer's business and fully understand its needs.

If time permits, it is possible to use the Custom Equipment (B) case which follows as a handout in this class. It is also possible to use Custom Equipment (B) as a follow-on class.

CUSTOM EQUIPMENT (B)

On August 18th, Matt Roberts chaired a meeting at which Eastern Electric (Eastern) proposed an in-house supplier store for wire and cable and other electrical products inside CE's warehouse.
Meeting with Eastern Electric

During the proposal review with Eastern Electric, a CE engineer made an interesting comment, almost jokingly. "With the total amount of electrical purchases we make each year, why not have one of these supplier organizations hold and distribute products from inside our facility?"

Matt was intrigued by the idea of locating a supplier directly inside CE's plant. This would strengthen supplier-customer relations and cut delivery times for the entire gamut of wire and cable products. However, it could also leave CE in a potentially awkward situation if problems occurred. Eastern Electric's account manager, who was also interested by the comment, asked for an opportunity to determine the feasibility and amend its proposal.

Eastern Electric returned two days later with an expanded proposal based on the idea from the initial meeting. The implementation decision would depend on the on-site distributor maintaining a 10 percent gross margin and 7 percent net margin. Estimating that wire and cable sales would amount to $75,000/month, and considering its required margins, Eastern calculated it could gross approximately $90,000 in 2000. Fixed costs would be approximately $37,000. Therefore, Eastern proposed to keep other commonly purchased products in the 'store'. It would be easier to spread cage costs over more products by adding other products from their line.

Eastern maintained that it could not achieve its margins supplying only wire and cable from the in-house facility, since labor and carrying costs would be too high. Therefore, Eastern proposed holding all commodity wires and cables, as well as other commonly-used electrical items inside the caged holding area. This would be to CE's advantage, since it would further decrease purchasing and inventory costs. It was beneficial to Eastern, since it could share some of the administrative and overhead costs of the 'store'. The store would be managed by one of Eastern's warehouse employees from another division.

CE Employees would simply walk to the supplier's 'store' and request items via authorized requisition sheets, specifying the items required and the job number. The job number was necessary to keep track of individual project costs. Matt thought that new receiving and requisition processes would have to be developed for the store. Eastern would be responsible for managing inventory, issuing materials upon request, and submitting a monthly invoice. Product ownership would transfer only when the required component was issued. The use of store inventory would not only decrease delivery time and transportation costs, but it would also help CE avoid incurring carrying costs. Store inventory would cut delivery time from an average of 2-5 days to 0 days for most common items.

Matt wondered what to do next.

Custom Equipment (B)

Teaching Note

IMMEDIATE ISSUE

How to respond to Eastern's in-house store proposal.

BASIC ISSUES

1. Allowing a supplier to alter a submitted quote.
2. Informing other suppliers of desired changes to the bid request.
3. Changing bidding procedures during the process.
4. Allowing a supplier to set up a store inside a buyer's facility → implications to competition.
5. Inventory management.

SUGGESTED STUDENT ASSIGNMENT

If you were in the position of Matt Roberts, what course of action would you take regarding Eastern Electric's proposal to implement an on-site store at CE.

POSSIBLE DISCUSSION QUESTIONS

1. Should all vendors be given the opportunity to re-submit their bids? Ie. Should Matt tell them? Is this fair to Eastern?
2. What is the next step? Does Matt need to get any approvals?
3. How would this affect workers and currently existing processes?
4. What if it doesn't work out?

ANALYSIS

During its post-bid meeting, Eastern offered to rework its initial bid submission based on a suggestion made by a CE employee. Eastern's management returned in two days with a modified proposal.

Eastern took the initial idea of supplying only wire and cable products from the 'store', as discussed in its post-bid meeting, and expanded it to include all electrical products. To justify its expense, Eastern claimed that it must be able to process more than just wire and cable. Although not mentioned, it may be possible for CE to share the costs of installation, thereby changing Eastern's justification to supply all of its electrical products to CE from the store. However, there are increased benefits for both organizations when considering the Eastern-tailored proposal.

Although Matt's "customers", CE's shop workers, would appreciate more material available upon request and the ability to order direct, Matt is not certain if the Eastern proposal will give them an unfair advantage over their competitors.

There is a likely possibility that Eastern could eventually eliminate all of its electrical products competition at CE by virtue of the store's accessibility to the shop workers.

Most shop workers who request a part require it at that moment. It seems logical for them to request it and receive it in person, rather than going through a purchasing agent. The process is more direct, but there may be less control. Purchasing agents do more than process requests. However, this process would not necessarily mean a loss of control for the purchasing agent. As new products are requested, negotiations on price could occur. This could occur for a single product or an entire product category.

Potential problems may occur if CE accepts Eastern's proposal, implements the internal store, and then finds that product quality diminishes. There may also be problems if the store cannot easily source a required product. Eastern could be given a reasonable time (1-2 days) to procure the product itself. After this time, Eastern would have to purchase the necessary part from an alternate electrical part source. Difficulty may arise if CE's former suppliers are reluctant to provide service, especially if the relationship ended poorly, due to CE's bid selection.

Other potential problems with the store may be: Theft, overcharging, and product returns

The initial store setup cost is expected to be $10,000. Included within this figure are costs for a new computer and printer, and the cage setup. An additional fee, similar to rent, may be required to cover CE's loss of space for the store and any overhead charges. Although relatively small, the space to be used for the new store would lessen the area available for CE manufacturing. Not only should Matt be concerned with the cost of the lost space, but he must also speak with the production manager regarding future shop floor plans.

Holding costs for material in Eastern's store should not be a consideration, since Eastern's would alternatively be stocking the items at another location. Included in the fixed cost would be an Eastern's store employee's salary.

CE's current carrying costs amount to 15% per annum. If an estimated $20,000 of wire & cable stock was held at all times throughout the year, CE's holding cost savings would amount to $3,000/year ($20,000 x 15%/year). At $50,000, the savings would be $7,500.

There are numerous savings to CE by the installation and use of the store, of which include the elimination of carrying costs on all wire and cable products, and the elimination of product delivery delays. CE's purchasing agents' time could be more effectively utilized when shop workers order their required products directly from the Eastern store.

With $90,000 as Eastern's estimated gross margin, its 10% requirement will be satisfied ($90,000/$800,000 total annual sales). However, with fixed costs of $37,000, Eastern's net margin would be 6.63% (($90,000-$37,000)/$800,000), compared with its requirements of 7%. Increasing the gross sales figure by selling more products from Eastern's store would help increase its net margin. An increase of $3,000, derived from stocking and selling other electrical products from the 'store', would allow Eastern to achieve its requirements.

ALTERNATIVES

1. Choose Eastern Electric

Eastern's willingness to implement the store, combined with its favorable bid score makes it the best candidate for the WMP. CE will accomplish its goal of cost reduction for wire and cable, and there will be further opportunities for substantial cost savings. Since Eastern is proposing a solution that goes beyond its original requirements, there are negotiating possibilities that were initially unseen. However, choosing Eastern on the basis of further savings from the store implementation may make justification to the other suppliers difficult.

It may be possible to further negotiate on pricing with Eastern.

2. Inform State, PCC, and Bannister of new developments

If the bid is to be considered a fair competition of proposals, then Matt must inform the suppliers of the changes which have been proposed. Suppliers that are unaware of CE's new expectations will not have a reasonable chance of selection without being updated on the new ideas that have developed. Therefore, Matt should arrange to meet with all three suppliers again and then give them some time to develop new proposals incorporating an on-site 'store' concept. By allowing the others to develop the idea, he may discover that an even better opportunity exists.

3. Gather more information

The final decision need not be made immediately. Matt should take some time to think through Eastern's proposal and thoroughly evaluate the potential savings of an on-site vendor facility. He should create best, worst, and likely scenarios to analyze objectively, since he is obviously currently 'caught-up' in the excitement of what the WMP has become.

The bottom line is that decisions of this magnitude and importance should not be rushed. All procedural changes must be assessed, from initial ordering to payment processing, and even products returns.

Recommendation – A combination of #2 and #3

To be a truly fair process, Matt should inform the other suppliers of the new proposal. Although time is a concern, an extra week of discussions will not impact CE negatively. In fact, as mentioned above, an even better solution may be discovered.

Currently, Matt is 'caught-up' in the WMP excitement. He will need some time to perform various quantitative and process analyses. Eastern seems like an excellent choice, unless another supplier makes a significantly improved proposal. Matt must be careful that State, PCC, and Bannister don't simply see this as an opportunity to improve their pricing in order to increase their chance of final selection. Matt must be explicit that only suggestions regarding store implementation or similar will be accepted.

Learning Points

1. Although for Matt Roberts the selection of either State or Eastern was almost certain, one innocent comment and some enthusiasm from both parties was all it took to sway the focus greatly toward Eastern.
2. The value of a post-bid meeting with each supplier is made obvious in this case. Basing a decision solely on the submitted quotes and personal interpretation of each supplier would not have enabled the opportunity for something much greater to be developed.
3. Ethical issues are personal. Disclosure of discussions with each supplier to the others is not required. Matt chose not to inform the other suppliers of his discussions with Eastern, because he was pleased with his expectations of the future relationship. Eastern had developed the idea, which could be regarded as intellectual property.
4. What started out as a project for cost savings on a commodity, developed into a potential solution to completely re-vamp some long-standing purchasing processes.

Follow-up

Given that Custom Equipment was its largest account, Eastern Electric determined the on-site store at CE to be both financially feasible and mutually advantageous. Eastern's eagerness to pursue the proposal easily made it the primary choice to manage the WMP.

Matt received approval for the initial layout relatively easily. The plant director immediately saw the organizational benefits of the proposal. However, more challenging aspects became evident as the program progressed. Assembling team members for meetings, assigning tasks, and ensuring work was completed took much of his time and energy. One frustrating aspect of leading the program was imbuing a similar sense of enthusiasm and urgency in other team members. Program members, who benefited indirectly, were less willing to make large time commitments, since they believed the returns would not justify their efforts.

Each day was a learning experience throughout the implementation period, and Matt noted which methods were most effective and those that failed. Involving all team members was a key aspect for achieving a positive group dynamic and avoiding potential disagreements. If problems arose, he had to decide the best course of action, always keeping in mind the best interest of both CE and that of the supplier. Matt learned techniques which allowed him to help these individuals understand each other's needs and to contribute their expertise for the benefit of the project as a whole.

Initially, attempts were made for specific items on the Bill of Materials to be requisitioned to the Eastern cage. However, client/server licensing agreements prevented any user other than CE from using the SAP system. Incorporating this step would have saved Eastern clerks from entering all the hand-written items submitted from the plant workers. All necessary stock items for each job could have be "kitted" together in anticipation of their demand. A worker would have then been able to pick-up, or have delivered, all necessary parts at once, thereby preventing further trips and ensuring the job received all required items.

The results have been impressive to date. The program is unique because it challenged CE's traditional business methods, and offers a more innovative and beneficial solution for both organizations. It is possible that this program will become a model for other CE Flexible Automation divisions, since Custom Equipment's location is regarded as one of the company's most successful business units worldwide. In fact, Eastern Electric has been so pleased with the results to date that it is applying a similar setup at a packaging company in Mississauga.

In the upcoming months, much time will be spent fine-tuning and monitoring the initial system. Informal contact with users will occur on a regular basis to obtain feedback. Scheduled meetings with Eastern Electric will be used to discuss potential difficulties and possible improvements to the process, such as the introduction of Electronic Data Interchange (EDI) for ordering and invoicing.

Industrial Products Corporation (IPC)

Teaching Note

IMMEDIATE ISSUE

What action to take with respect to a non-conforming supplier.

BASIC ISSUES

1. Supplier evaluation.
2. Single sourcing.
3. Continuous improvement.
4. Quality Measurement.

SUGGESTED STUDENT ASSIGNMENT

1. As Maggie Agnelli, what is your assessment of IPC's supplier evaluation program?
2. As Maggie Agnelli, what is your evaluation of Branco and what action would you take and why?

POSSIBLE DISCUSSION QUESTIONS

1. Does IPC's supplier evaluation scheme make sense?
2. Should the same evaluation scheme apply to all suppliers?
3. Why would a supplier start to slip on its ratings?
4. What incentives are there for a supplier to conform?
5. In a single source situation, what can a purchaser do to maintain supplier superiority?
6. Are there some unique features to custom packaging that are relevant here?

DISCUSSION

The purpose of this case is to take a hard look at a specific supplier rating scheme and also to deal with issues such as continuous improvement and corrective action.

IPC's Evaluation Scheme

It is useful to spend some time in class discussing IPC's supplier evaluation scheme. It is fairly comprehensive and it also includes continuous improvement. Let's take a look at each of its elements.

Quality — Rejected and Non-Conforming

This quality measure is based on percentage of shipments as are a number of the following measures as well. Theoretically, it would be possible to have a 0 in this category, provided the definition of non-conforming would be tight enough. A percentage of shipments measure assumes that there is a large number of shipments. One quarterly shipment, for example, would result in either a 4 or a 0 on this scale.

Process Capability, Data/Samples. This category of quality is concerned with two issues. One is the number of defectives. The other whether samples/data a received regarding the incoming shipment's quality.

It is surprising that up to 5% defects would still earn a 3 ranking on quality. This is a long way off zero defects! Moreover, the system does not indicate what to do if quality is less than 1% defects and sample/data regarding the quality of the incoming shipment is not provided. The 50% weighting of these two quality factors places the greatest importance on quality versus delivery and continuous improvement.

Delivery

Delivery is divided into four sub-categories: quantity, time, paperwork and shipment condition.

Quantity. It is unusual to see quantity as part of delivery, but it needs to be recognized as one of the basic supply requirements. Again, the 3 ranking for up to 5% non-conformance rate on quantity is surprising. Using the percentage of shipments way of measuring means that a supplier who misses by a minor amount regularly would get much lower ratings than one who missed by a large amount infrequently.

Time. Many of the comments under time are similar to those made under previous categories. No issue is made of the amount of delay. Therefore, one shipment five days late would be recorded in the same category as one shipment one day late.

Paperwork. The quality of supporting documentation is often overlooked in supplier evaluation, but not in this scheme. Without a full definition of error, it is difficult to comment on this category.

Shipment Condition. Much the same comments apply to shipments as the previous categories. No distinction is made whether 1 carton in a shipment of 100 is damaged or whether 50 cartons are damaged in the same shipment.

Continuous Improvement

Continuous improvement is separated into Corrective Action and Cost, Lead Time, and Lot Size Reduction.

Corrective Action. Clearly, corrective action and responsiveness to non-compliances are vital in an on-going buyer-supplier relationship. The length of time 30-60 days for a 3 ranking for both response and implementation seems rather long. What is considered "response" and "implementation" is not well defined in the case data and might well represent subjective judgement.

Cost, Lead Time, Lot Size Reduction. This is the second dimension of continuous improvement. It is the only one with a 4, 2, 0 scale, instead of the 4, 3, 2, 1, 0 scale used elsewhere. It is not clear how IPC would deal with an increase in cost and a decrease in lead time and no change in lot size.

Also, these categories as well as the other ones may require IPC input and cooperation. For suppliers such as Branco, for whom the raw material price fluctuates and is a large part of their total cost, cost reduction credits might be obtained when the market price of the raw material drops. Cost increases could also be beyond the control of the supplier. Is it wiser for the supplier to go for a big increase in price once, rather than frequent smaller increases?

CONCLUSION

The point of the above discussion is that the IPC system leaves a fair number of question marks in terms of fairness and appropriateness. How one standard rating system could be appropriate for every supplier of whatever good or part or service is problematic. For example — Branco supplies custom packaging. If it already delivers on a daily basis, lot size reduction may no longer be practical. Cost decreases in a market where prices are rising may be impossible. Lead times may already be as low as possible. What is the base of comparison, anyway? The previous quarter, year, original contract whenever it was signed?

The question whether IPC shoulders any blame for any of the supplier's shortcomings also needs to be carefully examined. Blaming a supplier for poor quality when IPC supplied unclear specifications is not a sound supply practice. On the assumption that there is a legitimate slide in Bronco's performance which cannot be traced to causes beyond the supplier's control or to IPC, then Maggie needs good documentation of what is going wrong and needs to find out why. The continuous stream of new problems suggests that Branco does not have its process under control and is strictly firefighting. How is it possible that a supplier who was once good enough to merit single source status would slip so badly? Perhaps a cause and effect diagram and investigative procedure needs to be initiated.

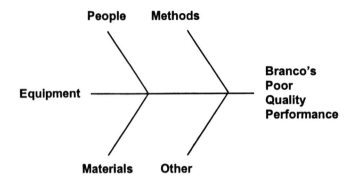

Perhaps IPC needs to supply some expertise to help the supplier pinpoint its difficulties and develop a program of continuous improvement. Having access to the plant manager directly gives Maggie the chance to get a commitment for demonstrable action, well beyond polite assurances that things will be looked into. Despite all of the potential pitfalls and unfairnesses of IPC's evaluation scheme, it, at least, forces the purchaser and supplier to communicate when performance goes off track.

If Maggie suspects that IPC assistance might be required to create a permanent change at Branco, she would do well to line up such resources inside IPC before the visit and have these IPC experts present at her meeting with the Branco group. Should Branco appear unresponsive, Maggie might well be forced to look for alternative suppliers who are more eager and better able to meet IPC's needs. In the new climate of cooperation and, apparently tough market conditions, it is important that Branco be given an opportunity to correct its ways. Should Branco identify specific IPC shortcomings which prevent it from supplying superior value, it is incumbent upon Maggie to address such issues serious and quickly.

CHAPTER 8

Outsourcing, Supplier Relations and Supply-Chain Management

Topics Covered

Make or Buy
    Reasons for Make instead of Buy
    Reasons for Buying Outside
    The Gray Zone in Make or Buy
Subcontracting
Outsourcing
    Outsourcing Purchasing and Logistics
Purchasing's Role in Outsourcing
Strategic Supply Base Management
Purchaser-Supplier Relations
    Supplier Goodwill
A Purchaser-Supplier Satisfaction Model
    Purchaser-Supplier Relationship
    Management

Partnerships and Strategic Alliances
    Strategic Alliances
    Co-Location/In-Plants
Reverse Marketing/Supplier Development
Supply Chain Management
    Supply Networks
Conclusion
Questions for Review and Discussion
References
Cases
    Saucy Foods Limited
    Paron Metal Fabricating Inc.
    Super Stamps and Products Inc.

QUIZ RESPONSES

B   1.   Which of the following is NOT a benefit of a buyer-supplier partnership:

                a. the buying organization can enjoy the benefits of vertical integration without the disadvantages.
                b. the amount of time committed to the buyer-supplier relationship is greatly reduced.
                c. internal barriers are removed and inter-corporate closeness is fostered.
                d. the design process and the introduction of new designs is speeded up.
                e. significant quality and cost improvements can result.

A   2.   A goal of supply chain management is to:

                a. reduce uncertainty and risks between and among members of the supply chain.
                b. drive down prices through competitive online bidding.
                c. push inventory as far down in the supply chain as possible.
                d. increase competition by increasing the number of suppliers in the supply chain.
                e. gain competitive advantage by acquiring confidential information from chain members.

D   3.   Outsourcing:

                a. of services is unrealistic because of the difficulty in measuring and evaluating performance of service providers.
                b. occurs primarily in large manufacturing firms in the private sector, but is rarely practiced in public purchasing.
                c. is a low risk venture because the firm can always revert back to performing the function in-house at low cost.
                d. is often chosen as a way for the organization to reduce or control operating costs, improve company focus, and gain access to world-class capabilities.
                e. decisions are based on financial factors that most organizations can easily access through their accounting system.

C	4.	Reverse marketing:

a. occurs when a purchaser sends a sales representative back for more information.
b. occurs when the seller is also a customer of the buying organization.
c. is an aggressive, purchaser-initiated, approach to developing suppliers.
d. requires that the marketer does sufficient homework to understand the needs of the buyer.
e. is most appropriate when used with local suppliers. |
| B | 5. | Early supplier involvement (ESI) and early purchasing involvement (EPI):

a. pulls both the buyer and supplier into the process of measuring results and developing action plans for performance improvement.
b. pulls both the buyer and supplier into the need recognition and description stages of the acquisition process.
c. pulls the buyer into the need recognition and description stages and pulls the supplier into the measurement stage.
d. pulls the buyer into the measurement stage and pulls the supplier into the need recognition and description stages.
e. pulls the buyer into relationship management stage and pulls the supplier into need recognition and description. |
| C | 6. | Trends in supplier selection include:

a. increasing the number of suppliers and developing closer relationships.
b. negotiating shorter term contracts but with fewer suppliers to increase purchasing's clout.
c. limiting the total number of suppliers and focusing on results from key suppliers.
d. greater concentration of the supplier selection decision in the purchasing department.
e. frequent switching of suppliers to capitalize on price variability among suppliers. |
| D | 7. | Strategic alliances:

a. are special arrangements to ensure access to raw materials deemed critical to national security.
b. are only possible when there is no intellectual property or technology involved.
c. do not require any contribution from top management.
d. reinforce the notion that supplier relationships contribute to corporate success.
e. are informal buyer-supplier relationships. |

A | 8. When deciding whether to continue making something inhouse or outsource it, purchasing and supply managers can:

   a. add value by aiding in the identification of potential sources, developing and negotiating the contract, and managing the relationship with the chosen supplier.
   b. add the most value by reviewing the analysis conducted by the outsourcing team and offering a critical assessment.
   c. add little value to the decision making process since the internal users have a much better understanding of their needs.
   d. add little value to the decision since it requires an understanding of the core competencies of the organization.
   e. add the most value by managing the contract once the decision has been made.

E | 9. One of the assumptions on which the purchasing-supplier satisfaction model is based is that:

   a. the satisfaction level cannot be assessed well enough to draw definitive conclusions.
   b. there are few tools and techniques available to assist parties in moving positions or improving stability.
   c. an unsatisfied party will see exiting the relationship as the only viable alternative.
   d. attempts to move to a different position fall only in the win-lose and win-win categories.
   e. purchaser and seller may have different perceptions of the same relationship.

D | 10. The steps in the developmental path to partnership occur in which order:

   a. supplier assessment, supplier rationalization, supplier improvements, supplier alignment, and supplier partnership.
   b. supplier assessment, supplier improvement, supplier alignment, supplier rationalization, and supplier partnership.
   c. supplier assessment, supplier improvement, supplier rationalization, supplier alignment, and supplier partnership.
   d. supplier assessment, supplier improvement, supplier rationalization, supplier alignment, and supplier partnership.
   e. supplier rationalization, supplier partnership, supplier alignment, supplier assessment.

True and False

T 1. Some of the reasons an organization may decide to make rather than buy are: greater supply assurance, stringent quality requirements, and very small quantity requirements.

T 2. Subcontracts are useful when the work is difficult to define, takes a long time to complete, and is extremely costly.

T 3. There are both negative and positive measures that buyers and sellers can take to shift the satisfaction level in the buyer-seller relationship.

F 4. Purchasing has had a leadership role in outsourcing decisions made by many organizations.

T 5. Strategic alliances are special arrangements to ensure access to raw materials deemed critical to national security reinforce the notion that supplier relationships contribute to corporate success.

F 6. Supplier goodwill, like customer goodwill, has real commercial value, and is recognized by courts of law.

T 7. Buyer-supplier relationships fall somewhere on a continuum from traditional, adversarial relationships to fully integrated, seamless relationships.

F 8. The perception of a buyer-seller relationship is based on the results obtained, but it is not impacted by the process used to attain those results.

F 9. Acceptable suppliers anticipate the operational and strategic needs of the purchaser, and are capable of meeting and exceeding them.

T 10. The focus on suppliers and supply management in many organizations is a result of recognition of supply's potential to reduce costs and improve profitability.

Saucy Foods Limited

Teaching Note

IMMEDIATE ISSUES

Should SFL make or buy its mustard requirements?

BASIC ISSUES

1. Make or buy.
2. Purchasing's role in make or buy.
3. Quality issues in make or buy.

SUGGESTED STUDENT ASSIGNMENT

1. If you were Denise Seidel what would be your analysis of the feasibility of making mustard in-house?
2. What information, if any, is still missing at this point and as Denise how would you go about collecting it? How might this information affect the proposal?
3. As Denise, what major topic areas would you address in your proposal to the CEO and what would be your main arguments?

POSSIBLE DISCUSSION QUESTIONS

1. Should it be purchasing's role to suggest insourcing?
2. What benefits would accrue to SFL from making mustard in-house?
3. What risks are there for SFL?
4. How long would it take to implement this kind of change?
5. Is the savings potential attractive enough?
6. Are there other alternatives?
7. What should purchasing's role be in make or buy?

ANALYSIS

Let us start with the proposal as it stands to make sure that financially, at least, it makes sense.

The Current Situation

SFL currently buys 500 drums (100,000) litres) of mustard per month--or 6,000 drums (1,200,000 litres) per year. Each drum has 200 litres.

The mustard costs $64/drum =	$.32/litre
Transportation $8/drum =	$.04/litre
Processing costs $20/hour - 1\6 hr./drum =	$.017/litre
Other costs and overhead =	$.02/litre

Whether other costs and overhead charges should enter into this calculation is open to debate. Purchasing costs will still be incurred under the new proposal, as the spice blend will have to be bought and the quantities of vinegar per month increased.

In any case, current mustard cost is about $.40-$.42 a litre. Apparently, there are no significant quality, taste, delivery or other problems encountered.

Mustard In-House

Under Denise's proposal the cost of making mustard in-house would be:

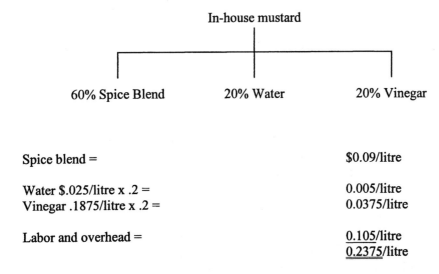

Spice blend =	$0.09/litre
Water $.025/litre x .2 =	0.005/litre
Vinegar .1875/litre x .2 =	0.0375/litre
Labor and overhead =	0.105/litre
	0.2375/litre

There is some question whether the $.105 per litre labor and overhead charge needs to be made since the labor already seems to be available. This is a touchy issue, because labor savings have been claimed on drum handling and to be on the safe side, given that this may well be a longer term proposal, labor time used to make mustard should be accounted for.

The interesting conclusion from these cost figures is that the savings come from a lower cost of making in-house. The supplier can make mustard from scratch and sell it with a drum for $0.40 a litre. In-house manufacture costs $0.24 a litre without a drum. Is the drum so expensive, or why is the supplier charging so much for this product? Is it possible Saucy Foods Limited has been paying too much, given that the mustard supplier's volume and process should result in costs lower than SFL's?

Assuming a purchased mustard cost of $0.40 per litre and an in-house cost of $0.24 per litre result in annual savings of 1,200,000 litre x $0.16 cents = $192,000. In a relatively small company and industry where price competition is tough, this has to be seen as a very attractive savings.

Financially, at least it appears that Denise is on the right track with her proposal.

OTHER ALTERNATIVES

It is reasonable to expect that other alternatives should be checked out before this proposal is finalized.

Given that the existing mustard supplier must be able to make mustard cheaper than SFL a different method of delivery, avoiding drums, might reveal a better option. For example, could mustard be delivered like vinegar in 15,000 litre lots and stored in a bulk container on the premises? This would save the cost of the drums, (not specified in the case, but likely at least $0.02-$0.05 cents a litre). It might also save on some of the transportation costs and the drum handling and disposal. It would be environmentally friendlier. The big question is whether the costs of a 15,000 litre storage tank would be too high and whether space is available on SFL premises. If investment in the storage tank itself is an issue, the supplier might be persuaded to provide it and recover the investment in the mustard price charged. For as far as SFL is confirmed, as long as the total point of use cost of custard is equal to $0.24/litre it should be indifferent. If the supplier could provide the mustard for less, staying with the outside supplier would be preferable. This could prove to be an interesting negotiation!

On the assumption of a 200 litre drum cost of $6.00 or $0.03 per litre, the supplier has $0.40 - $0.03 = $0.37 as a manufacturing cost plus profit.

At $0.24/litre as an indifference price to SFL, the supplier can be challenged to provide mustard at this price or lower. Assuming a bulk transportation charge of $0.03 per litre, and a variable manufacturing cost below $0.15/litre for the volume supplier, this would leave $0.06 per litre for a storage and pumping facility on the SFL property. On a two year pay-back basis this could sustain 1,200,000 litres x $0.06/litre x 2 years = $144,000 in investment. It is doubtful that a 15,000 litre storage tank would come close to that kind of installed cost. For example, a bulk truck could sit permanently on SFL grounds and pump in the mustard as required and the demurrage would not be $72,000 per year.

Another alternative would be to return the empty drums to the mustard manufacturer. This would save the $0.03 per litre purchase cost of the drum, but would incur extra haulage and cleaning costs. It could be environmentally friendlier, but would not make a significant difference in the financial picture.

OTHER ALTERNATIVES

Other alternatives might include making mustard from seed instead of a spice blend. Whether SFL's volume is sufficient is not possible to determine from the case. Switching to a closer by mustard supplier or to alternative packaging (not drums) may be other options.

Based on the information available in the case, the bulk delivery proposal along with negotiation appears to be the most serious option which should be investigated.

MISSING INFORMATION

Aside from the alternatives already discussed, the most serious missing information for the make proposal is whether in-house manufacture can produce the desired quality product. Quality in this case includes taste, blendability with other products, appearance, color and texture. Surely, this can and should be tested before any further steps towards in-house manufacture are undertaken.

Ultimately, future requirements for mustard need to be determined. Is future volume increasing, stable, declining? Each condition will affect the viability of this project.

Other information missing in the case deals with market conditions, price stability, quality of supplier and the nature of the current mustard and vinegar contracts.

Mustard seed is a commodity and will fluctuate and affect the price of purchased mustard as well as the spice blend. Vinegar prices are also relevant. Is there a chance that the increase in vinegar requirements of about 20,000 litres per month will offer an opportunity for a volume discount?

From the case it will be assumed that the current contract with the mustard supplier does not prevent SFL from moving into its own manufacture in the near future.

PLAN OF ACTION

It makes sense at this stage for Denise to check out the alternatives, particularly the bulk delivery of mustard option and to gather the missing information, especially the quality testing of in-house produced mustard. Based on a negative outcome for bulk delivery and renegotiation and a positive outcome on the quality testing, she would then be in a position to make a firm proposal for in-house production of mustard.

Her proposal to the CEO should stress the financial advantage to SFL, the minimal impact on quality of product and the case for switching to in-house manufacture. No investment other than testing, appears to be required and the hassle and non-value added activities associated with drums would be eliminated. There could also be labor safety benefits if drum handling could potentially be hazardous.

CONCLUSION

The interesting twist to this case is that in a time of outsourcing, it is purchasing's suggestion to make in-house. Traditionally, when it comes to make or buy, purchasing takes the buy alternative most of the time.

Paron Metal Fabricating Inc.

Teaching Note

IMMEDIATE ISSUE

Should Paron outsource the outrigger bracket to Mayes Steel Fabricators?

If the outrigger bracket was outsourced, how should concerns for lead times and order quantities be addressed?

BASIC ISSUES

1. Outsourcing.
2. Lot sizing.
3. Economic order quantity theory.
4. Cost analysis.

TEACHING OBJECTIVES

The case requires students to simultaneously evaluate the issues of outsourcing and inventory lot sizing. It can also be used to cover EOQ applications and supplier cost analysis.

SUGGESTED STUDENT ASSIGNMENT

1. What is your analysis of the opportunity to outsource the outrigger bracket? As Donald Mines what would you do and why?
2. If Paron was to outsource the outrigger bracket to Mayes, what lot sizes should Donald Mines specify and why? (Note: You must address this question, regardless of your response to Question 1.)

POSSIBLE DISCUSSION QUESTIONS

1. Do you think Paron should outsource the bracket? Why or why not?
2. What do you think of the quote from Mayes? How would you respond? What information would you request?
3. What would you say to the plant manager?
4. Is the cost savings sufficient enough to move the business to Mayes?

5. Can Donald Mines use the EOQ formula here to establish the lot size? Do all of the EOQ assumptions hold here?

ANALYSIS

This case requires some quantitative analysis if the students are going to develop a meaningful analysis. First, let's take a look at the cost data for the outrigger bracket. The case indicates that Paron produces 40 trailers per year, which suggests that it needs 800 brackets annually, assuming 20 brackets per trailer. Paron estimated its bracket costs at $150.10 each, for a total annual cost of $120,080. It is certainly worthwhile for Donald Mines and Linda Steadman to spend some time on this project.

Exhibit 1 in the case provides the data from the controller, Gerald Myers, and the detail from the quote from Mayes. Note the inconsistencies between the prices from Mayes and Paron's costs. Which raises the issue of the accuracy of the prices/costs. It suggests that either Paron doesn't have a good handle on its costs or Mayes has made some mistakes in their bid. It would be worthwhile to follow-up on this issue with the controller, Gerald Myers, and with Mayes. Students should be prepared to show how they intend to reconcile the inconsistencies. It would be useful to get more information, such as material and direct labor costs. Likely the material costs represent the bulk of the costs for the four subassembly parts.

Exhibit TN 1 provides analysis of the costs from the exhibit in the case, incorporating the fixed and variable components of Paron's costs. This analysis indicates a difference of $11.89 per part, or potential savings of $9,512 per year or 8 percent of the total current cost.

Lot Sizing and Inventory

The case infers that Paron's manufacturing and assembly operations do a pretty good job synchronizing their inventories and Paron carries very little finished inventory as a result. However, the case also suggests that Mines had to establish a lot size quantity in the event that Mayes was chosen as the source for the bracket. In any event, it would appear that finished component inventories for the outrigger bracket would be increasing.

There is sufficient information in the case for the students to calculate the EOQ. The following is provided in the case:

$$D = 800$$
$$i = 20 \text{ percent}$$
$$C = \$108.2$$
$$S = \$75$$

$$EOQ = \sqrt{\frac{2DS}{iC}}$$

$$EOQ = \sqrt{\frac{2(800)(75)}{.20(108.2)}}$$

$$EOQ = 74.5 \text{ brackets}$$

Before going any further, it must be made clear this situation breaks at least one of the underlying assumptions of the EOQ formula, constant demand. However, the EOQ formula is fairly robust and should provide a reasonable estimate of the appropriate order quantity.

The EOQ calculation suggests an order quantity of 75 brackets. Donald might want to adjust this slightly to match the 80 units needed for each trailer. Assuming an average inventory of 40 units, the carrying costs would be $865.60 (40 × $108.20 × 0.20) and the order costs would be $750 (10 orders at $75), for a total cost of $1,615.60 – not enough to reverse the verdict.

Other Considerations

There is a solid opportunity here for Donald Mines, assuming that the numbers from Gerald Myers and Mayes are accurate. However, this does not mean that Paron should outsource the bracket, at least right away. After checking the numbers with Gerald and Mayes, Donald might want to dig into process improvement opportunities before committing to outsourcing. For example, the case indicates that Paron is not getting full benefit from the eight station burn table machine. The threat of moving production out to a supplier might create some interest in the plant to changing the process to reduce costs. Either way, Donald might want to satisfy manufacturing that he gave them a fair chance to look at the process and its costs before pulling the business.

TEACHING STRATEGY

Class can start with a discussion of the motivation for the outsourcing. Touch on the annual costs of the bracket and what might be a reasonable cost savings to justify moving production to Mayes. For example, would you move it for a savings of 1 percent? How about 10 percent?

Next, look at the costs and prices in the exhibit in the case. Press the students on the inconsistencies and what they might do about it. A statement like this might be appropriate: "Just because someone gives you a number, should you trust it?"

Move into the cost analysis. Get out the fixed and variable components of Paron's costs and ask the students how they could use the data. Following this discussion, ask about lot sizing. The students should understand at this point that there are potential savings, so they should give some thought to how much should be ordered per batch. Someone should bring up the EOQ formula (especially if a reading about EOQs has been assigned), if not you might have to raise using this technique.

Near the end of class you can start to ask for what the students want to do and how they would implement their plan. Make them consider how they want to handle the matter with the manufacturing group at Paron and what information they may want from Mayes.

Exhibit TN 1

OUTRIGGER BRACKET COST ANALYSIS

Part	Paron Fixed Costs (20 % Total Cost)	Paron Variable Costs (80 % Total Cost)	Mayes Quote	Difference Paron Variable and Mayes Quote
T-67	$ 3.58	$ 14.34	$ 14.60	($ 0.26)
T-75	$ 3.58	$ 14.34	$ 21.10	($ 6.76)
T-69	$ 9.04	$ 36.16	$ 18.50	$ 17.66
T-77	$ 2.07	$ 8.30	$ 13.00	($ 4.70)
T-70	$ 11.74	$ 46.95	$ 41.00	$ 5.95
Total	$ 30.01	$ 120.09	$ 108.20	$ 11.89

Super Stamps and Products Inc.

Teaching Note

IMMEDIATE ISSUE

How to deal with an irate customer.

BASIC ISSUES

1. Outsourcing.
2. Partnership relations.
3. Quality conformance.
4. ISO-9000.
5. Supply chain management.

SUGGESTED STUDENT ASSIGNMENT

1. As Al Smith, why do you believe Quality Printers chose Super Stamps as a single source last September?
2. What is your assessment of what has transpired on your contract to date?
3. What proposals, if any, do you have for Thursday's meeting with Quality Printers?

POSSIBLE DISCUSSION QUESTIONS

1. Why would Quality Printers want to outsource their graphics department?
2. Why would Super Stamps take over both equipment and the artists from Quality Printers?
3. Why would both parties agree to a one year contract?
4. Could there be any explanations for the defective dies and the high non-conformance rate?
5. Could Super Stamps have taken different measures to ensure the success of this contract? If so, which ones? If not, why not?

DISCUSSION

This case has deliberately been chosen because it looks at the **supplier's** side in an outsourcing situation, rather than the purchaser's. It is a recent outsourcing decision, still in the first year of the contract, although both parties had established a buyer-seller relationship well before. Thus, the current problems cannot be attributed to a lack of familiarity between the two firms.

It is useful to take a look at the supply chain here to identify the roles of the various parties better.

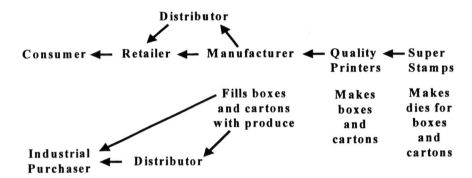

For Super Stamps to play its role as a superior supplier, it needs to ensure that the customers of Quality Printers and their customers assess Quality Printers as a highly preferred supplier. There is no evidence from the case that Super Stamps sees its role in this light. Super Stamps must have had an excellent supplier-buyer relationship and performance record to have been chosen by Quality Printers as its single source for dies. Super Stamps's willingness to take over Quality Printers' equipment and its two artists must also have weighed significantly in Quality Printers' decision to outsource.

What Has Changed?

It is, therefore, reasonable to ask what has changed since September 1st to create the kinds of problems that should never have happened in the past eight months. In the first place, it appears that Super Stamps has not changed. It is acting as if all of its commitments are identical to those before. Therefore, unless Super Stamps has had a significant turnover of staff (could it be the Quality Printers' artists take over?) or change in equipment (is it possible that Quality Printers' equipment is partially at fault?) it has been business as usual at Super Stamps.

At Quality Printers it is possible that things have changed a lot. Quite often in outsourcing situations, organizations discover what informal task or functions have been lost only after the outsourcing is complete. Is it possible that the two artists at Quality Printers performed communications, quality control, purchasing, scheduling, prioritizing and other functions they no longer perform on Quality Printers' behalf or only partially so? In the vacuum, have jobs slipped through that previously would not have?

Super Stamps is in the uncomfortable position where the cost of its dies is likely to be a very small portion of the cost of the cartons or boxes produced by Quality Printers. Thus, questions of consequential damages are really nasty ones to face. Far better to be doubly sure that such problems do not arise in the first place.

Die making is a fundamental step in printing, just as in metal stamping. A quality die will permit the user to turn out a quality job and, aside from quality, the die also has a major impact on productivity through reduced set-up time and higher machine speeds. Thus, a high quality source of dies is vital for Quality Printers. It believed that in Super Stamps it had that kind of supplier, but it certainly must have doubts at this point.

That Quality Printers started its own ISO-9000 program probably added to the confusion surrounding its outsourcing situation. Quality Printers' expectations have probably changed even since the signing of the contract eight months ago and it does not seem that Super Stamps has been a serious part of the loop.

Timing

Eight months have now passed and both parties are finally becoming serious about the situation. If Super Stamps is anxious to retain the business and $500,000 worth of die work is a lot of dies in this business, then it must show far greater concern for Quality Printers' needs than it has thus far.

Assignment of a high level individual, such as Al Smith, directly to the Quality Printers relationship and a team to work on various initiatives for improvement would be a good start. Development of a cause and effect diagram to pinpoint the areas of greatest need of improvement would be one of the first tasks of such a buyer-supplier team.

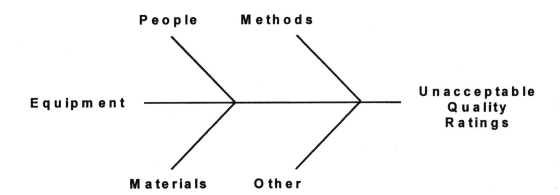

A similar diagram for both organizations might reveal where trouble spots occur. Certainly, the documentation area at Super Stamps does appear rather haphazard and could stand a more disciplined approach.

Weekly or even daily meetings between Super Stamps and Quality Printers staff to discuss current orders and projects for improvement would go a long way to get the relationship to where it should be. Whether four months is enough time to secure enough progress for a contract renewal is another question. It is likely that the one year contract, awfully short for an outsourcing situation involving transfer of people and equipment, was agreed to more as a "let's see how we are progressing and see where we should be going" kind of timeline, rather than a "you perform or you are out" kind of deal. Nevertheless, the former could change into the latter if bungles continue. Both parties were probably naive in their treatment of their new relationship over the past eight months. It is high time both become serious about it.

CHAPTER 9

Price Determination

Topics Covered

Relation of Cost to Price
    Meaning of Cost
How Suppliers Establish Price
    The Cost Approach
    The Market Approach
Government Influence on Pricing
    Legislation Affecting Price Determination
Types of Purchases
    Raw Materials/Sensitive Commodities
    Special Items
    Standard Production Items
    Small-Value Items
Methods of Price Determination
    The Use of Quotations and Competitive Bidding (Online or Offline)
    Firm Bidding
    Determination of Most Advantageous Bid
    Collusive Bidding
The Problem of Identical Prices
    Negotiation as a Method of Price Determination
    Provision for Price Changes
    Discounts
    The Price-Discount Problem
    Quantity Discounts and Source Selection
    Contract Cancellation
Cost Analysis
    The Learning Curve
    Total Cost of Ownership
    Total Cost Modeling and Reducing the Total Cost of Ownership
Target Pricing
    Activity-Based Costing
Negotiation Strategy and Practice
    Framework for Planning and Preparing for Negotiation
    Ground Rules for Successful Negotiation
Forward Buying and Commodities
    Forward Buying versus Speculation
    Speculation versus Gambling
    Organizing for Forward Buying
    Control of Forward Buying
The Commodity Exchanges
    Limitations of the Exchanges
    Hedging
Sources of Information Regarding Price Trends
Questions for Review and Discussion
References
Cases
    Global Heat Exchangers Inc.
    MasTech Inc.
    Chevron Corporation: The PC Selection Team
    Price Forecasting Exercise
    Commodity Purchasing Game

QUIZ RESPONSES

B   1.   The fairest possible means of treating all suppliers alike in a competitive bidding situation is to:

         a. allow all bidders to change their bids prior to the bid opening.
         b. establish a policy of firm bidding.
         c. allow for negotiation after all bids are received.
         d. relate imaginary bids to give prospective suppliers a ballpark figure to work with.
         e. none of the above.

E   2.   One of the main sources of reduction in total cost of ownership reported by Hendrick and Ellram was:

         a. short-term purchase agreements.
         b. multiple suppliers for each purchase category.
         c. arms-length relationships with suppliers.
         d. separate buyer and seller cost reduction programs.
         e. early supplier involvement in design.

C   3.   The Sherman Antitrust Act basically requires that a supplier:

         a. must adjust price so that profit on a given item is not over a specific percent of direct and indirect costs.
         b. not talk with competitors about price.
         c. must sell the same item, in the same quantity, to all customers at the same price.
         d. use standard grade descriptions in advertising products.
         e. meet competition, by adjusting price.

A | 4. A cash discount of 2/10, N/30 (2 percent cash discount if payment is made in 10 days, with the gross amount due in 30 days) is the equivalent of what approximate interest rate?

   a. 36.
   b. 18.
   c. 30.
   d. 45.
   e. 54.

B | 5. The prime function of an organized commodity exchange is to:

   a. furnish an established marketplace where commodity prices can be controlled.
   b. furnish an established marketplace where the forces of supply and demand operate freely.
   c. bring together sellers of the same commodity.
   d. furnish an established marketplace where products that are difficult to grade can be traded.
   e. furnish an established marketplace where there are only a limited number of buyers and sellers.

D | 6. The learning curve normally is applied to the analysis of:

   a. direct material costs.
   b. overhead costs.
   c. tooling costs.
   d. direct labor costs.
   e. profit rates.

E | 7. Target pricing:

   a. starts with the supplier's price, and works to determine the supplier's true cost structure.
   b. starts with the supplier's price, and works to determine the selling price of the buying organization's end product or service.
   c. starts with the buyer's lowest reasonable price target, and works to a negotiated price agreed on by the buyer and the supplier.
   d. starts with the selling price of the end product or service of the buyer's organization, subtracts off actual manufacturing, overhead, materials and services costs to determine operating profit.

e. Starts with the selling price of the end product or service of the buyer's organization, subtracts operating profit to establish cost targets for manufacturing, overhead, materials and services.

A   8.   Hedging is a way to:

     a. try to minimize price risks.
     b. make sure that the quantity ordered will be delivered.
     c. ensure delivery.
     d. guarantee maximum returns.
     e. obtain the quality that is needed.

A   9.   The process of attempting to determine all cost elements such as acquisition price, purchasing administration, follow-up, expediting, inspection and testing, rework, scrap, downtime, lost sales and customer returns is called:

     a. total cost of ownership.
     b. activity-based costing.
     c. target pricing.
     d. competitive bidding.
     e. learning curve.

E   10.   When developing a negotiation strategy, the negotiator should assess the positions of strength of both (all) parties to:

     a. decide if negotiation makes sense.
     b. establish negotiation points.
     c. avoid setting unrealistic expectations.
     d. b and c.
     e. a, b, and c.

True and False

F	1.	Competitive bidding, in general, is the most inefficient means of obtaining a fair price for items bought.
T	2.	In planning for negotiation, a factor or item of information over which disagreement is expected is known as an issue.
F	3.	Canceling a contract for a technicality when market prices are falling is considered an acceptable and ethical practice.
T	4.	A price protection clause gives the buyer the opportunity to renegotiate price with a supplier or buy from another supplier offering a lower price.
T	5.	Two approaches suppliers use to establish price are the cost approach and the market approach.
T	6.	An escalator clause provides for an increase or a decrease in price if costs change.
F	7.	A "fair price" is the lowest price that ensures a continuous supply of the proper quality where and when needed even if this means the supplier loses money on the deal.
F	8.	Educating suppliers about the buyer organization's operations is an example of a transaction cost in the total cost of ownership model.
F	9.	Activity based costing primarily is an accounting process that has little practical value for buyers.
T	10.	If the goal of negotiation is performance, then the process or tactics used during the negotiation are important because they may impact the intention to perform.

Global Heat Exchangers Inc.

Teaching Note

IMMEDIATE ISSUE

What should Deirdre do about the announced price increase from Titania?

BASIC ISSUES

1. Role of suppliers in gaining competitive advantage.
2. Pricing and estimating.
3. The marketing-purchasing connection in custom work.
4. Dealing with the unforeseen.
5. Use of top management in supply.

SUGGESTED STUDENT ASSIGNMENT

1. As Deirdre Collins, what alternatives do you believe you have regarding Titania and what are the advantages and disadvantages of each?
2. What action would you take and why?

POSSIBLE DISCUSSION QUESTIONS

1. Does the estimation process for custom work make sense?
2. Why might a price increase by 25% in a period of less than six weeks?
3. If this price increase had been sent three weeks earlier, would it make any difference?
4. If the price increase had been different, would your actions be different? 2%? 7%? 12%?
5. If a significant price decrease had been announced, say 10% or 20%, how would this affect your actions?

DISCUSSION

The Order

This is the first order with Japan. It is a large order compared to most business received. Moreover, it has the possibility of follow on orders. The Japanese are likely to use this order as a test with respect to such considerations as quality, timeliness, price and service. Therefore, it is clear that GHE must live up to its commitments under this order and ensure that full Japanese satisfaction will be achieved. For this reason, the idea of going back to Japan to announce a significant increase in price at this stage of the game does not seem to be a particularly wise action. If the price increase in titanium is realistic and supportable, however, future orders may have to be priced differently to reflect this. Therefore, if the price increase in titanium is legitimate and unavoidable, and if the quoted system sales price is maintained for good long-term customer relations with Japan it might be wise to start pre-conditioning the Japanese about the possibility that future prices may have to be raised to reflect higher titanium costs. It also would not hurt to let them know that you are absorbing the higher cost of titanium on this order for purposes of good will. Hopefully, neither of these will be necessary if Deirdre is successful in addressing the price increase in other ways.

The Announced Price Increase

Unfortunately, the Japanese order has taken more than 30 days to confirm. Therefore, the standard practice of expecting prices to hold for at least 30 days does not seem to apply in this particular situation. Nevertheless, a 25% increase in less than 6 weeks certainly sounds excessive. It is rather ironic that, had Deirdre confirmed her purchase orders before the facts arrived from Titania and not gone to the president's luncheon party, she might have had a much stronger case for not accepting the price increase. Titania might still have refused the order, but its timing would have been at a disadvantage.

Titania does not explain the reason for the price increase. This is a typical weakness in most marketing initiatives regarding price increases. The size of the increase 25% with an order of about $500,000 amounts to $125,000. The supplier's rather casual reference to this increase is particularly disquieting. They were well aware of the March 3rd quotation request and might have given advance warning to Deirdre that they were thinking about increasing prices. They certainly failed to do so. Titania, through its past relations with GHE, must have been aware that the particular order on which they quoted was an unusually large one for GHE. Warm buyer-supplier relationships are not built on these kinds of actions.

The Need for Additional Information

Clearly, Deirdre needs additional information before she can decide which action is most appropriate. It is not clear whether Titania's increase is because of an increase in titanium metal prices or other reasons. How much of the total cost of titanium sheet is for raw material as opposed to other costs? Supposing that raw material represents 60% of the cost, it would take a 40% increase in raw material ingot prices to warrant a 25% increase on sheet. Other components of sheet metal cost such as fixed costs in rolling equipment and variable costs in labor and energy are unlikely to have risen by this kind of amount in that short a period of time. The remote possibility that the earlier quote may have been a mistake does not seem relevant from the data in the case.

Certainly it would be useful for Deirdre to check alternate sources of supply for their prices on the required sheet metal of this titanium alloy. She should also check what has happened to commodity prices. Perhaps even the possibility of alternate materials, unlikely as it seems in view of the engineering considerations may have to be looked at. Perhaps at the higher price of titanium, other design options become economically feasible.

POTENTIAL ACTIONS

It behooves Deirdre to let Titania know immediately that the announced price increase is unacceptable and that she expects them to hold to their earlier quote. This will be a good starting position for any negotiations that might, in fact, follow. She should also immediately let the key parties inside her own organization, including the President, know what has happened. Along with this she should let them know what actions she can take, such as looking at alternative suppliers and checking commodity prices. If engineering redesign is an option, this should be undertaken quickly. I am presuming that the Japanese order has a fairly tight deadline and that quick action is vital on this order. She should also condition the president that she may need his help to bring pressure to bear on Titania. It may well be that Deirdre's position in the organization is too low to be able to bring real powerful pressure to bear on Titania. It should be pointed out that future orders from Japan may also benefit GHE's suppliers, such as Titania.

Under the new president, the likelihood that future additional international business may increase, but may also require longer lead times between time of quotation and actual placing of the order is high. Therefore, the old 30 day standard may no longer be realistic for maintaining quoted prices. On the assumption that it is unlikely that raw material prices for titanium have jumped 60% and that Titania is trying to pull a relatively fast one on GHE, it is important that a major effort to beat back the price be undertaken.

This is the kind of incident that requires that almost everything be dropped and that immediate action be taken. It is also a good lesson for GHE as to what kinds of suppliers it needs to be able to be competitive and effective itself in the years to come.

MasTech Inc.

Teaching Note

IMMEDIATE ISSUE

Should Robert Fisk recommend switching to a new supplier for steel and/or steel processing?

BASIC ISSUES

1. Price determination
2. Supplier selection
3. Total cost of ownership
4. Supply participation in target costing
5. Developing new suppliers
6. Supplier performance evaluation
7. Continuous improvement
8. Scheduling and delivery

TEACHING OBJECTIVES

This case is designed to highlight the complexities of total cost of ownership and the implications for supplier selection. Students are expected to evaluate the direct and indirect costs incurred in the supply chain and the cost reduction opportunities.

SUGGESTED STUDENT ASSIGNMENT

As Robert Fisk, what recommendations would you make to Andrew Ross and why? Support your recommendation with appropriate analysis.

POSSIBLE DISCUSSION QUESTIONS

1. How much money do you think Robert Fisk can save MasTech?
2. What do you think of the unreliable delivery issue? How should Robert Fisk address this problem?
3. How much inventory do you think Vaughan should carry?

4. What are your impressions of the quotes from Colgon and Ashgrove? Do you have any concerns about these two companies as potential suppliers?
5. What do you think of the way that Robert Fisk has handled the situation so far?

ANALYSIS

Quantitative Analysis

There are a few numbers in the case and it makes sense to work through the calculations to better understand Robert Fisk's situation. Let's look at what we know about MasTech and the importance of the Ford cross-member component to the plant. Assuming a 20 percent operating margin, MasTech costs of sales were sales were $225 million, based on revenue of $280 million. The case indicates that steel represents 60 percent of total costs, which suggests a total annual steel cost of $135 million per year. The case also indicates that the cross-member uses 130,000 tons of steel annually. At the current price of $30 per hundredweight (cwt), this represents a cost of $78 million, or roughly 58 percent of MasTech's total annual steel bill. Obviously the cross-member is a critical component for the plant in terms of sales volume.

Working backwards and assuming that the cost of the cross-member is 60 percent steel, with an 80 percent margin, annual sales of the cross-member are $162.5 million. Ford is expecting a 3 percent cost reduction, so to avoid margin erosion, MasTech needs to target annual savings of $4.9 million.

Robert has three primary pricing options. First, he could stay with Uxbridge and Vaughan, which has offered a revised price of $29.75 cwt. This translates into a total annual cost of $77.35 million ($595 per ton at 130,000 tons) and an annual savings of $650,000.

Second, Robert could source the cross-member steel with Uxbridge (cost $24.75 cwt), but use Ashgrove (cost $4.75 cwt) with a total cost of $29.50 cwt. This works out to a total annual cost of $76.7 million ($590 per ton at 130,000 tons), with a savings of $1.3 million.

Finally, Robert could use Colgon (cost $24.75 cwt) and Ashgrove (cost $4.75 cwt), which also has a total cost of $76.7 million and annual savings of $1.3 million.

Exhibit TN 1 provides a summary of the pricing alternatives and the associated costs and savings.

At best these options only get MasTech about 25 percent of the savings needed to hit the 3 percent cost reduction target stipulated by Ford and Robert needs to look for other opportunities.

Premium Costs

The case indicates that MasTech is paying premiums as a result of supply problems from Uxbridge and Vaughan. Using the 10 percent premium cost figure and 25 percent of the cross-member requirements, works out to total premium costs of $1.95 million ($78 million × .25 × .10). However, there are more opportunities for cost avoidance than cost reduction.

There are likely also costs that MasTech is incurring as a result of poor delivery reliability, beyond the premium costs of steel. It would be useful to have the students list possible costs at the appropriate time in the class discussion. The list might include:

- Opportunity costs of machine downtime @ $1,500 per hour
- Customer assembly line downtime @ $300,000 per hour
- Administrative costs for locating and purchasing new material
- Administrative costs for filing and payment of invoices and other paperwork, such as quality documents and certifications
- Scrap and production costs from the effects of the new material on the dies and equipment, such as trials and fine-tuning the equipment to accommodate the new steel that might have a slightly different chemical composition
- Quality cost for qualifying material and vendors
- Additional shipping, freight and expediting
- Additional inventory costs for bulk purchases (versus JIT shipments)

This analysis indicates the importance of taking a total cost perspective. Clearly negotiating with suppliers over piece price reductions alone will not support the $4.9 million in cost reductions needed. However, eliminating waste in the supply chain can help MasTech avoid or reduce costs, helping to protect its margins.

The instructor might want to ask the students how much these costs might represent. An easy approach would be to use a percentage of sales. Obviously there is no hard data in the case to quantify these costs, but an estimate of 10 – 20 percent would be reasonable. An implication is that Robert might have to dig into these costs before his meeting with Andrew Ross the next day.

What Should Robert Fisk Do Next?

Based on the quote in the case, Robert appears to think that the supply problem lies with Vaughan. However, Vaughan simply processes the steel and ships it to MasTech. The problem could originate with Uxbridge, or it could be a combination of both suppliers. Robert needs to understand the root causes of the problem and be prepared to take appropriate steps to address them. It might be useful in class to do a short brainstorming exercise regarding what might be causing the delivery problems, such as:

- Unreliable schedules from MasTech
- Insufficient capacity at Vaughan or Oxbridge
- Poor quality procedures
- Equipment breakdowns

There is likely more than one contributing cause, and this might be a good application for a Pareto Chart.

Until Robert can clarify the causes of the problems it doesn't seem reasonable to start negotiating alternative supply arrangements. Similarly, adding more inventories to the system, as implied in the case, might only add extra costs in the supply chain, without any appreciable benefits. In the end, Robert might be able to generate further price concessions by working with its steel and processing suppliers to reduce their costs.

There also appears to be some risks attached with changing suppliers at this point. First, it does not appear that Robert understands the switching costs. Will the tooling have to be fine-tuned or altered in any way? Will the quality be the same? Second, Colgon appears to be having financial problems. Will they stay in business? Will Colgon ask for price increases later? and, Will their financial problems affect their production commitments? Finally, Ashgrove does not have the capacity to handle the cross-member steel and needs to add a new line. It still remains to be seen how long this will take and what problems might be encountered. Furthermore, Ashgrove is a small company that likely does not have the resources and flexibility to react to problems and will be dependent heavily on MasTech's business.

Final Observations

If Robert Fisk is going to make a credible contribution to the cost reduction target he needs to look at total costs of ownership in the supply chain. It would be short sighted to change suppliers to save a few cents per hundredweight without understanding the full implications of the decision. It is frankly surprising that the delivery problem has been allowed to go on for two years.

In order to capture the potential benefits, Robert Fisk will need the support of others in the organization. The finance, operations and quality departments will all have to support the analysis and eventual action plan. Perhaps the most important accomplishment that can come out of his meeting with Andrew Ross is identifying the potential and getting his strong backing for attacking the supply chain costs.

It is interesting to note the approach taken by Robert Fisk so far. He has concentrated on the levers that he can pull without the involvement of others in the organization. Beating up suppliers on price and moving business around will not help support the continuous improvement philosophy needed to hit the aggressive cost targets set by Ford. Unfortunately this is an approach too often taken by supply managers.

TEACHING STRATEGY

Start the class off by clarifying the situation at MasTech. What are their annual revenues and what portion of sales does the cross-member represent? What are the industry characteristics and what does it take to be successful in this industry? Next move into a discussion of the cross-member. Clarify its annual material cost and the cost savings target.

Ask the class to explain what Robert Fisk has done up until this point. List the various sourcing options and associated costs and potential cost savings. At this point it should be evident that more savings have to be eked out of the system. Ask the students where else Robert can look. This should take you into the total cost or ownership analysis. Use mini brainstorming sessions to identify total cost of ownership issues and potential costs.

End the class with a discussion of what Robert Fisk should do next. First, what can be accomplished before his meeting with Andrew Ross and what does he need to accomplish in the meeting? Finally, talk about the need for cross-functional support and involvement. Success of Robert's cost reduction initiative will depend on active involvement and buy-in from others in the management group.

Exhibit TN1

PRICING AND COST OPTIONS

	Uxbridge/Vaughan	Uxbridge/Ashgrove	Colgon/Ashgrove
Steel	$24.75 cwt	$ 24.75 cwt	$ 24.75 cwt
Processing	$ 5.0 cwt (derived)	$ 4.75 cwt	$ 4.75 cwt
Total	$29.75 cwt	$ 29.50 cwt	$ 29.50 cwt
Savings	$650,000	$ 1.3 million	$ 1.3 million

Chevron Corporation: The PC Selection Team (Abridged)

Teaching Note

INTRODUCTION

This is case deals with supplier alliances and total cost of ownership. Students are asked to play the role of a Jean Wolcott, a member of the Chevron Desktop Life Cycle Management Team, who has been give the responsibility of leading the team through the a segment of the Chevron Supplier Quality Improvement Process (CSQIP) at the next team meeting on April 25th. The team has been given the mandate of selecting a desktop hardware supplier for Chevron's worldwide operations. The scope of the project involves developing a standard for 30,000 users, located in more than 700 sites in over 90 countries. The project has an initial cost of approximately $90 million in the first year, and approximately $250 million over five years. The primary objective of the case is to have the students evaluate potential total cost of ownership drivers and consider how such information can be used to evaluate potential suppliers.

Rather than have the students discuss potential total cost issues for a purchase decision, the Chevron case presents a model that attempts to link the concepts of total cost of ownership, supplier selection and supplier alliances. Students are asked to anticipate total cost factors then incorporate these into a supplier evaluation model. The case and subsequent events information in the teaching note provides an opportunity for the students to trace an actual total cost decision-making process.

IMMEDIATE ISSUE

List of total cost of ownership factors for the purchase of desktop computers at Chevron.

BASIC ISSUES

1. Total cost of ownership
2. Supplier alliances
3. Information technology purchasing
4. Supplier selection and evaluation
5. The use of a multi-functional team in equipment acquisition
6. Weighted average supplier evaluation systems
7. Total quality
8. Standardization

ASSIGNMENT QUESTIONS

If you were in the position of Jean Wolcott:
1. What factors do you feel would influence the total cost of ownership of desktop PCs and laptops at Chevron Corporation?
2. How would you envision the team could translate its total cost of ownership ideas into supplier selection criteria?

POSSIBLE DISCUSSION QUESTIONS

1. What do you think of the GIL Project? What are the potential risks and benefits?
2. What are your impressions of the CSQIP procedure?
3. What criteria do you feel are important for Chevron concerning the selection of a PC supplier?
4. What factors do you feel would influence the total cost of ownership for Chevron desktop computers in the GIL Project?
5. What is the structure of the computer industry? How many firms do you think Chevron should consider as potential suppliers?
6. Would you negotiate with GTC and Tricon or would you choose another approach? How would you proceed and what process would you follow? What are the advantages and disadvantages of this approach?
7. What additional information do you feel the team needs and where would you get it? What difference would it make?
8. Why is purchasing frequently excluded from IT purchasing decisions?
9. What is more important in this purchasing decision, product or supplier? Which would you focus on first?
10. What is your implementation plan? List the sequence of activities that you would recommend to the team.

ANALYSIS

Nature of the Challenge

It is important that the students appreciate the complexities of the challenges faced by the Chevron Desktop Life Cycle Management Team. By the time the project was completed, GIL would connect over 30,000 desks across more than 700 worksites in more than 90 countries, including some of the most remote parts of the world. Chevron had major exploration and production facilities in Mexico, California, Texas, Angola, Nigeria, Canada, the North Sea, Australia, Indonesia, Kazakhstan, the Republic of Congo and Papua New Guinea. It had major refining facilities in California, Mississippi, Utah, Texas, Hawaii, Canada, Asia, Africa, Australia and New Zealand. The marketing division had over 8,000 outlets in North America and more than 8,000 additional outlets in Asia, southern and eastern Africa, the Middle East, Australia and New Zealand. The Chemical Division (CCC) had plants in Brazil, Japan, Mexico, and Singapore, and operated or marketed in more than 80 other countries.

The main objective of the GIL Project was to "establish a flexible and reliable IT infrastructure by standardizing all aspects of the network and computing environment at Chevron Corporation worldwide". Given the range of company locations and diversity of its needs, this was a very significant task. For example, there would be unique challenges in terms of setting up and servicing the network in remote regions. Chevron was one of the first companies to attempt standardizing its IT network on a global basis. (According to Chevron, the other up until that time was Dow, which had completed a similar project about one year earlier.)

The implications for CITC also need to be considered. Tom Bell described this project as high risk/high reward proposition. It appears that Chevron personnel did not have much regard for corporate staff; the company had a very decentralized structure. The benefits, which are discussed in the next section, are substantial. However, the costs of failure for CITC could also substantial. Failure in could permanently damage the credibility of CITC.

The GIL Project and Benefits of Standardization

The GIL Project was a massive undertaking. Based on the business philosophy of its CEO, Chevron had a decentralized organization. Enforcing a standardized IT system might be difficult. However, momentum for GIL appeared to grow as the inadequacies of the existing approach became apparent to staff and executives in the business units and the corporate group.

It is a bit early at this point in the case to discuss the total cost of ownership (TCO) issues associated with a computer, but it is worth spending time discussing the potential benefits of the GIL Project. Possible examples include:

- Lower acquisition costs through high volume purchases
- Lower training costs for staff (single as opposed to multiple systems)
- Easier inter-company communication
- Lower system support/maintenance costs (expertise for single versus multiple systems)
- Better system reliability

Spend some time at the start of class discussing not only "what" Chevron is attempting to accomplish, but "why".

Selecting a Course of Action

Chevron Production Company (CPDN) had recently standardized its desktop systems with a PC and laptop from Global Technology Company (GTC). Furthermore, the OpCo had just leased approximately $20 million in equipment as part of the decision to standardize with GTC.

This event should be used to create a debate in class regarding future action. There are a number of reasons why GTC and Tricon Inc. should be selected without opening the process to other potential suppliers. First, timing was a major consideration. The team had only about eight weeks to evaluate suppliers and desktop operating systems and make their recommendation. Arguing that GTC has a preferred relationship with the company is a reasonable position given the recent $20 million purchase. Presumably they were evaluated and ultimately selected for good reasons. Second, a related issue is the cost implication of standardizing with another desktop system and writing-off a $20 million investment. Third, both Marjorie Ferrer and Pete Sandoval were both from CPDN and were involved in the decision to select GTC. They were likely to favor GTC. In fact, they had been placed on the team because of their experience with the CPDN project. Finally, GTC and Tricon both appear to be industry leaders with global organizations.

There are, however, several reasons why the team might want to consider other possible sources. First, the corporate review process will be very rigorous, and the safest approach would be to consider other possible suppliers in order to provide comfort that the team's evaluation was both fair and thorough. (Although not stated in the case, an interesting piece of information here is that an executive from Saba Computer Company, a competitor of GTC, was on the Chevron Board of Directors.) Second, the GIL system would be phased in over a period of several months. Conceivably CPDN could be scheduled at the end in order to minimize the penalties associated with canceling the lease early. Third, the CPDN situation was different from Chevron worldwide. CPDN was based in North America, while the situation at Chevron's international operations may legitimately necessitate the selection of a different supplier. Realistically, to decide not to consider sources other than CTG could be dangerous for Tom, Jean and the other members of the team.

The Desktop Lifecycle Management Team

One of the interesting aspects of this situation is that Chevron did not bring in a team of consultants to analyze their IT systems and make recommendations. The process was driven by the involvement of Chevron staff on several teams, including desktops.

The make-up of the team involved people from various business units, as opposed to only CITC staff. This helped gain organizational buy-in. Chevron has a very decentralized culture and the difficulty in setting a corporate standard should not be underestimated here. Furthermore, CITC was not highly regarded by most of the people in the business units, a reflection of the fact that the business units had created IT departments within their organizations. Note also that the team was cross-functional, involved staff from IT, finance and purchasing.

The Role of Purchasing

A central issue in the case is: What role can purchasing play? Jean Wolcott has been included on the team. Get the students to generate a list of the contributions that she could make to the team. Possible examples include:

- Familiarity with the supply base.
- Expertise in negotiating supply contracts.
- Expertise in evaluating potential products and services.
- Expertise in evaluating potential suppliers.

The case indicates that Jean does not have any particular experience in terms of IT acquisition. It is, therefore, best to assume that she is *not* an IT specialist, but she obviously does have purchasing expertise and CSQIP training.

An interesting aspect of this case is that, in some organizations, purchasing is excluded from IT purchasing decisions. It may be useful to discuss why this might happen. A reason often suggested is that while purchasing might be familiar with standard raw materials and supplies, IT is unique because of its sophisticated technical issues and the high level of change in the industry. For this reason, IT decisions at a lot of organizations are made under a cloud of secrecy.

CSQIP EXERCISE

The following process can be used in class to cover three steps of the CSQIP process with the students: internal business analysis, industry analysis and establish criteria.

First spend some time discussing CSQIP. What do the students think about CSQIP? Note that Chevron spent $2.6 billion in CSQIP alliances that year, and the amount of spending under CSQIP was increasing. The case also claims savings of 8 – 10 percent (and higher for services), which represents annual savings in the $208 million - $260 million range.

1. Perform Internal Business Analysis

The Internal Business Analysis segment includes: develop initial supplier selection criteria (Affinity Diagram Exercise) and evaluate total cost of ownership drivers (Brainstorming Exercise). Before discussing these issues, spend few minutes clarifying the current situation.

Price Determination 173

Clarify Current Situation

The case states that Tom Bell reviewed the team objectives and schedule at the first team meeting on April 22. A lot of information is provided in the case concerning the situation. What do we know:

- Chevron required approximately 30,000 computers (25,000 PCs and 5,000 laptops), for 700 worksites in more than 90 countries.
- GTC, Saba, Vytec and Cassin provide approximately 90 percent of the company's desktop machines. These are all large global manufacturers, based in North America.
- Many Chevron locations were remote.
- The project was to be completed by June 20, giving the team approximately eight weeks.
- Nothing close to a uniform standard existed, with the possible exception of CPDN. Chevron's current system consists of a variety of configurations and suppliers for both hardware and software.
- CPDN invested $20 million last year with GTC and Tricon.
- Industry appears to be made up of two segments, manufacturers and resellers/service providers/distributors.
- Initial budget of $90 million for desktops and $150 million for GIL.
- High risk/high reward project for CITC.

Total Cost of Ownership Drivers

Although Jean started with an affinity process (see next step), I prefer to start with brainstorming TCO drivers for desktops and laptops. Jean had the luxury of two days to work with the team, however, class time places limits on our process.

Jean Wolcott used a brainstorming process to gather ideas concerning total cost of ownership drivers. This same process can be used with the students in class. Expect to spend approximately 15 – 20 minutes, depending on the size of the group.

Brainstorming is used to create a large number of ideas on any topic through a process free of criticism and judgement. Ideas are never criticized. It encourages open thinking and attempts to get all team members involved. Ideally, team members build on each other's creativity. The process used here is structured brainstorming.

Based on the assignment questions, the students should be prepared with some ideas, but it might be wise to give them 4-5 minutes in small groups to discuss their ideas. This can be accomplished by having them work with the two or three students sitting in their general area.

The following process can be used in class:

1. Establish the issue clearly: What are the total cost elements associated with desktop PCs and laptops?
2. Have each student take a turn and give an idea. I go around the room to give everone a chance to give at least one idea.

    No idea is ever criticized. With each rotation a team member can pass at any time. Make sure each idea is recorded with the exact same words as the speaker – don't interpret or abbreviate (check with speak for if the idea has been worded accurately). Keep the process moving and keep it short (e.g., 10 – 15 minutes).
3. When all ideas have been exhausted review the written list for clarification and discard duplicated or those that are virtually identical. In some cases there may be important differences and some comments made be divided into two items.
4. Rank items: high/medium/low.
5. Determine influence: Which are influenced by the supplier, which by Chevron, which are influenced by both.

Criteria for Evaluating Suppliers

Jean Wolcott used an affinity diagram process to gather ideas concerning supplier selection criteria. This same process can be used with the students in class. Expect to spend approximately 10 - 15 minutes, depending on the size of the group.

Affinity diagrams are designed to allow team member to use their creativity and unique perspective to generate a large number of ideas and then organize and summarize them into natural groupings. This process encourages active participation of everyone in the team, prompts different methods of approaching issues, encourages ownership of results, and helps organize vast amounts of data and provides organization to vast array of options.

The following outlines the sequence that should be used:

1. Establish Issue: What criteria are important for the selection of a desktop computer supplier based on the TCO drivers already disucssed?

2. Brainstorm items and place each idea on the wall using large post-it notes. Avoid using single words, and try to use a verb and a noun. (Post-it note are not mandatory for the exercise. As an alternative, list the items on an overhead or on the board.)

3. Sort items into groups: Have class members take turns and silently sort the criteria into related groupings. Avoid discussion. As team members take turns the process will slowdown, until each person feels sufficiently comfortable with the groupings. It is okay for some notes to stand alone, as they might be important.

    Possible groupings might include company experience, equipment scope, service capabilities, quality/reliability, warranty, etc.

When working from an overhead or off the board in class, I place numbers in front of items to identify their groups. For example, quality items might be #1, experience items #2 and service #3.

4. Create a draft summary or header for each group using consensus and discussion. Start by gaining consensus on a draft word/theme/idea for each group. Next, agree on a concise sentence that combines this central word/theme/idea and what the items add to that idea. Replace the draft summary/header with the new final header card. Divide large groupings into subgroups as needed and create header cards.

There are typically 5 – 10 groupings of items in a typical affinity diagram process.

2. Perform Industry Analysis

This section is designed to incorporate industry factors into the supplier selection criteria. The industry analysis set is easy to skip, but is essential from this exercise.

Ask the students what they know about in industry in terms of the following:

- Major competitors.
- Product life cycles.
- Market structure (e.g., manufacturers and resellers).
- Existing alliances and partnerships (e.g., GTC and Tricon).
- What services the supply chain member provide.
- What market information do we need and where will we get it?
- Who do we want on the initial vendor list and why?

Most people in class will have a general understanding of the computer hardware industry and some might have a thorough understanding. Several things should become apparent after this discussion, such as, the industry is characterized by:
- Extremely short product life cycles driven by technological change.
- A few large companies, and many small ones.
- Wild variations in profitability.
- Manufactures tend to distribute through resellers, who also handle service. The services aspect of the industry is critical for this project and includes installation, maintenance and warranty repairs, help desk support and project management.

Return to the criteria and make changes. If not already on the list, criteria such as global network (Chevron will need to support approximately 700 locations in over 90 countries) and manufacturing capacity (Chevron will need about 30,000 identical machines) should be added to the list. Similarly, students should be made to recognize that Chevron needed to select both a manufacturer (e.g., GTC) and a reseller (e.g., Tricon).

3. Establish Criteria

At this point all that should be required is to review the suppler selection criteria established in step 1 and make some final changes. Then assign points for each category, with the most important receiving a larger number of points. The point assignment can either be based on an index, such as 100 or 1,000, or simply represent a relative scale.

NEED FOR DATA COLLECTION AND ANALYSIS

Since the Chevron had several weeks, they could collect data to validate their suspicions concerning TCO drivers. Students should be asked to indicate what data they would collect and how it could be used.

Understanding the total cost of ownership factors that Chevron faced helped guide them in crafting the supplier questionnaire by providing focus regarding important supplier capabilities that would reduce their 'total cost per seat'. The team collected data from two sources. The first was internal. Based on CITC costs, they found that the cost per seat was made up of approximately 24 percent of hardware costs and 76 percent of management costs, which included installation, administration and CITC support. The team also looked at the relationship between the number of PCs per IT support people and the number of different PC brands at each site, and found a strong correlation between increasing support costs and proliferation of PC configurations and brands. The team's second source of information was a major consulting company that specialized in information technology, and provided team results from their on going research in TCO for PCs and laptops. Their research basically validated the team's internal estimates, suggesting that the cost per seat was made up of capital costs, 21 percent, IT support, 27 percent, administration, 9 percent and end-use operations 43 percent. (End user operations: The time spent by end users on the non-job related PC activities that are necessary due to the presence of PCs, such as peer support and software management) These data very clearly indicated that the team needed to consider factors other than just purchase price, since it represented less than a quarter of the total cost per seat.

IMPLEMENTATION

Get the students to share their implementation plans. What will they do over the next eight weeks? Who will do it? An important issue here is, should the team concentrate on selecting a product or a supplier? If the product is important then the team should be focussing on performance differences between various supplier desktop operating systems. What criteria should the team use? What happens if the supplier of the "best" system cannot provide 30,000 standard machines? What if the supplier of the "best" machine cannot provide global service? Alternatively, what if the "best" supplier does not have a suitable product? At some point the team will have to reconcile the product – supplier issue.

SUBSEQUENT EVENTS

The following provides a list of subsequent events that can be used at the end of class to further stimulate debate and conversation:

- After internal analysis and benchmarking, the team found that capital costs (e.g., cost of the equipment) represented less than one-quarter of the total cost of ownership on a 'cost per seat' basis. Other costs included IT support, operator 'downtime' and administration.
- The team identified 20 potential suppliers, both manufacturers and resellers (distributors). Each was sent a 21 page questionnaire covering 14 different criteria established by the team. The suppliers were not asked to provide pricing or quotes. The questionnaires were sent to the potential suppliers on May 2 and returned 10 days later.
- The questionnaires were returned May 12th and reviewed by the team that week. Three suppliers were selected for the 'shortlist' and site visits by the teams: GTC, Saba and Tricon Inc. Tricon was a $4 billion annual revenue, technology services company and distributor.
- The team felt that because of the existing supply chain structure in the market, Chevron would need to partner with both a manufacturer (e.g., GTC and Saba) and a reseller/services company (e.g., Tricon).
- On May 16 Tom Bell received a call that GTC was partnering with Tricon on the Chevron project.
- On May 19 Tom Bell called Saba and asked if they would select a reseller partner for the project. Saba selected Axiom Inc, a $3 billion annual revenues technology services company and distributor.
- Site visits conducted at facilities of the two supplier groups, GTC/Tricon and Saba/Axiom, during the week of June 9. Two locations visited for each supplier group. Agendas were based on a formal request sent out by the team the week prior.
- The team selected Saba/Axiom. The initial vote of the team was unanimous. Although GTC/Tricon had been favored going into the site visits, Saba/Axiom did a much better job in the presentations and provided the team with a higher confidence level. The team also felt there was a better cultural fit.
- The team asked for pricing from Saba/Axiom and GTC/Tricon the week prior to the site visits. However, selection of Saba/Axiom did not factor in relative pricing, although Saba's quote was viewed as "competitive".
- The teams proposal was submitted on schedule (June 20) and Board of Directors' approval was received in late June, at which time deployment planning started. The total project was valued at $188 million in equipment and $58 million in services, over five years, more than double the original estimate because of the five year timeframe. Tom Bell and the deployment team were responsible for finalizing product design, testing, project planning and preparation for roll-out, and a pilot deployment. Deployment was scheduled for January – July the following year.
- In early October, Tom Bell received a request from the Kazakhstan affiliate to deploy 1,000 desktop machines, with a total value of $2.5 million. Kazakhstan was one of Chevron's most difficult to service affiliates because of its distant location, harsh climate and undeveloped economy. This affiliate had been waiting a year to refresh its computers, and deployment had to

be made before the end of December, since access was restricted due to weather between December and May. He had to decide to whether to deploy early, with machines not fully tested and the desktop design not finalized ('beta' machines).
- Tom Bell and Ed Miller decided to deploy in Kazakhstan early. Deployment was successful and raised the credibility of GIL/CITC considerably, reducing organizational resistance to GIL.
- Full deployment went as planned during January – July the following year, covering over 700 Chevron sites in more than 90 countries.
- Total annual savings of the GIL Project were estimated at $30 million. Jim Sullivan, vice chairman, Chevron Corporation, made the following remarks in a speech following completion of the GIL project:

> The GIL Project is unique within our industry. It has created a standardized computing environment for Chevron worldwide. Whereas our competitors have focused on the cost of the desktop, this project has driven out much larger costs and has paved the way for a more flexible and reliable infrastructure by standardizing on all aspects of the network and computing environment. Immediate impacts are an overall reduction in Chevron computing costs of about $30 million per year. The common infrastructure significantly improves communication within Chevron and supports improved work processes and applications deployment. Everywhere you work in Chevron today, the PC computing environment is the same, and anyone can use any PC in Chevron worldwide to do his or her work. GIL is a world-class organizational accomplishment for Chevron.

BUSINESS PLAN OBJECTIVES

Attached in Exhibit TN1 are the business plan objectives set-up with Saba for the GIL Project. This can be introduced during wrap-up discussion. Students can be asked to review the items on the summary and comment regarding the appropriateness of each. Several seem very broad. There is also an absence of quantifiable outcomes.

Exhibit TN1

CHEVRON GIL – SABA BUSINESS PLAN OBJECTIVES

OBJECTIVES AND STRATEGIES

1. Reduce the per seat cost of GIL

- Reduce support costs
- Supply very competitively priced hardware
- Expand the number of GIL seats

2. Improve key processes

- Develop and improve a post-project order process which can be used worldwide
- Create the process and team to manage the technology pipeline
- Improve break-fix processes worldwide
- Optimize supply chain logistics and inventory levels

3. Increase reliability of GIL

- Choose hardware with high reliability
- Build processes to identify hardware problem impact and work with hardware designers
- Improve systems management techniques for both servers and workstations (Toptools, Openview)

4. Identify ways to expand use and functionality of GIL

- Explore technologies to address current requirements and potential new opportunities with HP (e.g., biometrics?)

Price Forecasting Exercise

Teaching Note

This is an excellent exercise for accomplishing a variety of objectives:
1. It interests the student in some one commodity, a fact which can be used to advantage by the instructor throughout the course.
2. It brings out the problems of forecasting specific prices, including the necessity of reaching a definite decision even in the absence of wholly adequate data.
3. It should familiarize the student with sources of information as to current and probable conditions and prices, particularly for the chosen commodity.

PRICE FORECAST AND COMMODITY COMMITMENT

The following report is a modification of the exercise in price forecasting.

You and three other members of the class have been asked to forecast the price of a commodity on December 1, 2___. So that your organization may take the most advantageous procurement action possible, your organization needs $5 million worth of this commodity for delivery any time during the month of December. The amount, $5 million worth, is based on the spot price of this commodity on October 1, 2___.

Question 1

What is the current (October 1, 2___) spot price of this commodity, based on what quotation? What is the specification of the commodity and what is the minimum amount of purchase required for the quoted price to hold? How much in weight or volume does $5 million represent?

Question 2

What spot price do you forecast for this commodity on December 1, 2___. Why?

Question 3

In view of your forecast what recommendation would you make to the executive committee of your organization regarding the purchase of this commodity? Would you advise buying now and taking delivery now or later? Would you hedge? Would you delay purchase? Anything else? What savings do you forecast from your recommendation?

Qualifications

1. The commodity selected may not be a pegged price in the market at which you are purchasing. It must be a freely fluctuating price and it must be traded on a recognized commodity exchange with published prices for both spot and futures.
2. Approval for a selected commodity must come from the instructor. No two teams may select the same commodity. Commodity selection is on a first come first served basis.
3. It is not necessary to stay with the commodities listed in the text.
4. Foreign exchange rates may be an important consideration in your decisions.
5. This report has four parts.
    a. A written report (of at least two copies) to be handed in on October __ before 5 p.m.
    b. A 5-minute class report to be orally presented during class on October __.
    c. A written evaluation report (of at least 2 copies) to be handed in before 5 p.m. December __, including the December __ actual price. The evaluation should compare the actual price with forecast. It should also include a savings (loss) estimate in view of the recommended action in early October for the weight calculated in the October report.
    d. A 1-minute class report on December __, highlighting the evaluation.
6. Group names and commodity selections to be submitted no later than 5 p.m., September __.

Option

It is within the class's option to take two side actions to make this exercise more intriguing.
1. It is possible for each team to contribute $2.00 to $5.00 to a pot. The team realizing the greatest savings wins all or part of the pot. This makes it a competitive exercise.
2. It may be possible for the class to select one forecast and one commodity of those presented and by putting $10.00 to $20.00 on the line to play the market on that commodity. This would be a noncompetitive exercise.

It is up to the class as a whole whether it wishes to exercise any part of this option.

Special Remarks

1. The amount of $5 million is in U.S. dollars. Exchange rates with foreign currencies have to be considered as part of this problem.
2. There is a commission for every commodity.
3. In the case of purchase and storage ahead of December 1, the carrying cost is 1 1/2 percent per month. There are no savings by waiting to spend until December 1.
4. If the market has a daily variation and quotes high and low and closing for the day, please be consistent and use the same type of quotation throughout. For example, it is not right to use the low quotation on October 1 and compare it to the high on December 1.

This price forecasting exercise may be modified, of course, to suit the preferences of each instructor. A few additional comments may assist in getting the best out of the exercise.

1. *Group Size*

    Normally, it is difficult to have more than 10 groups per class. About six to eight groups are, probably, preferable. Thus, the number of students per group can be adjusted to end up with the desirable total number of groups.

2. *Dates*

    There are five key dates to identify in this exercise. The intent is to have the forecast done within the first few weeks of the course for a date which falls several weeks before the end of the course. This way, excitement can build about what is happening to actual commodity prices as the course progresses, and the forecasts will be compared with actual prices before the course is completed.

    The five key dates, then, are:
    a. Date when group composition and commodity choice are to be handed in to instructor. (Suggested within 10 days of course start.)
    b. Date when current spot is identified. (Suggested: a Thursday or Friday spot price within 10 days of date (1.) above.)
    c. A forecast hand-in and reporting to the class date. (Suggested within (7) days of date (2.) above.)
    d. A date for future spot price to be forecast. (Suggested within 18 days of last class in the course - preferably a Thursday or Friday.)
    e. A date when the final report along with a brief class presentation is due. (Suggested within 7 days of date (4.) above.)

3. *Presentations and Reports*

    During the first presentation to the class it is suggested to record key data on the current price and forecast on an overhead transparency (see Exhibit TN-1). This information can subsequently be typed and reproduced for all class members and reused during the final reporting session. Having the whole class vote and keeping track of the yes and no votes on the specific recommendation made by the forecasting group also adds interest and fun. This way, the class acts as a Commodity Committee, or a Board of Directors, approving specific expenditure commitments. Each student can be asked to use his or her own voting record (see Exhibit TN-2) until the day when the final result presentations are made.

    Two reports are requested, so that the instructor can keep a file for subsequent years of reports on specific commodities, while still handing back the original to the group. It is suggested that the grading of the reports be delayed until after the second report has been handed in.

4. *Instructor's final comments*

    At the end of the exercise the instructor may wish to comment on the size of the savings or losses incurred, the quality of the presentations, the difficulties of making a good forecast, even a short-term basis, and the variety of ways business tries to deal with the expertise required, the risks involved, etc., as discussed in the chapter.

Exhibit TN-1

COMMODITY FORECASTS

Commodity	Class Vote	Current Spot	Future	Spot Forecast	Spot Actual	Savings

NAME_____

Exhibit TN-2

COMMODITY FORECASTING EXERCISE

YOUR VOTING RECORD

Commodity	Your Vote		Were You Correct? December	
	Yes	No	Yes	No
Totals				

Commodity Purchasing Game

Teaching Note

GENERAL COMMENTS

This game usually requires about 3 hours, including the post mortem after the game and a ten-minute break in the middle.

IMMEDIATE ISSUE

How much cocoa should be purchased every month?

BASIC ISSUES

1. What purchasing strategy should be pursued in operating in the commodity market?
2. What are the various trade-offs in making these strategic decisions?
3. Relation between corporate profitability and purchasing strategy.

SUGGESTED STUDENT ASSIGNMENT

Please form groups of three to eight students each (depending on class size). Read the Commodity Purchasing Game and understand Exhibit 5. Be ready to make your decision for the month of October, knowing that the spot price is 48 cents/lb. and the contribution is, therefore, 13 cents/lb.

POSSIBLE DISCUSSION QUESTIONS (FOR USE AFTER THE GAME HAS BEEN PLAYED)

1. What was each team's strategy in playing the game?
2. What is your own evaluation of your decisions?
3. How important is cocoa-purchasing performance to this company?
4. Is it realistic to tie some personal incentive for Mr. Martin in with his cocoa-purchasing performance?
5. Had you been allowed to buy futures, what would you have done differently?
6. What was the key cost elements and trade-offs as you saw them?
7. Do you think a group best makes this type of decision?

Setup Instructions Before the Game

1. Identify each team by a letter A, B, C, etc. Try to keep the total number of teams to ten or less.
2. Review the decision process. On the basis of the October spot price of 48 cents and the contribution of 13 cents, you decide the quantity that you will purchase for October. You will hand in this decision on the decision report. I will then subsequently give you usage information and the new spot price for the next month. You will then have approximately 10 min. to decide how much to purchase in November.
3. The starting inventory is 200,000 lbs. and your starting cumulative cost is 0, calculate the October contribution before I give you the actual quantity used in October and the new November spot price.
4. If your team is incapable of making a decision by the time limit indicated you will automatically purchase 700,000 lbs. There is a $500 penalty in commission for a calculation mistake and the error will be corrected. For this reason at least two people should do the figure work on Exhibit 5. In column 5 of Exhibit 5 please note that there is a $1,000 commission loss if, at any time, your inventory exceeds 1,200,000 lbs. and you will not be able to claim any contribution on excess pounds purchased. Instead you will take a penalty of 6 cents/lb. on excess inventory sold off to bring the end of month inventory back to 1,200,000 lbs.
5. Make sure that every team has at least 13 report forms as shown in Exhibit 5. Each group may be asked to make up its own, or these may be printed ahead of time and distributed in the group.
6. Ask the teams if they wish to play for money. Almost always they want to play for $1 each with the winning team taking the whole pot and the second team acting as an auditor of all the winning team's figures.

Running of the Game

In the running of the game the following suggestions may be helpful.

1. For the first decision ask each team to submit its decision report. This first report will show no cumulative commission to date, but will show the number of pounds to be purchased.
2. After each team has submitted its decision report, show on an overhead transparency the November first data as enclosed. Show the October production first while covering the November price information. Allow the teams to go through their October calculations for several minutes, and then show the remainder of the transparency to allow them to work on the November decision. This procedure avoids confusion about the month to which the contribution needs to be applied. Occasionally, teams confuse November contribution with October contribution.
3. Announce the time allowed for the November decision, normally about 10 minutes, and collect the decision reports from each team. These reports should now show the October commission, which should equal the cumulative commission to date.
4. On the master transparency shown in the teaching notes record each team's cumulative commission on the period #1 and rank each team. Show the first month's results to the group.

5. This procedure is repeated month by month. In February, May, and July news bulletins are issued to the group. The content of these bulletins are shown in the instructor's notes on the following pages.
6. The instructor may wish to give the group a 15-minute break somewhere in the middle of the game. This depends on the schedule.
7. For the final period – September 1, remind the teams that the end of month inventory target is 200,000 lbs. There will be penalties for underages or overages. Those penalties will be disclosed only after the September 1 purchase decision has been made. (See final instructions)

NOVEMBER FIRST
Spot Price: 46.6 Cents per Pound   Contribution: 14.4 Cents per Pound

December	March	May
42.12	43.38	44.20
October Production: 650,000 Pounds		

DECEMBER FIRST
Spot Price: 49.8 Cents per Pound   Contribution: 11.2 Cents per Pound

December	March	May
44.90	45.90	46.80
November Production: 500,000 Pounds		

JANUARY FIRST
Spot Price: 53.2 Cents per Pound   Contribution: 7.8 Cents per Pound

March	May	July
49.64	50.54	51.40
December Production: 430,000 Pounds		

FEBRUARY FIRST
Spot Price: 61.0 Cents per Pound   Contribution: 0 Cents per Pound

March	May	July
54.24	55.18	56.02
January Production: 640,000 Pounds News Bulletin		

MARCH FIRST
Spot Price: 58.0 Cents per Pound Contribution: 3.0 Cents per Pound

March	May	July
50.50	51.46	52.38
February Production: 600,000 Pounds		

APRIL FIRST
Spot Price: 54.8 Cents per Pound Contribution: 6.2 Cents per Pound

May	July	September
48.42	49.22	50.08
March Production: 550,000 Pounds		

MAY FIRST
Spot Price: 55.2 Cents per Pound Contribution: 5.8 Cents per Pound

May	July	September
48.50	49.48	50.30
April Production: 280,000 Pounds News Bulletin		

JUNE FIRST
Spot Price: 55.6 Cents per Pound Contribution: 5.4 Cents per Pound

July	September	December
48.90	49.78	50.76
May Production: 160,000 Pounds		

JULY FIRST
Spot Price: 53.8 Cents per Pound Contribution: 7.2 Cents per Pound

July	September	December
46.48	47.48	48.88
June Production: 140,000 Pounds News Bulletin		

AUGUST FIRST
Spot Price: 55.8 Cents per Pound   Contribution: 5.2 Cents per Pound

September	December	March
49.68	51.10	52.12
July Production: 150,000 Pounds		

SEPTEMBER FIRST
Spot Price: 60.6 Cents per Pound   Contribution: 0.4 Cents per Pound

September	December	March
52.64	54.36	55.84
August Production: 400,000 Pounds		

FINAL INSTRUCTIONS

- Calculate Cumulative Commission as usual

  Then Adjust:

  For each 10,000 lbs. <u>over</u> or <u>under</u> 200,000 subtract: $30.00

  For Cumulative Commission

  September Production 900,000 lbs.

February 1

WALL STREET JOURNAL

SOME CANDY BARS ARE SMALLER AND DEARER AS A RESULT OF HIGHER COCOA AND SUGAR PRICES

- Hershey reduced the size of its chocolate bars.
- Cadbury increased the price of its chocolate bars.
- Nestle did not make any changes.
- Midwest is studying the situation.

Cocoa prices have climbed strongly in the past year and a half, reflecting the decline in world cocoa production to levels below the rate of consumption. Accra cocoa, a base African grade, is quoted at 61.0 cents a pound, for example, more than double the 19-year low of 22¾ cents a pound.

Record cocoa production of 1.5 million long tons last year depressed bean prices then, but succeeding smaller crops have forced manufacturers and importers to draw on reserve stocks to meet marketing needs. This has provided the base for the price rise.

May 1

BARRON'S

BULL MARKET IN COCOA BEANS COMES TO A HALT

The bull market in cocoa beans in which New York prices nearly tripled, from a nineteen-year low of 22¾ cents a pound in the middle of last year, to a seven-year, 61.0 cents high last February, has come to a pause. Part of the recent easiness is due to a sharp cutback, following the February price peaks, in European grindings. These may reduce this year's world grindings below expectations. Therefore, the size of the current year's crops, coupled with African government marketing policies, holds the key to future cocoa prices. Trade forecast on the new crops do not appear, however, until late summer, and reliable estimates are not likely before fall.

In cocoa futures market — used profitably and extensively by large manufacturers, dealers and brokers — distant deliveries are selling for below spot. The nearby May contract, already absorbing heavy deliveries, is traded around 48.50 cents a pound, following a slump from April 6's 51.82 cents to 47.40 cents on April 17. Similarly, the July delivery, which climbed from 41.92 cents on October 31 to a 56.48 cents high on February 14, now is selling at around 49.48 cents. Reflecting approximate carrying charges, the September futures sell at 50.30 cents, and the December new-crop option at 51.10 cents.

Tops and Bottoms

Current conditions could well bring a world crop as large as, or even in excess of the 1,507,000 long ton record (two years ago). Consumption appears to have leveled off at an annual average of just under 1,400,000 long tons. In that event, the price of cocoa (basis good, fermented Accra at New York), is likely to average close to or below 50 cents.

On the other hand, an explosive price situation would develop if adverse weather holds next season's world output considerably below anticipated grindings of around 1,400,000 tons. This possibility, plus the low level of manufacturers stocks, could combine to boost cocoa bean prices to or above the 80 cents mark — a level last seen nine years ago.

July 1

WALL STREET JOURNAL
DROP IN WORLD COCOA OUTPUT

Gill and Duffuss figures production in the last two sessions fell about 283,000 tons short of world consumption, pegged currently at more than 1,400,000 tons. Drawing from surplus stocks to meet demand, users in two years wiped out more than half the 450,000 tons build up during the preceding seven seasons.

Adverse weather and insects were important factors behind the production decline. But lower cocoa prices and higher costs also discouraged some grower efforts.

In Ghana, the largest cocoa producer, for example, an estimated 30,000 tons of beans from the last main crop weren't harvested because, growers complained, prices wouldn't cover their labor and other costs. Those unharvested beans about equaled the 8 percent decline in Ghana's last season productions, and cocoa officials say an additional 20,000 tons of Ghana cocoa were smuggled out of the country to fetch higher prices elsewhere.

Ghana buys all cocoa from its producers at a set price and then sells it in the world market. To boost production this year, the government raised the price paid to its growers (some producers complained the increase wasn't enough), and in the past 10 days devalued its currency 30 percent. This latest move will put more native currency in the hands of producers to pay higher wages and buy more fertilizer. Officials intend to keep selling cocoa for export at market prices.

Prices on the New York Cocoa Exchange have sagged recently. One reason: Traders suspected that consumption, as measured by cocoa grindings, is being slowed down by higher cocoa bean prices. However, last Friday, grindings figures for the United Kingdom and the United States large cocoa consumers, were released. The cocoa trade generally thought the figures indicate consumption is holding up well.

United States cocoa bean grindings in the second quarter of this year were 158,400,000 pounds, the Department of Commerce announced. This was 0.6 percent below the record high grindings in the second quarter last year of 159,300,000 pounds. The report confirmed a recent trade survey that grindings were only a fraction under a year ago of the second period.

The United Kingdom cocoa bean grindings in the second quarter were 26,700 long tons, off 2.6 percent from a year earlier. But dealers said this was a smaller decline than anticipated. In the first quarter this year, grindings fell more than 10 percent from last year's like period.

Meanwhile, long-range cocoa consumption is projected to rise steadily, with a big boost from communist countries, which heretofore bought very little. Says the foreign agricultural service of the United States Department of Agriculture: "Rising income levels in the U.S.S.R. and Eastern Europe have made this area a new and rapidly expanding market for cocoa use, while consumption in the traditional areas of Western Europe and North America will probably increase at a slower rate."

Team	1	2	3	4	5	6	7	8	Forecast 9	10	11	12	Final
A													
B													
C													
D													
E													
F													
G													
H													
I													
J													
K													

COMMENTS AFTER THE GAME HAS BEEN COMPLETED

Congratulate the winning team and remind everyone that the game is only a game with all its limitations. There are some special reasons for playing this game as part of this course. The case method allows everyone to walk away from decisions made without having to live with them. This is not true in this game. Chance events beyond purchasing control, and risk, are all part of the materials job. Almost nowhere is this more evident than in purchases in the commodity market. This game also forms a change of pace and an opportunity to test group work and each participant's personal involvement.

Now, let's take a closer look at the game itself. Let's also try to avoid hindsight. In view of the actual price information, it is very obvious how decisions should have been made. The art is in making reasonable decisions without perfect information. It is useful to remember that all the data given in this particular game is live data. Not one figure was altered from actual market reports. The articles were exact copies as they appeared in the magazines and so on. There is no disguise. It was an actual year in the cocoa market that we operated in. We did not give you the year mainly because we did not want people to start looking in the library.

At the start we knew the spot price as of October 1 and we had some idea of the world situation. We knew we had 200,000 lbs. of stock. We also had a fair idea on the consumption record and its variation. We also knew what the maximum limit on inventory was. We also knew stockout costs and inventory costs and the final inventory target. On the basis of these things we can see that the company got a contribution of 13 cents at the price of 48 cents. We also knew that the stockout costs compared to the inventory carrying cost was a ratio of 15 to 1. Therefore, dealing with a 12-month period, it is not particularly smart to stockout to save inventory carrying charges.

Now, the other decision and the far more difficult one is the strategy one. The two most obvious alternatives are to buy hand to mouth or to buy ahead. These we can put in a decision tree setting with the three chance events being an increase in price, price remaining the same, and price going down.

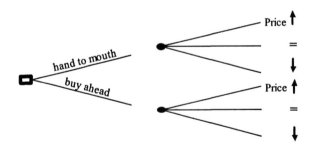

What are the consequences to management of these three events? Looking at the October 1 position, we can see that the company is in a reasonable profit position on cocoa at the moment at 13 cents contribution. If the price increases, what happens to our profit position? It obviously worsens substantially. If the price remains the same we'll continue to be in a reasonable profit position, and if the price goes down we'll be even better off. If we buy hand to mouth and the price increases we're going to be losing substantially. If the price remains the same, all we've done is incurred a minor inventory carrying charge of 0.4 cents/lb. If the price decreases we'll be able to take advantage of the further price decrease. Now, on the basis of the information available we have to put probabilities to each of these three likelihoods. Your own degree of risk aversion also comes into play here. How willing are you to gamble a good profit for an even better one? Are you the type that says: "A bird in the hand..." It seems that unless one is almost sure that the price will go down further, and substantially so, it is not particularly good strategy to start off with a hand-to-mouth philosophy. This is further reinforced by the high usage in the fall and early winter period. We're right at a time when some key decisions need to be made. A little later on, when usage is minor, it doesn't really matter how well we buy, because the profit impact will not be very great. Given the 1,200,000 lb. end of month inventory maximum, as of October 1, the opportunity to buy forward only extends as far out as December, since the fall is a high requirements period. Therefore, it is not unreasonable to ask as of October 1, what is the maximum increase in price possible by December and what is the maximum decrease possible?

It is not easy on the basis of the information to predict price reasonably. But, it is exactly this uncertainty that should lead to a reasonable insurance position. We see that an upswing starts to occur after November and this leaves every team in the uncomfortable position of having to decide whether to jump in now, or to try to ride out the price increase until it decreases again at a later date. And period by period the price gets worse.

It is almost impossible to predict short-term price movements. We see that in February they're talking about oversupply in the news and in May they're already starting to cry about a tightening of supply and an overestimation of production in May. It is impossible for someone to be able to predict these short-term moves exactly. It is the long-term trend which, therefore, is the one that needs to be observed most closely. The touchy questions regarding the long-term trend are whether turn-around periods are ahead or not.

It is possible for teachers who've played this game several times to share the performances of the current group with those of earlier ones by retaining the plastic score sheet of the type enclosed. It is suggested that the cumulative commission for every team be posted as soon as possible after every period on a transparency and projected onto a screen in front of the class. Each team should be ranked with a different color transparency pen to show its relative position to all other ones. This really adds to the competitiveness and excitement of the exercise.

In using the monthly information sheets to avoid confusion in the teams as to which period the contribution should be calculated for, it is a good idea to separate the usage information for the previous month from the new price information for the current month. Even if the usage is given 30 seconds ahead, this allows the teams to avoid that rather common mistake.

Since it is not possible to forecast either a decrease or an increase, the strategic perspective would be to ask if either event (price increase or decrease) is equally acceptable to the company.

CHAPTER 10

Purchasing Logistics Services

Topics Covered

Organization for Logistics Decisions
    Third-Party Logistics Service Providers
    Purchasing's Involvement in
        Transportation
FOB Terms and Incoterms
Freight Classifications
Selection of Mode and Carrier
    Inherent Advantages of Different
        Transport Modes
    Mode of Transport
    Freight Terminals
    Motor Carriers
    Less-than-Truckload (LTL) Carriers
    Truckload (TL) Carriers
    Rail Carriers and Intermodal Shipments
    Air Carriers
    Expedited Transportation
    Small-Shipment Services
    Same-Day Services
    Forwarders and Brokers
    Ocean Carriers and Ports
Freight Rates
Documentation in Freight Shipments
Expediting and Tracing Shipments
Loss or Damage Claims
Payment of Freight Bills
    Demurrage
Developing a Logistics Strategy
Questions for Review and Discussion
References
Cases
    Great Western Bank
    Geo Products
    Specialty Brewers

QUIZ RESPONSES

C | 1. Intermodal transportation refers to:

   a. the movement of goods in trailers or containers via at least two surface transportation carriers.
   b. the movement of goods in trailers or containers via at least two air carriers.
   c. the movement of goods in trailers or containers via rail coupled with at least one other transport mode, such as truck or air.
   d. the movement of goods in trailers or containers via at least two ocean shipping lines.
   e. the movement of goods in trailers or containers via truck and air carriers.

A | 2. Intermodal transportation has increased due in large part to:

   a. increased reliability from technological and operational improvements.
   b. the improved service levels from rail carriers following the consolidation of railways through mergers and acquisitions.
   c. the deterioration of roads, bridges, and highways leading to an increased reliance on rail.
   d. the improvements in roadways throughout North America.
   e. none of the above since intermodal business is declining, not increasing.

D | 3. A 1995 study by the Center for Advanced Purchasing Studies found that:

   a. the involvement of purchasing in inbound transportation decisions was insignificant.
   b. ninety percent of those surveyed use an outside agency to determine transport and routing.
   c. inbound transportation reported to purchasing in slightly more than half of the surveyed firms.
   d. the marketing department handled all inbound transport decisions.
   e. inbound transportation reported to purchasing in over 90 percent of the surveyed firms.

Purchasing Logistics 201

A | 4. In many large organizations:

   a. there normally will be full-time transportation or logistics specialists.
   b. transport decisions typically are handled by the marketing department.
   c. transport decisions on incoming items are handled by the buyer or purchasing manager.
   d. transportation decisions will not significantly affect costs.
   e. an outside agency typically is used to determine transport routings and rates.

E | 5. A transportation strategy should include consideration of issues such as:

   a. fuel/energy consumption and air and water pollution.
   b. setting realistic delivery schedules.
   c. consolidation of freight.
   d. alternative transport modes.
   e. all of the above.

E | 6. Integrated carriers (truck-air) like UPS and Federal Express are able to serve or provide provide which of the following:

   a. deferred services.
   b. heavy air cargo.
   c. time-definite services.
   d. a and b.
   e. a, b and c.

B | 7. When selecting freight carriers, buyers are most concerned with:

   a. intermodal capabilities.
   b. on-time deliveries.
   c. geographic coverage.
   d. shipment security.
   e. types of equipment available.

C | 8. A 1991 study by the Center for Advanced Purchasing Studies found that the most influential factor in determining the mode of transportation is:

   a. shipment size.
   b. cost of transport.
   c. required delivery date.
   d. reliability and service quality.
   e. time in transit.

B | 9. Classifications for rate-making purposes are driven by:

   a. size, shape, content, and weight.
   b. density, stowability, handling, and liability.
   c. stowability, handling, content, and distance.
   d. density, handling, size, and distance.
   e. handling, liability, shape, and distance.

E | 10. The selection of the FOB point is important to the purchaser, for it determines:

   a. Who pays the carrier.
   b. When legal title to goods being shipped passes to the buyer.
   c. Who is responsible for preparing and pursuing loss or damage claims.
   d. Who routes the freight.
   e. All of the above.

True and False

T	1.	Third-party logistics service providers are firms such as freight bill auditors, site selection consultants, and carriers (that may or may not own any assets) that act as intermediaries between trading partners, for example, shippers and carriers.
F	2.	Deferred service refers to the use of air transportation for ground packages so that the carrier can meet the buyer's schedule.
F	3.	The key document in the movement of goods is the bill of material (BOM).
F	4.	Two effective cost reduction strategies are use of a large supply base of carriers and short-term contracts.
T	5.	Congestion is one of the major issues faced by logistics decision-makers due to an aging air traffic control system, antiquated infrastructure (roads, bridges, tunnels, ports), citizens concerned about noise, traffic, and safety while also demanding low cost goods and services, and stiffer environmental regulations internationally.
F	6.	FOB Destination normally is the preferable freight method for the buyer to specify, because the buyer then has the legal right to specify how purchased items are to be shipped.
F	7.	The problem of selecting transportation suppliers is more difficult than that of selecting suppliers of product, since there is not yet available a supplier directory (such as Thomas Register) of freight carriers.
T	8.	The term FOB stands for "Free on Board."
T	9.	A recent study of large organizations using JIT found that savings in reduced inventory offset additional transportation costs.
T	10.	The practice of contracting with a core carrier, and having the carrier place staff on-site to manage day-to-day transport decisions is called co-location.

The Great Western Bank

Teaching Note

IMMEDIATE ISSUE

How can the buyer recover the funds spent for the twelve destroyed machines?

BASIC ISSUES

1. The interpretation of F.O.B. point.
2. The unilateral changes by buyer or seller.
3. Recovery procedures for claims.
4. The practice of paying for items not yet delivered.

SUGGESTED STUDENT ASSIGNMENT

1. If you were in the position of the buyer, what actions do you now take?
2. Did the buyer handle this situation correctly? What should have been said about the F.O.B. point and transport method in the purchase order?

SUGGESTED DISCUSSION QUESTIONS

1. What is the meaning of the F.O.B. terms in this case?
2. Who is right in this dispute?
3. What are the primary objectives of the buyer here?
4. What alternatives are open to the buyer here?
5. What is your assessment of the supplier's reaction to this situation?
6. Would you place an order for an additional 12 machines with this vendor?
7. Is this type of situation avoidable?

DISCUSSION

While the F.O.B. shipping point transportation terms do specify that the buyer owns the goods while in transit and must file and process any damage claims, if applicable, with the carrier, that would not apply in this situation. If the seller, Data-Max, had not complied with the terms of the purchase agreement, e.g., had not shipped the right merchandise or had changed the agreed-upon shipment method stated in the contract (without the assent of the buyer), then the purchase contract has been voided. Payment of the invoice is a clerical function and payment before receipt of merchandise is a common practice of many firms. The fact that the invoice was paid (in this case, in error) does not mean that the contract was completed.

If the P.O clearly spelled out the method of shipment and the seller deviated from that method without agreement of the buyer, the fact that a cheaper shipping method was used — and it actually turned out to be a much-more-expensive method since satisfactory goods were not received — then the responsibility of filing and collecting damages from the truckline falls on the seller.

The buyer should demand immediate replacement of the 12 machines, and perhaps attempt to negotiate a price adjustment in return for the advance payment of the invoice.

Geo Products

Teaching Note

IMMEDIATE ISSUE

Develop a transportation management strategy for review by the plant manager.

BASIC ISSUES

1. Outsourcing transportation
2. Customer order fulfilment
3. Distribution
4. Cost control
5. Customer service
6. Business planning and budgeting
7. Vendor selection and negotiation
8. Strategic use of logistics

SUGGESTED STUDENT ASSIGNMENT

As Sharon Lee, what is your assessment of how Geo manages its transportation activities? What recommendations would you make to the plant manager regarding Geo's transportation activities and why?

ANALYSIS

Overview:

Sharon Lee, supervisor of purchasing and transportation at Geo is faced with making a recommendation to the plant manager with respect to the company's future transportation needs. Expanding sales and production are the primary drivers behind the need to re-evaluate Geo's transportation activities.

Managing transportation activities for kitchen and bathroom cabinets can present some interesting challenges. First, size, as opposed to weight, represents the limiting characteristic. This may create a need for unique packaging and storage containers. Second, construction and renovation deadlines may drive expediting activities. Third, the transportation function can provide a competitive advantage through the development of low cost, timely delivery capabilities.

Geo's Competitive Position

Geo competed in the high end of the market and its customers were likely both in the new home construction and home renovation markets. Quality, design features (e.g. style) and availability are more important than cost in this segment. Geo produced based on confirmed customer orders only, and its customers likely include wholesalers, distributors and large retail operations. It is unlikely that these groups hold substantial inventory, and therefore, placed orders with Geo based on orders from their customers. Consequently, rapid delivery in Geo's market segment is a competitive advantage. Failure to provide the finished product quickly to the end customer, either homebuilders or renovators, could result in a lost sale. As a result, Geo cannot afford to sacrifice its delivery capabilities.

As one might expect, the cabinet market is seasonal, which has implications for production and customer delivery requirements. Note that Geo serves the southeast states, so factors such as weather are unlikely to affect sales, as might be the situation in the northern state. However, Geo's sales and production likely peak between March to October, slowing in the winter and Christmas period.

Evaluation of Geo's Current Transportation Activities

Geo changed its transportation strategy approximately nine years ago in an effort to reduce operating costs. It remains to be seen, however, if this was an appropriate decision given the transportation needs of the organization. The case provides some data with respect to transportation costs at Geo:

Service Provider	Current Total	Cost/Mile	Miles
Eastern	$160,000*	$1.00*	160,000
Trucking Services Company (TSC)	$200,000*	1.25	160,000
Total	$360,000	$2.25	160,000

* Data provided in the case

The case indicates that Geo produced 30,000 units last year, which would result in $330,000 in revenue from cabinet deliveries, based on the $11.00 delivery charge. Consequently, Geo failed to recover approximately $110,000 in delivery costs last year (costs of $360,000 + $80,000 compared to only $330,000 in customer revenue). With sales expected to increase, the magnitude of this loss can be expected in also increase. The breakeven point is $14.67 per delivery ($440,000/30,000) or $2.25 per mile (assuming equivalent cost for all shipments). It remains to be seen, however, if such charges are fair based on competitive cost structures.

The use of fixed capacity for transportation does not seem reasonable for a seasonal business. With only two trucks available, it appears that Geo does not have sufficient capacity to meet demand during peak months. This can be a critical problem for a business where delivery is important. A more appropriate arrangement would be to structure a transportation agreement that provides cost-effective, flexible transportation capacity, and would allow the company to meet delivery requirements in peak months while eliminating costs in non-peak months.

The current use of common carriers to back-up the existing fleet offers the worst combination of high cost and poor service. High cost because of a lack of pre-negotiated pricing arrangements and poor service due to late deliveries. As identified above, this also adds to the cost recovery problem.

Delivery Pricing Structure

Geo charges $11.00 per unit for delivery, regardless of size, number of units ordered or delivered, or shipping location. Note that such an arrangement penalizes customer located close to Geo, and offers an advantage to those located far away. Although not mentioned in the case, the delivery charge could be an industry standard, so not to disqualify Geo from supporting sales in more distant locations.

Despite the possible need for complying with industry standards regarding delivery charges, this situation does require some form of delivery pricing schedule. For example, Geo could provide volume discounts, based on making single versus multiple deliveries. This is obviously not a problem that Sharon could tackle alone; she would need to consult with the marketing department before any changes were made. However, this could be a win/win situation for Geo and its customers. By initiating a delivery fee schedule that encouraged more efficient delivery arrangements, Geo could pass on at least some of the savings through lower costs. Under the current situation there is no incentive for Geo's customers to consider the impact of delivery costs when placing orders. Therefore, they could place a series of small orders in order to keep their inventories low without a delivery cost penalty, as opposed to combining orders.

ANALYSIS OF ALTERNATIVES

The case offers three possible alternatives for Sharon to consider:

1. Status quo, using common carriers to support extra volume.
2. Lease an additional truck.
3. Re-structure the current agreement.

For reasons provided above, the first two alternatives are unlikely to address the transportation needs at Geo fully. A more feasible course of action would be to re-structure the current agreement to include the flexible capacity to allow cost effective, reliable deliveries during periods of peak demand, while still allowing the company to avoid unnecessary costs as a result of unused capacity during periods of low demand. Owning (or leasing) a fleet does not make sense for Geo, and working with a transportation service provider with the capability to dedicate resources based on the fluctuations in seasonal deliveries that Geo experiences is important.

As an aside, the home construction and renovation markets are very cyclical. A downturn in the market could put Geo in a cost-cutting mode. Keeping transportation costs flexible is also an important consideration. This was what happened nine years prior when Geo restructured its transportation strategy.

Sharon can either approach other vendors or negotiate a new agreement with the current TSC. The advantage of dealing with a large transportation service provider would be their ability to cover Geo's requirements during periods of peak demand and eliminating the need for Geo to own (or lease) trucks.

The case does not indicate if Geo has the ability to terminate the existing agreement without penalty, or if it is just obligated to provide reasonable notice to the TSC. Even if a penalty exists, there is no reason for Geo not to consider restructuring its transportation services agreement with the current vendor. For example, the two existing leased vehicles could be used by the current TSC as part of the new agreement. Maintaining control over a large account, such as Geo, would be a substantial incentive to any trucking company, especially given the opportunities for growth. This is an obvious opportunity for negotiation.

The case does not present any alternatives with respect to the pricing structure. However, this problem could also be addressed as part of Sharon's recommendations. By re-structuring its delivery fees Geo could recover its costs and potentially reduce transportation expenses by encouraging customers to plan shipments. Such an arrangement could also mitigate the need for additional trucking capacity. Consultation with sales and marketing would be required before such a proposal could go forward to the plant manager.

Specialty Brewers

Teaching Note

IMMEDIATE ISSUE

How to respond to the IHS offer to act as a single supplier of all hops requirements and to ship as required.

BASIC ISSUES

1. Single sourcing.
2. Transportation considerations and JIT.
3. Additional services provided by suppliers.
4. Implementing change.

SUGGESTED STUDENT ASSIGNMENT

1. As Al Mayfair, what is your assessment of the IHS proposal?
2. Do you have enough information now to be able to make a decision? If not, what additional information would you like and would it be available?
3. What do you suspect your answer would be to this proposal?

POSSIBLE DISCUSSION QUESTIONS

1. Why would IHS want to propose a deal such as this one?
2. What are the advantages of this proposal to Specialty Brewers?
3. What are the disadvantages of this proposal to Specialty Brewers?
4. How relevant are the transportation costs in this decision?
5. What are the key issues in this situation?
6. What are your major concerns with this proposal?
7. Where would the strongest opposition to this proposal come from within your own organization?
8. Who would be the strongest support for this kind of proposal in your own organization?

DISCUSSION

This is another one of those cases where some figure pushing is necessary to get a thorough understanding of the financial impact of the proposal. The calculations follow.

The Current Situation

Specialty is currently buying 1,039 pallets per year and storing the annual requirements of each brewery. In this process it is incurring the following costs:

1. Purchase cost - 1,039 x $2,900 per pallet = $3,013,100
2. Transportation cost - $79,389
3. Extra warehouse cost - 30% of 671 pallets (201 pallets for 3.6 months [say 4 months] at $6.00 per month per pallet is $24 + $4 per pallet one time extra charge is $28) so the total is $28 x 201 pallets is $5,600. (The assumption is made that outside storage is used up before inside storage is started.)
4. Money tied up in inventory is 1,039 pallets x $2,900 per pallet ☐ 2 x .12 = $180,786.
5. This comes to a total of $3,278,903 plus in-house warehousing costs which have not been identified and extra transportation costs to bring the hops in from outside storage to in-house for the 5 locations where some outside storage is used.

THE IHS PROPOSAL

The total costs previewed under the IHS proposal would be as follows:

1. Purchase costs - 1,039 x $2,900 per pallet = $3,013,100. This figure is exactly the same as the current purchase cost on the current plan.
2. The money cost would be - 1,039 pallets x $2,900 per pallet ÷ 2 x .08 = $120,524. (This assumes a prime rate of 7%).
3. Warehouse costs 1,039 pallets x $4 x 12 months ÷ 2 = $24,936.
4. The transportation costs if all shipments are moved in individual pallets would amount to $210,611. This is obtained by multiplying the last column in Exhibit 1 with the total number of pallets required shown in the first column on the same exhibit. These figures are reproduced in the table below. Obviously it does not make sense to ship to each location one pallet at a time and incur the very high freight charges. Therefore, it is necessary to look at shipping in larger quantities. Focusing on the larger breweries, first shows that Albany is using 308 pallets. At 46 pallets per truckload, this means about 7 full truckloads per year. Shipping in truckload lots would save almost $61,000 in freight cost alone. This would easily justify the additional investment in a truckload inventory as opposed to a one pallet inventory. The marginal additional investment is about $90,000 ÷ 2 = $45,000. Add a carrying charge of 12%. This would only amount to about $5,400 interest in inventory tied up.

However, since this would reduce the money paid to IHS, the marginal difference would only by 4% instead of 12% and amount to about $1,800 additional cost. The same reasoning could be applied to Cleveland and Dayton resulting in potential freight savings of about $23,000 at each location. Combining the 3 Florida locations in 1 truckload could probably save at least another $10,000 in freight. Using 1 trip to deliver to Boise, Billings and Cheyenne and, possibly, Omaha might also achieve further transportation savings.

The Trade-off Between Transportation Charges and Money Tied Up in Inventory

It is obvious from a comparison for the figures for the two situations that the major saving from the IHS proposal arises from their lower capital charge versus the internal Specialty Brewers 12% rate. Thus, if IHS holds the inventory for Specialty Brewers a saving of $60,000 is possible as long as the interest rate charged is 8%. If interest rates rise, this figure will become less attractive and if interest rates fall the savings would be greater. Much depends on the financial situation of Specialty Brewers. The supplier is offering to finance hops inventory and would free up about 3 million dollars capital at the beginning of the year for tie up in hops inventory. Over the year as a whole this would average out to about 1.5 million dollars of cash flow which could be used for other purposes in the brewery. If the return on this money is likely to be greater than what the supplier charges, then this may be an attractive proposition. The higher freight charges can be significantly offset if Al decides to ship in truckload lots, rather than less than truckload lots to each brewery. Shipping in individual pallet loads does not look attractive financially. For locations such as Albany, Columbus and Dayton individual pallet loads would represent one to two days inventory and might be considered too small a shipping quantity for these breweries, anyway.

INTERNAL WAREHOUSING COSTS

The way the case is written, it implies that no matter what quantity of hops are kept in storage, the full hops storage area represents a charge on each brewery. At the moment, no charge has been made under the current system for in-house storage of hops. This probably not realistic.

OBVIOUS CONCLUSIONS

1. The primary advantage of the IHS proposal is IHS' willingness to finance the hops inventory. This will be attractive only if the interest rates in New York prime + 1% is less than the internal rate of return and Specialty Brewers and/or the company is in a cash bind.
2. Freight rates are significantly higher unless shipments are made in full truckloads or shipments are combined to make a full truckload to roughly the same geographical areas.
3. The cost of outside storage now is minimal. There is no recognition currently of transportation costs from outside storage to each local brewery.

4. Unless local hops storage areas can be converted to other cold storage use (beer or other ingredients) or other uses (expansion), the supplier's willingness to store at $4 per pallet per month just adds extra out-of-pocket cost.
5. There is still a question of safety stocks as well. Presently each brewery would want to keep at least several weeks of hops supply in each location at a minimum.
6. At the heart of this problem is the issue that hops are harvested only once per year in the Northwest part of the country. This creates a need for storage. Is there any chance that anyone growing hops in the southern hemisphere might become a hops supplier?
7. Tying into one supplier for hops has some advantages, but also some standard risks associated with single sourcing.
8. The case already lists a number of pros and cons of each alternative.
9. If we assume that the internal storage costs for Specialty Brewers are about the same as for the supplier, then trade-offs between financing and transportation charges become the heart of this cases. If the suggested transportation changes are made it might be possible to ship for anywhere between $80,000 to $100,000.

Al would do well to find out from the finance area in the organization how welcome supplier financing of hops inventory would be due to the financial situation in the organization. Secondly, he should check out the local hops storage considerations and alternate usage of the space, should smaller quantities be ordered at one time. Thirdly, he should determine the optimal freight pattern for all of the breweries and a combination of the breweries to ensure lowest overall transportation costs for Specialty Brewers.

It is possible that some savings might accrue to Specialty Brewers from this action. They are likely to be relatively small, however. The key question of the price paid for the hops has not been addressed in the case itself. Concentrating all purchases with one supplier should be rewarded in some improvement in price. That might make the overall proposition substantially more attractive.

No mention has been made of quality considerations. Is it possible that hops stored by IHS might remain in better condition than hops stored at each individual brewery?

CONCLUSION

What IHS is proposing is a sort of systems contract. It is certainly in tune with the notions advanced under Just-In-Time, supplier based reduction and lowering of inventories. Because hops are a natural product, inventory level reductions are illusory here, however. It is more a matter of where in the supply chain they are being stored.

CHAPTER 11

Investment Recovery

Topics Covered

U.S. Environmental Initiatives
Canadian Environmental Initiatives
International Environmental Initiatives
Benefits of Effective Disposal
Categories of Material for Disposal
    Excess or Surplus Materials
    Obsolete Material or Equipment
    Rejected End Products
    Scrap Material
    Waste
    Hazardous Waste
Responsibility for Material Disposal

Keys to Profitable Disposal
Disposal Channels
Disposal Procedures
    Investment Recovery Examples
Selecting the Right Disposal Partner
Questions for Review and Discussion
References
Cases
    Nova Stamping Company
    Ornex

QUIZ RESPONSES

B   1. In order to return scrap to the manufacturer from whom it was purchased, either for cash or for credit on other later purchases:

       a. the material normally must be in short supply.
       b. the firm must be a large consumer.
       c. there normally must be at least two suppliers.
       d. the quantity involved must be small.
       e. all of the above.

D   2. Stock which is in excess of a reasonable requirement of the organization that arises because of errors in the amount bought or because anticipated production did not materialize is called:

       a. waste.
       b. obsolete.
       c. scrap.
       d. excess.
       e. rejected.

B   3. The Environmentally Preferable Purchasing Program:

       a. is an international initiative developed and managed by an agency of the United Nations.
       b. incorporates key environmental factors with traditional price and performance considerations in purchasing decisions.
       c. was developed by the Canadian parliament to encourage and assist provincial agencies in making purchasing decisions.
       d. was developed by the International Standards Organization and follows the format of ISO 9000.
       e. mandates the use of certain chemicals and compounds in a variety of industries around the world.

C 4. International environmental initiatives that affect supply management and investment recovery:

   a. are non-existent and unlikely to be enacted since it is difficult to get nations to agree.
   b. parallel the guidelines developed by the U.S. Environmental Protection Agency.
   c. include a certification process for environmental management systems known as ISO 14000.
   d. are codified as international law under the authority of the European Union.
   e. are in effect, but difficult to interpret because of different country standards.

E 5. Which of the following methods may be used to dispose of material:

   a. use elsewhere within the firm.
   b. return to the supplier for cash or credit.
   c. donate the material to a charitable organization.
   d. utilize a non-profit waste exchanger to find a user for the material.
   e. all of the above.

C 6. The Internet has:

   a. not been used widely in investment recovery initiatives.
   b. been used only as a marketing tool, but not for transactions.
   c. been used to locate and purchase used machinery and equipment.
   d. not been used to sell to another division of the company.
   e. been used for transactions, but not as a marketing tool.

E 7. Efforts to deal with hazardous waste include a:

   a. focus on highly visible sources of pollution, e.g. smoke stacks.
   b. focus on less visible uncontrolled sites, e.g. buried waste.
   c. focus on recycling.
   d. focus on substitution of non-hazardous materials for hazardous materials.
   e. all of the above.

C	8.	One of the reasons why companies have not given more attention to the problems of waste and scrap disposal is that:

a. the dollars involved are relatively small.
b. little scrap is generated.
c. many concerns are not large enough to have a disposal department.
d. scrap easily can be sold at the highest-possible price.
e. all of the above. |
| D | 9. | An integrated waste management system calls for:

a. reclaiming materials, recycling, stockpiling, and incinerating.
b. resource recovery, landfilling, incinerating, and donating.
c. source reduction, recycling, stockpiling, and donating.
d. source reduction, recycling, resource recovery, and landfilling.
e. source reduction, resource recovery, donating, and landfilling. |
| E | 10. | Investment recovery is often assigned to:

a. supply managers because they have knowledge of probable price trends.
b. salespeople because they have contact with buyers who may also use the material.
c. marketing managers because they are a good source of information as to possible users of the material.
d. engineers because of their familiarity with the company's own needs which may suggest possible uses for, and transfer of, the material within the organization.
e. financial analysts because they set the target return on all investments. |

True and False

F 1. Part of the reason why scrap disposal is a problem for many firms is that there are no detailed, extensive specifications governing the grading and shipping of scrap materials.

F 2. There is little material in electronic devices that can be reclaimed or recycled.

T 3. The total cost of hazardous waste for a company may include direct clean-up costs, disposal costs, administrative and legal costs, and new plant and equipment costs.

F 4. The return from the sale of material through a local scrap or surplus dealer likely will be quite high.

F 5. Escalator clauses in contracts for scrap disposal are unnecessary since the prices of primary metals rarely fluctuate.

T 6. If material has been declared obsolete, there is usually no logical reason to continue storing it.

F 7. The decision of whether to undertake the reclamation of any particular lot of material should be made by the purchasing department.

T 8. As more people come to believe that it makes economic sense to practice environmentally sound operations, business and government may be able to work together for common goals.

F 9. A 1995 study by the Center for Advanced Purchasing Studies found that purchasing was responsible for scrap/surplus disposal/inventory investment in less than half the surveyed firms.

F 10. Rejected stock is created when a change in the production process occurs, or when a better material is substituted for that material originally used.

Nova Stamping Company

Teaching Note

IMMEDIATE ISSUE

The disposal of obsolete equipment.

BASIC ISSUES

1. Equipment disposal criteria.
2. The role of purchasing in disposal.

SUGGESTED STUDENT ASSIGNMENT

1. As Sandra Glassford, what alternatives would you consider?
2. What criteria would you suggest be used in evaluating these alternatives?
3. What possible sources of information within the company would you investigate? Who can provide this information?
4. What would you recommend to Jim Armstrong?

POSSIBLE DISCUSSION QUESTIONS

1. Why should purchasing be involved in disposal?
2. Which three factors might be paramount in this disposal?
3. When does equipment become obsolete?
4. If equipment is obsolete, why might anyone else still want to use it?
5. How is equipment disposal different from surplus material, or scrap, or waste disposal?
6. Might there be any environmental issues here?

DISCUSSION

This case deals with the issue of obsolete equipment disposal and is suited for use in a class or seminar in purchasing and materials management.

Sandra Glassford, purchasing manager at the Nova Stamping Company Detroit plant has been asked by the plant manager, Jim Armstrong, to make a recommendation regarding equipment identified as obsolete. This equipment is currently supporting production, and is in working condition. Two new presses are expected in approximately eight months to replace the current machines. Sandra's alternatives include the following:

1. Selling the equipment for scrap value to a local scrap dealer.
2. Selling all or part of the equipment to an equipment dealer.
3. Transfer the equipment to another one of the two company facilities.
4. Selling the equipment to another stamping company.

In order to achieve maximum recovery value the equipment may have to be sold to different sources. For example, the sale may have to be split been an equipment dealer, competitor and scrap dealer.

Selling the equipment to a competitor raises a strategic issue; Nova will not want to add to the capacity of a competitor with low cost equipment, or alternatively, support the entry of a new stamper into the market.

When considering the various alternatives, Sandra must make sure that her implementation plan supports the transition with the new equipment, therefore, timely removal and avoiding production interruptions is critical.

Research indicates that management expects the purchasing function to be familiar with outlets for equipment and material disposal. A study by the Center for Advanced Purchasing Studies found that scrap/surplus disposal reported to the purchasing function in 63% of the firms surveyed, up from 57% in 1988 (Fearon and Leenders 1995). However, it can be implied from the case that Sandra does not have a great deal of experience with the issue of obsolete equipment disposal.

A good place for Sandra to start is to contact the corporate controller in order to identify company procedures for fix asset disposal. The controller can also provided relevant financial data, such as when the equipment was purchased, its acquisition value, and the current book value. This information is useful in determining tax implications of selling the equipment.

It would also be advisable for Sandra to talk to Alex Brown, the maintenance supervisor, regarding the condition and maintenance records of each machine. This will assist her in determining the condition of each piece of equipment and its potential marketability.

It is unlikely that management would want to see this equipment transferred to another of its facilities. Modern, state-of-art equipment and processes is a critical success factor in the automotive parts industry.

Regardless of which disposal alternative chosen, removal of the equipment should be carefully coordinated. The plant should avoid potential problems with unsupervised contractors and other personnel in the plant. Activities such as disconnecting power sources need to be controlled by plant management. Timing is also an issue that must be carefully planned in order to avoid production interruptions and free-up plant space for the new equipment.

WHAT HAPPENED

Although management expressed concerns regarding competitive implications of selling the equipment locally, most of the presses were sold to an equipment dealer in the area. Two machines were sold to a local tool and die shop for use in testing dies. Prices for the presses ranged from $1,250 to $5,000. Only one of the machines was sold as scrap.

Ornex

Teaching Note

IMMEDIATE ISSUES

1. How disposal of the surplus raw iron powder should be handled.
2. How to avoid reoccurrence of the ordering raw material that will not be used.

BASIC ISSUES

1. Surplus raw material disposal.
2. Forecasting and planning.
3. Risk management.
4. Inventory management.
5. The purchasing/sales interface.

SUGGESTED STUDENT ASSIGNMENT

As Greg Saunders, how what is your analysis of the situation regarding the surplus raw iron powder? What action would you take and why?

POSSIBLE DISCUSSION QUESTIONS

1. What are the costs of each of the options identified by Greg Saunders? Can you identify any additional options that he should consider?
2. Who is at fault here – purchasing, sales, the supplier or the customer – and why?
3. What would you do to prevent a reoccurrence of this problem?
4. What is your evaluation of the arrangements with the suppliers for consignment for raw material inventory? Would you want to make any changes?
5. What would you say to your customer regarding this matter? Do you think the customer has treated Ornex fairly?

ANALYSIS

There are two different, yet related issues in this case. The immediate problem is to decide what to do about the surplus raw material. It appears that the company is in a tight cash flow position and the supplier will be looking for payment by the end of the month. The second issue relates to preventing a reoccurrence of the problem.

It is useful to understand the sequence of events:

- July: Bid submitted for "races". Production expected to begin in March.

- November: Greg places order for custom raw iron powder. With a 16 week lead time, delivery of first 100,000 lbs scheduled for arrival in early March

- March: Receipt of 100,000 lbs of custom raw iron powder.

- April: Receipt of 100,000 lbs of custom raw iron powder.

- May: Receipt of 100,000 lbs of custom raw iron powder.

- June: Contract awarded to competitor

It would appear that Greg Saunders planned to have the material arrive based on the original expectation that Ornex would both receive the bid and production would start in March as scheduled. Assuming a 120-day consignment period, payment for the first 100,000 lbs would be due the end of June, consistent with the information in the case.

On June 3, Ornex had 300,000 lbs of inventory, representing a total value of $180,000, based on a cost of $0.60 per lb. The case identifies two options for Greg Saunders:

1. Return the Inventory to FE Metal Powders

In this scenario Ornex would pay $0.20 to FE Metal Powders and receive $0.40, representing a recovery of $120,000 and a cost of $60,000.

2. Hold and Use the Inventory

Greg expected to be able to use 100,000 lbs in the near future (presumably replacing raw material of equivalent value), but the balance would take 18 months out clear out. Using the 2 percent per month hold cost estimate given in the case and assuming an average inventory of 100,000 lbs ($60,000), the cost of holding the inventory would be $21,600. While financially more attractive, this option carries the risk of spoilage and the hassles of storage.

Additional Options

There are also a number of other options that Greg might consider. The instructor can get the students to brainstorm to generate a list in class, which might include:

- A hybrid of the two options identified by Greg: Sell 200,000 lb. now and use 100,000 lb. This option would pay $80,000 for the 200,000 lb (200,000 × $0.40) and cost $40,000 (200,000 × $0.20). It is more attractive than the first alternative, but still more costly than the second.
- Try to sell the raw material himself. Maybe Greg can get a better deal from a competitor. For example, Greg could contract the company that was awarded the business and investigate selling the material to them. Alternatively, Greg could advertise or ask the supplier's sales representative where the raw material could be sold.
- Ask the customer to sell the material or compensate Ornex for the cost of disposal. This might seem like a long shot, but ultimately the decision to buy the material was done to protect the customer. The customer could contact the supplier that won the contract and ask them to buy the raw material from Ornex.
- Look for new uses for the material. This option might require working with the engineers and operations staff.
- Hold on to the material and use it for new business.
- Sell to Simpsons Powders or ask Simpsons where the material can be disposed.

This is not necessarily a complete list and the students might be able to think of additional options. The point, however, is that several additional options do exist and should at least be considered.

The Bigger Picture

A far more serious issue relates to the root cause of the problem. According to the case, Greg understood that production would start in March and Ornex had a high chance of winning the bid. One difficulties of the automotive business is the high cost of stock-outs. OEMs would prefer to have suppliers hold inventory rather than risk a stock-out and idle an assembly plant. It would appear that Greg has been caught in a situation where the prospects for the award of the business and the anticipated start of production were both overly optimistic. If the business had been awarded on schedule or if Ornex had been awarded the "race" component, then the problem could have been avoided.

It would appear that Ornex has to watch its cash, since Greg is concerned about arranging a payment schedule. Clearly, the company cannot afford to make too many similar mistakes, both in terms of impact on cash flow and the high cost. It is worth asking the students how supply can help Ornex be successful. This is a low margin, high volume business and the company cannot afford to take financial hits on raw material disposal. Supply can help Ornex by keeping inventory levels to a minimum and raw material costs low. This situation runs counter to such objectives.

The problem demonstrates issues of poor coordination between supply and sales. There are number of questions that should be raised here: Was Ornex's sale manager aware that Greg had ordered 400,000 lbs of raw material for "races"? Did the customer know that Ornex had order the material expecting to receive the business? Why did the sales representative not notify Greg that award of the contract and production was delayed? Why did Greg not follow-up with the sales manager regarding the status of the contract? The supplier is not to blame in this situation, but some serious questions must be raised concerning coordination between sales and supply.

CHAPTER 12

Legal Aspects of Purchasing

Topics Covered

Legal Authority of the Purchasing Officer
Personal Liability of the Purchasing Officer
The Purchase Order Contract
    Acceptance of Orders
    Purchases Made Orally
Authority of Suppliers' Representatives
Inspection
Cancellation of Orders and Breach of Contract
Warranties
Acceptance and Rejection of Goods
    Protection against Price Fluctuations
    Title to Purchased Goods
    The Uniform Computer Information
    Transaction Act (UCITA)

Uniform Electronic Transactions Act
Electronic Signatures
The Electronic Commerce Enhancement
Act of 21
Antitrust and E-Marketplaces
Patents and Product Liability
Commercial Arbitration
Questions for Review and Discussion
References
Cases
    Brassco

QUIZ RESPONSES

A   1.   Both the Federal Trade Commission (FTC) and the U. S. Department of Justice:

         a. have raised questions about the potential for price-fixing and collusion in e-marketplaces.
         b. have ruled that e-marketplaces are inherently susceptible to price-fixing and collusion.
         c. have raised questions about e-marketplaces run by neutral third parties in which buyers pool their requirements for specific items, such as office supplies.
         d. have raised questions about a-marketplaces that are owned and operated by competitors who together represent more than 50 percent of an industry market share.
         e. have yet to address the questions concerning e-marketplaces and price-fixing and collusion.

C   2.   The legal authority of a salesperson normally is:

         a. the same as that of a buyer.
         b. to make legally-binding contracts for $500 or less.
         c. to solicit orders and send them to his or her employer for ratification and acceptance.
         d. to make legally binding contracts, if not for over $1,000.
         e. based on the length of time the supplier company has been in business.

A   3.   When a buyer relies on the seller's skill or judgment to select or furnish suitable goods, there is a(n):

         a. implied warranty of merchantability.
         b. express warranty.
         c. warranty of title.
         d. implied warranty of fitness for a particular purpose.
         e. implicit warranty.

E	4.	Common Law covers the purchase of:

a. all goods and all services.
b. goods and services, if the services portion of the contract is less than 50 percent.
c. only goods.
d. only services
e. goods and services, if the services portion of the contract is more than 50 percent. |
| A | 5. | When someone outside of the purchasing department, a marketing manager for example, agrees to buy something from a salesperson, and the material is received and paid for, the manager has:

a. apparent scope of authority.
b. actual scope of authority.
c. implied scope of authority.
d. conditional scope of authority.
e. strict scope of authority. |
| B | 6. | Which of the following is a factor in determining the validity of a contract?

a. incompetent parties.
b. legal subject matter or purpose.
c. offer and counteroffer.
d. employment in the purchasing department.
e. due process. |
| B | 7. | The concept of absolute liability:

a. is based on the idea that the injured party must prove that the product was defective when it left the manufacturer and that the defect caused the injury.
b. is based on the idea that the manufacturer is liable if misuse or abnormal use by the consumer should have been expected.
c. implies that the buyer is ultimately responsible for any injuries arising from the use of a legally purchased product.
d. varies according to the type of warranty that comes with the product.
e. limits the awards that injured parties may receive to a set percentage above the cost of the actual damage. |

Chapter 12

B | 8. Normally, if an offer to buy or sell is made:

    a. it must remain open for a reasonable time, which usually is six months.
    b. the contract is completed from the moment when the acceptance is transmitted.
    c. the offeror is prevented under the Uniform Commercial Code from specifying that the acceptance be communicated in any specific manner.
    d. the contract is completed at the time when the acceptance is received by the offeror.
    e. the acceptance must be communicated by the same means by which the offer was made.

D | 9. According to the UCC, an oral agreement:

    a. is never legally binding.
    b. may be revoked if the buyer sends a notice of objection within 30 days of receipt of the goods.
    c. that is partially performed (for example, one of ten lots is delivered) is automatically canceled under the doctrine of force majure.
    d. normally must include some written notation if the price of the order the sale of goods is $500 or more.
    e. is not valid unless and until some form of documentation is signed by both parties.

E | 10. Electronic or digital signatures for contractual purposes:

    a. are valid in all member countries of the United Nations.
    b. are valid in the U.S., Canada, and Mexico under the rules of origin of the NAFTA agreement.
    c. are invalid because there is currently no technological means available to authenticate signatures.
    d. are invalid in the U.S. because the UCC expressly prohibits them.
    e. have been given the same legal status as written ones by the European Union (EU), but must be approved by each EU government before going into effect.

True and False

T	1.	The doctrine of promissory estoppal says if one party "relied to its detriment" on the promises made by the other party in an oral agreement, the entire contract may be validated.
F	2.	In those infrequent situations where the buyer takes formal legal action to enforce a purchase contract he or she normally will not need legal counsel, since the Uniform Commercial Code is very specific.
T	3.	If a supplier fails to deliver goods which meet the contract agreement, one of the buyer's options is to reject the whole shipment.
T	4.	When both parties in a dispute agree to abide by the decision of an independent third party, this is called arbitration.
F	5.	Payment made to a supplier automatically constitutes an acceptance of the goods.
F	6.	It is the duty of the purchasing agent to provide written documentation to a seller outlining the purchasing agent's scope of authority.
F	7.	Article 2-B of the Uniform Commercial Code (UCC) was included in the 2000 revision of the UCC and addresses e-commerce.
F	8.	A valid offer can be made only by a purchasing agent or buyer.
T	9.	If the seller fails to make delivery by the agreed time, the purchaser may, without obligation, refuse to accept delivery at a later date.
T	10.	Under the Uniform Commercial Code, when the buyer has examined the goods as fully as he or she has desired, there is no warranty with regard to defects which an examination ought to have revealed to him or her.

Brassco

Teaching Note

IMMEDIATE ISSUES

1. The awarding of the hand towel contract.
2. The cancellation of the Riddirt contract.

BASIC ISSUES

1. Single vs. dual sourcing.
2. Contract cancellation.
3. Supplier selection.
4. Purchases of services.
5. Legal issues.
6. Pricing agreements.
7. Long term contracts.
8. Environmental improvement.

SUGGESTED STUDENT ASSIGNMENT

If you were in the position of Harry Jones what would be your analysis of the laundering contract situation to date and what action would you take and why?

POSSIBLE DISCUSSION QUESTIONS

1. What are the advantages/disadvantages of splitting the laundering purchases?
2. How do you determine a fair price for a service?
3. What should be a reasonable length of contract for a laundering service?
4. What is your interpretation of the contested contract clause?
5. How much time are you prepared to spend on this issue?
6. What are the alternatives here?

DISCUSSION

The following table provides the financial aspect of the laundering contract situation. Assuming no other launderer is able to provide linen service (a rather surprising and disquieting situation), the following options presumably exist.

	Option	Supplier(s)	Total Quote
1.	Single Source	Able	$78,500
2.	Dual Source	Able / Riddirt	$80,500
3.	Dual Source	Able / Cleano	$72,700
4.	Dual Source	Able / Wilkens	$70,600

It would be most useful to find at least one other option for Able so that the validity of their quote could be checked. No information is provided on the current cost of paper towels so as to be able to put a price tag on the extra cost, if any, of the environmental concern and benefit.

Since the current contract with Riddirt covers rentals as well as laundering, a switch of suppliers is not quite as simple as it would be if it covered laundering only. Presumably, there is a regular pick-up and delivery involved as well as determining appropriate sizes for new employees.

The Context

Given that Harry Jones purchases about $70 million per year, this contract is minimal and should not absorb a lot of his time. There is certainly no point in getting into a long and drawn-out legal battle over a few thousand dollars.

The Cancellation Clause and Term Length

Unfortunately, clause 5 is ambiguous and subject to the two interpretations provided. The suppliers' claim interprets it probably the way the original Brassco purchaser intended. Had Harry not gone out for quotes on the whole contract, he would never have found out that some cleaners were willing to under price Riddirt. Before acting hastily Harry would do well to ensure that we are really comparing apples to apples and that all of the specifications for rental, pick-up, response time, frequency of laundering, etc. would be identical. If employees are unhappy with the new uniforms or gloves or get a rash from a different detergent, the potential savings could be quite illusionary.

Potential Options

Harry Jones could try to find another cleaner who could supply linen towel service, or find out why Cleano, Wilkens and Riddirt are unable to quote on this business. Harry is right that a single supplier should be able to quote a lower price if linen towels and other laundry requirements can be delivered and picked up at the same time.

It is also useful to compare the current cost of paper towels to the linen service to establish whether real environmental savings would occur. If the linen service results in extra pick-up and delivery trips and water and air pollution, then Brassco is trading solid waste for liquid and air pollution.

One possibility is to sign a two year contract for linen towel service to coincide with the current other laundry contract so that the two contracts can be combined two years hence.

Riddirt's quick and harsh response tends to suggest this is not the first time its competitors have tried to steal business or buyers have tried to cancel contracts. Whether they would make a good long term supplier is something Harry needs to think over.

Getting a Legal Opinion

In any case, it would be useful for Brassco to get a legal opinion on the cancellation clause. This would confirm or disconfirm the current Brassco interpretation and also help ensure proper wording for other Brassco contracts. It is unlikely that this is the only contract on which ambiguous language exists.

CONCLUSION

Given the relatively low value of the contract involved, it is important that this issue does not grow out of proportion. If there is a genuine opportunity to improve the company's solid waste performance (without creating other environmental problems) and the cost of such an improvement is appropriate in view of the benefit, this opportunity should be pursued.

CHAPTER 13

Research and Measurement

Topics Covered

Purchasing Research
    Organization for Purchasing Research
    Cross-Functional Teams
    Identifying Opportunities
    Research on Purchased Materials, Products, or Services (Value Analysis)
    Target Costing
    Commodity Studies
    Supplier Research
    Purchasing Processes
    Assessing Purchase Research Results
Planning
Purchasing Budgets
Performance Measurement and Operations Reports
    Why Is Appraisal Needed?
    Problems in Appraisal
    Objectives
    Budgets and Standard Costs
    Procedures Used in Evaluation
    Operations Reports
    Types of Performance Measurement Systems
    Performance Purchasing Measurement
    Appraising Team Performance
Purchasing Performance Benchmarking
Questions for Review and Discussion
References
Cases
    Red Sea Corporation
    Chemical Treatment Company (CTC) Ltd.

QUIZ RESPONSES

D   1.   The budget which covers all of the expenses incurred in the operation of the purchasing function including salaries and wages; space costs; equipment costs; information technology charges; travel and entertainment expense; educational expenditures; postage, telephone, and fax; and office supplies is called the:

      a. materials (operations) purchase budget.
      b. MRO budget.
      c. capital budget.
      d. administrative budget.
      e. organizational budget.

C   2.   Purchasing process research:

      a. focuses on improving buyer-seller relationships.
      b. considers whether single or multiple sourcing is most advantageous.
      c. focuses on ensuring speed and cost-effectiveness by eliminating unnecessary steps in the process.
      d. compares cost and function to determine a lower cost alternative.
      e. is used to develop a strategy to reduce cost or ensure supply.

A   3.   Which of the following is necessary if purchasing is to develop a competitive supply base:

      a. encourage early supplier involvement.
      b. distance themselves from suppliers.
      c. increase the use of e-commerce tools.
      d. increase the supplier base.
      e. all of the above.

B 4. An efficiency-oriented performance measurement system:

   a. evaluates contribution to profit, quality of supplier relations, and levels of customer satisfaction.
   b. emphasizes material cost reductions and departmental operating costs.
   c. focuses on measuring direct contributions to profit.
   d. assesses and tries to reduce the time between receipt of requisition and order placement.
   e. might establish a goal of reducing the price of item A by 5 percent this year.

E 5. Value analysis:

   a. compares the actual performance of a good or service to the expectations of the internal users to determine if the supplier added value.
   b. compares the value-added at each step of a production process to calculate total cost of ownership.
   c. compares the function of a purchased item with the value required of that item to identify improvement opportunities.
   d. compares the design of an item or service to the needs of the internal customer to determine if value will be added.
   e. compares the function performed by a purchased item with the cost, in an attempt to find a lower cost alternative to attain the same or better functionality.

D 6. Purchasing performance benchmarks typically:

   a. analyze a firm's own internal trends.
   b. compare a firms current performance to past performance.
   c. provide industry standards for overall firm performance.
   d. give purchasing professionals a reference point to compare the firm's purchasing performance to that of its competitors.
   e. provide specific data about individual firms.

C | 7. Purchasing process benchmarking attempts to:

a. analyze a firm's own internal trends.
b. provide industrywide standards for overall firm performance.
c. determine how an organization achieves results in purchasing and supply.
d. determine what results organizations have achieved in their purchasing and supply activities.
e. give purchasing professionals a reference point to compare the firm's purchasing performance to that of its competitors.

D | 8. One of the principal disadvantages of having each buyer do his or her own purchasing research is:

a. it is cheaper, from an administrative cost standpoint.
b. the buyer likely will be more familiar with the items bought.
c. the buyer can make buying decisions faster.
d. the buyer likely will have a more narrow view of the effects of purchasing decisions on operating results.
e. the buyer likely will know the internal customers better.

B | 9. Cross-functional sourcing teams:

a. are often used because it is easy to assign accountability for results among the individuals on the team.
b. work best when performance evaluation and reward systems foster participation and overall team performance.
c. work best when no one member is stronger than any other member, and the leadership role is rotated.
d. work best when the team is given total autonomy to decide objectives and set expectations.
e. usually take less time overall to achieve results than if one individual performed the same task.

C 10. The five purchasing measures which had the highest value assessment *and* use as reported by CPOs in major firms were all related to:

a. price, service, and volume
b. quality, delivery, and service.
c. price, quality, and delivery.
d. quality, volume, and outsourcing
e. outsourcing, service, and price

True and False

T | 1. Key factors which must be looked at when evaluating the efficiency and effectiveness of a purchasing operation is purchasing policy, physical layout, purchasing procedures, and prices paid.

F | 2. One method often used in many organizations to evaluate the purchasing department's pricing performance is weighted point pricing.

T | 3. Industry benchmarking provides general comparisons, but does not allow an individual company to compare itself to its major competitor.

F | 4. Effectiveness performance measurement systems provide no goals or criteria against which a buyer's performance will be measured.

F | 5. Typically, the materials purchase budget has a planning horizon of three or more years.

F | 6. The best way to change the perceptions non-purchasing managers have of purchasing is to provide formal reports based on hard data.

T | 7. The standard approach to value analysis is to pose and provide detailed answers to a series of questions about the item currently being bought.

F | 8. *Value engineering* is done on purchased items used in the ongoing production process, while *value analysis* is done in the design stage, where items are being specified.

T | 9. The perceptions that non-purchasing managers have of purchasing are shaped by interactions with and observations of purchasing, tangible experiences with purchasing on a day-to-day basis, and the extent to which purchasing is seen as contributing to the firm's mission.

F | 10. Commodity study purchase research tends to be a major activity area for the internal user of the particular commodity.

Red Sea Corporation

Teaching Note

IMMEDIATE ISSUE

The value of industry benchmarks to Red Sea Corporation.

BASIC ISSUE

1. Benchmarking
2. Performance Evaluation

SUGGESTED STUDENT ASSIGNMENT

1. If you were Earl Jones, to what use might you put the CAPS Purchasing Performance Benchmarks for the U.S. Food Manufacturing Industry?
2. What would be the implications if Red Sea's results were:
   a. close to the industry average?
   b. all on the low side vs. the CAPS benchmarks?
   c. much higher than the CAPS figures?
   d. higher in some categories, lower in some and the same in the remaining ones?
3. Which of the 37 benchmarks would you consider most relevant and why?

POSSIBLE DISCUSSION QUESTIONS

1. Is benchmarking useful? Why?
2. Should Red Sea participate in the next round of CAPS' Food Manufacturers survey?
3. Is it a good idea to have an industry advisory group for a benchmarking survey like this? Why?
4. Is there an issue of statistical reliability?
5. Why would not all companies reply to every question?
6. For how long might this data be relevant?
7. What three measures might be most relevant?

DISCUSSION

The CAPS benchmarks have become an inexpensive, readily available set of data on purchasing across a wide range of industries as well as governmental buying. In the creation of a study, an industry advisory committee reviews the standard 19 common CAPS benchmarks and adds additional ones which they believe to be relevant for their own industry. As the low responses to some of the questions show, not all companies are unanimous in these measures and refuse the bother of determining them, when they are not an in-house standard.

It is doubtful that all 37 benchmarks are of equal importance in this study and, quite possibly, a smaller number might be quite appropriate. The size of the food industry makes it a particularly good benchmarking target and it is among those most frequently surveyed by CAPS for benchmarking.

CAPS has built a reputation for reliability, speed, and confidentiality that has made benchmarking possible. Only the absolute assurance that no one company's data will be divulged to another (and possibly a competitor) provides the basis of trust and the willingness to cooperate.

A unique feature of benchmarks is their ability to provide an historical record and to see over time what changes are taking place. Previous benchmarks may also indicate reliability, because unusually large changes in figures from survey to survey may make the data suspect.

Standard Concerns

There are a standard set of questions and observations that apply to most of the 37 benchmarks. It is useful to raise these once to avoid unnecessary repetition.

1. The question of the statistical validity is relevant. Even if all 14 respondents replied, are the numbers useful? For example, in an extreme example half the group might reply 10%, half the group 0% and the average would be reported as 5%, which not a single company would show as a percentage. If fewer companies replied to a particular question, the relevance of the numbers may be in question. The lower number may be an indication that for the non-respondents, at least, this may not be data they collect, or are willing to share.

   How the information provided is used is probably more important than the absolute statistical reliability of the data. Any one organization's data might be drastically different from the industry average for a number of good reasons including:

   a. The nature of the product line is sufficiently different. A chocolate bar manufacturer will show results different from a fish processor or a cereal producer for a number of categories.

   b. Corporate strategy may influence in a number of ways:

i) Make or buy stance may affect the percentage of raw materials, parts, etc.
ii) One centralized plant may require less maintenance than a large number of separate facilities.
iii) Location may effect wage rates, transportation charges, material and services prices, etc.
iv) The competitive premise of the organization — strong brand name, patented or unique product, quality, speed, price, taste, technology, or distribution may affect the demands placed on suppliers and the supply organization.
v) The status of the supply function in the total organization — reporting line, percentage of all acquisition handled by purchasing, quality and qualifications of supply staff, salary levels, etc. may vary.
vi) The growth rate and market share of the company may provide special challenges and opportunities.
vii) The future plans and objectives of the organization may require extra efforts and project involvement of supply.
viii) The organization's past may affect its current tasks, problems, costs, and abilities. A supply crew in need of substantial training might not be able to perform as one that is quite accomplished.
c. The way an organization keeps its records may be unique along with the definitions of purchasing, cost, professional, raw material, equipment, active supplier, etc.
d. The organization may be of a different size in number of employees, sales volume, profitability, debt structure, etc.

As is obvious from the foregoing comments, it is probably easy for any organization to pronounce its uniqueness and disclaim any relevance of the benchmarks provided. This is going too far. The benchmarks are useful to identify where differences exist and why they might exist. For example, a supply organization spending nothing on the training of its employees might ask why its competitors choose on average to spend 1.5 percent of operating expenses on training.

There is likely to be a desire in the class to avoid getting into the nitty gritty of the individual benchmarks, but there is usefulness to discussing them, in turn, and pushing the class into the challenge that Earl Jones faces. It is much better that Earl Jones asks himself what these numbers mean and what to do if his numbers were higher, lower, or the same as the industry average, than to have the president of the Red Sea Corporation sideswipe Earl sometime with a question about these CAPS Benchmarks that fellow presidents in the industry are talking about.

Ultimately, Earl has to decide how the supply function at Red Sea should contribute to corporate strategy and how he wants his performance measured. The CAPS benchmarks may be of assistance in helping him make up his mind about what he believes is relevant and if and how he wants to be different.

Specific Benchmark Comments

The following comments are made with reference to the Benchmarks as they are numbered in the summary of Food Manufacturing Purchasing Benchmarks.

1. The 28% of sales figure seems to be relatively low compared to other industries. The breakdown into the various purchase categories is probably also useful. It is not clear what percentage of non-traditional purchases are included in this industry in these figures. One might expect individual companies to vary significantly from these percentages for reasons such as a different make or buy strategy. Tracking its own figures might be important for an organization to see whether it is staying in line.
2. It is probably useful to have a benchmark on the expense of operating the purchasing function. As organizations move towards supply management organizations, tracking the purchasing personnel alone may become more difficult.
3. If we assume a purchasing operating expense to be primarily salaries at approximately 85%, about 10% of all salary income would be spent on travel and almost 2% of salary income on training.
4. One of the most basic benchmarks of all is the cost per dollar of goods or services purchased. Half a percent purchasing costs is an interesting benchmark and one that will be subject to considerable controversy. The general argument in the field is that spending some more on the cost of purchasing hopefully could reduce the total cost of what is acquired. This is one of the great paradoxes in the procurement field. A best in class benchmark on cost of purchasing might not produce optimal results for the organization.

5&6. A quick overview of worker productivity is given by benchmarks 5 and 6. Number 6 is acquired by multiplying the $62.9 million x 28%.

7. Under the assumption that a professional purchasing employee is supported by a number of nonprofessionals, it is interesting to see how many purchases these professionals are responsible for and their variation depending on the category of orders acquired.
8. It is not surprising that in the food industry, the food would be a high unit cost. These averages, when subjected to ABC analysis would show a surprisingly different picture.

9&10. The number of suppliers per purchasing employee and professional employee is still relatively large.

11. This is a derived figure from some of the earlier data. Total purchases with each supplier and by category are again average figures and ABC analysis would again show quite a different pattern.
12. This is an average figure obtained by taking purchasing department expense and dividing it by the total number of suppliers. It can be made to look better by increasing the number of suppliers and would look worse with relatively few suppliers.
13. This figure shows what impact an ABC type of analysis would have. It is interesting that the percentage of suppliers receiving 90% of all the purchases is almost the same regardless of the nature of what is acquired.
14. Number 14 shows some interesting trends in terms of number of suppliers.

15,16,17. Some data on minority-owned, women-owned, and small business suppliers is probably useful even in industries where government supply is not a major issue. It is assumed here that most minority-owned and women-owned suppliers are also small businesses and would be rolled into the 11 percent of all purchases.
18. A supplier certification seems to be an issue in many organizations.
19. EDI use seems to be significantly higher than some earlier surveys in other industries but still comes to less than 20 percent at this point in time.
20. Supplies further information on numbers 15, 16, and 17.
21. Direct material amounts to about half of all total purchases.
22. It is interesting that packaging materials turn over much faster than food. Is it possible that packaging purchases which run about half the total food purchases are being monitored better than inventory levels of food purchases.
23. It is suggested that almost three-quarters of all firms set purchasing savings targets.
24. It is interesting to note that almost three-quarters of all accounts payable activity originates in purchasing.
25. It is not surprising that in the food industry a number of risk management tools would be used to protect the organization from unexpectedly large swings in the market.
26. Slightly more than 21 percent of all organizations do not authorize forward buying or are limited to a maximum of 6 months. This is almost equivalent to buying hand to mouth.
27. This shows that environmental sensitivity is increasing.
28. This shows that the purchasing manager's overall cost savings and quality are by far the most important measures.
29. Some interesting data on outsourcing.
30. This shows payment practices and a tendency to extend terms.
31. This shows rather low percentages of purchasing initiative in activities which would typically expect high purchasing leadership.
32. This tends to suggest that few college graduates go for the CPM designation. More go for a graduate degree.
33. This shows that a reasonable number of purchasing employees participate in company bonus plans.
34. This shows that roughly 1 in 3 of professional purchasing employees participate in bonus plans.
35. Professional purchasing employees received an average 28 hours of annual training which amounts to about 3□ days. This is a long way off the typical 5 or 6 percent of total time normally cited as necessary in other functions.
36. This shows that slightly more than □ of professional purchasing employees are women and few are minorities.
37. This shows that organizations have not flattened out completely yet with the beginning buying position having 5 levels between it and the CEO.

Chemical Treatment Company (CTC) Ltd.

Teaching Note

IMMEDIATE ISSUE

Should CTC construct an on-site testing facility or continue to contract out to independent labs?

BASIC ISSUE

Make or buy.

SUGGESTED STUDENT ASSIGNMENT

1. As Stephen Wagner, what is your assessment of the current testing situation?
2. What action would you take regarding an on-site testing facility? Why?

POSSIBLE DISCUSSION QUESTIONS

1. What is the role of a testing lab for this kind of company?
2. What alternatives are open to Stephen Wagner at this point?
3. What are the pros and cons of running your own lab?
4. How does the financial side appear?
5. How does the non-financial side appear?

ANALYSIS

The analysis for this case can be broken into a financial and a non-financial one. On the financial side the following figures appear:

Differential Analysis

Recurring Cash Flows		New Lab
INFLOWS		
Savings on lab fees ($50/test x 2520 tests) (max).		$126,000
Elimination of surcharge		52,500
Total Inflows (max)		

OUTFLOWS		
Salaries		
Lab Technicians (2)	($44,000)	
Chemists (2)	(50,000)	
Supplies	(24,000)	
Utilities	(6,000)	
Insurance	(6,000)	
Total Outflows		(130,000)
Differential Cash flow		48,500
Investments		
Equipment	$160,000	
Portable	35,000	
Furniture	10,000	
Total	$205,000	

Different ROI = $\frac{48,500}{205,000} = 24\%$

Payback - minimum 4.2 years

Therefore, based on these numbers, the new lab facility seems not to be a good investment.

Breakeven Analysis:

Variable cost/test = $\dfrac{\$24{,}000 \text{ (supplies)}}{2520 \text{ (\# of tests)}}$ = $10/test

Therefore B/E (tests) = $\dfrac{\text{Fixed Costs}}{\text{Unit Contribution*}}$ = $\dfrac{\$106{,}000}{(\$50-\$20)}$ = 2650 < 2520 tests < last year

*Unit Contribution = Savings/test using in-house facility.

The conclusion of the financial analysis is that if the number of tests remains the same and if all of the surcharges can be avoided, the financial side still is not particularly attractive and has a payback of over four years.

However, a number of conditions might make the testing more attractive financially. These would include:

1. If total volume increases.
2. If second testing makes sense, CTC can check clients and surcharge clients.
3. If the reputation of CTC is at stake and their long-term viability depends on their ability to do testing in-house.
4. If they can sell access lab capacity to other users outside.
5. If they can reduce costs and possibly run the lab with fewer people.

Clearly, also, the question as to whether other opportunities exist for this organization in terms of their attractiveness as an investment also needs to be looked at.

ALTERNATIVES

CTC actually faces a number of alternatives in this particular situation. These include:

1. Switch disposal site. This may be difficult, given location and the general environmental concerns of society.
2. Change arrangement with disposal site. Possibly, CTC can negotiate to have the surcharges avoided or reduced.
3. Switch testing laboratory to a lab that can be a) faster and b) cheaper. The figures indicate that the variable cost per test might run about $10. This leaves a lot of negotiating range between this $10 variable cost and the actual $50 charge. Similarly, it is difficult to see why it should take an outside lab so long to perform these tests.
4. Find additional customers for their lab. These might possibly include their current clients or potential ones.

5. The opportunity might exist to ship materials more quickly if tests show that they are ready to ship. This might increase space utilization and allow them to expand with the existing space.
6. Increase total business because of the existence of the lab. If CTC becomes more attractive to clients because of its testing capability, then the testing lab may be easily justified.

FINAL REMARKS

There is something strange about the figures given in the case. If it is possible to do 8,000 lab tests in this lab with the crew configurations shown, it should be possible to do about half the number with half the crew. A saving of one lab technician and one chemist would come to $47,000 and make a lot of difference in the attraction of this proposal. It is not clear from the case why the minimum staffing has to consist of four people.

Although this looks like a simple make or buy type of decision, it probably has strategic overtones for the company as a whole. The case itself does not have enough information to come down to a definite yes or no answer. It is useful to recognize that some additional data gathering and thinking needs to be done before the decision can be taken. It is clear that the current supplier is not meeting the needs of this organization in terms of speed or cost. Therefore, either the market needs to provide a different offering or in-house starts to become attractive. On the market side finding another supplier or developing one appear to be the more realistic solutions. It may be possible that negotiation with the existing supplier may produce results, but this may be unlikely. They have been getting used to the prices and service times they have been supplying and may be difficult to move substantially from where they are now.

CHAPTER 14

Global Supply Management

Topics Covered

Globalization of World Trade
The Importance of Global Purchasing
    U.S. Imports
Reasons for Global Purchasing
    Price
    Government/Marketing Pressures
    Quality
    Unavailability of Items Domestically
    Faster Delivery and Continuity of Supply
    Better Technical Service
    Technology
    Marketing Tool
    Tie-in with Offshore Subsidiaries
    Competitive Clout
Potential Problem Areas
    Source Location and Evaluation
    Lead/Delivery Time
    Expediting
    Political and Labor Problems
    Hidden Costs
    Currency Fluctuations
    Payment Methods
    Quality
    Warranties and Claims
    Tariffs and Duties
    Paperwork Costs
    Legal Problems
    Logistics and Transportation
    Incoterms
    Language
    Communications
    Cultural and Social Customs
    Ethics

Information Sources for Locating and Evaluating International Suppliers
Global Sourcing Organizations
Intermediaries
    Import Brokers and Agents
    Import Merchant
    Seller's Subsidiary
    Sales Representatives
    Trading Company
Countertrade
    Barter/Swaps
    Offset Arrangements
    Counterpurchase
    Buyback/Compensation
    Switch Trade
    American Countertrade Association
Foreign Trade Zones
    Foreign Trade Zones Compared with Bonded Warehouses
    Maquiladoras
    TIBs and Duty Drawbacks
North American Free Trade Agreement
    Possibility of a Free Trade of the Americas
Questions for Review and Discussions
References
Cases
    Global Pharmaceuticals Ltd.
    Marathon Oil Company International

QUIZ RESPONSES

D	1.	Which of the following would be a situation encouraging countertrade? a. surplus of foreign exchange. b. plenty of available credit. c. desire to contract exports. d. need to develop export markets for new products. e. desire to standardize manufacturing methods of products.
A	2.	The really knowledgeable buyer, in dealing with an international supplier: a. may decide to deal in international currency options. b. will always state the price in U.S. dollars. c. will normally price in the currency of the seller's country. d. normally will attempt to negotiate a cost-plus-fixed-fee contract. e. will attempt to price in International Dollars or Euro Dollars.
C	3.	The most-cited reason for sourcing products outside North America is: a. more advanced technology. b. countertrade requirements. c. lower overall cost. d. better quality. e. only source available.
B	4.	The United Nations Convention for the International Sale of Goods (CISG): a. replaces the UCC as the worldwide body of law governing international buying. b. is automatically applied if both nations have adopted the CISG, unless another body of law is agreed upon in the contract. c. is automatically applied if both nations have adopted the CISG, and there can be no exceptions. d. should always be the preference for a buyer from the United States. e. always puts the United States buyer at a disadvantage.

E | 5. The structure of a global purchasing organization is influenced by:

  a. the location of the key suppliers.
  b. the location of the company operations.
  c. the overall organizational structure.
  d. the structure of the purchasing function.
  e. all of the above.

D | 6. In international buying, the type of entity that normally handles a wide spectrum of products from one or a limited number of countries is a(n):

  a. import broker.
  b. sales agent.
  c. import merchant.
  d. trading company.
  e. foreign import agent.

E | 7. The governing convention on shipping terms and responsibilities involved in international transportation is called:

  a. EXQ (Ex Quay).
  b. FOB terms.
  c. CIP (Freight carriage and insurance paid).
  d. ITAPS (International Transport and Payment Specifications).
  e. none of the above..

B | 8. The Foreign Corrupt Practices Act (FCPA):

  a. allows U.S. firms to prosecute foreign nationals on bribery charges.
  b. prohibits U.S. firms from making payments to obtain special advantages, but allows payment to facilitate the performance of normal duties.
  c. allows U.S. firms to offer payments to officials of foreign governments to obtain special advantages.
  d. attempts to persuade other nationals to adopt U.S. rules regarding payments to officials.
  e. none of the above.

B 9. When sourcing internationally:

   a. differing cultural and social norms will have little impact since most businesspeople are accustomed to working with North Americans.
   b. the buyer should learn about the culture, customs, norms, taboos, and history of the supplier's country.
   c. the global availability and use of email, fax, and phone has largely eliminated communication barriers.
   d. the buyer should immediately establish an informal first-name basis with the supplier's representatives.
   e. the need for personal space is generally the same in most regions of the world.

C 10. When one condition of the countertrade agreement is that government and/or military-related exports be purchased, this is:

   a. pure barter.
   b. mixed barter.
   c. an offset arrangement.
   d. co-production.
   e. buyback.

True and False

T   1.   The methods of obtaining data on international suppliers are not very different from those used for domestic suppliers.

F   2.   Countertrade historically has been very common in the sale by U.S. firms of armaments to other nations and its use has not been extended into civilian procurement projects.

F   3.   The North American Free Trade Agreement established complicated rules of destination which must be strictly adhered to if tariffs are to be avoided.

F   4.   Temporary importation bonds (TIB) and duty drawbacks allow a U.S. manufacturer to import materials, use them for manufacture, and export the finished product essentially without paying duty on the material as long as the finished products are exported within 10 years of the original TIB.

T   5.   Incoterms apply to contracts for goods and define contractual rights and obligations related to delivery.

T   6.   Despite growth in U.S. exports in the 1990s, the rate of growth has not been enough to shrink the trade deficit.

F   7.   One of the hazards of international purchasing agreements is the readiness of parties to settle contract disputes through courts of law rather than arbitration.

F   8.   U.S. Government import quotas and pressures have been major factors causing U.S. purchasing departments to buy outside the U.S.

T   9.   Three approaches to global sourcing are to establish (1) regional purchasing offices, (2) global commodity management organizations, or (3) International Purchasing Offices (IPOs).

T   10.   A foreign trade zone (FTZ) is a special commercial and industrial area in or near ports of entry to the U.S. where foreign and domestic merchandise may be brought in without being subject to payment of customs duties.

Global Pharmaceuticals Ltd.

Teaching Note

IMMEDIATE ISSUES

1. How to develop a procurement plan for the eight German products to be transferred to the London plant.
2. How to ensure quality and delivery within the tight time frame.

BASIC ISSUES

1. International sourcing.
2. Procurement planning.
3. International product transfer.

SUGGESTED STUDENT ASSIGNMENT

If you in the position of Ian Grant:
1. What would be the objectives of your procurement plan for the eight German products to be transferred?
2. What major options do you have?
3. What action would you take and why?

POSSIBLE DISCUSSION QUESTIONS

1. Had the two plant locations been different, would your answers to the above questions been different?
2. Would your answers be different if these products were not in the animal health sector?
3. Is this an easy task?
4. Does the acquisition of JCAH make any difference to this case?
5. What is the impact of the multi-language requirement?

ANALYSIS

This is a tricky little case dealing with an interesting procurement issue. Against a backdrop of major corporate acquisitions and realignment, what can and should a plant based purchaser do?

Some Quick Figure Work

Animal Health currently represents 8 percent of GLP's global business or about $640 million. This is before the Jones Clarke acquisition, the size of which is not disclosed, but sounds major.

The London plant is sourcing $11 million in Canadian dollars or about $8 million US. Assuming purchasing dollars at 33 percent of sales, this would give the London plant a sales volume of about $24 million US or about 4 percent of the Animal Health group's current total sales. The addition of the German product line is expected to increase production by 30 percent. If the sales volume is similar for the German products to the Canadian line, this would increase purchases by about $3.3 million in Canadian dollars or about $2.2 million USD and sales by about $32 million USD. It is beyond the scope of this case to discuss the rationale for closing the German plant.

Presumably, the availability of excess capacity in London, Canada, had something to do with making them responsible for the eight products key to this case. That the best laid plans for inventory build up did not materialize suggests that closing the German plant has run into some difficulties.

The eight products to be transferred from Germany represent 9 formulations, 13 different sizes and up to 13 label languages. No information is provided about the number of ingredients that each formulation represents, but at an average of 10 ingredients, they would represent about 80 ingredients (assuming Vitopax 1 percent and 10 percent would use similar ingredients.)

Given that the London plant already sources 1100 raw material and packaging items, the possibility might well exist that some ingredients and or packaging requirements could be identical.

Ian's Priorities

It is absolutely vital that the flow of high quality products with correct labeling be continued without interruption. Thus, materials and packaging have to be available in time to allow the London plant sufficient time for start-up, training, possibly some experimentation and setting up an effective distribution for finished product. No time limit is provided in the case, but Ian should be part of a Canadian planning and logistics team to ensure no hiccups will occur in the hand-over from the Germans.

Major Options

1. If timing is extremely tight, the simplest immediate procurement action might be to order sufficient ingredients and packaging requirements from the current German plant suppliers and assure continuity of finished product.
2. A slightly more sophisticated approach would be to check for overlap between the requirements for the eight German products, ingredients and packaging against the current Canadian requirements. For identical raw materials and packaging, substitution might be arranged, and the remainder ordered from current German suppliers.
3. If time permits, the current Canadian approved suppliers could be checked for ability to provide the ingredients or packaging for the eight German products.
4. It is possible that other GLP plants, and, possibly a GLP head office procurement group (no mention of such a group is made in the case) could be of assistance in locating suitable suppliers.
5. The soon to be accomplished merger with Jones Clarke represents another potential long term possibility for creating a central procurement group for common requirements or, at least, coordination of purchases on a worldwide basis. On the assumption that, at least, Animal Health is currently totally decentralized in its purchases, each plant's purchasing manager is on his or her own.

The Type of Product and Size

It is not clear from the case whether the London plant currently produces a similar profile of products to the German range, and injection, tablets, suspension, or paste. Presumably, these are common forms of animal health types of presentations and should not, in themselves, represent huge barriers.

The same can probably be said for the size range. In either case, should anything be particularly unusual, this might require special attention.

Label Languages

Label languages may represent some unusual challenges. Extreme care needs to be taken to ensure no mistakes are made in any transfer of responsibility regarding languages. It sounds as if GLP is moving toward world or regional mandates for its production facilities in an effort to rationalize where this makes sense. Language watchdogs may have to be appointed to ensure faultless execution.

Quality Control

The quality requirements in the pharmaceuticals area are such that traceability and formulation integrity are vital. This means that any supplier chosen needs to prove capability over time and supplier switches are not simple and quick.

FINAL COMMENTS

The German plant sourced its requirements for these eight products in Europe. It is reasonable to expect that in the long run new North American suppliers need to be found to shorten supply lines and simplify logistics. In this case there is a big difference between the immediate need to avoid finished product shortages and the longer term goal of developing a suitable North American or worldwide supply base.

With the scarcity of information in the case about GPL's and Animal Health's procurement activities, it is difficult to comment on how much procurement responsibility each plant in the system should have. It is likely that sooner or later, corporate-wide questions regarding supply will be raised and the role of the plant purchaser might change substantially.

Marathon Oil

Teaching Note

IMMEDIATE ISSUE

The immediate issue is the location of the IPO for Sakhalin.

BASIC ISSUES

1. Organization for international procurement.
2. Project procurement.
3. Procurement for resource based organizations.
4. Procurement in a consortium.
5. Purchasing strategy.

SUGGESTED STUDENT ASSIGNMENT

If you were Bob Engel:
1. What factors would influence your decision on the location of the IPO for the Sakhalin Island Project?
2. What would you do next and why?

POSSIBLE DISCUSSION QUESTIONS

1. Does a separate IPO for Sakhalin make sense?
2. Would changes in partners in the project make a difference?
3. What is the significance of the Sakhalin location?
4. If the Sakhalin project lay off the Louisiana coast how would this affect your answers? Off Kuwait? Off Nigeria?
5. What relations should this IPO have with other IPOs of Marathon? Head office?
6. Would you like to work in an IPO like this? Why?

DISCUSSION

A large number of factors may influence the decision on the Sakhalin Island IPO location:

1. The project itself and its requirements.
2. Project phases.
3. Project location.
4. Environmental aspects.
5. Project planning and managerial team location.
6. Consortium members.
7. Location of suppliers.
8. Existing supply strengths at Marathon.

1. The Project Itself and Its Requirements

The Sakhalin project sounds like an oil industry dream. A brand new rich discovery in a remote location with both oil and gas in abundance. Off-shore, however, is more expensive than on-shore and Sakhalin is part of what used to be the USSR with everything that implies in terms of political instability and risk. Even though the oil industry is well acquainted with such risks, it pays not to underestimate them.

A 12 billion dollar project like this represents significant financial exposure, even for the consortium members. At this point the date of the rights approval is unknown. The construction season is short. A lot of infrastructure needs to be put in place. It is safe to assume that for the consortium members delays in bringing the project in once the rights have been granted will be very costly, both in ROI and increased political risk. The two bright spots, presumably, are the richness of the deposits and the Russian government need for royalty income.

By the way, this is the region of the world in which Russia and Japan have been squabbling over what territory belongs to whom. The presence of Japanese members in the consortium, necessary though they may be for market and financing reasons, probably adds to the political sensitivity on this deal. The absence of any Russian partner on the consortium is another matter.

2. Project Phases

The project is really composed of five major phases:

1. The planning phase.
2. The construction phase.
3. The start-up phase.
4. The running phase.
5. The shut-down phase.

At this point the IPO will be primarily concerned with the planning and construction phases. In the longer haul, the start-up and running phases will require continuing support to ensure effective performance and maintenance of equipment and facilities, quite a different role from the project nature of planning and construction.

Start-up will require fast response to problems as they crop up. Presumably this will occur in stages and may well happen in parallel with some construction activities. For example, one platform may start well ahead of others. Natural gas may lead or lag the oil production side.

3. Project Location

The remote location of the Sakhalin Island and the lack of local industry creates some special problems. These are well familiar to the oil industry, where remote locations are often the norm. Some local supply presence will eventually be required to ensure that those requirements which can be locally obtained □ food, lumber, accommodation, gravel, sand and a variety of services □ will be obtained locally. Such local purchases become very important to ensure local political support for the project. Local employment will also be a vital factor.

4. The Environmental Aspects

Despite the remote location of Sakhalin, the size of the project, the international sensitivity, plus the off-shore nature will require careful environmental management. Oil or chemical spills would be very damaging to consortium members, both in the short term as well as the long term. Suppliers of equipment, suppliers of transportation, and the consortium members will all have to exercise extreme caution in this regard.

5. Project Planning and Management Team Location

The location of the project management team will clearly influence the location of the IPO. Once the project starts, local management at Sakhalin Island will be required to supervise construction, subcontractors, etc. Some local supply presence will have to be provided at that time to support local activities. Some personnel with Russian language skills and local familiarity, as well as supplier expertise will be useful to provide the necessary local supply support. Such people may not be easy to find!

However, in the planning and engineering stages of this project, where the major decisions will be made regarding requirements and specifications, it is important that supply be intimately involved and in close proximity to the engineers and other planners. For this planning phase, the IPO staff should be wherever the engineering decisions are made.

6. The Consortium Members

It is not unusual for consortium members to have influences and requirements for supply priorities on projects such as this. It appears that the Japanese have a fairly straight-forward piece of the action with heavy focus on natural gas. Shell's role seems to be primarily in engineering. McDermott as the platform builder has another key piece of the project. It does not appear, at first glance, that Marathon's supply hands are severely tied in terms of its procurement options but they do have to be checked out to ensure that consortium sensibilities are recognized.

7. Location of Suppliers

McDermott as the supplier of the platforms is both a consortium member and a supplier of some of the key equipment that will be used. Under extreme conditions, platforms may well cost 2 to 3 billion dollars each. Therefore, proximity to McDermott will be a significant factor to consider, especially if McDermott takes over full responsibility for drilling platform maintenance and/or operation as soon as the project starts.

For production, pipelines, tanks, and pumping stations, along with tanker filling facilities will require suppliers capable of meeting deadlines, as well as technical specs. It is expected that a significant number of North American suppliers exist that can supply these needs. Therefore, a US location and, especially Houston with its proximity to McDermott and specialized skills at headquarters and other Marathon supply and technical personnel appears attractive at first glance.

8. Existing Supply Strengths at Marathon

The location of the IPO office could, theoretically, be anywhere in the world. Some locations appear to be better, however. Scotland has already an IPO and connections and would be close to Shell in Holland. Houston would be close to headquarters, McDermott, procurement talent, and engineering talent. Japan would be physically close to the project and to consortium members. The presence of experience supply personnel in the area of the IPO location would be a factor, especially if significant delays before project start permit alternative use of these people. Proximity to the Sakhalin Island project team, project engineering and project management is probably a major plus, as would be quick access to major suppliers.

Given today's communication technology and the relatively low cost of personal travel compared to the cost of this project, mean that factors somewhat different from the traditional proximity to the project itself can have a greater significance. The specific supplier expertise for off-shore drilling and exploration is quite different from that for roads and buildings.

IMPLICATIONS FOR PURCHASING

The implications of the above remarks for the task facing Bob Engel are obvious. The procurement role on this project will be to help ensure project completion early, or at least on time, to specification and to budget. Supply and delivery assurance are probably of greater significance than price, particularly if project start-up might be delayed.

The uncertainty about the project commencement date means that a lot of planning needs to be done ahead of time and suppliers must be ready to start as soon as they get the go-ahead. Obtaining supplier priority and flexibility will be part of the supply challenge. Since Marathon is taking on the lead role in engineering and construction, it is vital that they provide top notch people for the supply team.

ACTION

A discussion with Sakhalin Island project managers might be a very good start to clarify objectives, timing and the type of supply expertise required. A key decision that needs to be made deals with the extent that Marathon insiders will be used for the IPO team versus outsiders specifically hired on a contract basis. Also, for subcontractors, will Marathon do the buying or will they be in charge of securing their own requirements?

The advantages of using Marathon personnel to occupy key positions in the IPO team are obvious. Experience will be a key requirement. The disadvantage is the loss of these personnel from their current duties and the need to substitute for them. The early stages will require fairly large numbers of people in the IPO, while ongoing requirements probably require different and fewer people, more geared to MRO supply. Eventually, disposal may require a different expertise again. For a project this size that might be decades away as continued exploration will probably develop further opportunities over the years and extend the life of the project.

Chapter 15

Public Purchasing

Topics Covered

Characteristics of Public Purchasing
    Source of Authority
    Budgetary Restrictions/Limitations
    Outside Pressures
    Greater Support of Public Service
Programs
    Perceived Absence of Interest Costs
    Little Formal Inspection
    Lack of Traffic Expertise
    Time Required to Modify the Organization
    Salary Levels
    Lack of Confidentiality
    Importance of Specifications
    Acquisition Procedures
    Emphasis on the Bid Process
    Difficulty in Recognizing Past
Performance
Trends in Public Purchasing
Federal Government Purchasing
    History
    Small Business Favoritism
    Labor Surplus Area Favoritism
    Buy American Act

    Preference for Environmentally Preferable
Purchases
    Renegotiation
    General Services Administration (GSA)
    Military Purchasing
    Postal Services (USPS)
State and Local Government Purchasing
    History
    Participant in GSA Contracts
    Prison-Made Goods
    Cooperative Purchasing
    Local-Bidder Preference Laws
Innovations in Government Purchasing
    Longer Term Contracts
    Use of Automated Systems
Model Procurement Code
Health-Care Purchasing
Questions for Review and Discussion
References
Cases
    City of Roxborough
    Don Willit Associates
    TriCity

QUIZ RESPONSES

C | 1. One of the intents of the Competition in Contracting Act (CICA) of 1984 was to:

   a. increase the requirements for formal advertising.
   b. reduce the requirement for more procurement planning and research.
   c. promote full and open competition where all responsible offerers are allowed to compete
   d. discourage use of commercial, as opposed to specially-made, products.
   e. discourage the use of performance specifications.

A | 2. In the CAPS benchmarking study on state and local government purchasing:

   a. most of the respondents reported utilizing some form of centralized purchasing.
   b. most of the respondents reported utilizing some form of decentralized purchasing.
   c. none of the respondents reported using centralized purchasing.
   d. most reported utilizing virtual centralization, in which there is a centralized contracting process with decentralized execution.
   e. no one reported using virtual centralization, in which there is a centralized contracting process with decentralized execution.

B | 3. The guarantee that if the order is awarded to a specific bidder, it will accept the purchase contract; and if the supplier refuses, the extra costs to the buyer of going to an alternative source are borne by the insurer, is known as:

   a. performance bond.
   b. bid bond.
   c. security bond.
   d. payment bond.
   e. guarantee bond.

C | 4. | The Model Procurement Code:

   a. was started in the late 1990s by the National Institute of Governmental Purchasing for state and local purchasing activities.
   b. established legally binding statutes to ensure uniform purchasing procedures across all fifty states.
   c. was designed to provide policy guidance, remedies for controversies, and a set of ethical guides for public buyers.
   d. has not been widely accepted.
   e. has been abandoned by most of the early adopters.

B | 5. | In public sector purchasing, when deciding to keep an existing supplier or switch to a new supplier, the past performance of a supplier:

   a. is heavily weighted in the evaluation.
   b. is often difficult to recognize, particularly if it has been excellent.
   c. may be considered in the evaluation as long as the information is quantifiable.
   d. may be considered as long as multiple people in the buyer's organization offer the same evaluation.
   e. may never be considered as part of the evaluation.

A | 6. | In a 1999 study, *Purchasing Performance Benchmarks for State and County Governments*, conducted by the Center for Advanced Purchasing Studies (CAPS), a comparison of public and private procurement revealed:

   a. two similarities, (1) the use of automated purchasing systems to process transactions and track purchasing activities, and (2) multiple-year contracts.
   b. no similarities.
   c. one similarity, the use of automated purchasing systems to process transactions.
   d. one similarity, multiple-year contracts.
   e. one similarity, strategic alliances/partnering.

E | 7. | The "Buy American Act" passed by Congress provides that on certain government purchase requirements:

   a. international suppliers can bid only on items with a unit purchase price of under $15,000.
   b. international suppliers can bid only on items with a unit purchase price of under $100.00.
   c. only international firms with a plant in the United States are eligible to bid.
   d. all purchases must be made from suppliers who are in a labor surplus area.
   e. the purchase order will be awarded to the domestic supplier if its price is not over a given percentage amount over that of the international supplier.

E | 8. Public sector purchasers are mandated to:

   a. select the lowest priced bidder in all circumstances.
   b. limit the number of solicitations to reduce bureaucracy.
   c. issue a formal bid solicitation for every purchase.
   d. only buy from U.S. suppliers in all circumstances.
   e. seek maximum competition.

D | 9. The emphasis on the bid process in public purchasing:

   a. makes it difficult for the smaller supplier to compete for sales to the government.
   b. minimizes the administrative paperwork required.
   c. typically permits the purchase of materials within a very short period of time.
   d. tends to put undue weight on price as the basis for supplier selection.
   e. makes it somewhat easier for the buyer to favor a particular supplier than if it were a negotiated purchase.

C | 10. Trade groups representing small and minority-owned businesses believe that efforts to streamline government procurement, incorporate best-value considerations, simplify procedures, and encourage an electronic marketplace:

   a. may favor small businesses over large businesses.
   b. will have no effect on supplier selection decisions.
   c. threaten to dilute or eliminate legislation that awards contracts to small and minority businesses.
   d. will result in cosmetic changes only to the supply base of most public purchasing entities.
   e. will usually resulted in higher prices paid for items bought.

True and False

F	1.	Governmentwide acquisition contracts (GWAC) in which one agency pays an administrative fee to use contracts for information technology products and services operated by another agency are no longer allowed by the GSA.
F	2.	Most public purchasing professionals support the adoption of a "Local Bidder Preference Law" since it simplifies the acquisition process.
T	3.	Privatization refers to the practice of the government getting out of a business altogether and turning it over to private enterprise.
T	4.	In public purchasing, normally all information on prices submitted by suppliers, and the price finally paid, must be made available to any taxpayer requesting it.
F	5.	CAPS benchmarking studies found that a large portion of public funds are spent to purchase services, and these purchase decisions are being made primarily by buyers in the purchasing department.
F	6.	Cooperative purchasing contracts, used by public purchasing agencies, have the greatest advantage for larger purchasing units, such as large cities and states.
T	7.	The application of Diagnostic-Related Groups (DRGs)-based payment system provides an incentive for holding down costs and improving efficiency in the U.S. healthcare system.
T	8.	The public buyer generally must be willing to consider any supplier who requests to be put on the bid list.
T	9.	The General Services Administration (GSA) is the U.S. federal government's biggest e-commerce success with GSAAdvantage.gov, which lists more than a million items.
F	10.	A *responsible* bidder is one who has submitted a bid that conforms to the invitation for bid.

City of Roxborough

Teaching Note

IMMEDIATE ISSUE

To whom should the sodium hypochlorite contract be awarded?

BASIC ISSUES

1. Public bidding process.
2. Multiple bids from the same supplier.
3. Cash discounts.

SUGGESTED STUDENT ASSIGNMENT

1. As Joe Graham, what is your assessment of the sodium hypochloride bid situation?
2. What action would you take and why?

POSSIBLE DISCUSSION QUESTIONS

1. Why might a supplier accidently submit two bids?
2. Why might a supplier intentionally submit more than one bid?
3. Why might a supplier appear twice on the City's bidders' list?
4. Does the variation between the first and second bid signify anything?
5. What is the significance of the 2/10 terms offered by James Corporation?
6. In private industry would the situation be handled differently and how and why?

DISCUSSION

Which of the Two Ryerson Bids Counts?

The decision as to which of the two bids of the Ryerson Company prevails is trivial. By the City's own by-laws the latest bid governs. Unfortunately, for the City this one is the higher of two bids. For 132,000 litres the sales manager's bid amounted to 132,000 x 0.1710 = $22,572. The sales representative's bid amount to 132,000 x 0.1760 = $23,232. The difference of ½¢ a litre amounts to $660.

Is Ryerson the Lowest Bidder?

Now that the question has been settled as to which of the Ryerson bids applies, the next question centers on which supplier should be selected. To review, here are the quotes

Ryerson	James Corp.	JON
.1760 / litre	.1770 / litre 2/10 or net 30	.1771-.1803 / litre depending on load size

JON can, therefore, immediately be eliminated as the high bidder. James Corp., however, has offered a 2/10 discount. This brings the early payment price down to $.1770 - .00354 = .17346, which is below the .1760 price quoted by the sales representative of Ryerson!

The question now remains whether this price with the early payment discount is better than the net 30 price quoted by Ryerson. For this we need to know the cost of money for the City of Roxborough. We can assume that the 7.5% figure given in the case is one appropriate reference point. Theoretically, short term money should be less expensive than this. Therefore, if at a 7.5% rate it is cheaper to go to James, it clearly would be better to do it at a lower rate.

A monthly delivery of 132,000 litres ÷ 12 months = 11,000 litres per month. Under Ryerson's offer this would cost 11,000 x .1760 = $1,936. Under James Corp.'s offer it would cost 11,000 x .17346 = $1,908.06. The difference = $27.94 per month. At a 7.5% cost of money for the City of Roxborough the cost of being 20 days early on the James Corp. offer amounts to .075 x 20 ÷ 364 x $1,908 = $7.86. Thus, we can see that by $27.94 - $7.86 = $20.08 the James Corp. offer is the better one. Had the sales manager's bid not been superseded by the sales representative's, Ryerson Company would have been the low bidder.

AN OVERVIEW

It is true that this is a bit of a tempest in a tea pot. The total amount of money is relatively trivial. The principles involved are not, however, and that is one of the key points in public procurement.

How the City could have sent out two different bid requests to Ryerson is a good question. This kind of inattention does not stand the supply function in good stead. Similarly, it is interesting that Ryerson responded twice. The probable explanation is that the sales manager and the representative acted independently, because of the two different bid requests. It shows that coordination of bids is also not a strong point at Ryerson. Perhaps it is a poetic justice that their mix-up cost them the contract.

It should be emphasized, however, that there is a very legitimate reason for allowing bidders to change their quotes up to bid submission deadline. Should an error be found in the earlier quote, this can still be corrected. (Submitting the first bid 5 minutes before the deadline removes this option.) Rejecting the bids and asking for new ones doesn't make any sense here because (1) there are no grounds, (2) the small size of the total contract, (3) it's likely to delay delivery of the material. Because of the chemical nature of the product, it is undoubtedly environmentally sensitive. This means that both the supplier and the transportation company delivering it are subject to special conditions and scrutiny.

It is interesting that it was not necessary to use the full bidding procedure at the City for this requirement. The annual amount of money falls below the $56,000 limit that requires a bidding process. It is not explained in the case why this decision was taken.

A Comparison to Private Practice

A comparison to private practice may be enlightening here. It would be normal, particularly if Ryerson had been the incumbent supplier, to phone them to clear up any misunderstanding. Second, in either private or public procurement the first question should be why sodium hypochlorite was not made part of a larger bid for all older control chemicals? The cost of a separate contract and the possibility of lower transportation savings (this is certainly identified in the JON bid which recognizes volume differences) might well suggest that a total chemicals contract might make more sense. Nickel and diming pieces of the total half million dollar requirement may prevent significant overall savings and total cost of ownership of the whole chemical package.

On this kind of contract, quality, delivery, supplier reliability, and environmental considerations as well as, possibly, particular technical expertise and assistance to the operators may be very useful. Could this possibly have been a long term contract for the whole package?

Don Willit Associates

Teaching Note

IMMEDIATE ISSUE

Is Supplier C still a potential candidate for the computer hardware and software contract?

BASIC ISSUES

1. The role of a consultant in a procurement situation.
2. The role of additional information once a supply decision has been taken.
3. Supplier reliability and financial status.
4. The uniqueness of hardware and software from a procurement prospective.
5. Dealing with difficult financial conditions and supplier relations.

SUGGESTED STUDENT ASSIGNMENT

1. As Don Willit, what is your analysis of the computer systems re-engineering project supply decisions to-date?
2. As Don Willit, how would the news of Supplier C's financial difficulties affect your recommendations in your report?
3. What action would you recommend and why?

QUESTIONS FOR DISCUSSION

1. Is the steering committee an appropriate means to deal with a re-engineering study such as this one on computer systems?
2. Why is compatibility of such relevance here?
3. If Supplier C went bankrupt how could the city protect itself?
4. Why might the financial condition of Supplier C not have been apparent before?
5. What is the role of a consultant on a project such as this?
6. What could happen to Supplier C if it did go bankrupt?

DISCUSSION

This case, although it is set in a public setting, is the potential nightmare of most supply people. It also represents a significant challenge for Don Willit. Can he still recommend Supplier C as the best source, despite its financial difficulties?

THE PROJECT

The total re-engineering project involves at least 8 million dollars worth of purchases plus a tremendous amount of people, resources, and time. With 5 million dollars in personal computers and a communication network, and another 2 million dollars in computers and 1 million in software and training, this represented a major undertaking for the city. The use of a massive steering committee including 20 people, give some indication of the scope of this project. It is already behind schedule and further delays may significantly affect the city's administrative system.

Supplier C

If Supplier C was able to garner sales of only 1.9 billion on an asset base of 1.5 billion dollars, this may well explain the loss of 750 million dollars. It sounds as if Supplier C has high fixed costs. It behooves Don Willit to find out whether this loss has been incurred because of the introduction of a new product, or whether other explanations for such a massive loss are in order. Clearly, the key question is whether this is a one time loss or whether it is likely to recur. Any significant recurrence will force Supplier C into bankruptcy. It may be difficult for an outsider like Don Willit to get the full scoop on all the details regarding Supplier C. It is probably wise to take a fairly pessimistic perspective. The computer industry has been going for some time through a period of rationalization and contraction. It is not at all unusual for organizations to be successful one year and to be in significant financial difficulty in the next period. It is obvious that Supplier C has some significant strengths as its high quality hardware and software tend to imply.

It should also be recognized that whether the city likes it or not it is already heavily into C at this point. It has its hardware standardized with C hardware and its software is extensively used inside also. Therefore, even if they do not go with C for this next phase of the re-engineering project, the question of C's survival will have to be addressed in view of its installed base within the city.

KEY QUESTIONS

The key questions at this point become: (1) Should Supplier C be ruled out as a potential supplier for the 3 million dollar contract? If so, how should the city proceed? (2) If C should not necessarily be ruled out, how can the city protect itself from its potential financial difficulties and might the city possibly profit from C's uncomfortable financial position?

To address these questions, it might be useful to have a look at what is happening in the computer industry. It is not at all unusual for the stronger players to acquire their weaker rivals. Such may well be the case with Supplier C. It must have a substantial customer base using hardware and software developed by Supplier C. Service contracts alone must represent a significant asset. Even in the worst case scenario where Supplier C went bankrupt, someone would have to keep servicing this installed base.

POTENTIAL OPTIONS

There are a few potential options available to the city at this point. One would be to bite the bullet and select one of the alternate supplier options with all of the attendant problems of training, compatibility, and higher cost. It also might delay the total re-engineering project significantly. The net result might well be an adverse effect on customer service and the city's own productivity and effectiveness.

The option of selecting Supplier C is no longer as simple as it seemed to be originally. Given the precarious financial position of Supplier C, it is vital that the city protect itself in case of Supplier C's future demise. This might require Supplier C to set up a service office in the city, staffed with appropriate personnel to ensure that the city would be able to continue using Supplier C's hardware and software in the future. Another option might be to try to hire some of Supplier C's more knowledgeable people onto the city staff and its own information systems area to assure continuity and expertise. Don Willit would do well to talk to the major users within the city to find out what the minimum amount of outside support required would be and whether it is reasonably feasible to consider Supplier C as a supplier.

Ultimately, Supplier C's financial condition may put the city in a tremendous bargaining position. It might be able to profit from Supplier C's difficulties and negotiate itself an even better deal than it thought it had on it's original bid.

If Supplier C's Management Systems package for municipalities is a particularly attractive one, other municipalities using the supplier may be interested in assuring the continuity of these systems. Perhaps the city can combine with others to ensure continuing updating of the software. The hardware may be less critical than the software in this particular application. Some supplier development work may well be in order, should the city want to avoid increasing its own staff levels.

CONCLUSION

Obviously, the new twist will require a reassembly of the advisory steering committee. It is probably useful to do that once a feasible solution to the challenge has been found. Since the next step is to bring the package to City Council, it will be necessary to persuade the elected officials that your plans are foolproof. It is important that they be protected from looking ridiculous in the public eye by approving a contract with a near bankrupt supplier.

TriCity

Teaching Note

IMMEDIATE ISSUES

1. Elaine Carter needs to decide how to ensure the new procurement system functions properly.
2. She also needs to think of possible safety nets she needs to design into the workflow to ensure such issues are caught ahead of time.

BASIC ISSUES

1. Procurement processes.
2. Issues arising from changing methods of buying.
3. Change management in a public sector setting.
4. IT issues related to new technology implementation and resistance to change.
5. Managerial issues of creating innovative solutions to unexpected problems.

SUGGESTED STUDENT ASSIGNMENT

1. If you were in Elaine Carter's position, what would you do?
2. What kind of safety measures would you take to avoid similar mishaps?

ANALYSIS

1. Elaine is facing a customer service issue. The implementation of Integrated Procurement has seen resistance from several stakeholders, certain customers who lost on-line ordering facilities are already feeling alienated, and the credibility of the new system is at risk.
   a. Students should identify the importance of the procurement role to this organization.
   b. The role of everyday inventory (wiper blades) in large dollar concerns (snow-truck) should also be noted.
   c. Elaine has to take immediate action to provide wiper blades to her customer. Since the purchase amount for such items should be minimal, she can initiate a Purchase Order immediately.
   d. The vendors of the new system should be asked to come in and immediately check for technical problems with the system. They should also be asked to check other orders that have been entered to check for the integrity of the system.

2. Elaine can take the following actions:
   a. Inform her customers about the possible problem in the short-run. This will allow her the time to mitigate any further problems.
   b. Continue with the old system of ordering on-line to ensure the process works. The new system has only been in implementation for over a month so technical issues may continue to arise.
   c. Request additional budget to provide human resources to monitor the process. Although difficult to sell, due to budget constraints in the public sector, this may be justified due to the importance of the ordering process, and the impact malfunction can have on the operations of TriCity.

The student should also think about the issues involved with change in this situation. The diagram below suggests a possible thought process:

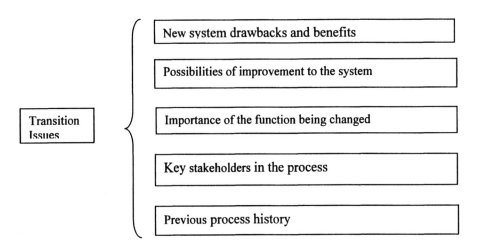

Possible Recommendations:

- Elaine should launch an effort to inform all customers about the new system.
- The Vendor should be required to help resolve basic problems.
- Elaine can request increased budget to revamp the system entirely. However, with limited budgets, this may not be possible.
- Elaine can also recommend that the system be eliminated and the previous one installed. However, it is important to remember that it has only been just over a month since its implementation, and that the learning curve may be a large part of the reason for problems.

FINAL COMMENTS

Unfortunately, in many IT decisions, purchasing tends to have little input and receives often inadequate attention. It is possible and actually likely, that the fleet manager is overstating the case. Wiper blades can be obtained in a hurry from appropriate sources. His complaint can be seen more as frustration with the new system, as he is one of the 10 lucky ones who do have direct access to the new integrated procurement system.

CHAPTER 16

Capital Goods Acquisition

Topics Covered

New Equipment--New Technology
    New Equipment Acquisition
    Special Problems of Equipment Buying
    Importance of Cost Factors
    Life Cycle Costing or Total Cost of Ownership
    Engineering Service
Selection of the Source
    Design and R&D Considerations
    Some Legal Questions
    Special Budgeting Procedures
    Disposition of Obsolete or Replaced Equipment
Procurement of Used Equipment
    Reasons for Buying Used Equipment
    Sales Contracts Terms
Leasing Equipment
    Advantages and Disadvantages of Leasing
    Types of Leases
    Categories of Leasing Companies
    Lessor Evaluation
The Acquisition of Construction
    The Traditional Approach to Construction and Pitfalls
    Different Approaches to Construction Acquisition
    On-Site Considerations in Construction
    Purchasing Involvement in Construction
Questions for Review and Discussion
References
Cases
    Mark Appleton
    Casson Construction

QUIZ RESPONSES

B   1.   The total cost of equipment is:

      a. quickly offset by the income derived from the use of the equipment and therefore of little importance.
      b. composed of initial equipment cost and a series of estimates, such as the effects of idle time, obsolescence, maintenance and repair, displaced labor, and even direct operation factors.
      c. unaffected by such elements as plant layout, kind of power used, and types of machines used for other operations.
      d. easier to determine with exactness than, for example, the total cost of raw materials.
      e. composed of two quantifiable cost elements: purchase price and after-sales service.

D   2.   A turnkey supplier:

      a. normally provides training for purchaser personnel so that they can work on the turnkey project during its construction phases.
      b. usually has access to capital funds at lower rates of interest than the purchaser.
      c. usually provides the maintenance on all equipment after the project is completed.
      d. relieves the purchaser of substantial subcontract responsibilities and risk.
      e. normally finances all phases of the project until it is completed.

D   3.   The purchase of used equipment:

      a. should only be considered if the price differential between new and used is at least 30 percent.
      b. can never be justified in a well-run organization.
      c. makes sense when the machine will be used continuously.
      d. may be considered for use in a pilot or experimental plant
      e. should not be considered when time is essential because of the long lead times associated with delivering used equipment.

E | 4. Multipurpose equipment:

   a. is not easily disposed of and has a low salvage value.
   b. usually is available from a narrower range of suppliers than single purpose equipment.
   c. may require extensive consultation between technical personnel of both buyer and supplier to determine specifications.
   d. has a short technological life.
   e. may have a variety of uses in many industries.

B | 5. Buying capital equipment differs from other types of purchases because:

   a. the selection of the supplier is a tactical corporate decision.
   b. determination of final cost includes estimates over the life of the equipment.
   c. tax considerations may not significantly affect delivery and transfer of title.
   d. a and b.
   e. a, b and c.

A | 6. In the office equipment field:

   a. it is normal for the lessor to purchase the equipment to the buyer's specifications and perform all services.
   b. it is normal to find finance lease companies.
   c. leases are normally written so that the purchaser pays a hidden premium of 11 to 12 percent.
   d. there are strong advantages for dealing directly with international suppliers.
   e. rapid change of technology makes leasing highly preferable to buying.

E | 7. For tax purposes, a transaction likely would be considered a purchase rather than a lease if:

   a. the agreed rental payments exceed the current fair rental values.
   b. the lessee will acquire title on payment of a stated number of rentals.
   c. the total amount which the lessee pays for a relatively short period of time constitutes an inordinately large proportion of the total sum required to transfer title.
   d. some portion of the periodic payments is specifically designated as interest.
   e. all of the above.

C | 8. Total cost of ownership:

   a. is used to determine the amount of capital appreciation a real estate property is likely to face in a certain market.
   b. requires that the purchase cost of a capital asset be divided into total years of service to end up with a purchase cost per year.
   b. requires that future costs and benefits be discounted to establish a current expected value.
   c. is used to build up a reserve fund to replace all their obsolete equipment.
   e. recognizes that every product on a piece of equipment has its own life cycle which can be constant over time.

A | 9. In the acquisition of construction:

   a. special contract provisions normally deal with on-site regulation governing construction personnel.
   b. it is usually best for the purchaser to perform the role of prime contractor.
   c. cost over-runs are uncommon.
   d. it is preferable to avoid architectural costs by dealing directly with a contractor.
   e. it is useful to recognize that there are no bargains in constructions.

B | 10. A full-service lessor:

   a. is uncommon in the automotive, office equipment, and industrial equipment fields.
   b. generally obtains discounts or rebates from equipment manufacturers which are not disclosed to the lessee.
   c. uses outside sources of financing.
   d. mainly obtains its profits from maintenance and service charges which are in addition to the lease rate.
   e. does not purchase or maintain the equipment.

True and False

F	1.	One disadvantage of leasing is an increased risk of obsolescence.
T	2.	Having a continuing relationship with the supplier of capital equipment is a primary consideration in selecting a source for capital equipment.
F	3.	The decision whether to lease or not is heavily driven by quality considerations.
F	4.	For balance sheet purposes, capital assets are normally expensed rather than depreciated.
F	5.	The book value of equipment is a significant consideration at the time of its disposal.
F	6.	Leasing is a cost effective way for departmental heads to acquire equipment for long-term use when no capital budget exists.
T	7.	In the Construction industry, an e-commerce provider can link the entire construction team with passwords enabling differing levels of access to information and services related to the project.
T	8.	New technology frequently permits an organization to gain competitive advantage on the bases of different products and services at significantly lower cost.
T	9.	In construction buying there is great incentive for the purchaser to consider requests for proposals.
T	10.	Since equipment is not commonly bought until needed, it is seldom bought during periods of business recession, although prices for equipment normally are low at such times and many good arguments can be advanced for buying then.

Mark Appleton

Teaching Note

IMMEDIATE ISSUE

Should Mark Appleton acquiesce to the project engineer's vendor preference?

BASIC ISSUES

1. The sharing of responsibility and authority with regard to supplier selection between purchasing and engineering.
2. The role of purchasing in broadening lists of potential vendors.
3. The treatment and evaluation of low bidders.
4. The role and ethics of bidding.
5. Acquisition of capital assets.

SUGGESTED STUDENT ASSIGNMENT

As Mark Appleton, what action would you take on the construction project and why?

POSSIBLE DISCUSSION QUESTIONS

1. What should engineering's role be in the selection of construction contractors?
2. What should purchasing's role be in the selection of construction contractors?
3. How should disputes between engineering and purchasing be settled?
4. How should trade-offs between economics, corporate peace, risk, etc., be assessed in a reasonable fashion?
5. Was Mark Appleton correct in suggesting two additional vendors?
6. What is a meaningful bid?
7. What is comfort level?
8. What alternatives are open to Mark Appleton?
9. What action will you take and why?

DISCUSSION

The purchasing/engineering interface is often a difficult one for many organizations. Ideally, the strengths of each should be brought to bear on purchases with engineering content. It is not at all unusual for engineering to try to carry the ball completely, leaving, at most, a paperwork role for purchasing.

For Browne and Coulter Engineering (BCE), the proposed building itself is a relatively minor capital project. Nevertheless, the total dollars are still in a significant range and the difference between the low bidder and the next one is a sizeable $168,000, or about 42 percent of the bid from Andrews Construction as shown below:

Bidder	Bid	Recommended for Bid List By
Andrews	$404,000	Appleton
Foster	$572,000	Forker
Moore	$604,000	Appleton
3 Bidders	>$650,000	Forker

This case is classic in the use of the term "high level of comfort" by engineering. It is not clear whether this comfort level refers to quality, delivery, or just past record. Obviously, the project engineer is willing to pay a substantial premium for this designation of comfort.

It might be useful to go back over Mark Appleton's actions in this case. Presumably, the project engineer had "high comfort level" with four vendors. Was this the total extent of her prior experience? Mark Appleton from his experience questioned the original list proposed by engineering and, presumably, called correctly on three out of the four instances. Mark Appleton's assumption may have been that once the project engineer accepted the addition of two more vendors to the bidder's list, she implied acceptance of these vendors if they made an acceptable bid. Apparently, this assumption was not correct. It is possible that the project engineer agreed to this suggestion of more bidders knowing full well she would not accept either anyway? This, then, raises the question of corporate ethics. Disagreements on bid lists should be settled in-house before bids are submitted. In the preparation of a bid, the vendor incurs significant cost and should have the assurance the bid has a reasonable chance of acceptance if it is competitive. By acquiescing to Mark's request, the engineer did Mark, her own organization, and the two vendors a disservice, if she had no intention of accepting their bids.

Since Mark Appleton is a senior contracts buyer, it is safe to assume he has at least reasonable experience and that his suggestion as to alternate sources was realistic. His two suggested vendors turned in substantially different bids, about $200,000 apart. However, they were both among the three low bidders.

The case indicates that technical competence is important and that the project had a tight schedule. Both probably influenced the bids provided by the contractors. However, any delays may hold-up completion of a current project and potentially damage relations with a customer.

NEXT STEPS

Mark Appleton now has to make a judgment call. Does he feel strongly enough about this purchase to make an issue of it? He could go back to the project engineer and try to argue it out further. He could also at the same time indicate he is not satisfied with the engineer's reasons. Obviously, BCE is a large, engineering-based organization, and may well be engineering dominated. Nevertheless, unless purchasing does make a stand on issues where it knows it is right, BCE's procurement effectiveness might well be impaired. The art is in picking the issues, the people, and the times where it makes good purchasing, engineering, and corporate sense to proceed along the lines purchasing recommends.

Mark Appleton would also do well to discuss the situation with his superior in the purchasing department for advice and support. Perhaps this issue may have to go up the ladder if it cannot be resolved between Mark Appleton and the project engineer. Mark Appleton may wish to double check if BCE has prior experience with his recommended supplier and if he can find appropriate documentation on their prior performance. If his choice of contractor was not based on prior experience with BCE, does he have adequate proof that his recommended source can handle the job adequately?

One possibility may well be that the proposed laboratory structure is part of a larger project with requirements Mark may not be fully familiar with at this point. If, for example, significant time or quality trade-offs are at risk here, he should be ready to change his mind on relevant additional information. It is also possible that in the engineer's mind the cost of the building is not significant in relation to the total project.

The difficulty with issues of this sort is that precedence is always established. If purchasing's role in supplier selection is limited to paperwork only, it is doubtful the job would be attractive to energetic and well-qualified staff. Under those circumstances, the engineering department might well have a purchasing clerk in its own office to process the paperwork.

Casson Construction

Teaching Note

IMMEDIATE ISSUES

1. How to deal with a late and uncooperative subcontractor on a construction project?
2. How to leave an audit trail for potential subsequent legal action?
3. How to deal with a high profile customer when a supplier's inaction threatens on time project completion?

BASIC ISSUES

1. Prime contractor – subcontractor relations.
2. Project management.
3. Managing schedule compliance.
4. Legal aspects of supply.
5. Dealing with broken promises.
6. Working in a family business.

SUGGESTED STUDENT ASSIGNMENT

If you were in the position of Robert Casson:
1. What would be your analysis of the Langford Precast situation to date?
2. On reflection, might Casson Construction have proceeded differently with respect to Langford Precast since Casson was awarded this contract by the university?
3. What action, if any, would you take now and why?

POSSIBLE DISCUSSION QUESTIONS

1. Are purchaser-supplier relations in construction different from relations with suppliers in manufacturing, in the public sector?
2. At what point in a project do you decide to change subcontractors?
3. At what point in a project do you threaten legal action?
4. How much should the prime contractor get involved in the subcontractor's business?
5. Would you like to work for your father in the family business?

DISCUSSION

An academic visitor from England specializing in construction purchasing said, "Constructon is purchasing and managing supplier relations." The very nature of the construction business has evolved into one where the general contractor's expertise lies in securing contracts on the one hand and, on the other, managing its supply base to assure a quality product, meeting all specifications, on time delivery and on budget. The highly competitive nature of the construction industry and the unique, customized design of each project require a general contractor with sharp quality, time and cost management skills.

It is interesting to note that the father of Rob Casson has tried to introduce a philosophy of cooperation and flexibility with customers and suppliers to build a unique reputation for his firm. Robert Casson should try to resolve the current challenges at Langford Precast within that philosophy, if at all possible.

The current situation is serious because no resolution is yet in sight and the precast delays threaten successful and timely completion of the Family Law Library renovation and addition. Late completion may not only cause serious penalty charges, but also harm the reputation of Casson Construction with the University and the community at large. The project is similar to the Olympics. Late delivery is not an option. This is an important starting point because it dictates priorities for Robert Casson at this time. While it is important to have appropriate documentation for eventual legal action, should it ever come to that, it is far more important to assure successful, on time project completion.

In retrospect, it sounds as if Casson Construction has been lax in responding to early danger signals with Langford Precast. For example, after a March 2 meeting at which it was agreed that a color and texture sample was due on March 8, this sample was only submitted two months later on May 6. Similar slippages allowed on other promises may have lulled the subcontractor into believing that schedules need not be kept.

The role of promises, kept and broken is at the heart of the subcontracting business, indeed, in all of purchaser—supplier relations. In the construction industry it is normal practice for general contractors to enlist bids from subcontractors prior to preparing a project bid. Unfortunately, upon winning a project bid, the general contractor often engages in a second round of bidding with the subcontractors trying to squeeze prices. Thus, trust is lost between general contractors and their subcontractors. No evidence of this practice is suggested in the Langford Precast situation. It may, however, explain to some extent the inability of Robert Casson to move Langford to a more cooperative mode.

Part of the difficulty clearly lies in Robert Casson's lack of understanding as to what is causing Langford's reluctance to fulfill its obligations. Is Langford secretly hoping to get out of this contract because:

A. It lacks the capability to meet the exact requirements of the window precast units?
B. It lacks the capacity to meet all of its commitments and is favoring its more profitable business over its less lucrative contracts?
C. It fails to understand the criticality of its commitment both to the university and Casson?
D. It does not see Casson as a desirable or potential long-term client and has, therefore, low priority for this job?
E. It is in financial difficulties?
F. It is Robert Casson's personality?
G. Something else?
H. A combination of the above?

Notice, that as long as Robert Casson does not understand the nature of the challenge he faces at Langford, the only option he can offer is threats of dire consequences such as legal action. Even non-payment for work already completed is ineffectual, since Langford has not invested much in the up front work on this project to date.

The letter, at least, gives Robert Casson a legitimate reason for requesting an immediate meeting with Langford. It may well be that Robert will have to enlist the help of his father, who, surely, has faced similar challenges in the past. Maybe his father, alone, or together with Robert can engage in the: "Let's cut out all of the bullshit, what's really going on here" type of discussion that needs to take place. Once the real cause has been identified, then the appropriate remedy can be developed. For example, if it is a lack of technical expertise, experts or consultants may be able to help or the job may have to be moved to another contactor or the architect may have to relax some specifications.

If Langford is not making any money on the job, perhaps ways of cutting costs can be explored. The idea of paying more is obviously not appealing, because it sets a bad precedent and eats at vital margin. It may be necessary, however. If the problem is one of capacity, working overtime, or subcontracting out the less difficult parking bumpers may help.

The key point is that extracting promises has proven to be meaningless so far. Therefore, the core cause of Langford's reluctance to meet its commitments needs to be determined and appropriate and speedy corrective action developed.

A successful resolution of this bind in which Casson is seen as a problem solver rather than as a bully may well strengthen relations between Langford and Casson, so that future cooperation will be a realistic possibility as both sides gain trust and confidence in each other. These latter statements are based, of course, on the presumption that Langford has key skills and capabilities in the precast area that could be successfully improved with better management.

THE LEGAL SIDE

It is well beyond the coverage in this textbook to worry about what exact legal language would be considered appropriate for Robert Casson's letter. Clearly, he needs advice from Casson's legal counsel if he really wants to be on safe legal ground. Unfortunately, by the time the legal views would be raised in court, the project would and should be completed. Thus, it is the threat of legal action that Robert Casson wants to employ. It is not at all clear from the case that this threat will induce Langford to perform. It certainly is a strong warning that should be applied carefully. In the language of the supplier relations coverage of this text — legal action is a "crunch" tool.

THE FINANCIAL IMPLICATIONS

Admirable as Robert Casson's concern over not spending extra money on this project is, given the consequences of late delivery on Casson's reputation, he may well have to consult with his father and siblings on the need to spend beyond budget. Given that precast is now a critical item on the critical path it is no longer appropriate to assume that budget integrity will be preserved.

Chapter 17

Services Purchasing

Topics Covered

Services
- How Significant Are the Dollars Spent for Services?
- Purchasing Department Involvement
- What Makes Services Different?

A Framework for Analyzing Services
- Value of the Service
- Degree of Representativeness
- Degree of Tangibility
- Direction of the Service
- Production of the Service
- Nature of the Demand
- Nature of the Service Delivery
- Degree of Standardization
- Skills Required for the Service

The Acquisition Process for Services
- Need Recognition and Specification
- Developing the Statement of Work (SOW)
- Analysis of Supply Alternatives
- The Purchase Agreement
- Service Contract Administration

Getting Greater Supply Involvement
- Process for Obtaining Results

Questions for Review and Discussion
References
Cases
- Erica Carson
- Talbot County School Board
- Scope Repairs

QUIZ RESPONSES

B   1.   The statement of work (SOW) is:

       a. the legal document provided by potential suppliers guaranteeing they have the capability to meet the buyer's requirements.
       b. the document that describes the needs of the internal customer, communicates those needs to the supplier, and ultimately becomes the basis of the service contract.
       c. the document that provides the buyer with the supplier's rationale for being awarded the service contract.
       d. the document that clarifies the internal user's role in continuous quality improvement with the specified service provider.
       e. the supplier's action plan for service quality improvement to become a certified supplier.

C   2.   Services directed at people:

       a. are of high tangibility.
       b. are of low value.
       c. normally require the involvement of the ultimate user in both the specification and assessment of the service.
       d. can often be measured by standard statistical control means.
       e. require little interaction between supplier personnel and purchaser personnel to determine compatibility.

A   3.   The tangibility of a service:

       a. may affect the ease of evaluation of potential suppliers.
       b. has low impact on its price.
       c. can best be handled letting the users specify a preferred supplier.
       d. is easily measured.
       e. is best ignored at the time of acquisition.

B   4.   In the acquisition of repetitive services:

         a. the acquisition process is best left to the user of the service.
         b. a high value could be acquired under a long-term contract.
         c. it is useful to try out a large number of different suppliers to determine which one is the best.
         d. if demand is discrete, on-time delivery performance is relatively unimportant.
         e. if directed at equipment, will require low technical skills of the purchaser.

E   5.   Purchasing's low involvement in buying services may be explained by:

         a. the complexity of specifying service needs and analyzing potential service providers means that the user has greater expertise than the purchasing department.
         b. the buying of services involves more of a personal relationship between the service supplier and user.
         c. many services in the past have been available only in a governmentally regulated environment, in which the price and service-delivery requirements were essentially the same from all suppliers.
         d. a and b
         e. a, b, and c.

E   6.   ABC analysis:

         a. allows the purchaser to separate the low tangibility services from the high ones.
         b. allows purchasers to evaluate the performance of service suppliers.
         c. allows the purchaser to separate discrete demand services from continuous services.
         d. is inappropriate in a service context.
         e. is entirely appropriate in a service context.

D | 7. High labor intensity services:

a. are normally best done in-house because it is too hard to evaluate employees of outside suppliers.
b. require special materials management skills.
c. are best contracted to small suppliers.
d. may require the purchaser to pay special attention to the capability of the supplier to supply a sufficient number of people of the right skills.
e. are very difficult to cost out.

C | 8. Make or buy in service acquisition:

a. should be of low concern to the purchaser.
b. is most common in services of high intangibility.
c. is a significant consideration.
d. is basically a financial consideration.
e. is of little concern in services purchasing.

C | 9. Competitive bidding in the acquisition of services:

a. is most appropriate when there are relatively few potential sources of supply.
b. is a quick and easy way to determine which suppliers are potentially interested.
c. can easily be justified when the degree of customization is low and supplier skills required for the service are low also.
d. is most appropriate when the tangibility of the service is high.
e. is a quick and easy way to determine which suppliers are potentially interested.

B | 10. Quality control in services:

a. is relatively simple.
b. tends to be difficult if the service is to be evaluated during delivery.
c. does not require statistical analysis.
d. is particularly difficult for services of high tangibility.
e. is most easily done on the buyer's premises.

True and False

T 1. In the need recognition and description stages of service purchasing, two things are defined: (1) exactly what the supplier will provide, and (2) what the purchaser will do to help the supplier perform as required.

F 2. It is normally best practice to place full responsibility for all aspects of service delivery on the internal customer.

F 3. Samples are not of any use in the acquisition of services of high tangibility.

T 4. Quality control in service acquisition is quite different from quality control in materials acquisition.

F 5. Recent research indicates that corporate outsourcing will decline since it offers few advantages as a a competitive tool.

T 6. One type of formal service quality evaluation process measures the gap between service expectations along five dimensions and the perceptions of actual service performance.

T 7. The notion of "best buy" applies to services.

T 8. The ability of the buyer to negotiate a warranty for a consultant's work depends on the clarity of functional requirements and the availability of objective criteria for assessing performance.

F 9. User specification is most common when the degree of standardization of the service is high.

F 10. When buying services, the buyer should always insist on a fixed price contract.

Erica Carson

Teaching Note

IMMEDIATE ISSUE

What action would you take on Killoran's attempt to secure some check printing business?

BASIC ISSUES

1. Purchasing for a service organization.
2. The price, quality, delivery, service trade-off.
3. Supplier selection and splitting of business.
4. The purchase of services.
5. Treatment of unsolicited proposals from suppliers.

SUGGESTED STUDENT ASSIGNMENT

If you were Erica Carson, what action would you take on the quotation received from Killoran?

SUGGESTED QUESTIONS FOR DISCUSSION

1. What importance is the check printing to the bank?
2. How would you do a cost analysis on a check printing order?
3. How would you evaluate a supplier of check printing for this bank?
4. How many suppliers are desirable for check printing?
5. What alternatives are open to Erica Carson here?
6. What action will you take? Why?

DISCUSSION

Erica Carson's first objective must be to assure that the flow of printed checks continues uninterrupted and with high quality to the bank's customers. A delay in check forms may well mean that the customers do not use the bank's services and create frustration on their part. Misspelled names and addresses would also cause customer frustration and reflect on the bank's image of reliability. Since each printing order is a small custom job, special attention to detail and rapid service are of vital concern here as compared to price. It is reasonable to assume that courier charges paid by the two current suppliers are significant. The recent cost study also showed that prices paid to suppliers were fair and that their cost performance was in line. Given this background, the low bid by Killoran becomes suspect.

KILLORAN'S BID

As long as Killoran's bid is unsolicited and unofficial it falls into a very special category. It seems clear from the case that Killoran's low price is an attempt to gain at least part of the check writing business. It also appears clear that Killoran's recovery of its costs would have to come from their promotion of "scenic checks". What is it that Killoran proposes to do with our customers that our current printing firms are not doing? Is there a possibility that they may pursue our customers more aggressively? Is there any possibility that they might turn-off some of our existing customers? Is there also a possibility that they might be charging more for scenic checks than our current suppliers to make up for the losses on the regular check business? Provided that the answers to the above questions are not negative, there might be an advantage to our bank of having more scenic checks sold. This would mean that we would not have to pay for the standard personalized checks and it might help cut down on our annual commitment of $8 million per year. If one third of our customers who are currently using standard personalized checks would be switched to scenic checks, this might represent a saving of $2.7 million dollars per year. If such an opportunity realistically exists, perhaps the bank itself should be investigating ways and means of accomplishing this. Leaving it to a printing supplier to accomplish this task might not be in the bank's best interest.

Purchasing personnel are always bombarded by unsolicited, unofficial quotations. How to handle these "feelers" is part of the good buyer's art. Unless a supplier is willing to commit on paper the details of an offer it can only be assumed as non-existent. If Killoran represents a reasonable source, perhaps they should be given a chance to quote on the next round. No new suppliers such as them should be given a significant round of business until they have proven they can handle all the intricacies very well. Thus, it could be several years at least before they could be considered a sound and proven supplier.

The one exception to the above remarks deals with the possibility that Killoran might have more advanced equipment, or better systems, to handle this type of work. If so, the question can be raised why they were not selected for this kind of work before. Also, what was the quality of our cost analysis study that it did not reveal this kind of information?

If buyers started giving business to every supplier who came in with a low or unofficial quote, the world would be full of disappointed buyers. It is normally understood that a supplier, to take away business from well performing and established suppliers, must make it attractive enough for the buyer to switch. The easiest way to draw a buyer's attention is with a low price. Only when that price appears to have a longer time horizon attached to it, and the back-up of all of the appropriate services necessary to satisfactory completion of the order, should the supplier be seriously considered.

In this case the service aspect is at least as important as the printing of the checks. Faultless electronic transmission of data, security, rapid response and high quality printing to assure proper machine reading of checks are all part of a complex requirement in which supplier reliability and trust are vital.

Talbot County School Board

Teaching Note

IMMEDIATE ISSUE

What should be done about the elementary school photocopier service contract?

BASIC ISSUES

1. Managing supplier relationships.
2. Customer service impact.
3. Public versus private acquisition.
4. The role of Purchasing as a specifier.
5. Legal/contractual issues in supply.
6. Selection of appropriate methods of price determination.
7. Budgeting.
8. Acquisition of services.
9. Consortium buying.

SUGGESTED STUDENT ASSIGNMENT

What is your assessment of the current situation at the Talbot County School Board regarding photocopier servicing? As Paul Travers, what action would you take next and why?

QUESTIONS FOR DISCUSSION

1. As an employee at Talbot County School Board, what are your purchasing needs here?
2. What are the economics of the situation? How significant is this matter?
3. What are the major budgetary items in a school board's budget?
4. How effectively has Paul Travers performed his job regarding the photocopier service contract?
5. How do you define quality here?
6. Do you think Paul should negotiate a contract for photocopier services? How long do you think it should be?
7. What do you think of the option to recycle toners?
8. Should Paul send the contract out for bid?
9. Should Sigma receive a retroactive price adjustment?

10. Why did Paul continue to use Sigma when he suspected or knew their prices were 50 percent below the market cost?

ANALYSIS

This case deals with several issues that are fundamental to purchasing: price determination, customer service, budgeting, negotiation, and cost control. An appropriate place to start is with some calculations:

At 0.9 cents per copy for 8 million copies, the Talbot County School Board (TCSB) was paying $72,000 per year to Sigma. At the new price of 1.4 cents each, the total cost comes to $112,000 per year, or an increase of $40,000. The recycling alternative will provide a savings of 0.2 cents, or $16,000 per year.

Consequently, the net price increase is $24,000. With thirty schools in the district, this is only $800 per year per school. So why not just pay the extra cost and move on?

Two important issues must be taken into consideration. First, this can be a potentially embarrassing situation for Paul. He may be asked to explain why he missed his budget by so much, and why he can't find another supplier at the same price. It seems that he they have had an artificially low price for several years, and a big jump may reflect poorly on Paul.

Second, most of a school board's costs are salaries and wages, maybe as high as 90%. Since these are fixed, based on negotiated and binding contracts, opportunities to control costs are limited to a relatively limited number of controllable items, such as service contracts. In other words, even a small reduction in a school board's budget, will put tremendous pressure on the purchasing department.

The other side of this argument is that the 90% of the budget must be properly supported. This relates to the issue of service to Purchasing's customers: teachers, support staff and administration personnel. At 8 million copies, and a total of 30 elementary schools, each school produces an average of 267,000 copies annually, on one copier per school. Assuming an average of 50 teachers per school, this represents an average of 5,340 per teacher each year. Copier downtime, poor quality, and other problems will result in inefficient use of staff time. An important issue in this case is that Paul should keep focused on the larger picture: how can he adequately support the needs of his customer at an efficient price? Cheaper toner or recycling systems will not be answer here if it results in copier breakdowns and inefficient use of staff time. A $40,000 price increase is only a fraction of the annual cost of one teacher (especially with benefits included).

Other Considerations

There are several other factors that must also be taken into consideration. First, why has the TCSB been paying for the service contract up-front? The case indicates that the service contract was paid in advance. At 12% cost of capital, this represents an annual cost of $8,640. This does not seem like good business practice, especially when you suspect your supplier has priced the work under cost. It is, however, especially dangerous taking into consideration the fact that a formal contract does not exist. However, if the fee has already been paid, it may be worthwhile for Paul to question whether Sigma has a legal obligation to fulfil the service contract for the balance of the year. This may provide a good bargaining chip in negotiations. The flip side is that any decisions to switch will need to take this issue into consideration.

Second, how are the contracts for the secondary schools handled? Better still, how do other school boards or public organizations handle their copier contracts? A popular way for public organizations to deal with budget cuts is through the use of consortiums. It makes sense for Paul to at least investigate how similar arrangements are handled for the other schools boards and local public institutions such as hospitals, municipalities and federal government offices. Volume is a good motivator to suppliers for price reductions.

Third, how much time does Paul want to devote to this problem? Other areas may provide greater returns. However, a $40,000 problem is definitely worth straightening-out. Ongoing administration and follow-up after a decision has been finalized should be minimized. The system should function effectively.

Fourth, the clock appears to be running in terms of retro adjustments. Although the request to make the adjustment effective the beginning of the year may be a bargaining ploy, any delays may result in a financial obligation.

Evaluation of Alternatives

At the end of the case, three alternatives are presented: agree to pay, pay and use the recyclable toner, and look for a new supplier. A reasonable way for the students to approach this is an advantages/disadvantages or pros/cons analysis.
Agree to pay is the least attractive. Paul would likely face difficult questions and scrutiny if he simply accepted the proposal. The advantages are that he would protect a relationship with a good supplier and he would not have to spend much time distracted by this problem. Accepting the new price scheme with recycled toner helps demonstrate that he has reacted to the problem, although only partially.

It seems logistical here to at least consider the alternative of a new vendor. Ultimately someone will ask Paul if he considered this option. It is likely that Sigma will expect Paul to look around, so any bad blood should be minimal. Such an investigation will either justify Sigma's position or help identify another vendor.

Students should not be limited to these options. Several other viable alternatives exist.

Next Steps

Clearly Paul should not let this problem drag-on. The costs of having the new owner of Sigma get frustrated and withhold services would represent a significant problem. Furthermore, there is the issue of retroactive pricing. The longer things go, the weaker Paul's argument becomes.

Paul should consider the following:

1. Has the service fee been paid and for what period? What are the implications if it has been paid? Paul can find this out with a quick call to the legal and accounts payable departments.
2. How are similar service contracts handled by other school boards and local public institutions? Is there an opportunity here for a consortium arrangement? This should also be fairly easy information to locate.
3. Meet with the owner of Sigma and explain that he will have to market-test the contract in order to justify a price increase.
4. Before implementing toner recycling, or other cost saving measures, the new system should be tested to ensure that it does not result in extra downtime or inferior quality.
5. This is definitely a situation where negotiation comes into play. Everything should be on the table for negotiation here: the advance payment at 9 cents per copy, potential for lost business for the supplier, and the cost of recycled toner systems. Combining the recycled toner savings with the savings from not re-paying make-up more than half of the original price increase.
6. In the long-term, Paul can look for other opportunities for cooperative buying with other school districts, and perhaps, other public organizations, such as hospitals. These efforts do not have to be limited to copier services, but can be extended to other areas as well

When the students present their action plans, watch for timing mismatches: long-term solutions for short-term problems. Students should first deal with the short-term aspect of this case before suggesting solutions that have long-term implications, such as consortium buying.

Scope Repairs

Teaching Note

IMMEDIATE ISSUES

1. What to do about scope repairs in the short run.
2. Where to move on scope repairs in the longer term.

BASIC ISSUES

1. Supplier dishonesty and malfeasance.
2. Dealing with OEM's.
3. Cooperative purchasing in the public sector.
4. Make or Buy.
5. The acquisition of services.
6. Purchasing responsibilities and involvement in technology.

SUGGESTED STUDENT ASSIGNMENT

As Mark Greig, what is your analysis of the scope repair situation at Victoria Hospital and what action would you take and why?

POSSIBLE DISCUSSION QUESTIONS

1. Is there anything fishy here?
2. What do you think of Barton?
3. What do you think of Larson?
4. What is going to happen to the use of scopes in hospitals?
5. What are the costs of scope failure?
6. Where is the purchasing department?

ANALYSIS

This case has a lot of angles which may not be apparent on first reading. A good place to start is with endoscopy itself.

THE USE OF SCOPES

As the case suggests, the use of rigid and flexible scopes permits exploratory and corrective surgery without full anaesthesia and without major incisions. Therefore, it is safe to assume that future use of scopes is likely assured and may well expand as the technology becomes more reliable and further applications are found.

Currently, a lot of problems still appear to be present with the technology. Scope break-down during surgery requires delay or abandonment of the operation, surely expensive to both patient and the hospital, not even counting the psychological costs. With an average operation cost of $1,000-$2,000 (pure guess--no data given in the case) and a patient loss of time and productivity at $250, avoidance of abandonment, or 100% scope performance has high rewards attached to it. This can be achieved through provision of a high quality scope at the start of the operation and constant availability of a back-up scope for every operation. The cost of providing such a back-up is relatively minor given the high cost of abandonment or even delay. the reluctance to VH to invest in additional scopes and to prefer borrowing at the last minute from other local hospitals gives an indication of the tightness of funds.

The case description suggests that currently an endoscope, particularly a flexible one, is a highly sensitive, state of the art type of equipment, requiring very careful handling, frequent repairs and continuous inspection and maintenance. Presumably, at some time in the future they may become more reliable, more technicians will be able to perform minor repairs, at least, and some standardization will take place. Apparently, despite the equipment's sensitive nature, Victoria Hospital does not keep many spares around for every type of scope used, requiring going without until after repairs have been completed, or borrowing from another hospital.

FIGURE WORK

No data are provided regarding the number of operations delayed or aborted because of scope problems. Some guestimates may help, however. Total scope repairs of $60,000 at $300 per repair average amounted to 200 interruptions of operations. At a cost of $1000 per operation, this would incur a $200,000 interruption cost. Obviously these figures need to be checked. The principle, however, that scope repairs cost is relatively low compared to OR disruption is probably sound. Another argument for life cycle and activity based costing information!

A decision rule that at least one back-up scope be provided for every operation would cut down drastically on the number of aborted operations. If scope failure happens to be 200/2500 or 8% as suggested above, dual failure would be 8% x 8% or .64% and reduce the number of aborted operations from 200 per year to .64% of 2500 or 16 per year. Note that complete prevention of scope failure gets to be expensive. A two scope back-up policy would reduce the .64% to about .05% or about 1 interruption per year, but would save about $15,000 in aborted operations.

The total inventory of scopes currently available is not given. An examination of the records and the operations schedule would indicate how much of an additional scope investment would be required to be able to provide at least one back-up scope during each operation. If coordination between the three hospitals is a possibility, a combined scope inventory might make such a back-up system more easily possible than if each hospital had to have its own private back-up inventory.

The length of time that a scope is out of commission for repairs is obviously a factor also in this deliberation. Assuming one scope under repair, one scope for operation, and a third for back-up would require a minimum scope inventory of three of each type of scope on average. Fast repair would greatly reduce the need for a third scope.

In a total London perspective, each individual hospital might require three scopes of each type. If operations can be scheduled in advance, avoiding use of the same scopes simultaneously at all three hospitals, the need for 9 scopes centrally could easily be avoided and an inventory level of 5 scopes would permit two operations simultaneously (1 scope each for operation and backup) and still allow for one scope on repair. This does assume standardization is possible, as well as coordination across the London area.

A look at the dollars and numbers provides a useful preliminary insight. VH spends about $60,000 per year in outside repairs and performs about 2,500 operations requiring scopes. Therefore the outside repair cost comes to about $24/scope use. This does not count the routine preventive maintenance, inspection and preparation of a scope just before an operation. New scopes and allied equipment cost another $90,000 per year for a total of $150,000 per year for VH. At 2,500 operations per year that comes to an outside capital and repair cost of $60/scope. Inside costs in terms of management and technical support are not identified but are probably significant.

In the scheme of things, relative to the hospital's total budget the amount of money spent on scope and scope repair is not huge. It is probably a B item in total hospital perspective. Nevertheless, if significant savings potential exists, given the tightness of hospital budgets, it should be explored.

SCOPE REPAIRS AND MARKET DEMAND

Scope repairs currently cover four areas: (1) preventive maintenance, (2) screening before repair (estimates), (3) minor repairs, and (4) major repairs. If 80% of the repair work covers the first three categories, about $48,000 of the $60,000 currently spent might be a candidate for in-house work.

Apparently, the other two London hospitals use scopes more extensively as their repairs combined total $180,000.

If London is about one thirtieth of Ontario's population, then Ontario scope repair demand would total about $7 million and Canada about $21 million. And if the ratio of new equipment vs. repairs at VH is indicative of the demand for new scopes and associated equipment, then the total London market for equipment would be $360,000, the Ontario market about $10.5 million and the Canadian market about $31.5 million. Even though in only one hospital neither the equipment or its repairs represent a huge outlay, on a provincial or national base the market for repairs and equipment are significant. For the US these numbers can be multiplied by at least ten.

WHAT'S WRONG?

What's currently wrong with repairs by Barton and others? Repairs seem to be expensive, they take a long time and the integrity of suppliers is in doubt. That the Toronto connection could reduce repair costs by 40% is an indication that repairs were too expensive and that non-OEM's can do decent repairs.

Speed of repair cuts down on the need for spares, important from a capacity investment and technological obsolescence perspective. Since each scope needs at least $20,000-$30,000 of associated equipment, it is really a $50,000 piece of equipment with a replaceable scope of $20,000.

The really disturbing aspect of this case deals with supplier integrity. Overcharging is one thing. Claiming for unnecessary repairs is another. And wilfully damaging scopes to scare purchasers into staying with the OEM is absolutely criminal. At the moment, the behavior of Barton is very suspect. And, unfortunately, Larson's behavior as a new untried supplier in Manitoba is incomprehensible. When a client brings a screwed-up scope they should be able to prove that this is not their doing and their quality of work is beyond any shadow of doubt. Also, their three week repair far exceeded the promises of their sales rep. Therefore, currently, VH does not have a satisfactory repair service available and could well have a case for criminal behavior with at least Barton, who also supplies OEM equipment.

ALTERNATIVES

Alternatives at this point include:

(1) Do nothing; (2) Straighten out Barton; (3) Straighten out Larson; (4) Perform minor repairs in-house; (5) Set up a London connection repair service; (6) Use Toronto's repair service; (7) Develop another supplier; (8) Standardization and simplification; (9) Go to the US; (10) Some combination; (11) Other?

1. Do nothing is not acceptable based on the information available.

2. Straightening out Barton would involve obtaining satisfactory explanation of the criminal activity, evidence of corrective and disciplinary action, and agreement that future repairs would be fair and reasonably priced and fast. This might take a substantial effort and results are not guaranteed. Conceptually, it would make sense to contract for repairs and price at the time of purchase of the new equipment rather than treating purchase and repair as independent buying decisions.

3. Straightening out Larson would make sense if they were the only Canadian option. They are far away and have not performed satisfactorily so far, even though their first scope repair performed OK for 25 operations over three weeks. (With a scope out for three weeks of repairs and three weeks use, its effective capacity is only 50%).

4. Minor repair capability in-house would, hopefully, speed up scope return and improve availability and start to build up expertise which would cut down on supplier overcharging. For $48,000 of repairs, it is doubtful this is sufficient to justify this option.

5. A cooperative venture to set up separately or in-house a London scope repair facility might come closer to being economically viable. With $240,000 of total repairs or $192,000 of minor repairs, a 40% saving would be $79,000, sufficient to warrant the $10,000 equipment investment and $2,000 in training. At a technician cost of about $40,000 per year, this might be doable if all three hospitals cooperate and suppliers were willing to supply parts at reasonable prices.

    If the London shop could also service the rest of South-Western Ontario, the volume might triple and make the venture more attractive.

6. Use of Toronto's repair service, if possible, would at least reduce costs by about 40% and avoid having to establish a London shop. It would build on Toronto's established expertise and increase their volume so as to improve buying power and learning curve performance. The existence of a Toronto facility makes the Manitoba option much less attractive.

    If Toronto is willing to give London access to their service, setting up a London shop would have to be compared to the Toronto option, rather than the status quo. If Toronto cannot accommodate the London volume, maybe Toronto could set up a satellite operation in London and then London could benefit from Toronto's expertise and buying power and yet receive the benefits of having a local source.

7. Developing another supplier would make sense if no reasonable alternative existed in the market place. Currently, the Canadian market for both repairs and new equipment is sufficiently large to have at least a number of repair facilities and several OEM suppliers.

The current repair volume for VH does not justify a large amount of VH staff time on this option.

8. Standardization and simplification. This is the kind of situation where with a large number of types of scopes standardization and simplification could potentially contribute, provided medical performance would not be compromised. Repair service would become more focused and efficient, spare inventory would be reduced and training cost minimized.

No matter which of the other options is chosen, standardization and simplification should be pursued where possible.

9. Given the size of the US market, there have to be reliable sources of equipment and repair service. Understanding what the options are helps sharpen the reasons for any decision. Even though there might be some cross-border hassles (repair services have been troublesome in cases), the North Americana Free Trade Agreement (NAFTA) is supposed to make cross border trade more feasible and easier. If reliable, high quality suppliers in the US can give fast service at good price, it is their performance that sets the benchmark for what any Canadian option has to meet or beat.

10. Combination of the above options are clearly a possibility and desirable.

11. Other options may well exist. Eliminating scopes had better not be one. A more interesting one follows.

DEALING WITH OEM'S

Hospitals are surely not the only purchasers in the world who have to deal with OEM's and repair service. There is lots of experience in the field outside of medicine that can be brought to bear on the scope situation. Anyone who buys equipment faces the same situation.

If VH had a reliable, high quality supplier of scopes and repairs, they might envision a purchasing arrangement as follows.
The supplier would charge a specific price for each scope use, be responsible for all repairs and be subject to penalty for every operation in which a scope failed during use. The supplier could provide an in-house technician (or in-town technician) or in-town technician to service one or more hospitals) and also be responsible for training of doctors in scope use.

VH is a long way away from that kind of partnership or alliance at this point but it could be considered as a long term target, not just for scopes, but other equipment as well. Given the status quo, it is in the supplier's interest for equipment to break down, rather than perform, the exact opposite of what the hospital needs. Synchronizing hospital needs and supplier interest would have beneficial results for all. (And angulation wires would be a good start).

WHO BUYS?

What is interesting in this case is that the purchasing department is not involved in this purchase. Mark Greig is a highly qualified individual in a technical and education sense, but his purchasing expertise is probably not there. He would do well to consult his hospital's purchasing group for advice. Perhaps the Biomedical Engineering Department should have its own buyer attached to it. Frequently, in technical areas the assumption is that purchasing has no meaningful involvement and contribution to make. As a result, purchasing is shut out and technical people bungle on the procurement side. They would be horrified if the tables were reversed, yet have difficulty accepting the notion that purchasing expertise is just as relevant as technological expertise in services of this kind.

CHAPTER 18

Strategy in Purchasing and Supply Management

Topics Covered

Definition of Strategic Planning
Levels of Strategic Planning
Supply's Contribution to Business Strategy
Major Challenges in Setting Supply Objectives and Strategies
    Social Issues and Trends
    Government Regulations and Controls
    Financial Planning with Suppliers
    Product Liability Exposure
    Economic Trends and Environment
    Organizational Changes to Facilitate
Long-Term Productivity and Efficiency
    Product or Service Line
    Competitive Intelligence
    Technology
    e-Commerce
    Investment Decisions
    Mergers/Acquisitions/Disinvestment
    Time-Based Competition
Risk Management
    Supply Interruptions and Delays
    Direct Increases in Cost
    Managing Supply Risks
    The Corporate Context

Strategic Planning in Purchasing and Supply Management
Major Purchasing Functional Strategy Areas
Strategic Components
    What?
    Quality?
    How Much?
    Who?
    When?
    What Price?
    Where?
    How?
    Why?
Trends in Purchasing in Supply and Supply Management
The Future
Questions for Review and Discussion
References
Cases
    Saint Mary's Health Center
    Heat Transfer Systems Inc.
        Custom Windows Inc.

QUIZ RESPONSES

B   1.   A supply strategy that is just in an embryonic form is the trend toward:

        a. increasing the number of third- and fourth-tier suppliers.
        b. the development of a network of suppliers around a central customer.
        c. further definition and strengthening of functional lines in an organization.
        d. Increases in cycle time as supply lines lengthen.
        e. separation of supply strategy from organizational strategy.

E   2.   Trends already underway in supply management include:

        a. movement of managers from other functional areas into supply management and elimination of requirements for technical credentials such as a science degrees.
        b. a concentration of professionals educated specifically in supply management with no technical credentials or previous employment in other functional areas.
        c. a concentration of information technology specialists who can automate the purchasing process so the organization can reduce headcount.
        d. an emphasis on transactions rather than process as organizations focus on using e-commerce applications to eliminate the purchasing department.
        e. an emphasis on the process used in acquisition, and the use of e-commerce applications as tools for simplifying and reducing transactions.

D   3.   In terms of supply management's role in strategic planning, studies done in the 1980s and 1990s by the Center for Advanced Purchasing Studies:

        a. dispelled the notion that linking supply strategy to corporate strategy is needed.
        b. reported that most firms have mechanisms in place to link supply strategy to corporate strategy.
        c. reported that only firms in the manufacturing sector need to link supply strategy to corporate strategy.
        d. reinforced the notion that linking supply strategy to corporate strategy is needed.
        e. reported that only firms in the non-manufacturing sector need to link supply strategy to corporate strategy.

A | 4. The primary purpose of a firm using a strategy of selling production equipment to a third party and then entering into a lease-back arrangement is to:

   a. free up capital for more productive uses.
   b. minimize user liability.
   c. obtain a lower purchase price.
   d. shift the risk of obsolescence from the original manufacturer.
   e. simplify equipment maintenance procedures.

D | 5. The purchasing quality strategy which emphasizes "Do it right the first time" is known as:

   a. process quality control.
   b. supplier certification.
   c. statistical process quality control.
   d. zero defects.
   e. ultimate cost-based buying.

A | 6. Normally, most organizational objectives can be summarized under four categories:

   a. survival, growth, financial, and environmental.
   b. marketing, management, financial, and operations.
   c. profitability, return on investment, liquidity, and earnings per share.
   d. survival, market share, earnings per share, and return on investment.
   e. growth, maintenance, new products, and asset management.

C | 7. In regards to environmental protection, a long-term strategic question for the organization is:

   a. are there any current environmental laws which our organization isn't following?
   b. is there any pending environmental legislation that our organization should be lobbying against?
   c. how can we redesign products to eliminate the use of environmentally unsafe materials?
   d. should we include additional clauses in our contracts to put the burden of environmental responsibility on our suppliers?
   e. should we increase our spending on governmental affairs to have a greater influence on legislation?

C | 8. | Which of the following is *not* one of the five major purchasing substrategies:

a. Assurance-of-supply strategies.
b. Cost-reduction strategies.
c. Performance strategies.
d. Supply-support strategies.
e. Competitive-edge strategies.

B | 9. | Peter Drucker defines strategic planning as:

a. a discrete process.
b. doing things today to obtain tomorrow's objectives.
c. taking big risks to maximize current period benefits.
d. delegating decision-making authority to employees throughout the organization.
e. a procedure for allocating resources to appropriate functions in the organization.

E | 10. | Three major strategic challenges facing the supply manager are:

a. (1) How many suppliers should we do business with? (2) Which suppliers should we select? and (3) What type of relationship should we have with these suppliers?
b. (1) Should we have a centralized or decentralized purchasing structure? (2) should we hire managers trained in supply management or in technical fields? and (3) Should we outsource any or all of the purchasing function?
c. (1) How can we simultaneously provide uninterrupted supply and minimize inventory? (2) How can we improve quality while reducing our supply base? and (3) How can we increase our involvement in outsourcing decisions?
d. (1) Should we precertify suppliers? (2) Should we allow internal users to purchase certain categories of purchases? and (3) Should we increase or decrease the number of suppliers in our supply base?
e. (1) What is the effective interpretation of corporate objectives and supply objectives? (2) What is the appropriate action plan or strategy to achieve the desired objectives? and (3) How can supply issues be identified and integrated into organizational objectives and strategies.

True and False

T	1.	The strategy of deciding to buy an item that previously was made in house is known as outsourcing.
F	2.	Time has become a less important factor in product differentiation because of the proliferation of choices available to the end consumer.
F	3.	Supplier development is an aggressive process where the seller takes the initiative to create a buyer where none currently exists.
F	4.	To align supply strategies and objectives with those of the organization, the supply manager must wait for someone from top management to translate corporate objectives into supply objectives, and designate a strategy.
T	5.	If an automobile manufacturer buys a radio producer and also produces its own semiconductor devices, this would be an example of a strategy of vertical integration.
F	6.	Consignment buying arrangements allow the buyer to avoid product liability obligations.
T	7.	A purchasing strategy is an action plan designed to achieve long-term goals and objectives.
F	8.	The payment terms agreed to by a buyer can have no real impact on A the buying and selling firms' cash flow picture and overall profitability.
T	9.	Supply can contribute to technology by (1) providing technology information to their design/process/ production people, (2) working with their own suppliers to develop new technology, and (3) helping to "lock up" new, advantageous technology through exclusive agreements with suppliers.
T	10.	Risks in the supply chain can be classified into two main categories. (1) The risk of interruption of the flow of goods or services, (2) The risk that the cost of the goods or services will be higher than expected.

Saint Mary's Health Center

Teaching Note

IMMEDIATE ISSUE

1. To develop a plan to achieve 15% in purchasing savings.

BASIC ISSUES

1. Purchasing's bottom line impact.
2. Organization of purchasing.
3. Alternatives to achieve savings.
4. Purchasing in health-care.
5. Setting savings targets.

SUGGESTED STUDENT ASSIGNMENT

1. If you were John Smith, what would be your analysis of the purchasing situation at Saint Mary's?
2. What would be your plan of action to address the 15% savings target?

POSSIBLE DISCUSSION QUESTIONS

1. Is the 15% savings target realistic?
2. What is purchasing's role in the health-care field?
3. What about the trade-off between the costs of purchasing vs the cost of what is purchased?
4. Are there other alternatives?
5. Do you have any feel for the major obstacles that might be encountered?
6. How would you get started?

ANALYSIS

Some Figure Pushing

Let's start with some figure pushing. Saint Mary's has a total budget of $150 million purchases of 30% will amount to $45 million and a projected deficit for the coming year of $9 million or 6%.

A 15% savings target for purchasing exceeds the 6% deficit projected by about 150%! Accumulated deficit over the past two years is $12 million or about 4% of two years or 8% of one year's budget. If Saint Mary's can achieve an across the board improvement of 15% this year, it would wipe out the accumulated deficit built up over the last two years and prevent a deficit this year. It would also leave Saint Mary's with a $20 million surplus the following year, if it could run at the coming year's level of costs and income. This suggests that a 15% across the whole organization is highly unlikely and that the purchasing area's target of 15% improvement may not be typical of all functions.

THE 15% TARGET

There is no indication in the case where the 15% target came from and by whom it was set. Is this one of those situations where the target is set at 15% in the hopes that 5% will actually be achieved? Or is it serious and heads will roll if the target is not met? A 15% improvement on $45 million of purchases amounts to a $6.75 million improvement or about 75% of the projected $9 million deficit! At first glance, without having a clear indication of the status quo at Saint Mary's — 15% appears to be an extremely ambitious target. Since the last two years have already been very tough financially, it is safe to assume there already has been pressure on purchasing to achieve significant savings.

The setting of savings targets is in itself an interesting exercise and may well affect the likelihood that savings will be achieved. If requisitioners, specifies and purchasers together agree to work towards a specific savings target, the organizational climate will at least, be supportive of whatever target is set.

At Saint Mary's it sounds more like a desperation target set from the top. It falls from a funding shortfall and an attempt to survive financially. The question is not — "Is this target realistic?" The demand is, "We need this money to be able to survive or to balance the budget or to live without our financial means." Given that survival is the first and foremost objective of most public and private organizations, it is appropriate that purchasing and suppliers heed that call. In industry, the Chrysler request from its suppliers in the early 1980s for a 10% price reduction was a prime example of this, "You won't have any business if we don't survive" is a strong message. The trouble is that organizations can only pull this one out of the hat once every thirty years or so.

What is also disturbing about the Saint Mary's situation is that John Smith has to come up with a plan very quickly. The more ambitious the improvement target, the more care should be taken in planning.

THE ALTERNATIVES

John Smith has identified three options. These will be discussed first, followed by further suggestions.

1. Centralization of Purchasing

At the moment purchasing is spread into three major areas reporting to two different vice presidents. At first glance it does not appear that there should be a major overlap of suppliers or purchasers between nutrition, service and pharmaceuticals. Even if we assume that the costs of purchasing are running at about 2% of what is purchased or about $900,000, the major saving will have to come from what is bought, rather than the cost of buying. This is not to suggest that centralization should be completely ignored. It may be possible to eliminate some supervisory levels, have one manager of purchasing and buyers in nutrition, service and pharmaceuticals. The point is that even total elimination of all people associated with purchasing will only save about 2%. Therefore, this alternative in itself will not be sufficient to come even close to the 15% target.

If, among the staff in the three functions some special skills exist at negotiation, or identifying savings opportunities, or working on improvement projects with people in other departments at Saint Mary's, being able to assign purchasing people to those areas where their skills are most valuable now, may be a major benefit from rethinking the current organizational structure.

Clearly, if there is duplication of items or services bought, or the potential to combine volume to achieve greater clout, this should be identified with, or without centralization.

In today's world "doing more with less" is standard across all functions and rethinking the staffing needs and the organization of purchasing at Saint Mary's is one fundamental task to be done now, in any case.

2. Supplier Base Reduction

Getting rid of all suppliers with less than $100,000 per year may be a bit too mechanical. It would not be difficult to dream up some rather exotic hospital needs which can only be met by one source at less than $100,000 per year.

The idea of reducing the supplier base, often driven by quality or strategic needs rather than cost alone, has been well tested in the private sector. The notion of clout, or price reductions for a high volume of business, is one of the oldest purchasing ploys around. The idea that suppliers could provide "free" product at possibly inflated prices to achieve tax write-offs needs to be monitored carefully to stay clear of the law. In the health field this has become a rather standard practice and is favored by suppliers over direct price reductions. Certainly volume discounts might be possible if supplier rationalization takes place.

Part of the problem is that giving suppliers a 15% savings target will mean that 15% will never be achieved. For every supplier that agrees to 15% another one will hold the line, or come in at 5%.

Obviously, increases in volumes will result in more single sourcing and flexibility, an implied purchasing benefit, will be lost.

3. Computerization Or Warehouse Sharing

An EDI system with bar coding and direct supplier connection sounds fantastic. Setting up such a system is time consuming and expensive and may not be currently the highest priority. Warehouse sharing with other hospitals might be a preferable option if such a warehouse is currently in existence and is "shareable."

Setting up a new warehouse to service a number of hospitals may be a longer term project, if it is proven that it is the best alternative available. In any case, reductions in inventory, while freeing up current capital, are unlikely to provide the full savings target in themselves.

OTHER ALTERNATIVES

4. Hiring Consultants

Saint Mary's might well benefit from a thorough review by some knowledgeable consultants which can assess not only the three alternatives, but also propose others. In the last decade a large number of purchasing professionals have joined the consulting ranks. Given the hospital's current organization and climate, depending on internal staff to focus on genuine reductions, rather than saving their jobs, may be difficult. Also, given the ambitious target of 15%, spending some money to save a lot should be a realistic option.

5. Systems Contracting

Systems contracts could solve some of the computer inventory and warehouse problems and also achieve clout with suppliers and reduce small volume buying.

6. Internal Task Force

The basic point is that reductions of 15% in total purchases are not possible without full cooperation from users at Saint Mary's. Therefore, any changes from the existing mode need approval and support from the various internal stakeholders affected. Given that it is very much in the interest of the stakeholders to assist purchasing (the alternative would be additional staff reductions in this area), purchasing may have a better chance to achieve significant changes than might at first be imagined. The advantage of such a task force, if properly constituted with the major stakeholders, is that a realistic plan can be laid out and followed with the commitment of future cooperation. Care needs to be taken that quality of health-care be maintained. Some key professional judgements will be called for to assess the impact of proposed changes in systems, requirements, suppliers and people.

7. Value Analysis, Standardization and Simplification

Some of the old standby's value analysis, standardization and simplification should not be overlooked as potential major saving improvement techniques. If the necessary skills are lacking to implement such programs, bringing in knowledgeable outsiders to train and assist should be considered.

8. Supplier Appeal

Inviting key suppliers in for a round table discussion with the president to request proposals for major value improvements may well bear fruit. Sending a letter to less important suppliers at the same time may assure that no stone is left unturned.

It would be highly unlikely that these would turn up sufficient savings to solve all problems, but could generate a few happy surprises. This approach would certainly force senior managers, to take an active role in dealing with suppliers and help them assess how realistic the 15% savings target is.

9. A Combination

Given that almost no alternative holds sufficient promise to achieve the savings target, a combination of alternatives makes eminent sense.

10. Timing and Plan

Given the very tight timing at this point and John Smith's own obvious limitations in understanding the options (he could only generate 3), the idea of a comprehensive plan of action is not realistic. John would do well to call for an internal task force, and knowledgeable consultants to get his program started. There is no way currently to tell whether the 15% savings target is realistic and what might be appropriate timing for the various portions of the plan. The manager of purchasing and the three supervisors should be fully aware of what he wants to do, why, and what the alternatives are.

Ironically, it may well take more purchasing staff, rather than fewer, to pull this program off. Aside from keeping Saint Mary's supplied with its daily needs, a lot of analytical, investigative and negotiation type of work will have to be done. It is doubtful that the current staff will be able to handle the full load. Whether the current staff has the competence to work on this initiative is not clear from the case. If certain skills are lacking, others may have to be brought in, on a contract, temporary, or permanent basis to provide the training and skills required.

Heat Transfer Systems Inc.

Teaching Note

IMMEDIATE ISSUES

1. How to reduce inventory.
2. How to reduce prices paid for aluminum tubing.
3. How to ensure on-time deliveries.

BASIC ISSUES

1. Inventory reduction.
2. Price improvement.
3. Changing role of purchasing.
4. New person on the job.
5. Strategic supply.

SUGGESTED STUDENT ASSIGNMENT

If you were Stan Durnford, what would be your analysis of the purchasing and inventory management of aluminum tube at Heat Transfer Systems Inc. and what action would you take and why?

POSSIBLE DISCUSSIONS QUESTIONS

1. How do you know how much inventory is too much or too little?
2. What it the impact of delivery uncertainty on HTS?
3. What is the impact of long lead times on HTS?
4. Does multiple sourcing for aluminum tube make sense?
5. How does Stan's newness to the job affect this situation?
6. What would be ideal supply situation for aluminum tube for HTS?
7. What are the alternatives here?
8. Is it possible to get lower prices and faster delivery and inventory reduction at the same time?

ANALYSIS

Stan Durnford is lucky. His predecessor in purchasing at HTS has left room for improvement which should give him a chance to establish credibility as a necessary component to lifting purchasing's role at HTS.

THE CURRENT SITUATION

It appears that the current situation left by the previous purchasing manager stressed availability, supply security and initial price, rather than total cost of ownership, inventory minimization and strategic purchasing.

THE INVENTORY SITUATION

A $6 million inventory of raw materials and components for a business which has only $16 million in sales is very high. Allowing a total manufacturing cost of about $12-13 million gives a turnover of two, which is terrible. Moreover, valuable space is occupied, it is probably difficult to access inventory and easy to lose track of what is where under the current system.

Why is inventory so high? There are a number of explanations. The need for different wall widths and diameters creates a need for sub groups of tubing inventory. Lengths are another matter. Since each job requires different lengths of material stock, it is likely that a fair amount of tubing gets wasted if the proper length is not available. It seems obvious that if a customer order would be delayed because of unavailability of economic lengths of material, high scrap losses would be preferred, provided the right wall thickness and diameter tube is available in lengths longer or shorter than optimum.

There is no indication in the case about potential design and manufacturing trade-offs which would allow for a smaller diameter tube to be wound more tightly than a bigger diameter aluminum tube with larger fins. In other words, could engineers design around inventory availability?

Uncertainty about demand for certain diameters and wall thicknesses create a need for safety stock. Similarly uncertainty about supply--particularly for European tube with up to three months delay-- would create a need for safety stock.

Container load ordering from Europe would also create extra stock which would have to be justified on the basis of transportation savings.

A $3 million aluminum tube inventory represents about 86% of annual requirements or about ten months stock! This clearly is far too high even given the factors above.

From the case data it is difficult to tell what the exact amount of aluminum tube inventory should be. Perhaps it is better to start with an ideal target of operations to see what the end goal calls for.

THE IDEAL ALUMINUM TUBE SUPPLY SITUATION

The ideal tube supply situation would permit HTS to order the aluminum tube requirements after the customer order has been confirmed. This would permit HTS to order the right lengths of the right wall thickness and diameter in the right amount to fit each job. Theoretically, this would permit a zero inventory, other than a slight build-up of jobs which are not run completely in one day and delivery is on a job lot basis.

What would be necessary for this to work? In the first place, the quality of the tube would have to be assured. No impurities, weak walls or off-spec material or the wrong lengths or amounts could be tolerated. Delivery would have to be quick, probably two weeks or less to permit time for manufacture and shipping to customer. And the price would have to be competitive so that HTS would be able to compete effectively in the quotes.

Is this vision impossible? It would mean that no European supplier could be considered. North American wholesalers or distributors could possibly meet the delivery and cut-to-length requirements, but might be suspect on quality and price. The ideal sources would be a North American producer who would cut to length and provide the necessary quality and dimensions quickly. Either of the current two sources might fit the bill. HTS might have to offer an alliance or preferred supplier, single source incentive to get an improved price and better delivery and service.

The benefit to HTS could be substantial. Reducing the $3,000,000 aluminum tube inventory to two months requirements would free up $2,400,000 of working capital, space, and save bout $600,000 in carrying costs per year. Disposal of odd lengths left over could be eliminated and decrease new material costs. Control over raw material usage would be substantially improved and the hassle of dealing with container loads of European material continually arriving late would be eliminated along with the currency exchange risk.

A 10% decrease in price for increased volume would reduce the North American price to about $1.35/lb., below the current average price of $1.38 paid. Once transportation and inventory costs are factored into the European price moreover, the $1.20 price per pound is likely to be illusionary. Safety stock requirements of three months add 6% to the cost and transportation probably another 15% minimum.

MAKING PURCHASING AND SUPPLIERS PART OF THE COMPETITIVE ADVANTAGE OF THE FIRM

Stan's aspiration should be to make purchasing and suppliers part of the competitive edge of HTS. Currently, neither purchasing or suppliers contribute effectively to organizational goals and strategies. In fact, the contribution is negative, saddling the firm with too much inventory, high prices and long lead times. If HTS can still be successful despite such drawbacks, its competitiveness could be drastically improved through strategic, value focused purchasing. In an organization where raw materials and components account for 65% of sales it is vital that suppliers and purchasing contribute the very best. Unusually fast delivery and good price, minimum inventories and top quality on the supply side will permit HTS to take on rush orders at premium prices and make extra profits which can be partially applied to rejuvenating the organization through technology, training and continuous improvement and partially to reward investors with better return.

ACTION PLAN

If the vision is clear, then the next step should be planning of how to accomplish it.

The first step has to be a thorough review of past requirements for aluminum tube and a discussion with marketing and engineering to get a feel for future changes in demand, if any. Particular focus should be on total volume expectations, quality requirements and dimensional requirements in terms of lengths, wall widths and diameters. The concern is to understand requirements fully.

The next or simultaneous activity has to be on the current inventory. What is available and where is it located? Because the intention is to start decreasing this inventory, it has to be used up as jobs come in. It is entirely possible that because of wall width and diameter requirements, some of this inventory may take several years to deplete, while in some sizes shortages may exist.

The two existing North American suppliers need to be evaluated along with others to determine their ability to meet the "vision" described previously. If one of the existing suppliers appears capable and willing to take on the challenge of becoming a preferred single source, willing to supply quickly, cut to length material, then this supplier can be placed into that mode for requirements not available in stock.

Similarly, if neither of the current suppliers fits the bill, a new supplier will have to be developed to replace all existing ones.

If the temporary target of two months inventory is appropriate, eight months of requirements will be supplied from stock over the next year or so, cutting HTS' tube requirements to about four months ,not all that different from what each of the current North American suppliers provides. Thus, any major volume increases would not appear until the second year, giving HTS a chance in the first year to get its house in order, to test the new approach, and to become comfortable with operating on a lower inventory level.

Clearly, this idea needs to be sold to production, marketing, engineering and quality control before any supplier is approached with a proposition. This cooperation is vital, but the benefits to all are too great to ignore. The original investigative phase is a good one to plant seeds of the new direction and to determine which people in particular have to support the new direction. The previous purchasing manager obviously received support internally for multiple sourcing and high inventories. These supporters now need to review their earlier persuasion and have to be converted to a more aggressive and strategic purchasing stance.

AFTER ALUMINUM TUBE

The approach developed for aluminum tube might also be followed for other new materials and components. Although not quite as bad as aluminum the $3 million in inventory represents over four months in sales and is also excessive. More product categories and supplies will be involved and the aluminum experience, if successful, can increase Stan's credibility of HTS to tackle the other requirements strategically also.

POST SCRIPT

What happened in this situation is interesting. The proposal to cut inventory was welcomed by the CEO and most others because it would free up cash and space and reduce carrying costs. In the end Stan and the production manager agreed to get two short racks instead of the previous three long ones plus parking lot plus open space in the plant. The maximum amount of aluminum tubing which could be carried would have to fit the two short racks available. This was a good visual and physical constraint which everybody could understand.

The quality issue was a vital one. One of the current North American suppliers offered to make some process modifications to ensure high quality finning tube and to cut length as required. For the producer cutting to customer lengths created very few difficulties, whereas HTS would invariably be faced with numerous tube lengths left over, which significantly increased new material costs. In return for increased future volume and single sourcing the supplier was also persuaded to drop prices and speed up deliveries. Aside from inventory reduction benefits, Stan figured price and lengths and quality savings at more than $800,000 per year!

The other materials and components were tackled similarly. Despite an increase in sales of about 25% inventory was reduced below $1.5 million and Stan is still continuing to see if he cannot do better. The strategic purchasing approach has paid off handsomely for Stan and HTS as its competitiveness has drastically improved along with its profitability.

Custom Windows, Inc.

Teaching Note

IMMEDIATE ISSUE

What supplier or which suppliers should be chosen to supply glass to Custom Windows for the coming year?

BASIC ISSUES

1. Single versus multiple sourcing.
2. Buying from manufacturers versus distributors.
3. Inventory reduction.
4. Purchasing strategy.

SUGGESTED STUDENT ASSIGNMENT

1. As Caroline Joseph, which supplier or which suppliers would you choose for glass for the coming year?
2. Do you think it might be possible to achieve a 30-35 turnover rate on raw material glass?
3. What is your analysis of the past glass supply practices at Custom Windows?
4. Where would you like to go in the future with your glass supply strategy?
5. What short-term or long-term action would you take for glass at Custom Windows and why?

POSSIBLE DISCUSSION QUESTIONS

1. What are the advantages to Custom Windows of having four different suppliers for glass?
2. What are the advantages of dealing with a glass distributor? Disadvantages?
3. What are the advantages of dealing directly with a glass manufacturer? Disadvantages?
4. Does single sourcing make sense in a situation such as this one?
5. What is the interaction between lead time, minimum order quantities, and inventory levels?
6. How is it possible that a distributor can price lower than a manufacturer to the same customer?
7. What are the key differences between the short and long term in this case?

DISCUSSION

This little case is full of snakes. Even though glass to this point has been a relatively minor percentage of total sales at less than 5%, it appears to be growing significantly in the future as expensive low energy glass expands significantly in the future.

The tradeoffs in this case deal with short and long-term needs and strategies, price, inventory levels, minimum order quantities, and single versus multiple sourcing as well as distributor versus manufacturer. The increasing importance of low energy glass means that glass purchases in total dollar volume will increase sharply. If all 15.3% annual growth is from low energy glass, while clear glass remains the same, this means that low energy glass volume will go from 99 blocks last year to 99 blocks plus 66 blocks this coming year. This 66% increase in low energy glass purchases will increase dollar volume by about $180,000 to $725,000 next year. If this trend continues over the five year period (104% volume increase over 433 blocks would be 450 additional blocks of low energy glass raising total low energy purchases to 550 blocks) total low energy glass purchases would be about 1.5 million dollars (if the cost of low energy glass per sq. ft. per block stays the same). Being able to source low energy glass effectively will become a key purchasing factor.

In the short term for next year the supply solution chosen may not be the most appropriate for the longer term. Going for quotes annually without looking at the longer term implications is not likely to be a sound purchasing strategy.

QUOTE OBSERVATIONS

Exhibit 2 provides a summary from which the following observations can be made:

1. On the whole, there is not much difference in price from year to year or between suppliers.
2. The only one to lower one price significantly was Travers Glass in the case of 3 mm glass by 2.73¢ per sq. ft. per block or about 8.8% on its own quote. Because this is a large volume requirement, this lower price is significant. Ross lowered its quote by about 1¢ per sq. ft. per block. The net result is that if clear glass volume remains the same for next year, and if all clear glass were purchased from Ross, it would cost Custom Windows about $243,096. From Travers, the equivalent price would be $235,236. The following table TN-1 summarizes the quotes in terms of total annual dollar volume. Travers clearly comes in at the lowest price of $711,126.

	Clear		Low Energy		Total
	3 mm (309 blocks 2400 ft²/bl)	4 mm (25 blocks 1600 ft²/bl)	3 mm (152 blocks 2400 ft²/bl)	4 mm (13 blocks 1600 ft²/bl)	
Clear View	244,728	17,600	430,464	31.408	724, 200
Travers	235,236	17,556	426,816	31,518	711,126
Ross	243,096	17,484			
Jackson	244,728	17,600			

It is interesting the Caroline Joseph did not approach a low energy glass producer herself, given the increasing importance of low energy glass. Also, her desire to avoid getting a quote from West Bend makes it difficult to compare her options, given that the only manufacturers she asked to quote cannot currently supply low energy glass.

THE DISTRIBUTOR VERSUS MANUFACTURER

Theoretically, at least, Custom Windows should be in the position to deal with glass manufacturers instead of through distributors. Since of the four supplier options, only distributors offer both clear and acceptable low energy glass, this means that in the short term, at least, Caroline is forced to used distributors anyway. Therefore, the only remaining question is whether she should use a manufacturer/distributor option, a distributor/distributor option or only one distributor?

MULTIPLE VERSUS SINGLE SOURCING

Caroline is currently using four different sources of glass. No explanations are given for so many sources. It may have been price related in the case of Ross Industries and availability related in the case of the two distributors, Clear View and Travers. Given the minimal price differences between suppliers, other considerations become more important.

INVENTORY CONTROL AND TURNOVER RATES

Splitting orders between four suppliers and trying to order in truckload quantities is not the most effective way to control inventories. The ability to combine 3 mm and 4 mm clear and low energy glass in a truckload is very useful to minimize total inventory. A quick look at order quantities and prices reveals the following. With daily requirements of 2.6 blocks in the high season for the next year, a seven day supply would require 18 blocks in inventory. With a two-day safety stock of 5 blocks, this means order size could be up to 26 blocks and still meet the average inventory target (26 ÷ 2 + 5 = 18). This would result in a 27 turnover rate.

A turnover of 30 times would require an average inventory of 16.5 blocks and a turnover of 35 would require an inventory of 14 blocks. With anticipated daily use of 2.6 blocks of glass in the six months summer season and 1.36 blocks in the winter season, some variation in inventory could be expected. For example, carrying 18 to 20 blocks of inventory in the summer and 8 to 10 blocks in the winter would come close to the targeted number of turns. 18 to 20 blocks in the summer would amount to 7 to 8 days of production and 9 blocks would come close to 7 days of production in the winter period.

Since fast delivery is becoming an important competitive factor for Custom Windows, availability of glass on short notice is going to be a vital competitive factor. Unfortunately, low energy glass currently cost about 3½ times as much as clear glass. Therefore, inventory control of low energy glass will become increasingly important even though for some time the physical bulk of glass sold will be clear.

Safety stock of glass will have to relate to demand uncertainty as well as delivery uncertainty. With 10 days delivery time of vinyl windows and same day production, some leeway exists for bringing in glass after the order has been received, if the order quantities and delivery time can be fast enough.

Some Financial Figures as They Relate to Inventory

For the coming year Table TN-2 shows what might be the cost of carrying inventory.

Table TN-2

CAPITAL TIED UP PER BLOCK FOR THE COMING YEAR

Clear		Low Energy		Total
3 mm (309 blocks 2400 ft^2/bl)	4 mm (25 blocks 1600 ft^2/bl)	3 mm (152 blocks 2400 ft^2/bl)	4 mm (13 blocks 1600 ft^2/bl)	
$777	$700	$2829	$2423	
61.8%	5%	30.4%	2.6%	99.8%

Given next year's expected mix of blocks this puts an expected value per block in stock of $1,438.

The past year's tie up in inventory at 14 times turnover represented 31 blocks at $1,225 average value for $37,975. The coming year's tie up at 14 times turnover would amount at 499/14 times $1,438 is $51,254. This not only would represent an increase of about $14,000 but would also exceed the inventory space available. If we can achieve a 35 times turnover this would represent about 7 days inventory or 7 times 2.6 blocks in the high season = 18 blocks and 7 times 1.2 blocks for the low season is about 8 blocks for an average of about 13.2 blocks per year. This would represent a capital tie up of 13.2 blocks times $1,438 = $18,982. Therefore, this would free up almost $19,000 in working capital compared to last year and a substantial amount of space.

Theoretically, with the local distributor option discussed subsequently, Custom Windows should be able to do substantially better, provided complete order flexibility exists.

THE LONG TERM

The long term ideal goal would be to have one manufacturer who is a leader in both clear and low energy glass and who is willing to give preferential pricing to Custom Windows in return for a single supplier position. The current situation is a far cry from this ideal. It is not clear from the case whether the 5 year projected volume of glass for Custom Windows of about $1.8 million per year is sufficient to warrant that special customer status with a manufacturer.

The alternative would be to have special status with a distributor for whom the volume might be more attractive. Such a distributor could use Custom Windows's volume to combine with other customers to gain more clout with glass manufacturers than Custom Windows could ever expect to get. This second alternative is certainly realistic now. Travers Glass and Clear View could both potentially fill this role. The advantage of Clear View is its location. As a local supplier they should be able to offer small, quick, daily delivery without significant transportation penalties. Travers Glass appears to be slightly more aggressive in its pricing currently, but is at least 2.5 hours away, a significant enough distance to make real JIT a bit less realistic.

SUGGESTED ACTION PLAN

Caroline should sit down with managers from Clear View and explore the possibilities of single sourcing provided: (1) Clear View improves its pricing; (2) Clear View is willing to work on a JIT delivery system which allows Custom Windows to keep its raw materials glass inventory in-house to a maximum of 5 to 7 days supply. Given high season requirements next year of 2.6 blocks per day or 13 blocks per 5 day week, this would translate into weekly requirements of 8 blocks of 3 mm clear, β of a block of 4 mm clear, 4 blocks of 3 mm low energy, α blocks of 4 mm low energy. In the low season these weekly requirements would halve.

Therefore, in high season daily delivery during the week could be Monday 3 blocks, Tuesday 2 blocks, Wednesday 3 blocks, Thursday 2 blocks, and Friday 3 blocks. If an 8 block minimum is required for transportation efficiencies, deliveries would have to be every 3 days. In the low season the delivery could be every second day with a 3 block delivery followed by a 2 block delivery, or an 8 block delivery every 6 days. This should allow Custom Windows to lower its in-house inventory substantially and meet its turnover targets.

What is missing in the case is the fluctuation in demand between 3 mm and 4 mm and between clear and low energy glass. Provided the glass supplier maintains sufficient inventory of each kind, Custom Windows should only need to order sufficient glass to see it to its next delivery. Given that a block of glass may be the minimum order quantity and that 4 mm clear and 4 mm low energy are low volume requirements, these two would lie around in partial block form for some time (in high season 4 mm clear 12 weeks, 3 weeks in low season; and 4 mm low energy 3 weeks in high season and 6 weeks in low season).

TRAVERS ALTERNATIVE

Should Clear View fail to arise to the challenge, the same proposition could be put to Travers. Given the higher delivery distance, the minimum order size for transportation might be the 12 blocks quoted. This translates into weekly delivery in high season and bi-weekly delivery in the low season. This should still permit the 35 turn target, provided demand instability is not too great.

DURING THE COMING YEAR

During the coming year Caroline should carefully investigate the producer side of glass. Is Ross working to improve its low energy glass? Is Jackson's of satisfactory quality? How come Travers can get West Bend clear glass so much cheaper than Custom Windows? Are other manufacturers available and interested? Does it make sense for Custom Windows to concentrate on distributors or manufacturers? Given the high growth in low energy glass, who will be the world beaters in that material? Why is low energy so costly and are improvements in price and quality likely to occur and how and why? In a few years time, low energy glass may become the largest single cost component for Custom Windows and it deserves special attention.

Until now, Caroline has treated glass as something to be quoted on an annual basis. Apparently, given the minor price differences between one supplier and another, transportation considerations have been more important than suppliers selection and supply strategy. She has to change her perspective and has to become much more knowledgeable than she is at this point. The extra pressure from inside to improve raw material turnover provides even more impetus to take a very serious look at glass supply and start to develop a short-term and long-term strategic perspective on it.

APPENDIX

Power Point Presentation

Website

http://www.mhhe.com/leenders12e

Corporate Supply Challenges

- Need to control unit costs
- Need to reduce the total cost of acquisition
- The increasing influence of suppliers on the purchaser's ability to respond to end-customers needs
- Increased reliance on fewer suppliers
- Trend towards reliance on suppliers for design and build responsibilities for complete subassemblies and subsystems

The Evolution of the Supply Function

- *The Handling of Railway Supplies – Their Purchase and Disposition*
  - Published in 1887
- Attention in first half of 1900s to reliable access to supply of raw materials, supplies and services
- Two vexing problems in the decade of the 1970s put senior management attention on the supply function:
  - international shortage of basic raw materials
  - pricing inflation

The Evolution of the Supply Function

- By 1990s firms faced challenges of global "supply chains" and an increased reliance on suppliers
  - Outsourcing has led to increased reliance on suppliers for key components and services
- Technological developments in the early 21st century provides expectations for supply chain integration, lower transaction costs and faster response times.
  - The Internet and B2B e-commerce

The Evolution of the Supply Function

- Clerical and tactical
- Focus on policies and procedures
- Key challenge: availability of supply and cost management

- Strategic orientation
- Global supply chains
- Executive level leadership
- Key challenge: Technology and the Internet

early 1900s → early 21st century

Evolution of the Supply Chain

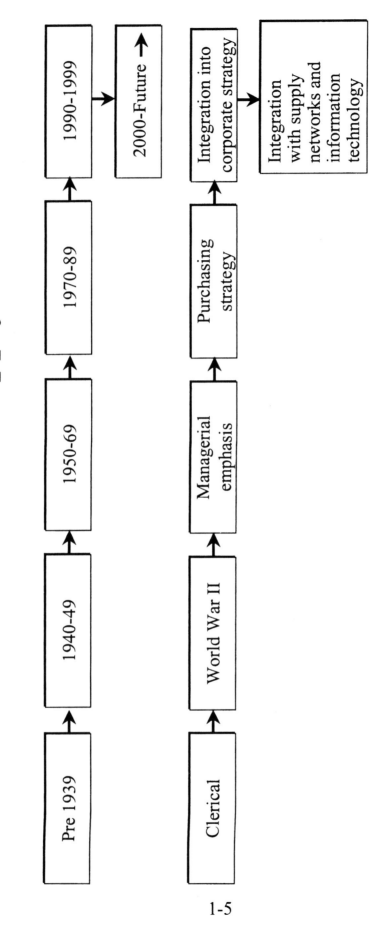

The Buyer/Planner Concept

- Combines planning and purchasing functions into one position
  - Planners: Determine what materials are needed and when
  - Buyers: Handle sourcing and buying
- Charged with responsibility for a specific line of inventory
- Duties may include: establishing schedules, issues and analyzes quotations, places orders, monitors supplier performance, and keeps abreast of market trends, supplier capacities and technologies.

Major Logistics Activities

- customer service
- demand forecasting/planning
- inventory management
- logistics communications
- material handling
- order processing
- packaging
- parts and service support
- plant and warehouse site selection
- purchasing
- return goods handling
- reverse logistics
- traffic and transportation
- warehouse storage

Supply Chain Management

"The design and management of seamless, value-added processes across organizational boundaries to meet the real needs of the end customer. The development and integration of people and technological resources are critical to successful supply chain integration."

Simplified One-Stage Decision Tree

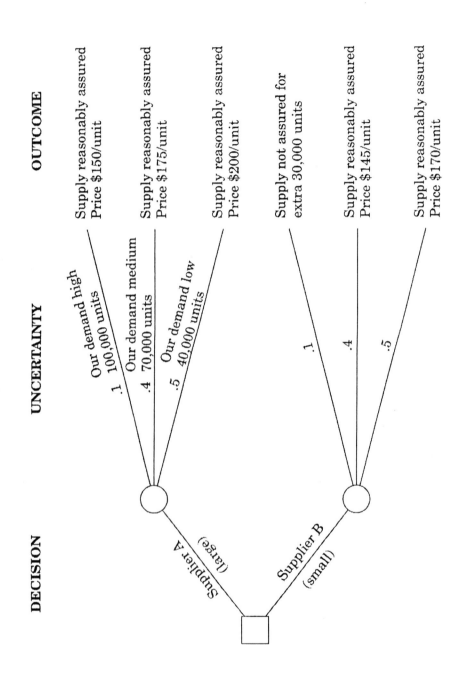

Purchasing's Operational and Strategic Contributions

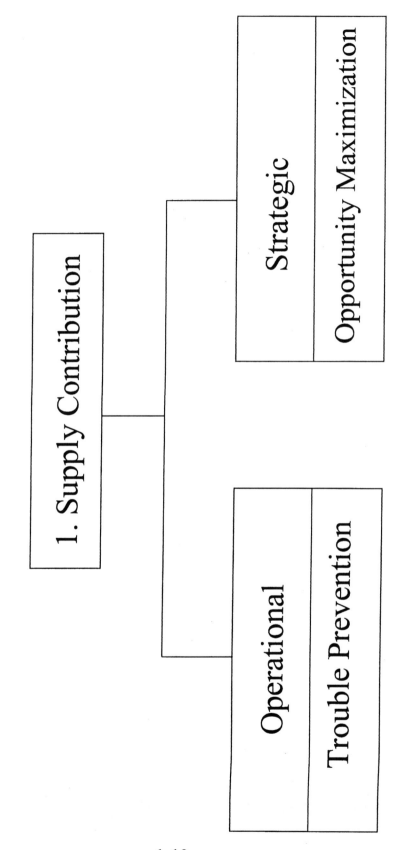

Purchasing's Operational and Strategic Contributions

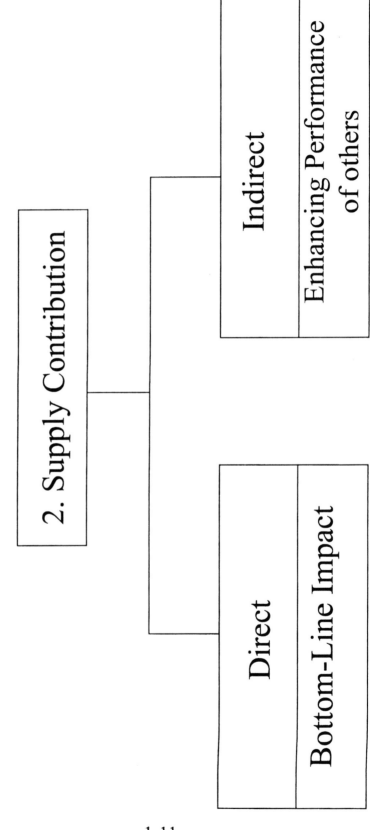

Purchasing's Operational and Strategic Contributions

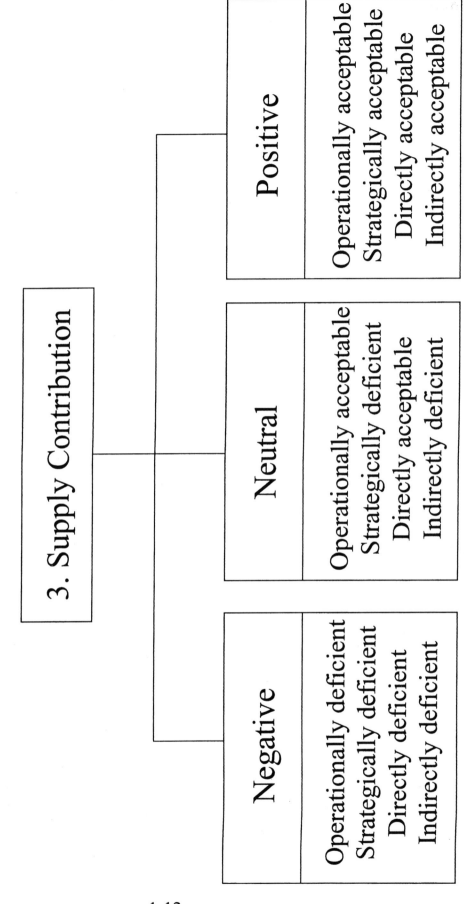

Return on Assets Factors

```
                                    ROA
                                    10%
                                  (20.6%)
                                    ↑
                              Multiplied by
                    ┌───────────────────────┐
                    │                       │
            Investment                  Profit
            turnover 2                  margin
                                          5%
              (2.06)                    (10%)
            ↑         ↑              ↑         ↑
         Divided by               Divided by
         ┌──────┐                  ┌──────┐
         │      │                  │      │
       Sales  Total              Profit  Sales
       $1     assets             $50,000 $1 million
       million $500,000          ($100,000)
              ($485,000)
                 ↑                  ↑
              Inventory          Sales      Total cost
              $150,000           $1 million  $950,000
              ($135,000)                    ($900,000)
                              Minus
```

* Inventory is approximately 30% of total assets.
† Purchases account for half of total sales, or $500,000.
†† Figures in parentheses assume a 10% reduction in purchase costs.

The Opportunities for Contribution of the Purchasing/Supply Function

- Profit-leverage effect
- Return-on-assets effect
- Information source
- Effect on efficiency
- Effect on competitive position and customer satisfaction
- Effect on image
- Training ground
- Management strategy and social policy

Characteristics of an Integrated Strategic Procurement and Sourcing Function

Executive Leadership

- Executive committee support for integration across company and strategic business unit corporate plans

Functional Leadership

- Company-wide customer-focused leadership
- Establish integrated visions workers at results and processes
- Drives supply base/supplier management strategies company-wide

Strategic Positioning

- External/internal customer focus
- Matrix management
- High-level positioning - second, third or fourth levels

Integration

- Cross-functional, cross-location teaming
- Part of the technology, manufacturing and SBU planning process

Characteristics of an Integrated Strategic Procurement and Sourcing Function

Supply Base Strategy

- Quality driven
- Design standardization
- Concurrent engineering
- Supply base optimization
- Commercial strategy emerging

Supplier Management

- Focused on supplier development
- Joint performance improvement efforts
- Value focused
- Total cost improvement
- Supplier benchmarking

Measurement

- Customer orientation
- Total value/cost focused
- Benchmarking with best in class

Systems

- Global databases
- Historical performance data
- Strategic
- EDI, Internet, EFT, CAD, CAM

Professionalism in Purchasing

- New assignments
- Education
- College recruitment
- Training programs
- Salary levels
- Professional associations

Challenges Facing Purchasing

- B2B e-commerce
- Supply chain management
- Measurement
- Purchase of non-traditional goods and services
- Contribution to corporate strategy
- Recognition by senior management

Goals of the Purchasing Function

- Provide an uninterrupted flow of materials, supplies and services required to operated the organization
- Keep inventory investment and loss at a minimum
- Maintain and improve quality
- Find or develop competent suppliers
- Standardize, where possible, the items bought
- Purchase required items and services at lowest cost

Goals of the Purchasing Function

- Achieve harmonious, productive working relationships with other functional areas within the organization
- Accomplish the purchasing objectives at the lowest possible level of administrative costs
- Improve the organization's competitive position

Purchasing's Prime Decision Authority

- Select the supplier
- Use whichever pricing method is appropriate
- Question the specifications
- Monitor contacts with potential suppliers

Various Titles of the Chief Purchasing Officer

- Director of Purchasing
- VP of Purchasing
- Manager of Purchasing
- VP of Materials Management
- Materials Manager

Purchasing Reporting Relationships

Position to Whom the CPO Reports	1988 %	1995 %
President	16%	16
Executive VP	19	15
Senior VP/Group VP	*	19
Financial VP	7	10
Manufacturing/Operations VP	24	15
Materials/Logistics VP	8	7
Engineering VP	1	1
Administrative VP	13	9
Other (many of whom were VPs)	12	8

* category not identified in study

Functions that Report to Purchasing: CAPS Study

Function	1988 %	1995 %
Scrap/surplus disposal	57	63
Materials and purchasing research	*	60
Inbound traffic	40	51
Stores/warehousing	34	41
Inventory control	37	41
Material planning	*	40
Outbound traffic	31	39

* category not identified in study

Purchasing Activities

- Purchasing/buying
- Purchasing research
- Inventory control
- Transportation
- Environmental and investment recovery/disposal
- Forecasting and planning
- Outsourcing and subcontracting
- Nonproduction/nontraditional purchases
- Supply chain management

Typical Purchasing Organization Structure - Medium Sized Company

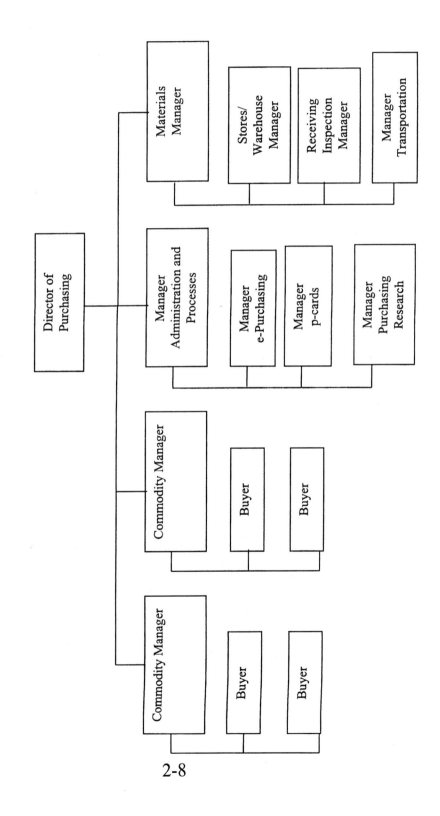

Potential Advantages and Disadvantages of Centralization

Advantages

- greater buying specialization
- ability to pay for talent
- consolidation of requirements - clout
- coordination of policies and procedures
- effective planning and research
- common suppliers
- proximity to major organizational decision makers
- critical mass
- firm brand recognition and stature
- reporting line - power
- strategic focus
- cost of purchasing low

Disadvantages

- narrow specification and job boredom
- lack of job flexibility
- corporate staff appears excessive
- tendency to minimize legitimate differences in requirements
- lack of recognition of unique needs
- focus on corporate requirements, not on business unit strategic requirements
- even common suppliers behave differently in geographic and market segments
- distance from users
- tendency to create organizational silos
- customer segments require adaptability to unique situations
- top management not able to spend time on suppliers
- lack of business unit focus
- high visibility of purchasing costs

Potential Advantages and Disadvantages of Decentralization

Advantages

- easier coordination/communication with operating department
- speed of response
- effective use of local sources
- business unit autonomy
- reporting line simplicity
- undivided authority and responsibility
- suits purchasing personnel preference
- broad job definition
- geographical, cultural, political, environmental, social, language, currency appropriateness
- hide cost of supply

Disadvantages

- more difficult to communicate among business units
- encourages users not to plan ahead
- operational versus strategic focus
- too much focus on local sources - ignores better supply opportunities
- no critical mass in organization for visibility/effectiveness - "whole person syndrome"
- lacks clout
- suboptimization
- business unit preferences not congruent with corporate preferences
- small differences magnified
- reporting at low level in organization
- limits functional advancement opportunities
- ignores larger organizational considerations
- limited expertise for requirements
- lack of standardization
- cost of supply relatively high

Potential Advantages of the Hybrid Structure

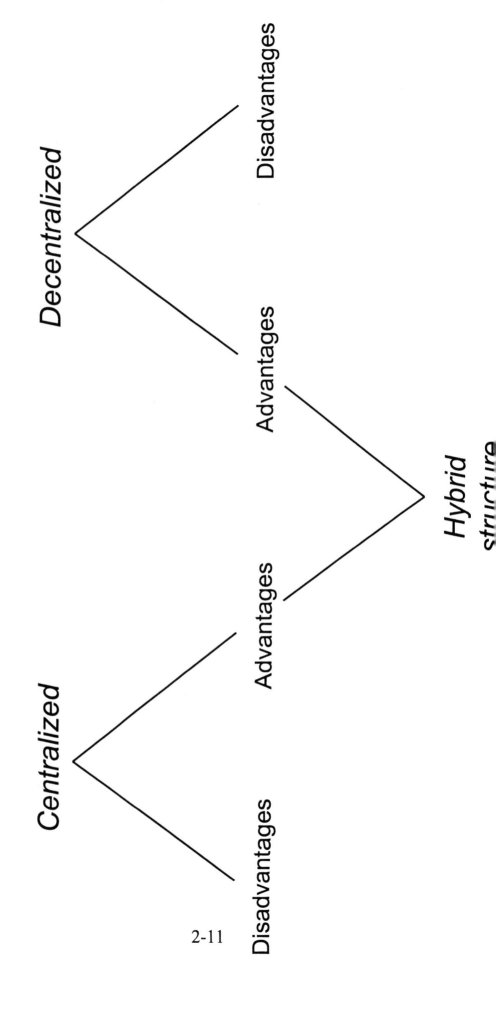

Purchasing and Supply Teams

- Cross-functional teams
- Teams with suppliers
- Teams with customers
- Teams with suppliers and customers
- Supplier councils - key suppliers
- Purchasing councils - purchasing personnel only
- Commodity management teams
- Consortiums

Team Leader Responsibilities

- Work with the team to establish and commit to performance goals
- Secure individual member involvement and commitment
- Manage internal team conflict
- Help maintain team focus and direction
- Secure required organizational resources

Team Leader Responsibilities

- Prevent team domination by a member or function
- Deal with internal and external obstacles confronting the team
- Coordinate multiple tasks and manage the status of team assignments
- Clarify and help define each team member's role
- Provide performance feedback to members

Keys for Successful Consortiums

- Reducing total costs for the consortium members
  - Through lower prices, higher quality and better services
- Eliminating and avoiding all real and perceived violations of anti-trust regulations
- Installing sufficient safeguards to avoid real and perceived threats concerning disclosure of confidential and proprietary information

Keys for Successful Consortiums

- Mutual and equitable sharing of risks, costs and benefits to all stakeholders, including buying firms/members, suppliers and customers
- Maintaining a high degree of trust and professionalism
- Maintaining a strong similarity among consortium members and compatibility of needs, capabilities, philosophies and corporate cultures

The Essential Steps in the Purchasing Process

1. Recognition of need
2. Description of need
3. Determination and analysis possible sources of supply
4. Determination of price and terms
5. Preparation and placement of the purchase order
6. Follow-up and/or expedite the order
7. Receipt and inspection of goods
8. Clear the invoice and pay the supplier
9. Maintain records and relationships

A Sample Sourcing Process Flowchart

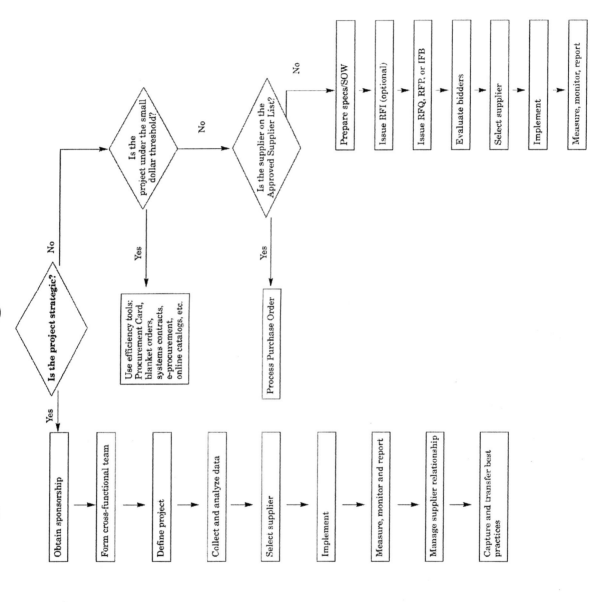

Some Possible Methods of Reducing Small Order Transaction Costs

- Stockless buy and systems contracts
- P-cards
- Blanket P.O.s
- EDI- and Internet-based systems
- Reverse auctions
- Changing authority levels and bidding practices
- Single sourcing
- Outsourcing small value order processing
- Standardization
- Batch orders
- Set requisition schedule
- Invoiceless payments
- Users pay directly

Information Needed for Requisitions

- Date
- Number (identification)
- Originating department
- Account number
- Complete description of material or service and quantity
- Date material or service needed
- Any special shipping or service-delivery instructions
- Signature of requisitioner

Internal Information Flows to Purchasing

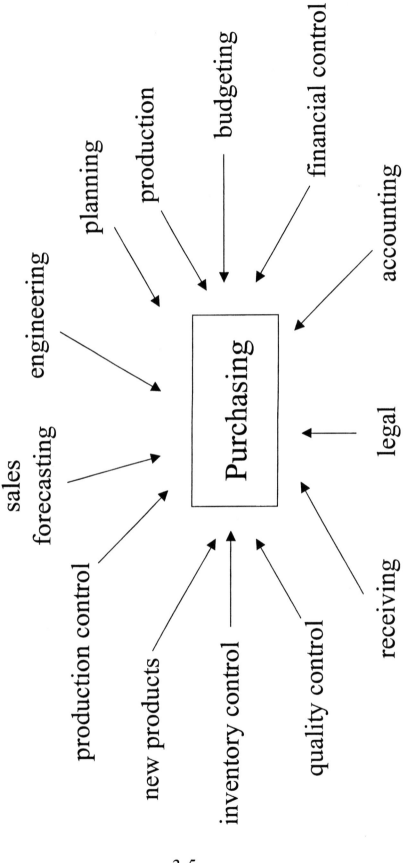

External Information Flows to Purchasing

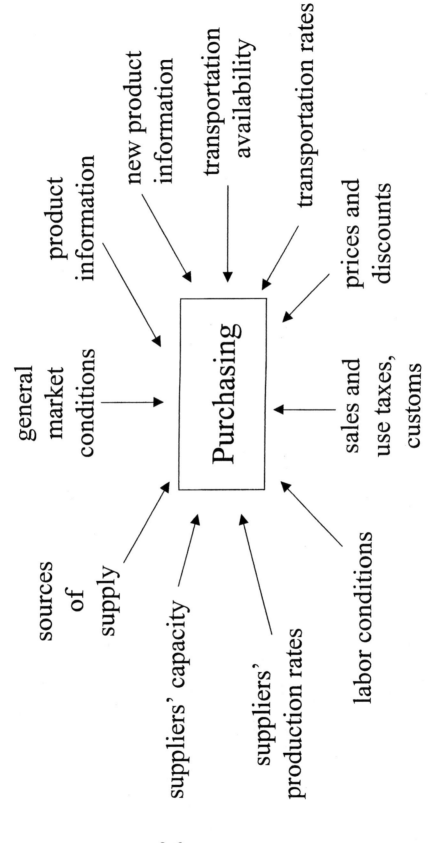

Internal Information Flows from Purchasing

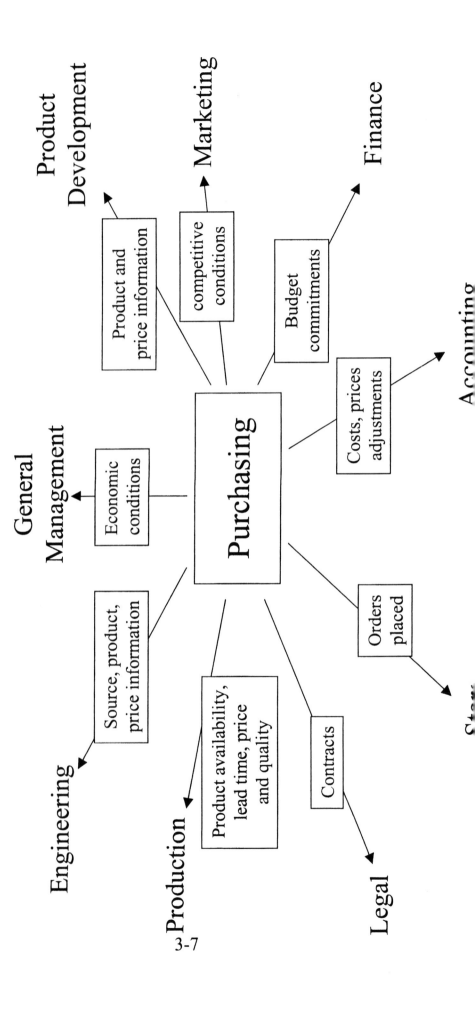

Adoption Rate of Internet-Based Procurement

- To identify new suppliers: 80.7%
- Purchasing indirect materials: 70.9%
- As part of RFP 48.8%
- On-line collaboration with suppliers: 42.8%

Examples of the Potential Contribution of a Computerized Purchasing System

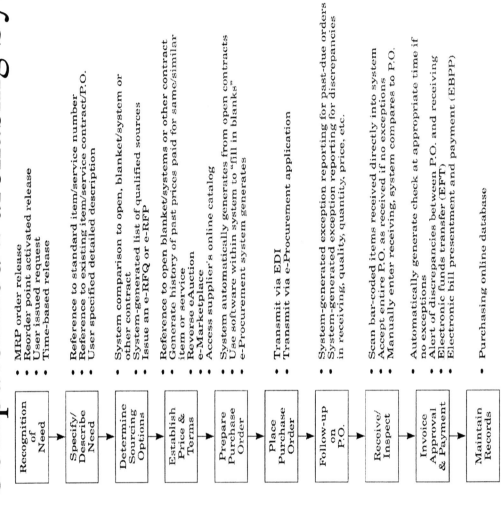

Source: Adapted from Lisa Ellram and Laura Birou, *Purchasing for Bottom-Line Impact: Improving the Organization through Strategic Procurement* (Burr Ridge, IL: Irwin Professional Publishing, 1995), p. 135.

Simplified Flowchart of an Automated Purchasing System

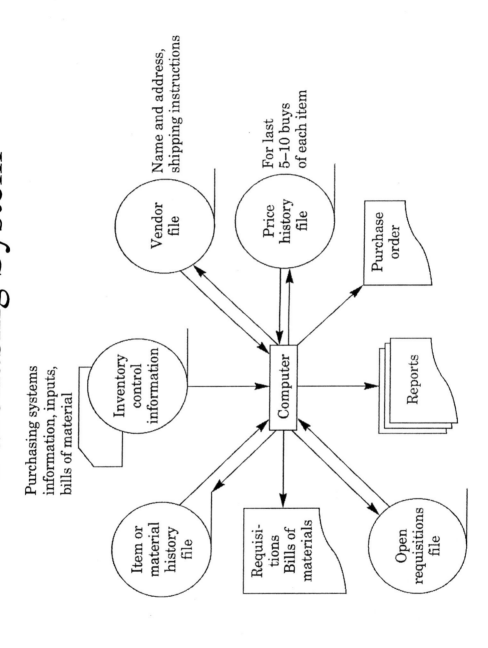

EDI Benefits

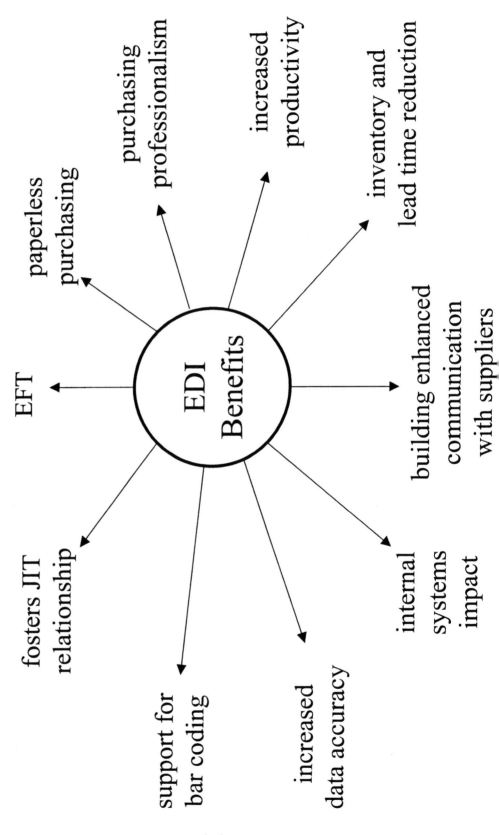

EDI Versus XML

	EDI	**XML**
Optimized for:	Compressed messages	Easy display and programming
Requires:	Dedicated EDI server	Web server
Server costs:	$10,000-$100,000	$5,000
Uses:	Value-added network	Existing Internet connection
Message format:	Months to master	Learned in hours
Requires:	C++ programmers	JavaScript, Visual Basic, Python or Perl script writers
Readable by:	Machine	Human and machine

Source: Gartner Group, found in Anne Chen, "Getting to XML," *eWeek*, August 6, 2000

Problems Related to Implementing e-Procurement

- The requirement for explicit approval prior to making an on-line purchase
  – e.g., manual sign-off
- Reliance and comfort with fax and email lead to clumsy links between buyers and suppliers
- Transaction-by-transaction review prior to payment rather than paying on proof of shipment
- Haphazard review of buying and supplying behavior that leaves people unsure of the degree of success of e-procurement

E-Procurement Applications

- The buying organization can purchase and install on its servers a package from a solutions provider
- The buying organization can use a third-party to host the e-procurement application for the organization
- An e-marketplace serving multiple buyers and multiple sellers can purchase and operate the e-procurement application
- "Content Vendors" may supplement the e-procurement package by creating catalogs or providing access to existing ones

Steps for Setting up an e-Procurement System for Indirect Materials

1. Selecting a solutions-provider and determining the type of relationship
2. The buyer(s) determines how many suppliers and which suppliers to keep in its supply base for indirect purchases
3. The buyer(s) negotiates terms and conditions with the chosen suppliers, including deeply discounted prices in return for volume
4. Digitized versions of the suppliers' catalogs are loaded alongside the e-procurement application

Steps for Setting up an e-Procurement System for Indirect Materials

5. Employees use computer browsers to search the catalogs of designated suppliers, selected items for purchase, and create requisitions and a P.O. is generated

6. The P.O. is streamed directly into the supplier's inventory application and the order is processes, and the goods shipped

7. Invoicing and/or payment is made; sometimes through and electronic bill presentment and payment process

When to Use Online Auctions

- The good or service has the characteristics of a commodity
  - e.g., there is a clear and unambiguous specification
- There are multiple suppliers available and willing to compete for business
- The organization has access to the technology necessary to run the auction

Three Types of e-Auctions

- Open offer negotiations
  - Suppliers select items for bidding and enter as many offers as they want until closing
  - Names not disclosed to other bidders
- Private offer negotiations
  - Suppliers review offers from the buying organization that includes target price and quantity
  - Suppliers select item(s) and offer prices
  - Status levels: accepted; closed; BAFO; open
- Posted price
  - Buyer posts price and first supplier that meets price is accepted

e-Commerce Implications for Purchasing

- Should we be a leader or a follower?

- What should be acquired through e-commerce?

- What tools should we use to acquire those items?

- Who should we use as service providers?

The Transformation and Value-Added Chain

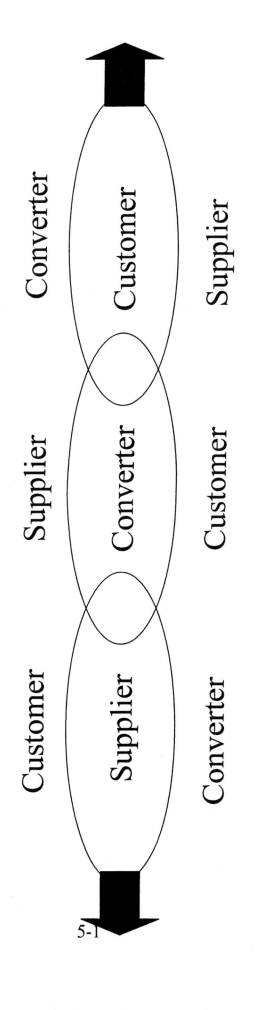

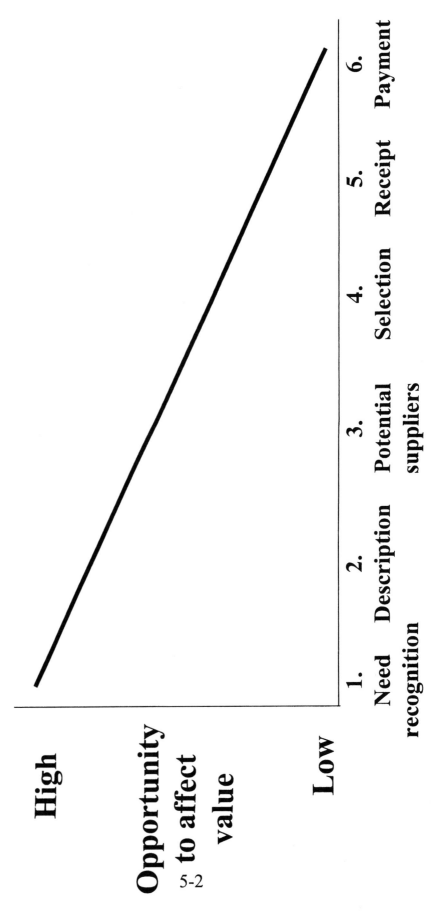

Methods of Description

- By brand
- "Or Equal"
- By specification
  - Physical or chemical characteristics
  - Material or method of manufacture
  - Performance
- By engineering drawing
- By miscellaneous methods
  - Market grades
  - Sample
- By a combination of two or more methods

Standardization and Simplification

- *Standardization*: Agreement on definite sizes, design, quality, or other aspects of the product or service.
  - A technical and engineering concept

- Simplification: A reduction in the number of sizes, designs or other aspects of the product or service.
  - It is a selective and commercial problem
  - It may be applied to articles already standardized or as a step preliminary to standarization

Total Quality Management

- Quality must be integrated throughout the organization's activities
- There must be employee commitment to continuous improvement
- The goal of customer satisfaction, and the systematic and continuous research process related to customer satisfaction, drives TQM
- Suppliers are partners in the TQM process

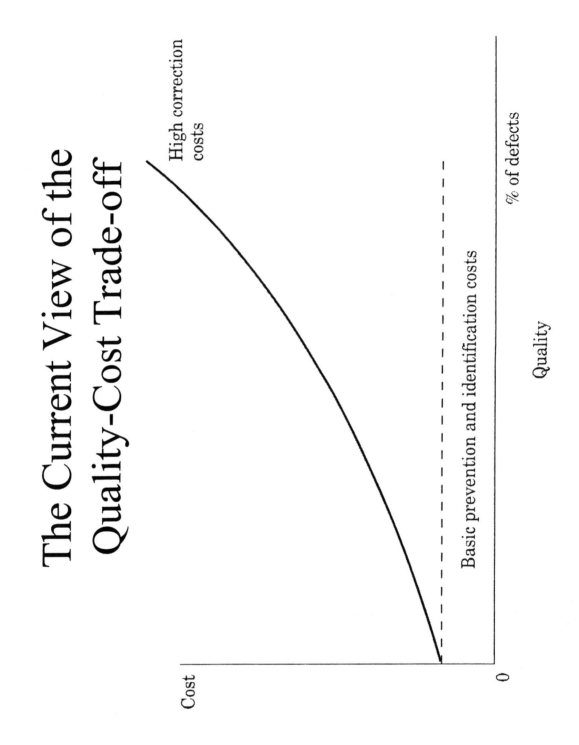

The Four Major Cost Categories for Quality

- Prevention costs
- Appraisal costs
- Internal failure costs
- External failure costs

The Four Integrated Stages of Quality Functional Deployment

- *Product planning* - to determine design requirements
- *Parts deployment* - to determine parts characteristics
- *Process planning* - to determine manufacturing requirements
- *Production planning* - to determine production requirements

The Role of Suppliers in QFD

- *Product planning* - Provide expertise in analyzing customer requirements and generating a list of new product ideas

- *Parts deployment* - Provide alternative design concepts and estimate the manufacturing costs of various parts

- *Process planning* - Suppliers can determine their existing processes' constraints

- *Production planning* - Help develop performance measurement criteria for production planning

Process Control

- *Process capability* - The ability of the process to meet specifications consistently

- *Statistical process control (SPC)* - A technique that involves testing a random sample of output from a process in order to detect if nonrandom changes in the process are occurring

  – common causes versus special or nonrandom causes

Control Chart

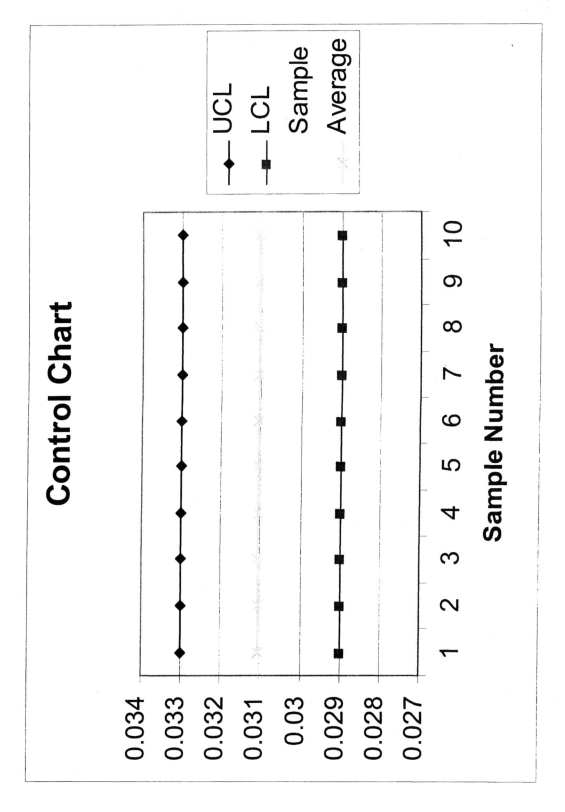

ABC Classification of Purchases

Class	Percentage of Total Items Purchased	Percentage of Total Purchase Dollars
A	10	70-80
B	10-20	10-15
C	70-80	10-20

Example of ABC Analysis

Number of Items	Percentage of Items	Annual Purchase Value	Percentage Annual Purchase Volume	Class
1,095	10.0%	$21,600,000	71.1%	A
2,168	19.9	5,900,000	19.4	B
7,660	70.1	2,900,000	9.5	C
10,923	100%	$30,400,000	100%	

Purchase Value is a Combination of Price and Quantity

Category	Unit Value	Annual Volume	Annual Value
A	high	high	high
A	medium	high	high
A	low	very high	high
B	high	low	medium
B	medium	medium	medium
B	low	high	medium
C	medium	low	low
C	low	medium	low
C	low	low	low

Forecasts Showing Uncertainty

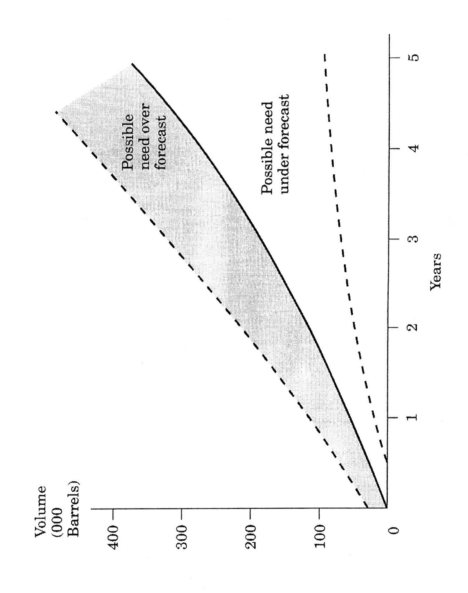

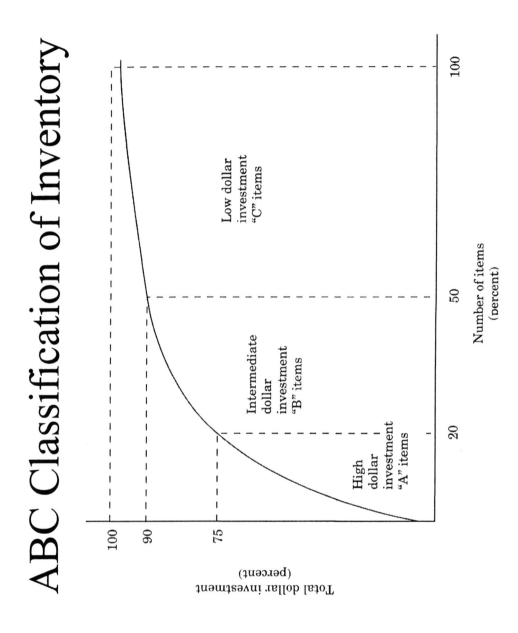

The Forms and Functions of Inventory

Functions of Inventories

- Transit or pipeline inventories
- Cycle inventories
- Buffer or uncertainty inventories or safety stock
- Anticipation or certainty inventories
- Decoupling inventories

Forms of Inventories

- Raw materials, purchased parts and packaging
- Work-in-progress
- Finished goods
- MRO items
- Resale items

Inventory: Types, Functions, Objectives

TYPE	FUNCTION	OBJECTIVE
Transit or Pipeline	It takes time to move products (transit time, handling time, delays)	Balance in-transit inventory costs against cost of reducing delays
Cycle	Demand pattern does not equal supply pattern (goods produced in lot sizes)	Balance cost of ordering (or setup) and cost of carrying inventory
Buffer or Safety	Demand pattern varies. Customer service levels must be maintained.	Balance cost of carrying extra inventory against cost of stocking out
Anticipation	Variations in demand relative to productive capacity or significant cost advantages to holding supply in anticipation of demand	Balance inventory costs against production costs, transportation costs, purchase discounts, and costs of avoiding price changes
Decoupling	Distribution and production efficiency gained from independence between stages of production and distribution	Balance efficiency of production - distribution activities against costs

Examples of Inventory Functions

TYPE	EXAMPLE
Transit or Pipeline	• parts on trains, forklifts, etc. • paper forms being moved between departments
Cycle	• a retail store that orders furniture by the truckload to save ordering and shipping (set-up) costs • student buys $25 of credit instead of $10 for a photocopy card to reduce trips for extra credit
Buffer or Safety	• extra shirts ordered for unanticipated demand by a retailer • extra bottles ordered by a brewery to allow for unexpected breakage
Anticipation	• air conditioners produced and stored during winter • sandwiches assembled during the morning and stored for lunch
Decoupling	• plastic moulding machine produces at 100 parts/hr, assemblers work at 50 parts/hr, parts are held in operations to balance production rates (and moulding is shutdown periodically).

Inventory Forms and Functions

FUNCTION	WHY	ELIMINATE REASON BY
Transit	move speed/distance	make moves faster/shorter
Cycle	make/use batch	reduce onetime batch costs
Buffer	cope with variability	reduce variability
Anticipation	smooth peak demand	increase volume flexibility
Decoupling	reduce dependence	coordinate/schedule

The EOQ Model

$$EOQ = \sqrt{\frac{2RS}{KC}}$$

where:

R = annual demand
S = set-up or order cost per order
C = delivered purchase cost
K = carrying cost percentage

therefore:

KC = unit holding cost

Economic Order Quantity Model

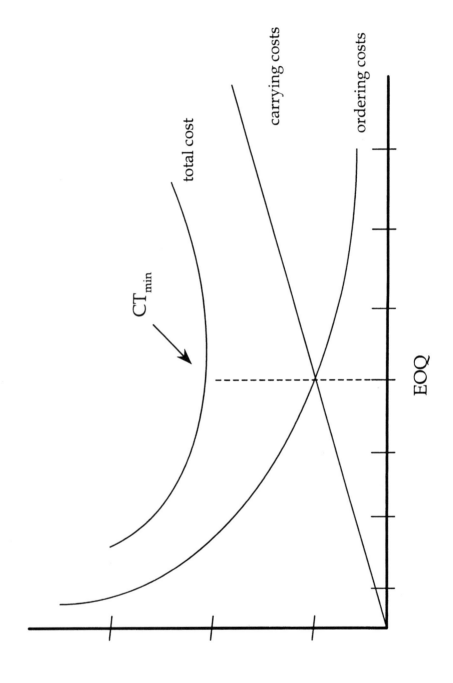

Fixed order quantity system

- Perpetual inventory system
- Event triggered: Initiates order when stock depleted to a specific level.
  - Reorder point
- Inventory replaced in fixed amounts
  - Economic order quantities
- Issues: visual signals, IT applications

Fixed Order Quantity System

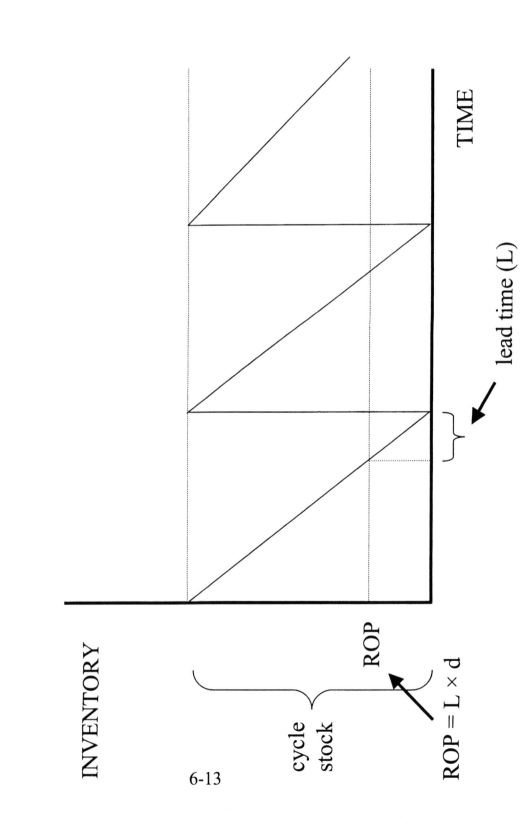

Safety Stock

- Safety stock is held because of uncertainty in supply and/or demand

- The trade-off is the cost of stocking out versus the cost of holding inventory

- Safety stock levels can be calculated using statistical techniques.
  - e.g., Take into account standard deviation of demand

Fixed Order Quantity System: Cycle Stock, Safety Stock and Lead Time

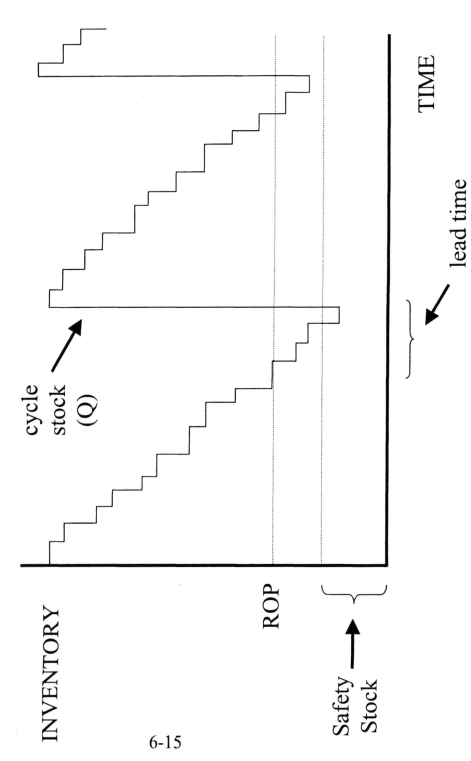

Fixed time period systems

- Inventory on-hand counted at specific time intervals and replenished to a desired level

- Only the passage of time triggers the model

Fixed Time Period System:
Cycle Stock, Safety Stock and Lead Time

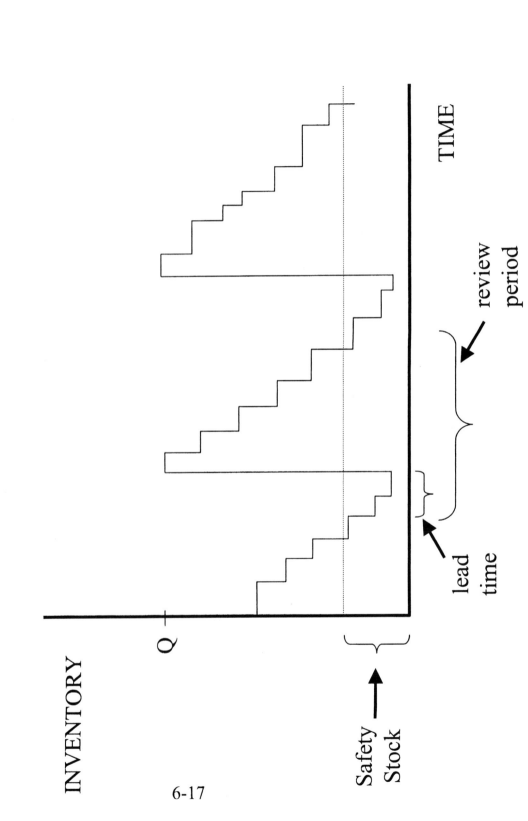

Which system is better?

- Fixed order quantity system
  - Higher maintenance costs
  - Every transaction logged
  - Inventory controlled precisely

- Fixed time period
  - Minimal record keeping
  - Higher average inventories to protect against stock-outs
  - Higher stock-out rates
  - Different order quantities for each cycle
  - Ability to batch orders to suppliers

Materials Requirement Planning (MRP)

- Based on a master production schedule, a material requirements planning system:
  - Creates schedules identifying the specific parts and materials required to produce end items
  - Determines exact numbers needed
  - Determines the dates when orders for those materials should be released, based on lead times
- "Get the right materials to the right place at the right time."

Key Inputs to MRP

- Master production schedule (when do we need it)
- Inventory record file (what do we have and what do we need)
- Bill of material (how does it get made)

Distribution Resources Planning (DRP)

- DRP developed after MRP
- Applies the same concepts to meeting a market demand for various products
- Started with a basic model and has become more sophisticated
- Goal: Plan and monitor the resources required to meet anticipated market demands
- Leading DRP and MRP systems are integrated but the two terms are still found

MRP Implications for Purchasing

- Accurate records for quantities, lead times, bills of material, and specifications
- Tight control of inventory
- Cooperation from suppliers for on-time delivery, proper quantities and batch sizes, exacting quality (zero defects)
  - May need to re-evaluate existing contracts
- Long-term planning horizon
- Less "slack" in the system

What is JIT?

- JIT is characterized by providing the *exact* quantity needed at the *precise* moment it is required

- However, to be able to support JIT firms require certain capabilities
  - short production lead times
  - economical small batch production
  - flexible resources (labour, material and equipment)
  - exacting quality

What is JIT?

- True *JIT production systems* strive to eliminate waste
  - Waste includes: inefficient set-up procedures, inventories
  - Focus on all aspects of the production system: human resources, supply, technology, and inventories
- JIT is based on the logic that nothing will be produced until it is needed
  - When a unit is sold, the system *pulls* a replacement unit from the last position in the system
  - This process continues throughout the system

Kanban

- Kanban means "sign" or "instruction card" in Japanese
  - A number of visual methods can be used
- Authority to produce come from downstream operations
- Kanban cards represent the number of containers used in the system
  - Dictates the lot size production levels and inventory

JIT Imposed Supplier Activities

- Frequent deliveries
- Small lot sizes
- Exacting quality
- Long-term relationships/contracts
- Reduced number of suppliers

Supply Managers' JIT Expectations

- Reduction in number of suppliers
- Reduction in supplier lead time
- Improvement in supplier quality
- Improvement in supplier delivery
- Increased inventory turnover
- Inventory reduction in total dollars

Supply Risks and Dollars Extended

Bottleneck • Unique specification • Supplier technology important • Production-based scarcity • Substitution difficult • Usage fluctuates • Potential storage risk	**Strategic** • Continuous availability essential • Custom design or unique specifications • Supplier technology important • Few adequate suppliers • Changing source of supply difficult • Substitution difficult
Non-Critical • Standard or commodity type • Substitute products available • Competitive supply market	**Leverage** • Unique cost management important • Substitution possible • Competitive supply market

Risk: High / Low

Value: Low / High

Source: Peter Kraljic, Purchasing Must Become Supply Management," *Harvard Business Review*, September-October, 1983

Numerous Potential Sources of Information

- Catalogs (online and printed)
- Trade Journals
- Advertisements
- Supplier and commodity directories
- The Internet
- Sales contacts and interviews
- Colleagues, networking, professional contacts
- Your own records

Supplier Evaluation

- Informal evaluation
- Executive roundtable discussions
- Formal supplier evaluation and rating systems

Formal Supplier Evaluations

- Quality
- Price
- Delivery
- Service

Good Performance → *Fair Performance* → *Unsatisfactory Performance*

Weighted Point Evaluation Systems

- Identify suppliers
  - Important suppliers and/or critical goods and services
- Identify factors or criteria for evaluation
- Determine the importance of each factor
- Establish a system for rating each supplier on each factor

Evaluation of Potential Sources: Two Key Questions

1. Is this supplier capable of supplying our requirements satisfactorily in both the short- and long-term?

2. Is this supplier motivated to supply these requirements in the way we expect in the short- and long-term?

Evaluation of Potential Sources

- Technical, Engineering and Operations
  - Quality systems and performance
  - Engineering and technical strengths
  - Capacity and flexibility to meet demand (lead time)
  - Process capabilities
- Management and Financial
  - Mission, corporate culture, values and goals
  - Organization structure and decision-making
  - Management controls, information systems, policies and procedures
  - Qualifications and background of managers
  - Financial analysis; e.g., profit, inventory turns, receivables, current ratio
  - Procurement systems

Arguments in Favor of Single Sourcing

- Exclusivity: The supplier may be only available source
  - patent protection, exclusive distributorship
- Outstanding quality or service → value
- Order too small to split
- Opportunities for discounts or lower freight costs
- More important customer → more attention from supplier
- Cost of duplication prohibitive
- Easier to schedule deliveries
- JIT, stockless buying or EDI arrangements
- Focus on one, not many suppliers
- Prerequisite to partnering

Arguments in Favor of Multiple Sourcing

- Traditional practice
- Keep suppliers "on their toes"
- Assurance of supply
- Capable of dealing with multiple suppliers efficiently
- Avoid supplier dependence on one customer
- Obtain a greater degree of volume flexibility
- Strategic considerations; e.g., military preparedness
- Government regulations
- Limited supplier capacity
- Opportunity to test a new supplier
- Supply market volatility

Customer Service Inputs

Total Customer Satisfaction ↔ { Other, Quantity, Delivery, Cost, Quality } ↔ **Suppliers**

Simplified Supply Chain Perspective: The Three Core Links

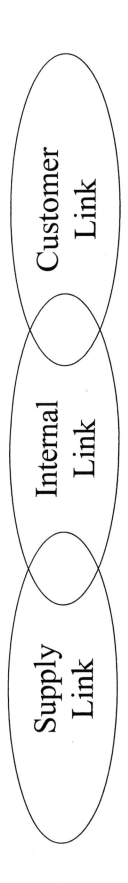

Reasons to Make Instead of Buy

- Quantities are too small and/or no supplier is interested
- Quality requirements are too exacting or unusual and require special processing methods
- Greater assurance of supply
- Closer coordination of supply and demand
- Preserve technological secrets
- To take advantage of unused capacity
- Keep our capacity utilization high and outsource the rest
- Avoid supply dependency
- Competitive, political, social or environmental factors
- Personal preference
- Preservation of the status quo: Decisions to make are hard to reverse

Reasons to Buy Instead of Make

- Lack of administrative or technical experience
- Excess production capacity
- Customer preference for a particular brand
- Problems maintaining technological leadership for a noncore product
- Preservation of the status quo: Decisions to outsource are hard to reverse
- Flexibility
- Trend to outsourcing: Focus on core activities and outsource the balance of the company's requirements
- Superior supply management expertise
- Lower overhead costs

Research: Reasons for Outsourcing

1995

- Cost reduction
- Headcount reduction
- Focus on core competencies
- Acquire and deploy peripheral knowledge or process technology
- Minimize inventory and materials handling
- Reduce development and production cycle times
- Improve efficiency
- Reaction to positive media reports

1998

- Reduce and control operating costs
- Improve company focus
- Gain access to world-class capabilities
- Free internal resources for other purposes
- Resources are not available internally
- Accelerate reengineering benefits
- Function difficult to manage/out of control
- Make capital funds available
- Share risks
- Cash infusion

Risks of Outsourcing

- Loss of control
- Higher exit barriers
- Exposure to supplier risks
  - e.g., financial, commitment to relationship, response time, quality, service
- Unexpected/unanticipated costs
- Difficulty quantifying economies
- Conversion costs
- Supply restraints
- Possibility of being tied to obsolete technology
- Concerns with long-term flexibility

The Outsourcing Matrix

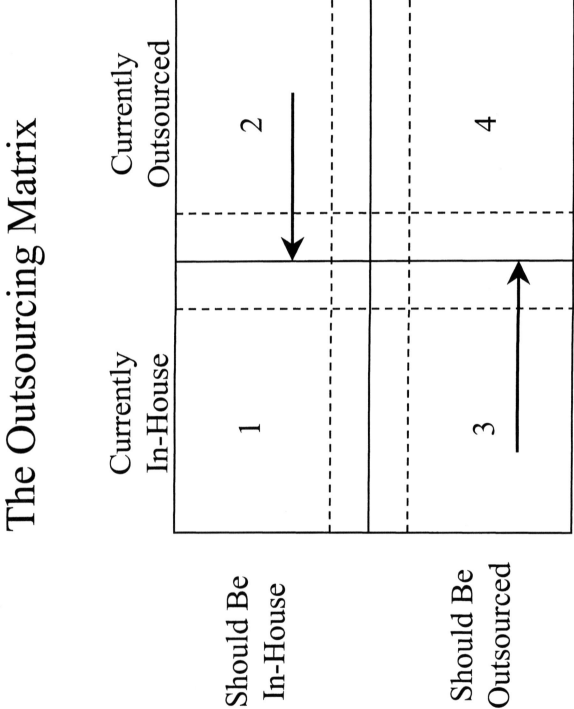

The Outsourcing Decision

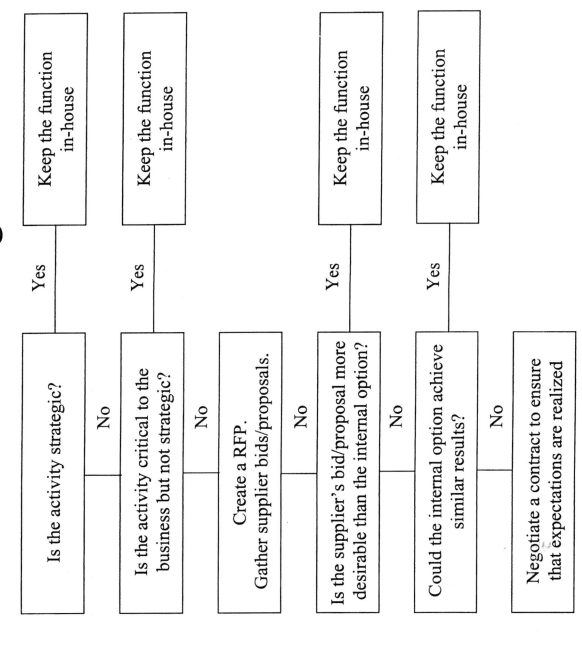

8-8

Purchasing's Role in Outsourcing

- Providing a comprehensive, competitive process
- Identifying opportunities for outsourcing
- Aiding in selection of sources
- Identifying potential relationship issues
- Developing and negotiating the contract
- Ongoing monitoring and management of the relationship

Source: Lisa Ellram and Arnold Maltz, *Outsourcing: Implications for Supply Management*, Tempe, AZ: Center for Advanced Purchasing Studies, 1997.

A Simple Purchaser-Supplier Satisfaction Model

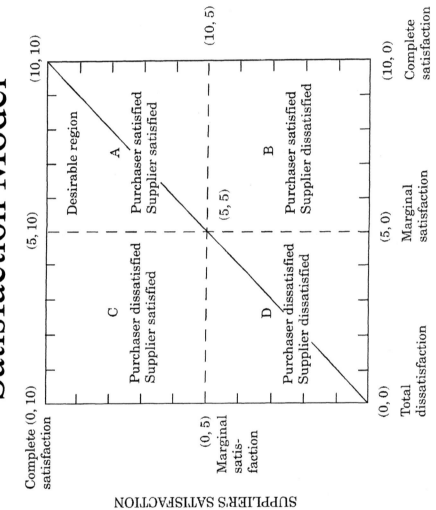

Purchaser-Supplier Satisfaction Model: Congruent and Noncongruent Perceptions

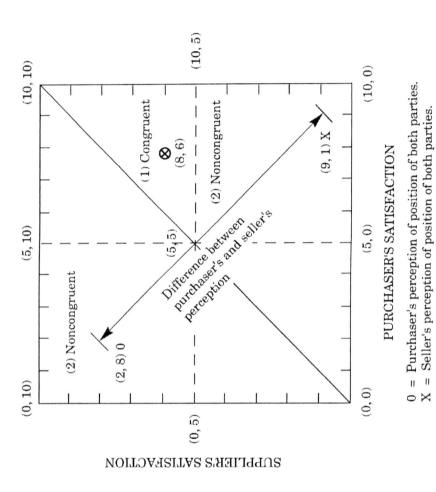

Buyer-Supplier Relationship: Investment Versus Rewards Obtained

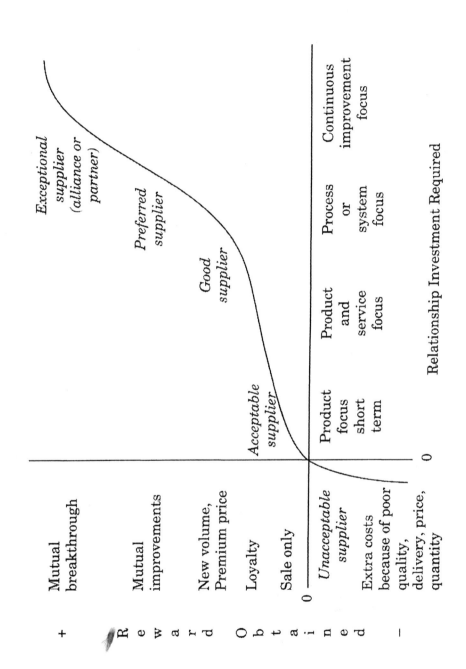

Adapted from C. Michael Stralkowski and S. Alexander Billon, "Partnering: A Strategic Approach to Productivity Improvement,"; *National Productivity Review*, Spring 1988.

View of Buyer-Supplier Relationship: A Paradigm Shift

Traditional

- Lowest price
- Specification-driven
- Short-term, reacts to market
- Trouble avoidance
- Purchasing's responsibility
- Tatical
- Little sharing of information

Partnership

- Total cost of ownership
- End-customer driven
- Long-term
- Opportunity maximization
- Cross-functional teams and top management involvement
- Strategic
- Both supplier and buyer on both sides share short- and long-term plans
- Shared risk and opportunity
- Standardization
- Joint ventures
- Share data

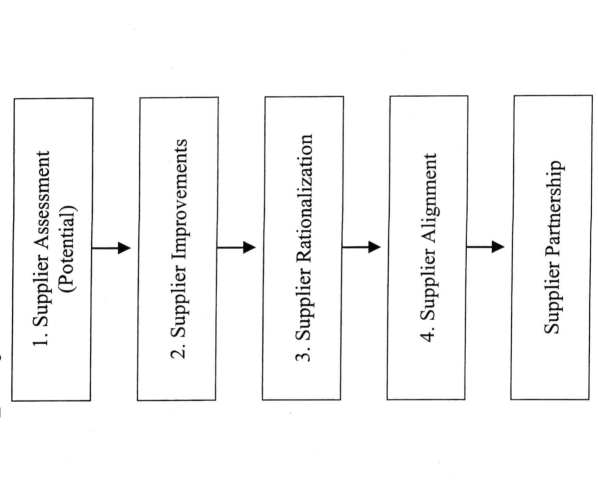

Partnering Strategies and Outcomes

Strategies

- Decrease average delivery lot size
- Decrease total number of suppliers
- Decrease average number of sources used per purchased item
- Increase average contract/agreement length
- Increase average frequency of delivery to the plant
- Increase supplier involvement in quality certification programs

Outcomes

- Improve quality of the supplier's operations/processes
- Improved quality of oncoming goods
- Decreased supplier's total costs
- Decreased buying organization's total cost
- Improved supplier's ability to handle buyer-initiated changes to the agreed-to delivery date
- Improved buyer's ability to handle supplier-initiated changes to the agreed-to delivery date

Source: T. Scott Graham, Patricia J. Daugherty and William N. Dudley, "The Long Term Strategic Impact of Purchasing Partnerships", *International Journal of Purchasing and Materials Management*, Fall 1994..

Some Indicators of a Successful Partnering Effort

- Formal communication processes
- Commitment to our suppliers' success
- Mutual profitability
- Stable relationships, not dependent on a few personalities
- Consistent and specific feedback on supplier performance
- Realistic expectations
- Employee accountability for ethical business conduct
- Meaningful information sharing
- Guidance to supplier in defining improvement efforts
- Non-adversarial negotiations and decisions based on total cost of ownership

Source: SEMATECH

Supplier Development

The Marketing Context

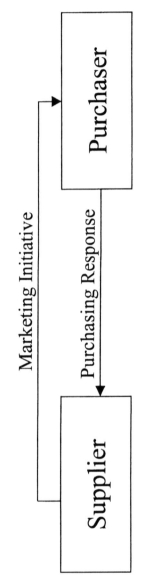

The Supplier Development Context

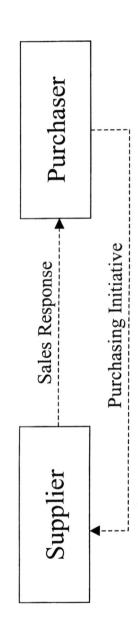

Meaning of Cost

- *Direct Costs: Costs that can be specifically and accurately assigned to a given unit pf production*

- *Indirect Costs: Costs incurred that normally cannot be related directly to any given unit of production.*

When evaluating costs as either direct or indirect, the issue is the ability to trace the costs directly to a unit of production

Meaning of Cost

- *Variable Costs:* Vary directly and proportionally with the number of units produced
- *Fixed Costs:* Remain the same regardless of volume produced (over the relevant range)
- *Semivariable Costs:* Partly variable and partly fixed

When evaluating costs as either variable or fixed, the issue is how costs change as volume of production changes

Seven Types of Purchases

- Raw materials
- Special items
- Standard production items
- Items of small value
- Capital goods
- Services
- Resale

Competitive Bidding

- Bidders must be qualified to make the item in question in accordance with the buyer's specifications and to deliver it by the date required
- Bidders must be sufficiently reliable in other respects to warrant serious consideration as suppliers
- Bidders must be numerous enough to ensure a truly competitive price
- Bidders must not be more numerous than necessary

Conditions for Competitive Bidding

- There must be at least two, and preferably more, qualified bidders
- The suppliers must want the business
  - a "buyer's market"
- Specifications must be clear
- No collusion between bidders

Any Aspect of the Purchase Agreement is Subject to Negotiation

Quality

- specification compliance
- performance compliance
- test criteria
- rejection procedures
- liability
- reliability
- design changes

Support

- technical assistance
- product research, development, and/or design
- warranty
- spare parts
- training
- tooling
- packaging
- data sharing, including technical data

Any Aspect of the Purchase Agreement is Subject to Negotiation

Price

- purchase order price
- discounts (cash, quantity and trade)
- escalation provisions
- exchange terms
- import duties
- payment of taxes
- countertrade credits

Transportation

- FOB terms
- carrier
- commodity classification
- freight allowance/equalization
- multiple delivery points

Supply

- lead times
- delivery schedule
- consignment stocks
- expansion options
- supplier inventories
- cancellation options

Problems Using Cost Analysis

- Suppliers may not know their costs
- Interpretation of cost calls for an exercise of judgment
- Some suppliers are not willing to divulge cost information
- The seller's costs do not determine the market prices
- The buyer is not interested in the supplier's costs, the primary concern is getting the best price

The 90 Percent Learning Curve Plotted on Standard Graph Paper

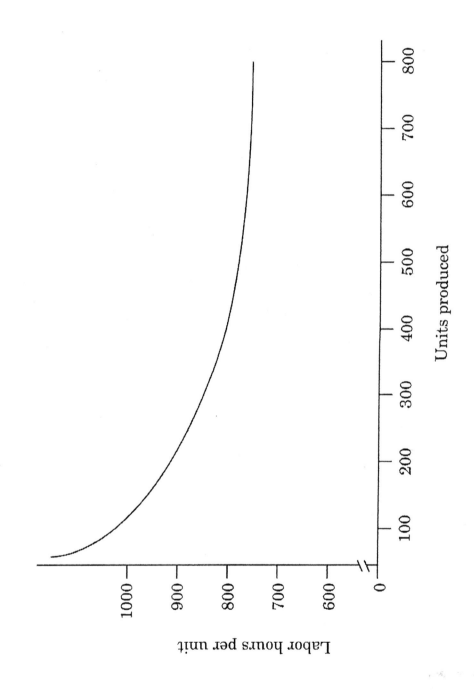

The 90 Percent Learning Curve Plotted on Log-Log Paper

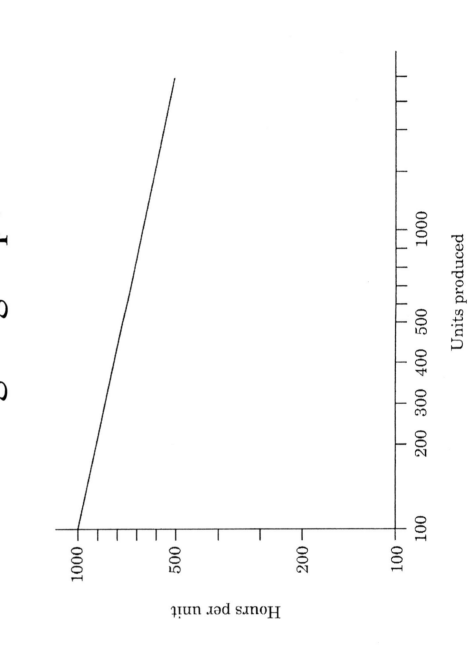

Major Categories for the Components of Total Cost of Ownership

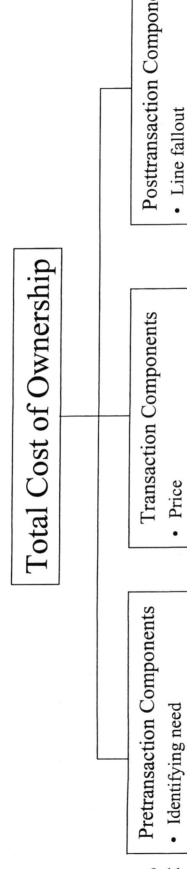

Source: Lisa Ellram, "Total Cost of Ownership: Elements and Implementation," *International Journal of Purchasing and Materials Management*, Winter 1993.

Situations Where Negotiation May Provide Value

- Any written contract covering price, specifications, terms of delivery and quality standards
- The purchase of items made to the buyer's standards
- When changes are made in drawings or specifications
- Following an unsuccessful bidding process
- When problems of tooling or packaging occur
- When changing economic or market conditions require changes in quantities or prices
- When problems of termination of a contract involve disposal of facilities, materials or tooling
- When problems arise under the various type of contracts used in defense and governmental contracting

Model of the Negotiation Process

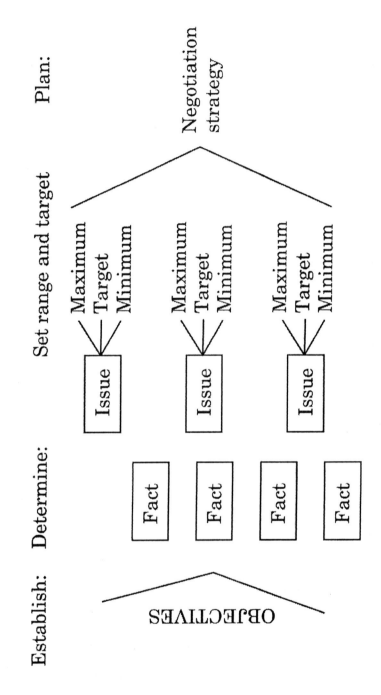

9-13

The Basic Steps in Developing and Negotiation Strategy

1. Develop the specific objectives (outcomes) desired from the negotiation
2. Gather pertinent data
3. Determine the facts of the situation
4. Determine the issues
5. Analyze the positions of strength for both (or all) parties
6. Set the buyer's position on each issue, and estimate the seller's position on each issue based on your research
7. Plan the negotiation strategy
8. Brief all persons on the negotiation team
9. Conduct a dress rehearsal
10. Conduct the actual negotiations with an impersonal calmness

Total Transportation Costs for 1999

	United States*	Canada*
Highway	$ 450	$ 12.5
Railroads	36	4.5
Water	22	2.4
Pipelines	9	N/A
Air	26	4.3
Freight forwarders	6	3.6
Shipper related	5	N/A
Total	$ 554	$ 27.3

* In Billions

Major Issues Facing the Logistics Industry

- Congestion
- Mergers and anti-trust concerns
- Cargo and liability concerns
- Safety regulations

Transportation Industry Segments

- Air cargo
- Air passenger
- Motor freight
- Railroad
- Marine
- Intermodal
- Pipeline

Third-Party Logistics Suppliers

- Integration of services desirable
  - transport and logistics
- Opportunity for logistics/transport companies to provide more value-added services under deregulation
- Outsourcing issue for manufacturers
- $50 billion industry
  - Growth market

Third-Party Logistics Suppliers

- Facilitated by advances in information technology
  - Logistics deals with the flow of goods and information
- TPL providers differentiated on the basis of:
  - geographic scope
  - industry specialization
- Potential economies of TPL
  - economies of scale
  - economies of scope
  - specialized expertise

The Selection of the FOB Point Determines Four Things

1. Who pays the carrier

2. When legal title to goods being shipped passes to the buyer

3. Who is responsible for preparing and pursuing claims with the carrier

4. Who routes the freight

Since deregulation of the transport sector, purchasers are increasingly taking control of transport arrangements as a means of controlling costs

Terms of Sale: Possible FOB Points

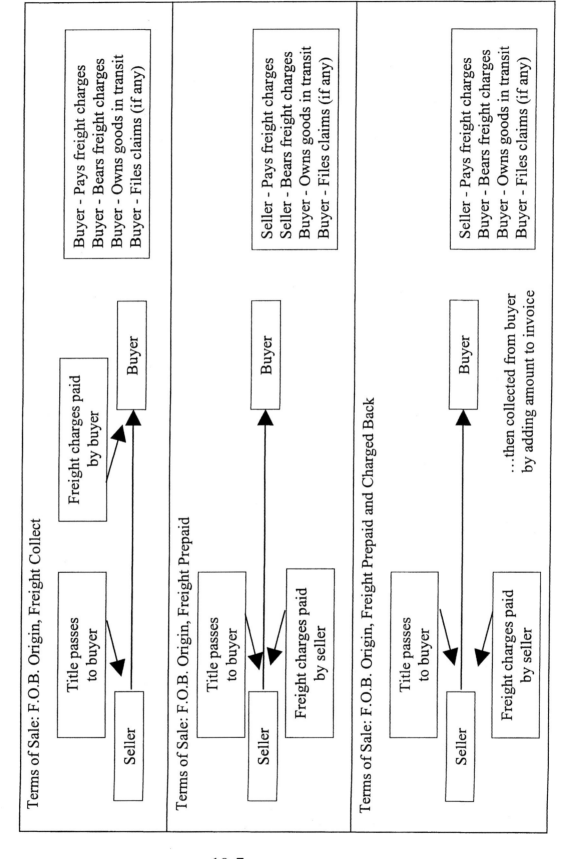

Terms of Sale: Possible FOB Points (continued)

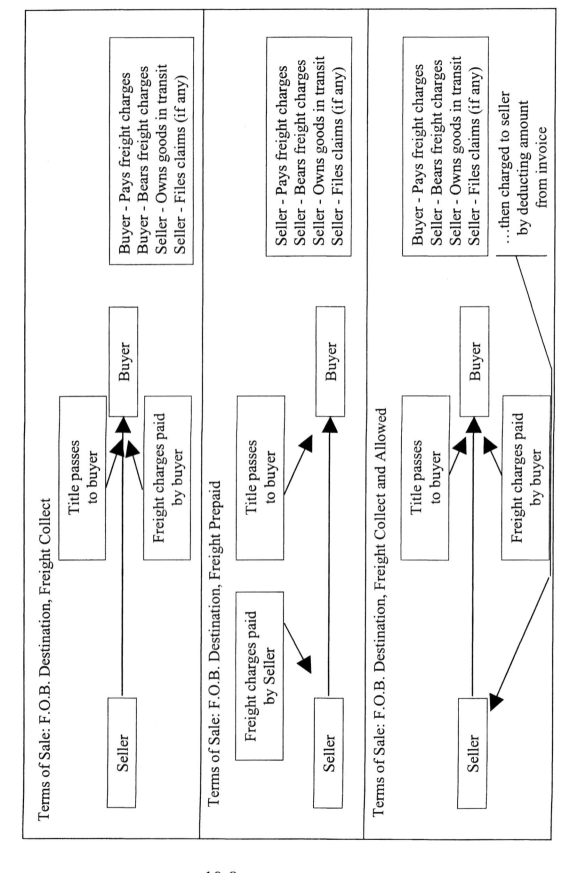

The Effects of Transportation Deregulation

- Greater innovation and efficiency
  - by carriers and shippers
- Wider range of services available to shippers
- Carriers free to experiment with geographical extent and nature of services
- Restructuring of transport industry
  - true of all modes
- Greater pressure on all suppliers to carriers to be more efficient
- Decreases in actual or real transport costs

Scrap Recyclers Handle 120 Million tons/year

- 60 million tons of scrap iron and steel
- 47 million tons of scrap paper and paperboard
- 5.1 million tons of scrap aluminum
- 1.7 million tons of scrap copper
- 1.1 million tons of scrap stainless steel
- 1.4 million tons of scrap lead
- 248,000 tons of scrap zinc
- 2.3 million tons of scrap glass
- 745 million tons of scrap PET plastic bottles
- 734 million tons of scrap HDPE plastic bottles

Source: Institute of Scrap Recycling Industries (ISRI)

Four Pieces of Federal Legislation Impact the Scrap Disposal Market and Sourcing Procedures

- Resource Conservation and Recovery Act (RCRA)
  - Ensure that suppliers are competent and reputable and have an EPA permit
  - Require the supplier to warrant that employees are trained in handling the specific waste
  - Insist on the right to inspect the facility and the EPA permit
- Toxic Substances Control Act (TSCA)
  - Requires suppliers to warrant that any chemical or chemical mixture they provide is listed by the EPA

Four Pieces of Federal Legislation Impact the Scrap Disposal Market and Sourcing Procedures

- Comprehensive Environmental Response, Compensation and Liability Act (CERCLA)
  - Purchasers must track the amount and type of chemicals that enter and leave the plant and consult the Material Safety Data Sheets (MSDS)
- Clean Air Act Amendments
  - Purchasers can choose environmentally friendly products, establish criteria for supplier selection that limits purchases from suppliers that sell damaging products, and be alerted to alternatives, substitutes or new technology that may help their companies meet the goals of the act.

The EPA's Voluntary Compliance Programs

- Climate Wise
- Commonsense Initiative
- Design for the Environment
- Electronic Commerce/Electronic Data Interchange
- Environmental Accounting Project
- Environmental Leadership Program
- National Environmental Performance Track Team
- Sector Facility Indexing Project
- Sustainable Industry Project
- WasteWise

Environmentally Responsible Purchasing Practices Can Reduce Costs

- Reducing the obsolescence and waste of MRO supplies through better inventory management
- Reducing costs from scrap and materials losses
- Lowering costs of handling hazardous materials
- Increasing revenues by converting wastes to by-products
- Reducing the use of hazardous materials through more timely and accurate materials tracking and reporting systems
- Decreasing the use and waste of chemicals and solvents
- Recovering valuable materials and assets with efficient materials recovery programs

Environmental Management

- Reduce
- Reuse
- Recycle

→ *less risk*
less complexity
easier to implement
smaller environmental benefits

Materials Recaptured from a Computer

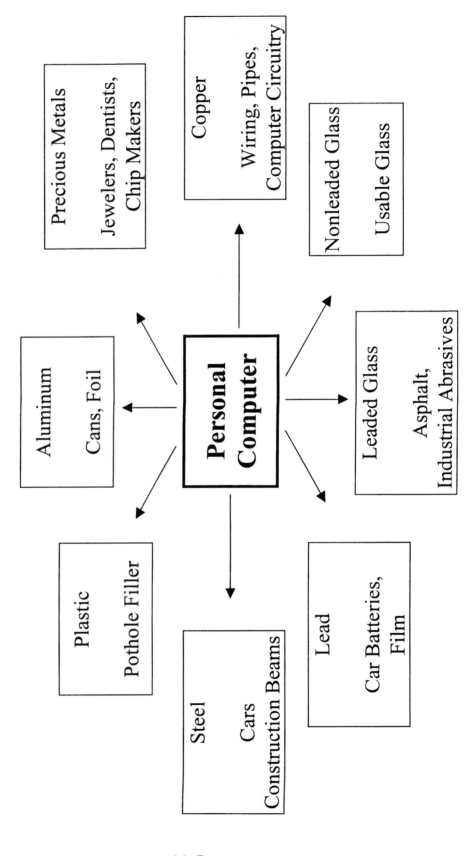

ISO 14000 Framework

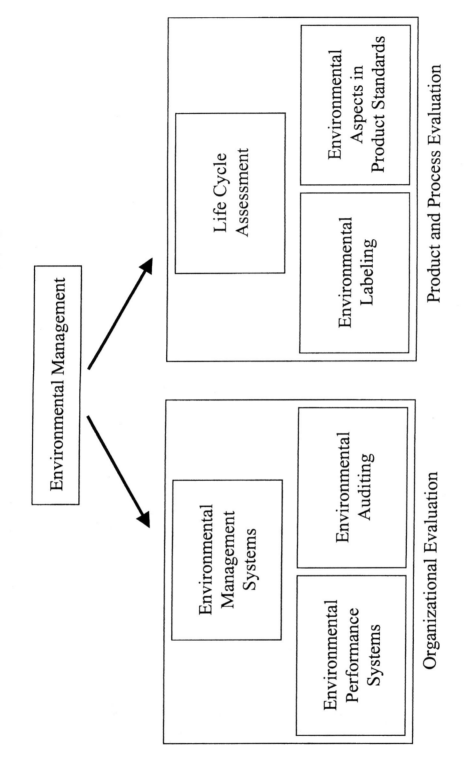

Source: Melnyk et al., *ISO 14000: Assessing Its Impact on Corporate Effectiveness and Efficiency*, Tempe, AZ: Center For Advanced Purchasing Studies, 1999.

Benefits of Effective Disposal Programs

- Cost recovery
- Cost reduction and avoidance
- Customer service
- Quality control
- Protect intellectual property and brand identity
- Comply with government regulations
- Reclaim valuable materials from customers
- Control product liability
- Improve public image

Categories of Material for Disposal

- Excess or surplus materials
- Obsolete material or equipment
- Rejected end products
- Scrap material
- Waste
- Hazardous waste

Reasons for Assigning Disposal of Materials to the Purchasing Function

- Knowledge of the materials, equipment or substances being disposed
- Knowledge of price trends and the market
- Contact with salespeople and information as to possible users of the material
- Familiarity with the company's own needs for the material
- The company may not have a surplus material disposal group

Disposal Channels

- Use elsewhere in the firm "as is"
- Reclaim for use within the plant
- Sell to another firm for use on an "as is" basis
- Return to the supplier
- Sale through a broker
- Sale to a local scrap or surplus dealer
- Donate, discard or destroy the material or item

The Reverse Flow of Materials in the Supply Chain

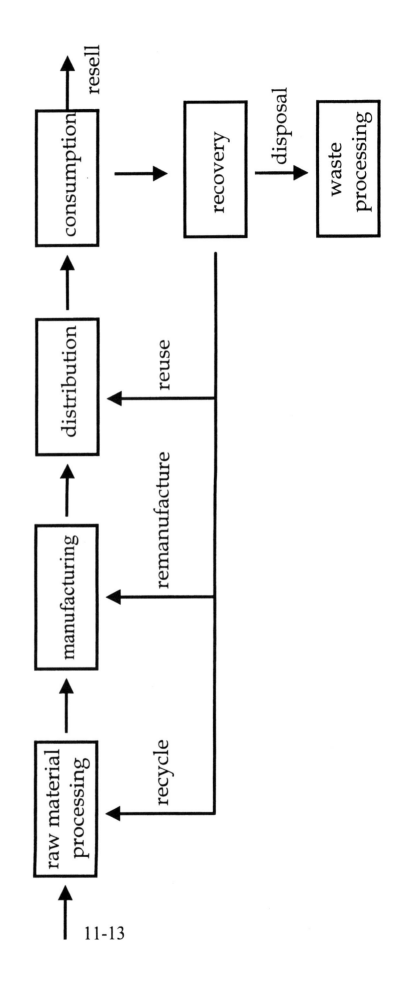

Selecting Disposal Partners

- Selling, not buying materials places the purchaser in a new role
- Understand regulatory issues
  - fines, penalties
- Disposal practices have implications for operations
  - impact on processes, labor costs
- Use appropriate segregation and transportation methods based on volume of material
- Internet and technology applications
  - Internet marketplaces provide access to a large number of potential bidders

The Purchasing Officer May Be Personally Liable Under Certain Conditions

- When making a false statement concerning authority with intent to deceive or when the misrepresentation has the natural and probable consequence of misleading
- When agents perform a damaging act without authority
  - Even though believing they have such authority
- When performing an act which is itself illegal
  - Even on authority from the employer
- When willfully performing an act which results in damage to anyone
- When performing damaging acts outside the scope of authority
  - Even though the act is performed with the intention of rendering the employer a valuable service

A Valid Contract Is Based on Four Factors

1. Competent parties - either principals or qualified agents
2. Legal subject matter or purpose
3. An offer and an acceptance
4. Consideration (bargained-for exchange)

Purchases Made Orally

- Normally there must be some written notation if the price of the order for the sale of goods is $500 or more.

- If the seller supplies a memorandum which is not in accordance with the buyer's understanding of the oral order, he or she must give a notice of objection to the supplier within 10 days of receipt of the memorandum to preserve his or her legal rights.

Four Types of Warranties

1. Express warranty
2. Implied warranty of merchantability
3. Implied warranty of fitness for a particular purpose
4. Warranty of title

The Buyer Has Three Options When Delivery Fails to Conform to the Contract

1. Reject the whole shipment

2. Accept the whole shipment

3. Accept part of the shipment and reject the balance

The goods may be late, may be delivered in the wrong quantity, or may fail to meet specifications

E-Commerce and the Law

- The Uniform Computer Information Transaction Act (UCITA)
  - Commercial code that would provide uniform rules and standards
- Uniform Electronic Transactions Act (UETA)
  - Validates the use of electronic records and electronic signatures
- The Electronic Commerce Enhancement Act

Commercial Arbitration

- Is your clause in proper form under the appropriate arbitration laws?
- Does your clause fully express the will of the parties or is it ambiguous?
- Does your clause ensure the appointment of impartial arbitrators?
- Does your clause provide for a method of naming arbitrators?
  – By reference to the rules of an association or otherwise
  – Safeguarding against deadlocks or defaults in the proceedings

Ingredients of Effective Buying

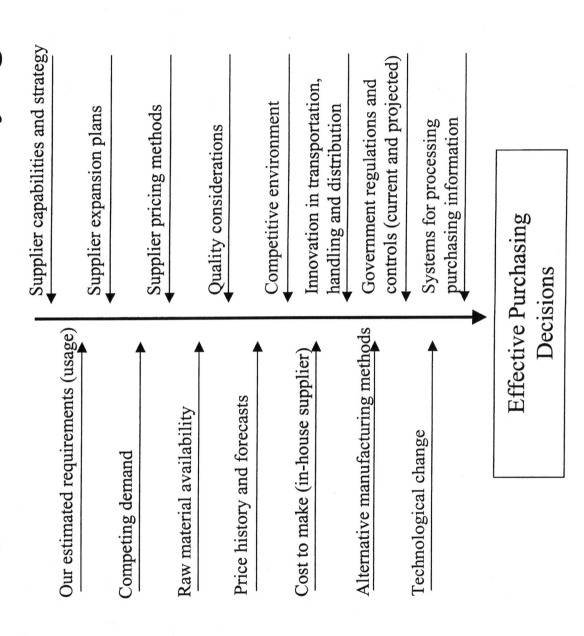

Conditions Necessary for Effective Cross-Functional Teams

- Team members are carefully selected to ensure that each really has something to contribute
- Strong leadership
- Specific objectives and expectations, communicated to each team member
- Each team member's normal job responsibilities are rearranged to provide necessary time and resources
- Performance evaluation and reward systems foster team participation and overall team performance

Criteria for Deciding Where to Direct Research Efforts

- Value of product or service - top dollar

- Product profitability - red dollar

- Price/cost characteristics

- Availability

- Quality

- Data flows

Purchasing Research

→ *What is Acquired*
- value analysis
- commodity studies

→ *From Whom*
- supply base analysis

Value Analysis

- Value analysis compares the function performed by the purchased item with the cost in an attempt to find a lower cost alternative
- Value analysis is done on purchased items used in the ongoing production process
  - *Value engineering* looks are cost saving possibilities in the design stage

Possible Value Analysis Research Topics

- Investment recovery
- Lease or buy
- Make or buy and continue making or outsource
- Packaging
- Specification
- Standardization
- Substitution
- Supplier switching

Commodity Studies

- Should provide the basis for making sound procurement decisions

- Should present purchasing management and top management with information concerning future supply and price of purchase items

Major Areas in a Commodity Study

- Current and future status of our company as a buyer
- Production process alternatives
- Uses of the item
- Demand
- Supply
- Price
- Strategy to reduce cost and/or ensure supply

Topics in Supplier Research

- Analysis of financial capacity
- Analysis of production facilities
- Finding new supply source
- Supplier cost analysis
- Single sourcing
- Supplier-purchased material quality assurance
- Supplier attitude survey
- Supplier performance evaluation
- Supplier sales strategy
- Countertrade

Four Common Purchasing Budgets

- Materials (operations) purchase budget
- MRO Budget
- Capital Budget
- Administrative Budget

Common Purchasing Activity Reports

- Total dollar volume of purchases
- Total dollars spent for department operating expenses
- Total number of purchase orders issued

These figure are sometimes related to each other by calculating average figures and percentages, such as:

- average dollar cost of purchase orders written
- operating costs as a percentage of total dollar volume purchases
- operating costs as a percentage of total dollar volume of sales

Major Sections for Purchasing Operating Reports

1. Market and economic conditions and price performance
2. Inventory investment changes
3. Purchasing operations and effectiveness
4. Operations affecting administration and financial activities

Four Types of Performance Measurement Systems

1. Efficiency-oriented
   – Emphasizes cost and departmental operating efficiency
2. Effectiveness-oriented
   – Measure of direct and indirect contributions of supply
3. Multiple objectives
   – Considers both efficiency and effectiveness measures
4. Naïve
   – No goals, objectives, or pre-set performance measures
   – Supply managers told that an appraisal will be made of their performance

Problem Areas in Purchasing Performance Measurement

- There are no industry-wide standards of functional performance
- A lack of management information systems support
- Differences in the scope and sophistication of supply
  - Even within the same firm
  - Operational versus strategic
- An historical focus on functional goals without linkages to the corporate goal-setting process

12 Guidelines for Establishing a Purchasing Measurement System

1. Measures need to be designed for use at a point in time
2. Each organization has specific measurement needs at a given point in time
3. Measures should address financial results, supplier performance, computer systems and internal practices and policies
4. Measures must change frequently
5. Trend analysis is often useful
6. Measures should not be overdone or underutilized

12 Guidelines for Establishing a Purchasing Measurement System

7. Measures are only tools
8. Benchmarking is a source of new ideas and measures
9. Senior management must see value in the measures used
10. Measures can show the effectiveness of purchasing and identify areas needing improvement
11. Ensure the credibility of measures
12. Continuous improvement in purchasing depends on measurement

Growth in World Trade

- Total value of world merchandise exports in 1999 was $5.47 trillion
- World commercial services exports in 1999 was $1.35 trillion

The WTO estimates that total trade in 1997 was 14 times the level of 1950

U.S. Imports and Exports and Merchandise Trade Balance 1950-1999

Year	Imports ($ millions)	Exports ($ millions)	Surplus or Deficit ($ millions)
1950	$ 8,984	$ 10,282	$ 1,298
1960	15,075	20,612	5,537
1970	39,756	42,590	2,834
1980	256,984	220,786	(36,198)
1990	495,300	393,600	(101,700)
1995	743,543	584,742	(158,801)
1996	795,289	625,075	(170,214)
1997	869,704	689,182	(180,522)
1998	911,896	682,138	(229,758)
1999	1,024,618	695,797	(328,821)

U.S. Imports and Exports by Country for 1999

Year	Imports ($ millions)	Percent of Total Imports	Exports ($ millions)
Canada	$ 198,711	19.4	$ 166,600
Japan	130,864	12.8	57,466
Mexico	109,720	10.7	86,909
China	81,788	8.0	13,111
Germany	55,228	5.4	26,800
United Kingdom	39,237	3.8	38,407
Taiwan	35,204	3.4	19,131
South Korea	31,179	3.0	22,958
France	25,708	2.5	18,877
Italy	22,357	2.2	10,091

U.S. Imports by Selected Commodity

Commodity	$ Millions	Percent
Agriculture commodities	$ 36,681	3.7
Television, VRC, etc.	50,936	5.1
Clothing	56,412	5.7
Chemicals	63,825	6.4
Mineral fuels	75,803	7.6
ADP equipment, office machinery	84,430	8.5
Electrical machinery	88,620	8.9
Machinery	91,396	9.2
Vehicles	145,927	14.7
Other manufactured goods	300,467	30.2

Reasons for Global Purchasing

- Price/cost
  - labor costs, exchange rates, equipment and processes, product and pricing focus
- Government/marketing pressures
- Quality
- Unavailability of items domestically
- Faster delivery and continuity of supply
- Better technical service
- Technology
- Marketing tool
- Tie-in with offshore subsidiaries
- Competitive clout

Potential Problem Areas in Global Purchasing

- Source location and evaluation
- Lead/delivery time
- Expediting
- Political and labor problems
- Hidden costs
- Currency fluctuations
- Payment methods
- Quality
- Warranties and claims
- Tariffs and duties
- Paperwork costs
- Legal problems
- Logistics and transportation
- Language
- Communications
- Cultural and social customs
- Ethics

Potential Hidden Costs

- Commissions to customs brokers
- Financing charges, letter of credit fees, exchange rate differentials
- Foreign taxes imposed
- Extra inventory and carrying costs
- Extra paperwork/documentation
- Inventory obsolescence, deterioration, spoilage, pilferage
- Travel

- Packaging
- Fees for consultants, inspectors
- Marine insurance
- Import tariffs
- Transportation
- Freight forwarder
- Warehousing
- Port handling

General Guidelines for Dealing with International Suppliers

- Even if English is spoken, speak slowly, use more communication graphics and avoid use or metaphors and jargon
- Bring an interpreter to all by the more informal meetings
  - Allow extra time to educate interpreters on issues
- Document in writing the main conclusions and decisions
- Learn about the country's history and taboos
- Do not use first names unless invited to
- Get cultural advice from professional or your own company employees, not from supplier representatives in the U.S.
- Expect negotiations to last longer with some cultures
  - Suppliers must learn to accept you and your company as a customer

Source: Dick Locke, *Global Supply Management*, New York: McGraw-Hill, 1996

Incoterms

- Developed by the International Chamber of Commerce
- Updated: Incoterms 2000
- Internationally recognized standard definitions that describe the responsibilities of a buyer and seller in a transaction
  - Variations across regions and among carriers possible so make sure to specify conditions
- 13 standard Incoterms
- Each term must be followed by a geographic location, such as a port or city

Incoterms: Departure

- EXW: Ex Works (*named place*)
  - Buyer takes title when goods picked up at the supplier's factory and is totally responsible for shipment, customs clearance and duties.
  - Places greatest responsibility on the buyer

Incoterms: Main Carriage Unpaid

- FCA: Free Carrier (*named place*)
  - Goods have cleared by the seller for any export customs procedures and the seller is responsible for loading the goods
  - The buyer takes possession at the named place in the seller's country
- FAS: Free Alongside Ship (*named port of shipment*)
  - The seller clears the goods for export and delivers them to the port of export
  - The buyer takes possession at the dock at the port of export

Incoterms: Main Carriage Unpaid

- FOB: Free on Board (*named port of shipment*)
  – The supplier clears the goods for export and is responsible for the costs and risks of delivering the goods past the rail at the named port of shipment
  – The buyer takes responsibility for the goods as they pass over the ship's rail during the loading process.
  – Note: This term is used differently from the conventional North American term "F.O.B."

Incoterms: Main Carriage Paid

- CFR: Cost and Freight (*named port of destination*)
  - The supplier clears the goods for export and arranges and pays freight as far as the port of entry
  - Title and risk of loss transfer to the buyer from the time the goods go over the ship's rail in loading - the buyer owns the goods on a carrier selected by the supplier.

Incoterms Main Carriage Paid

- **CIF: Cost, Insurance and Freight** (*named port of destination*)
  - The supplier clears the goods for export, arranges and pays the freight and marine insurance for the goods
  - Title and risk transfer once the goods clear the ship's rail while being loaded

- **CPT: Carriage Paid To** (*named port of destination*)
  - The supplier clears the goods for export, delivers the goods to the carrier and pays for carriage to the port of destination, unloading customs clearance and duties
  - Title and risk risk of loss transfers when goods are transferred to the carrier

Incoterms Main Carriage Paid

- CIP: Carriage and Insurance Paid To (*named port of destination*)
  - The supplier clears the goods for export, delivers the goods to the carrier and is responsible for paying carriage and insurance to the named port of destination
  - The seller is also responsible for costs of unloading, customs clearance and duties
  - Title and risk risk of loss transfers when goods are transferred to the carrier

Incoterms: Arrival

- **DAF: Delivered at Frontier** (*named place*)
  - The supplier clears the goods for export and is responsible for making them available to the buyer at the named place at the frontier, and not cleared for import.
  - Title transfers at named place and time at the frontier.

- **DES: Delivered Ex Ship** (*named port of destination*)
  - The supplier is responsible for clearing the goods for export and for making them available to the buyer on board the ship at the port of destination, not cleared for import.
  - Title transfers from time the goods are made available at the named port

Incoterms: Arrival

- **DEQ: Delivered Ex Quay** (*named port of destination*)
  - The supplier is responsible for clearing the goods for export and making them available to the buyer on the warf at the named port of destination, not cleared for import
  - The buyer is responsible for import clearance, duties and other costs upon import and transport to the final destination
  - Title transfers from time the goods are made available at the warf

Incoterms: Arrival

- DDU: Delivered Duty Unpaid (*named place of destination*)
  - The supplier clears the goods for export and is responsible for making them available to the buyer at the named destination, not cleared for import.
  - The buyer is responsible for import clearance, duties and associated administrative costs.
  - Title transfers at the named place of destination

Incoterms: Arrival

- DDP: Delivered Duty Paid (*named place of destination*)
  - The supplier clears the goods for export and is responsible for making them available to the buyer at the named destination, cleared for import, but not unloaded
  - Title transfers at the named place of destination.

Organizational Considerations

- **Assignment within the Purchasing Department**
  - Organized by commodity or geographic region
- **Subsidiary**
  - Subsidiary supply organization responsible for local suppliers
- **International Purchasing Office (IPO)**
  - Separate purchasing organization usually reporting to head office purchasing department

Intermediaries

- Import brokers and agents
  - For a fee will assist in locating suppliers and handling the paperwork
- Import merchants
  - Buys the product, takes title and delivers it to buyer
- Supplier's subsidiary
- Sales representatives
- Trading companies

Countertrade

- Countertrade is the practice of a company promising to buy material, products or services from a country in return for the privilege of selling there
- The supply function may be called to:
  - Use material acquired through a barter/swap
  - Identify cost-effective sourcing alternatives to fulfill offset agreements
  - Identify goods and services to fulfill counter purchase agreements

Foreign Trade Zones (FTZ)

- FTZ: isolated, enclosed area in or adjacent to a port of entry, used to used to import, process, and reship products to foreign markets.
- Main purpose for using FTZ's are to avoid, postpone, or reduce the tariff on imported goods
- FTZ's differ depending on their major functions.
  – transshipments, storage, exhibition and display, manufacturing

Government Purchases of Goods and Services
($ billions)

Year	Federal	State and Local	Total
1933	$ 2.0	$ 6.0	$ 8.0
1941	16.9	7.9	24.8
1950	18.4	19.5	37.9
1970	96.2	123.3	219.5
1985	353.9	464.7	818.6
1990	424.0	674.1	1098.1
1995	439.2	694.7	1133.9
1996	445.3	726.5	1171.8
1997	456.9	766.5	1223.3
1998	453.7	808.4	1262.1
1999	470.8	855.0	1325.7

The Objectives of Government Supply are Basically the Same as the Private Sector

- Assurance of continuity of supply
- Avoidance of duplication and waste through standardization
- Maintenance and improvement of quality standards
- Development of a cooperative environment between supply and the agencies and departments served
- Obtaining maximum savings through innovative supply and application of value analysis techniques
- Administering the supply function with internal efficiency
- Purchase at lowest like cycle cost

Characteristics of Public Purchasing

- Source of authority established by law
- Budgetary restrictions/limitations
- Outside pressures
- Greater support of public service programs
- Perceived absence of interest costs
- Little formal inspection
- Longer time required to modify the organization
- Lower salary levels at senior ranks
- Lack of confidentiality
- Importance of specifications
- Acquisition procedures determined by established dollar thresholds
- Emphasis on bid process
- Difficulty recognizing past performance

Acquisition Procedures Determined by Established Dollar Thresholds

1. Small-dollar purchases for item below the threshold for competitive bids or quotes

2. Request for quotations (RFQ) for items below the threshold for issuing a formal bid solicitation but high enough to require competitive quotes

3. Invitation for Bids (IFB) for items above the threshold to issue formal bid solicitation, normally for a product or contractual (nonprofessional) service

4. Request for proposal (RFP) for professional services or high-tech needs when formal bid solicitations are required

Acquisition Procedures Determined by Established Dollar Thresholds

5. Emergency purchases for unplanned needs to protect public health, life or property

6. Sole-source purchases for high-tech or mechanical needs where compatibility is required, to purchase a unique item or service

7. Negotiated acquisition, usually part of an RFP or sole-source purchase, or to acquire exempt services such as utilities, power or landfills

Source: Ron Gauthier, "Purchasing in the Fishbowl", *NAPM Insights*, March 1990, p. 21-22.

Three Types of Bonds

- *Bid (or Surety) Bond:* Guarantees that if the order is awarded to a specific bidder, it will accept the purchase contract

- *Performance Bond:* Guarantees that the work done will be done according to specifications and in the time specified

- *Payment Bond:* Protects the buyer against liens

Trends in Public Purchasing

- Centralization
  - centralized: 35%
  - centralized/decentralized: 37.5%
  - virtual centralization: 22.5%
- Privatization or Outsourcing
  - reduce costs, gain shorter implementation times, better quality services
- Commercial Practices
  - payment processes, contract types, electronic procurement and investment recovery programs

Issues in Federal Government Purchasing

- Small business favoritism
- Labor surplus area favoritism
- Buy American Act
- Preference for environmentally preferable purchases
- Renegotiation to recover "excess profits"
- The General Services Administration
- Military Purchasing
  - firm fixed price contract, cost plus fixed fee contract, cost no fee contract, cost plus incentive fee
- U.S. Postal Service - a quasi-governmental organization

Issues in State and Local Government Purchasing

- Prison-made goods
- Cooperative Purchasing
  - Joint buying
  - Formal, separate cooperative buying agency
- Local-bidder preference laws

Advantages and Disadvantages of Cooperative Purchasing

Advantages

- Lower prices
- Improved quality through improved testing and supplier selection
- Reduced administrative costs
- Standardization
- Better records
- Greater competition

Disadvantages

- Inferior products
- Longer lead times
- Limited items available
- More paperwork
- Inability of small suppliers to compete due to larger quantities

Special Problems of Equipment Purchasing

- Strategic considerations and high cost of failure
- Substantial amounts of money for a single purchase
- Long life and infrequent purchases
- Difficulty estimating the total cost
- Derived demand
- Environmental impact and disposal
- Significant tax considerations
- Technology forecasting
- Dedication of time and resources during start-up
- Commitment to process, cost, product line and plant space
- Coordination with existing processes and operations

Reasons for the Purchase of Capital Goods

- Capacity
- Economy in operation and maintenance
- Increased productivity
- Better quality
- Dependability in use
- Savings in time or labor costs
- Durability
- Safety, environmental and emergency protection

Source Selection

- Total cost of ownership (TCO) analysis
  - Purchase cost may only represent 20 to 60 percent of TCO
- Engineering Service
  - Presale and postsale service
- Design and R&D capabilities and costs
- Legal considerations
  - patents, liability for lost sales, health & safety
- Disposal at end of useful life

Reasons for Buying Used Equipment

- When price is important
  - Differential between new and used is great or
  - Limited funds available
- For use in a pilot or experimental plant
- For use with a special or temporary order
- Where the machine will be idle for a substantial amount of time
- For use with apprentices
- For maintenance departments, not production
- For faster delivery/availability
- When a used machine can be modernized easily or is already the latest technology

Conditions of Sale

- "As is" and "where is"
  - "No warranty, guarantee or representation of any kind, expressed or implied, as to the condition of the item offered for sale"
- With certain specific guarantees
- Guaranteed and rebuilt

Sources for Used Equipment

- Dealers and manufacturers that accept used equipment as trade-ins
- Directly from users/owners
- Equipment brokers
- Auctions
- Equipment dealers

Advantages of Leasing

- Tax considerations
  - Lease rentals are expenses for income tax purposes
- Small initial outlay
- Availability of expert service
- Reduced risk of obsolescence
- Adaptability to special and seasonal jobs
- Test period provided before purchase
- Burden of investment shifted to supplier
- Leasing company has greater purchasing clout
  - e.g., automobiles

Disadvantages of Leasing

- Final cost may be higher
  - Higher financing costs, fees
- Surveillance by lessor entailed
- Less freedom of control and use
- Tax considerations
  - Some leases may not be deductible
- Penalties and fees for early lease termination
  - Limits flexibility

The Full Service Lessor

```
         Manufacturer
              |
Bank ————— Lessor ————— Lessee
```

The Finance Lease Company

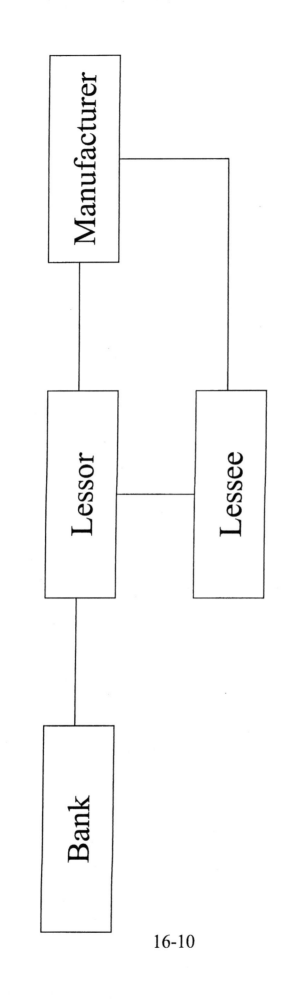

The Captive Leasing Company

```
┌─────────┐             ┌──────────────┬────────┐     ┌────────┐
│  Bank   │─────────────│ Manufacturer │ Lessor │─────│ Lessee │
└─────────┘             └──────────────┴────────┘     └────────┘
```

Bank Participation

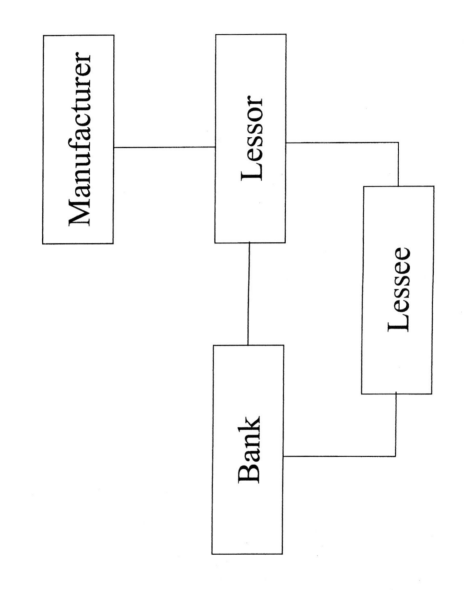

Reasons for Captive Leasing

- To secure wider distribution or a higher margin
- To reduce credit risk
- To sell a full line or to increase the volume of sales of supplies
- To control the secondhand market
- To stabilize growth
- To control servicing
- To protect a patent position

Lessor Evaluation

- Reasonable and fair in dealing with customers?

- Devoting as much attention and money to research as alleged?

- Strong financially?

- If a sole source, prone to be arbitrary in the periodic adjustment of rental and other fees?

Issues for RFQs and RFPs in Construction Purchasing

- Include appropriate drawings
- Identify when and how work changes are determined and accepted
  - include costing procedures
- Acceptance criteria
- Procedures for submitting and pricing modifications
- Clearly identify decision criteria
  - e.g., cost, completion time frame, expertise, past history

Issues for RFQs and RFPs in Construction Purchasing

- Payment process
- Insurance and bonds
- Establish termination criteria including violation of contract requirements
- Establish project schedule, including start and completion dates
- Site inspection/walk-through
- List of subcontractors

Issues for RFQs and RFPs in Construction Purchasing

- Liquidated damages in the event of delays
- List of acceptable pricing options
- Clearly define the supplier's responsibility in a statement of work

Goods Versus Services Spend

	Goods	Services
Manufacturing firms (N = 59)	61%	39%
Service firms (N = 23)	19%	81%
Governmental organizations (N = 34)	19%	81%
Total (N = 116)	38%	62%

Source: Harold E. Fearon and William A. Bales, *Purchasing of Nontraditional Goods and Services*, Tempe, AZ: Center for Advanced Purchasing Studies, 1995.

Dollars Spent for Purchase of Services

Total and Top 10 Categories	Percent of Total	Percent of Total Services	Percent of Dollars by Purchasing
Total services	54.0%	100.0%	27%
Utilities	4.8	9.0	26
Insurance	4.4	8.2	6
Sales/promotion	3.9	7.2	48
Health benefits plans	3.3	6.1	5
Travel: air tickets	3.1	5.8	12
Construction	2.6	4.9	42
Consultants	2.6	4.8	55
Transport of goods	2.5	4.7	33
Banking	2.2	4.2	0
Copying	2.0	3.6	19

Source: Harold E. Fearon and William A. Bales, *Purchasing of Nontraditional Goods and Services*, Tempe, AZ: Center for Advanced Purchasing Studies, 1995.

Reasons for Lack of Purchasing Involvement in Service Acquisition

- Complexity of specifying service needs and analyzing potential service provides means that the user has greater expertise than purchasing

- The buying of services involves more of a personal relationship between the supplier and user.

- Many services in the past have been available only in a regulated environment, in which price and service-delivery was essentially the same for all suppliers

What Makes Services Different?

- Intangible
  - Cannot touch it
- Perishable
  - no inventories
- Heterogeneous: The "service package"
  - high levels of customization
- Customer participation in the production process
- Simultaneous production and consumption
- Difficult to measure quality

A Framework for Analyzing Services

- Value of the service
  - high, medium low
  - Pareto/ABC analysis
- Degree of repetitiveness
  - repetitive versus unique
- Degree of tangibility
  - Low versus high
- Direction of the service
  - Directed towards people or assets

Source: William B. Martin, Quality Service: *The Restaurant Manager's Bible*, Ithaca, NY: Cornell University, School of hotel Administration, 1986.

A Framework for Analyzing Services

- Production of the service
  - People, equipment or people and equipment
  - Skill level of people
- Nature of demand
  - Continuous, periodic or discrete
- Nature of service delivery
  - Location, time
- Degree of standardization
  - Standard or customized
- Skills required for the service

The Acquisition Process for Services

1. Need recognition and specification
   - Key questions:
     - Why is this service necessary?
     - What is important about this service?
     - What represents good value?
     - How is quality defined for the service?
     - How is the service produced?
     - How do we know we received what we expected?
   - Developing the statement of work (SOW): Describes the needs and becomes the basis of the contract

The Acquisition Process for Services

2. Analysis of supply alternatives
   – sourcing, pricing, other terms and conditions, source options and make or buy

3. Purchase agreement
   – Short versus long term; standard versus custom
   – Service level agreement (SLA): means, method, organization, processes and material requirements
   – Pricing structure
   – Special provisions

The Acquisition Process for Services

4. Contract administration
   – Follow-up
   – Quality control
   – Payment
   – Records maintenance
   – Supplier management and evaluation

Service Quality Evaluation

- Reliability: Ability to perform the promised service dependably and accurately
- Responsiveness: Willingness to help customers and provide prompt service
- Assurance: Knowledge and courtesy of employees and their ability to inspire trust and confidence
- Empathy: Caring, individualized attention the firm provides its customers
- Tangibles: Physical facilities, equipment and appearance of personnel

Source: A. Prasuranman, V.A. Zeithaml and L.L. Berry, "A Conceptual Model of Service Quality and Its Implications for the Future", *Journal of Marketing* Fall 1985, p. 41-50.

Process for Obtaining Results in Service Acquisition

1. Do the people now in the purchasing department have the skills needed for purchasing services?

2. Do they have the time? Can they make the time?

3. Obtain data on what services are bought by whom and dollar amount.

4. Take one area at a time.

5. Establish the team: user(s) possibly finance, quality and purchasing

Process for Obtaining Results in Service Acquisition

6. Determine if the buying service satisfies the user and represents effective spending.

7. Purchasing should ensure the use of a logical process and arrive at the contract or agreement.

8. All parties must agree on the specification

9. Explain why any changes are required in supplier, specification, price, terms, etc., to users and senior management

10. Do not interfere with effective service acquisition activities handle by other departments

Summary of Service Characteristics and Acquisition Process Implications

Service Characteristic		Acquisition Process	Need Recognition, Description	Sourcing Alternatives Pricing, Analysis	Agreement, Contract Provisions	Contract Admin., Follow-up, Q.C., Payment, Records
Value		High	high attention	careful price sensitive make or buy	likely negotiated	high attention
		Low	lesser attention	low acquisition cost local source	standard if possible	low attention
Repetitiveness		High	develop standard	test	standard longer term	standardize
		Low	seek expert assistance	seek expert assistance	custom or one shot	custom
Tangibility		High	specs important	pretest, samples	similar to product purchase	control for physical characteristics
		Low	references user involvement	personalities important	specific persons	User involvement high

17-13

Summary of Service Characteristics and Acquisition Process Implications

Service Characteristic		Acquisition Process	Need Recognition, Description	Sourcing Alternatives Pricing, Analysis	Agreement, Contract Provisions	Contract Admin., Follow-up, Q.C., Payment, Records
Direction of		equipment	equipment familiarity	equipment familiarity	specified equipment performance	control process quality
		people	user involvement high	user involvement high	people skills important	control quality at user interface
Production by		equipment	specify equipment capability	specify equipment capability	specify equipment performance	conditional on equipment use
		people	specify people capability	worry about capacity	specify availability	user provides
Demand		continuous	continuity	reliability and continuity	complete coverage	control quality by sampling
		discrete	availability during need	availability during need	specify delivery	control quality by delivery

Summary of Service Characteristics and Acquisition Process Implications

Service Characteristic	Acquisition Process	Need Recognition, Description	Sourcing Alternatives Pricing, Analysis	Agreement, Contract Provisions	Contract Admin., Follow-up, Q.C., Payment, Records
Delivery	at purchaser	user interface important	user interface important	access clauses	in-house Q.C.
	at seller	good description	location	purchase access and progress reports	concern over service completeness
Customization	high	user specification	custom capability	special contract	quality control very specific and may withhold a large % of payment
	low	standard specs	competitive bid	standard contract	standard Q.C.
Skills	high	user specification	specify specific persons	availability of individuals	professional standards, regulations, user involvement
	low	standard specs	competitive bidding	standard contract	minimize use hassle

An Organization Must Approach Strategic Planning on Three Levels

- *Corporate:* Decisions and plans that answer the questions of *what business are we in?* and, *how will we allocate resources among these businesses?*

- *Unit:* Decisions mold the plans of a particular business unit, as necessary to contribute to corporate strategy.

- *Function:* Plans concern the "how" of each functional area's contribution to the business strategy and involve the allocation of internal resources.

Key Strategy Questions

1. How can the supply function contribute effectively to organizational objectives?

OR

2. How can the manager of purchasing make sure the supply function contributes effectively to organizational objectives?

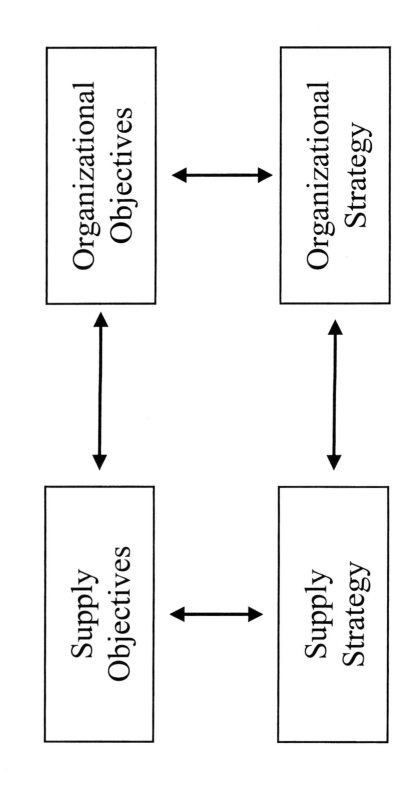

Supply Strategy Links Current and Future Markets to Current and Future Needs

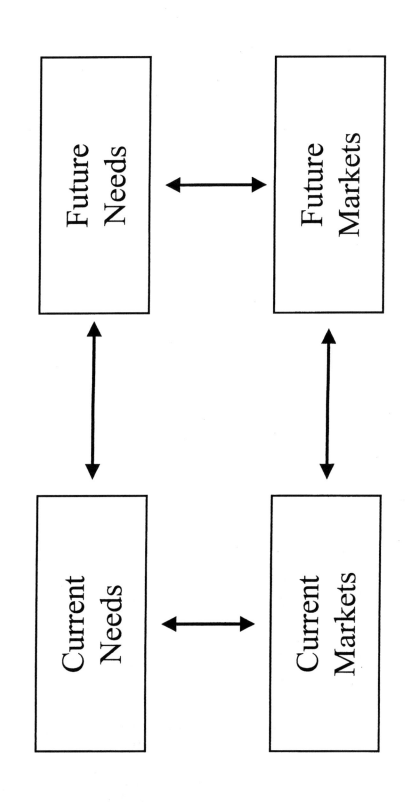

Normal Organizational and Supply Objectives

<u>Organizational Objectives</u>

1. Survival
2. Growth
3. Financial
4. Environmental

<u>Supply Objectives</u>

1. Quality
2. Quantity
3. Delivery
4. Price
5. Service

Potential Business-Strategy Contribution Areas

1. Social issues and trends
2. Government regulations and controls
3. Financial planning with suppliers
4. Product liability exposure
5. Economic trends and environment
6. Organizational changes
7. Product or service line
8. Competitive intelligence
9. Technology
10. e-Commerce
11. Investment
12. Mergers/acquisitions/disinvestment
13. Time-based competition

Four Possible Changed Organizational Strategies Involving Purchasing

1. Materials management
2. Project management
3. Logistics management, or supply chain management
4. JIT purchasing/production

Three Ways for Supply to Contribute to Technology Strategy

1. By providing information to their own design/process/production staff on development in technology

2. By working with suppliers to develop new technology that can be incorporated into the buying firm's operation

3. By assisting to "lock-up" new, advantageous technology through exclusive agreements with suppliers

e-Commerce Issues

- Which exchanges should our company participate in?

- Should our company form a B2B exchange with our competitors?

- Should we demand that our suppliers conduct business with us on-line?

- What software should we be committing to?

Risk in the Supply Chain

1. The risk of interruption of the flow of goods and services

2. The risk that the cost of the goods or services will be higher than expected

Managing Supply Risks

1. Identification and classification of the risks

2. Impact assessment

3. A risk strategy

Major Purchasing Functional Strategy Areas

1. Assurance of supply strategies
2. Cost reduction strategies
3. Supply support strategies
4. Environmental change strategies
5. Competitive edge strategies

Strategic Purchasing Planning Process

```
Restate                  Determine supply           Isolate factors
organizational    →      objectives to contribute → affecting achievement
goals                    to organizational goals    of supply objectives
                                                            │
                                                            ↓
Identify and      →      Determine        →    Review          →  Gain commitment  →  Evaluate
analyze alternatives     supply strategy        implementation      and implement
     ↑                                          factors                                   │
     └──────────────────────────────────────────────────────────────────────────────────┘
                                                                                          │
     (loop back to Restate organizational goals) ←──────────────────────────────────────┘
```

Supply Strategy Questions

- What
  - Make or buy
  - Standard versus special
- Quality
  - Quality versus cost
  - Supplier involvement
- How much
  - Large versus small quantities (inventories)

Supply Strategy Questions

- Who
  - Centralized or decentralized
  - Quality of staff
  - Top management involvement
- When
  - Now versus later
  - Forward buy
- What Price
  - Premium, standard, lower
  - Cost-based, market-based
  - Lease/make/buy

Supply Strategy Questions

- Where
  - Local, regional
  - Domestic, international
  - Large versus small
  - Multiple versus sole source
  - High versus low supplier turnover
  - Supplier relations
  - Supplier certification
  - Supplier ownership

Supply Strategy Questions

- How
  - Systems and procedures
  - Computerization
  - Negotiations
  - Competitive bids
  - Fixed bids
  - Blanket orders/open orders
  - Blank check system
  - Group buying
  - MRP
  - Long-term contracts
  - Ethics
  - Aggressive or passive
  - Purchasing research
  - Value analysis

Supply Strategy Questions

- Why?
  - Objectives congruent
  - Market reasons
  - Internal reasons
  - 1) outside supply
  - 2) inside supply

Trends in Purchasing and Supply Management

- Nontraditional people will be in many supply management positions
- Technical entry route into purchasing
- Emphasis on total quality management and customer satisfaction
- Emphasis on the process used in acquisition, rather than the transactions
- Purchase of systems and services, as well as products

Trends in Purchasing and Supply Management

- Strategic cost management
- Design engineering and purchasing capitalize on their potential synergy
- The supplier base will be reformulated
- Longer term contracts
- e-Commerce
- Global supply management
- MRO items handled by a third-party contractor

Trends in Purchasing and Supply Management

- Sourcing will include the complete end product or service and be done proactively
- Closer supplier relationships
- Teaming
- Empowerment
- End-product manufacturers will focus on design and assembly
- Consortiums for purchasing

Trends in Purchasing and Supply Management

- Separation of strategic and tactical purchasing
- Greater purchasing involvement in nontraditional purchases
- Environmental purchasing
- Value enhancement versus cost reductions

The Future of Supply Management

1. Supply chain management
2. Cycle time reductions
3. Video communication with suppliers
4. Integration into business strategy
5. Outsource the procurement process
6. Functional lines blurred or even eliminated
7. Design for procurability
8. "Pull systems" become common in manufacturing
9. Reduction of third- and fourth tier suppliers
10. Networking of suppliers
11. Contract with two suppliers simultaneously to design and build
12. Rationalization of B2B marketplace
13. Expert systems/artificial intelligence